Being Single in Georgian England

Being Single in Georgian England

Families, Households, and the Unmarried

AMY HARRIS

OXFORD
UNIVERSITY PRESS

Great Clarendon Street, Oxford, OX2 6DP,
United Kingdom

Oxford University Press is a department of the University of Oxford.
It furthers the University's objective of excellence in research, scholarship,
and education by publishing worldwide. Oxford is a registered trade mark of
Oxford University Press in the UK and in certain other countries

© Amy Harris 2023

The moral rights of the author have been asserted

All rights reserved. No part of this publication may be reproduced, stored in
a retrieval system, or transmitted, in any form or by any means, without the
prior permission in writing of Oxford University Press, or as expressly permitted
by law, by licence or under terms agreed with the appropriate reprographics
rights organization. Enquiries concerning reproduction outside the scope of the
above should be sent to the Rights Department, Oxford University Press, at the
address above

You must not circulate this work in any other form
and you must impose this same condition on any acquirer

Published in the United States of America by Oxford University Press
198 Madison Avenue, New York, NY 10016, United States of America

British Library Cataloguing in Publication Data
Data available

Library of Congress Control Number: 2023930844

ISBN 978-0-19-286949-4

DOI: 10.1093/oso/9780192869494.001.0001

Printed and bound by
CPI Group (UK) Ltd, Croydon, CR0 4YY

Links to third party websites are provided by Oxford in good faith and
for information only. Oxford disclaims any responsibility for the materials
contained in any third party website referenced in this work.

For Barbara, Susan, and Alan, who make sure I never stand alone

In memory of Jenice (1928–2020) and Anne (1987–2021)

Acknowledgments

I first encountered the Sharps while conducting dissertation research in the Gloucestershire Archives in 2003. That work eventually turned into a book about siblinghood and the Sharps appeared occasionally in its pages. In the ensuing years I have accrued intellectual, emotional, and social debts to a variety of people and institutions who have supported this work.

My family's unhealthy obsession with garden produce might not rival the Sharps' musical talents, but traveling life together with them, through rough waters and smooth sailing, has made the journey richer and safer than I could have imagined. Some of them even helped me with this book, answering questions about audience, mulling over word choices, and offering suggestions about how to clearly identify the four separate Catherine Sharps. My unwavering thanks to my siblings, appropriately listed in birth order: Alan, Deborah, Susan, David, Fred, Peter, Shelley, Betsy, Leslie, Barbara, and Tom. And thanks for producing children and grandchildren who love and amuse me.

Friends near and far have been an unremitting gift. My thanks to Karen Auman, Heather Belnap, Lindseay Brown and Niven Wofford, Karen Carter, Jill Crandell, Cacey Farnsworth, Don Harreld, Alicia and Matt Hastings, Kari and Adam Hauert, Valerie Hegstrom, Andy Johns, Christopher Jones, Heather and Ben Lawrence, Jenny Ostermiller, Jan and Brad Phillips, Sarah Reed, and Clark White.

I am also grateful to friends and colleagues who generously read drafts and provided insightful comments. The book is far better than it would have been without your contributions: Karen Carter, Rachel Cope, Rebecca de Schweinitz, Amy Froide, Craig Harline, Jane Hinckley, Kate Holbrook, Matt Mason, Francesca Morgan, Jenny Pulsipher, Kate Retford, Brent Sirota, Paul Westover, and the BYU History Department writing group. I'm also thankful for the years of support from Deborah Cohen and am grateful to her, Tom Silfen, and Alice for their kind sociality while I was in Chicago.

I presented early research findings to various groups, who also helped me conceptualize the book. In particular, Anu Lahtinen and the Gender and Family Relations, Medieval to Modern Conference at the University of Turku in 2015; Deborah Cohen and the Newberry Library British History Seminar in 2016; and Karen Harvey and the Barber Institute of Fine Arts at the University of Birmingham in 2019.

In addition, the blind reviewers' helpful comments were crucial to refining the book. Editors at Oxford University Press, particularly Stephanie Ireland, Cathryn

Steele, and Tom Stottor as well as the copyeditors were unstinting in their support and patient with my many queries. My thanks to the efficient and insightful Rachel Nishan at Twin Oaks for compiling the index. I also have a debt of gratitude to Kristine Haglund for her crucial editing help and warm encouragement in the final stages of revision.

My thanks to Paul Evans and the staff at Gloucestershire Archives, who have been supporting my research for two decades and to the Lloyd-Baker trust and the National Portrait Gallery who have kindly tolerated my repeated requests to use the Sharp family portrait for nearly the same length of time. I also appreciate the support unstintingly given by the staff at Bamburgh Castle, Durham Cathedral Archives, Durham Record Office, University of Durham Palace Green Library, Lord Crewe's Charity, London Metropolitan Archives, the Newberry Library, New York Historical Society, Northamptonshire Record Office, Northumberland Archives, Society of Genealogists, the William Andrews Clark Memorial Library at UCLA, the Borthwick Institute at York University, and York Minster Archives. My special thanks to Lynne Cleaver and Patricia Phillips who helped me acquire additional digital images. And thank you to Susan Barwood who photographed Catherine Sharp's portrait and memorial to her family so they could be included in these pages.

John Heward and other Northumberland local historians generously shared sources about local features and landscape. The effort they put into sharing sources and telling stories, which they then freely share online, not to mention answering my email enquiries, is one of the things that makes historical research in the digital age so rewarding.

Staff at my own institutional library have been enormously helpful. Years of investment in electronic databases and book collections meant I had access to any scholarly resources needed for this project and staff consistently went out of their way to facilitate my access. The Faculty Publishing Service at BYU helped me revise my writing, FamilyChartMasters helped me with lineage charts, and the BYU Geography Department's Think Spatial Lab designed the maps for me.

I benefited from the conscientious and talented work of research assistants. Shelby Shoaf in 2016 who compiled probate information; Ally Patterson in 2020–21 who compiled a database of Sharp records; and Ellie Hancock, Amy Stoddard, and Kaitlyn Richardson in 2021–22 who helped with last-minute research needs.

This project has been funded by the William Andrews Clark Memorial Library and Center for 17th and 18th Century Studies at UCLA, the American Society for Eighteenth-Century Studies Fellowship at the Newberry Library, BYU's College of Family, Home, and Social Sciences, and BYU's Gerontology Program. I'm grateful to the college for a professional development leave and to Brian Cannon and the BYU History Department for a teaching release during the final stages of writing the manuscript. I'm indebted to Jen Nelson who helped me navigate the load-bearing red tape necessary to acquire image permissions.

Sadly, the years spent on this project were also years colored by many losses. Lenore Davidoff (1932–2014) kindly and with stunning generosity in her last months talked with me at length on the phone when her declining health would not permit a visit. I am still saddened by her loss and by the loss of Dallett Hemphill (1959–2015) who I got to know through our mutual interest in sibling studies and who was so supportive of this book's early stages. I especially want to recognize George (1950–2022) and Peggy Ryskamp for three decades' support and mentorship and Kate Holbrook (1972–2022) for a decade of insightful leadership of our writing group and for her steady and deeply kind friendship.

I end with words from Thomas Sharp Sr.'s introduction to his father's biography, with slight alterations. It captures my thoughts on describing the experiences of people so distant from me in time and place. From the *Life and of John Sharp*, p. xxiv:

> The writer has this, however, to say, in behalf of [her]self... that how imperfect and unfinished soever the piece may seem, the outlines and main strokes are just... And as to the disposal of the colours, and lights, and shades, in which something must be allowed to fancy, which naturally would act a kind part, there is yet this justice done throughout the whole, that nothing is either falsified or knowingly disguised.

I might not have managed to capture all of the Sharps' colors, lights, and shades, but I hope that I have provided a just portrait nonetheless.

Contents

List of Figures	xiii
List of Plates	xv
List of Abbreviations	xvii
Note on Sources and Interludes	xix
Introduction	1
1. Prehistory	17
Interlude 1: Meeting of the Minds	33
2. Growing Up Sharp	35
Interlude 2: Common Letters	60
3. To Marry or Not to Marry	66
4. Living Single	97
Interlude 3: Portrait	137
5. Aunting and Uncling	141
6. For All the World	169
7. Leaving a Legacy	198
Interlude 4: Epitaphs	221
Epilogue: An Afterlife in Documents	227
Select Bibliography	235
Index	241

List of Figures

1.1	Sharp siblings with parents, spouses, and children	19
1.2	Wheler family chart	21
1.3	Sharp family chart	22
2.1	Sharp siblings: infant and childhood mortality	42
2.2	Sharp cousin network	48
3.1	Sharp family residences, 1720–1843	70
3.2	Map of Sharp family residences	71
4.1	Map of Sharp family travels, 1750–1809	107

List of Plates

1. Family portrait by Johan Zoffany, on loan to The National Gallery, London; © Lloyd-Baker Estate, used with permission

2. Sharp family pedigree, D3549/1/2/4, Gloucestershire Archives, used with permission

3. (Upper image) Sharp family pedigree (detail), Gloucestershire Archives, used with permission; (lower image) Whitton Tower sketched by Granville Sharp, 1754, Northumberland Archives, used with permission

4. (Upper image) sketch of William Sharp's organ, "Miss Morgan," by a Sharp sibling, c.1750s, D3549/7/2/15, Gloucestershire Archives, used with permission; (lower image) pencil sketch of Wicken Park by Charles Fitzroy, c.1818–27, Northamptonshire Archives, used with permission

5. (Upper image) first entry in the Sharp boat books, 1753, D3549/12/1/1, Gloucestershire Archives, used with permission; (lower image) drawing of Hartburn vicarage and grounds, Northumberland by Judith Sharp, D3549/8/1/6, Gloucestershire Archives, used with permission

6. Elizabeth Sharp Prowse, memorandum and commonplace book, D3549/14/1/1, Gloucestershire Archives, used with permission

7. (Upper image) miniature of Judith Sharp (1733–1809), Lord Crewe's Charity, used with permission; (lower image) miniature of Thomas Sharp (1725–1772), Lord Crewe's Charity, used with permission. [The Charity indicated that the miniature of Thomas was not labeled and they determined it was of James. However, the collection of miniatures, other than the one of Granville, are exclusive to the family members who lived together in Northumberland: John, Mary, Judith, and Jemima. Thomas would be the obvious brother to include in the group and the miniature depicts a man wearing a clerical style wig.]

8. (Upper image) Sharp family monument, Bamburgh parish church, photograph © Susan Barwood, 2022; (lower image) portrait of Catherine Sharp by Margaret Carpenter, Bamburgh Castle, used with permission, photograph © Susan Barwood, 2022

List of Abbreviations

BIY	Borthwick Institute, University of York
BL	British Library, London
DCL	Durham Cathedral Library
DRO	Durham County Record Office, Durham
ECCO	Eighteenth Century Collections Online
FHL	Family History Library, Salt Lake City, Utah
GA	Gloucestershire Archives, Gloucester
HL	Huntington Library, San Marino, California
LMA	London Metropolitan Archives
LPL	Lambeth Palace Library
NA	Northamptonshire Archives, Northampton
NAW	Northumberland Archives, Woodhorn, Northumberland
NL	Newberry Library, Chicago
NYHS	New York Historical Society, New York City
PGL	Palace Green Library, Durham University
SoG	Society of Genealogists, London
TNA	The National Archives, Kew
WACML	William Andrew Clark Memorial Library, University of California, Los Angeles
YMA	York Minster Archives

Note on Sources and Interludes

The Sharps' extraordinary lives left an extraordinary and rich archive. Their collected papers and possessions offer a chance to see the contours of singleness and family life in the eighteenth century. Like any family, they chose what to write down and what to preserve as evidence of their most valued ideals. As Patricia Crawford described it, "the records which survived had been self-consciously created and preserved. What individuals revealed in their diaries was what they were prepared to allow other family members to see or transcribe...letters...were written in the knowledge that they would be read to others and circulated."[1] Their family archive, spread over multiple archival collections and expanded through digital reproduction not just of records but of detailed catalogs, as well as databases of original records on genealogical websites means we have unprecedented access to their lives.

Elizabeth's family chronicle is particularly complex. It is clear that she must have kept a diary—perhaps as early as 1743 when she was 10 years old—because the content of what is now labeled, alternately, "memoradum," "diary," and "commonplace book," reflects specific details that could only be recorded at the time and not remembered at a distance of decades. Probably beginning in the 1790s, she and niece Catherine transcribed a copy of this account, inserting clippings, obituaries, and transcription of funeral monuments, as well as a hand-written copy of a cousin's account of his family. This seems to have been the principal source for a twentieth-century typescript copy made by a descendant of another niece. That typescript version, however, has some content not found in the late eighteenth-century copy, suggesting that additional documents no longer available were used. This possibility is further confirmed by a microfilm copy of Catherine's memorandum/commonplace book which had pages and pieces of information not found in the other copies. In the footnotes I have followed the archive's label, "memorandum and commonplace book" for all of her writings and indicated when the typescript was used.

Between them, the Sharps kept pocketbooks, letters, diaries, and accounts, many of which they also copied and edited later in life. None, however, wrote an autobiography or personal memoir, despite having that tradition within their family. The siblings preserved their records, but always as a means for preserving their *collective* identity. To highlight their collective family archives, I have placed

---

[1] Patricia Crawford, "Katherine and Philip Henry and Their Children: A Case Study in Family Ideology," *Transactions of the Historic Society of Lancashire and Cheshire*, 134 (1984): 61.

XX NOTE ON SOURCES AND INTERLUDES

brief interludes between some chapters. These are short narrative accounts about a particular document or artifact that warranted its own treatment, but which did not fit within the larger chapter's structure. They are designed to highlight particular moments in the Sharps' lives and to provide readers samples of the documents they produced.

Note that the surviving correspondence from and by the sisters is limited. It might be in private hands, but more likely it was not preserved as well as their brothers' or it was dispersed among their niece's descendants. To fill some of those gaps I used traditional genealogical methods, tracking women in probate and church records. For example, John Thomlinson, a one-time suitor of Judith Wheler (the Sharps' mother), kept a diary recording his professional and marital ambitions. In 1722, after Judith had already married Thomas Sharp, Thomlinson debated which of two women he should court. He settled on a woman from London, though he does not name her, instead emphasizing that her inheritance could be increased if some of her sisters were to die. In order to flesh out the story, I employed traditional genealogical techniques to learn the woman's name (Catherine Winstanly), find her parents, and learn details about her birth, her marriage to Thomlinson, and the number and ages of her sisters.

Analyzing genealogical details also reveals how families change over time. For example, most treatments of the Sharps have relied on their letters and diaries and on published genealogies from the eighteenth or nineteenth century. These sources, however, often neglect to mention descendants who never married or had children. They hide from view the experiences of those who left no genealogical evidence, thereby erasing the impact those individuals had on family relationships and economics. Additionally, tracing out genealogical details exposes the wider kinship network and prevents a particular family from appearing like a static entity.

The Lloyd-Baker Family of Hardwicke Court Collection at Gloucestershire Archives contains the bulk of Sharp family papers. To avoid repetitious citation content, the specific catalog number (within collections D3549 and D6919) is cited each time, but the collection and archive name is not.

Newspapers: Unless otherwise indicated, all newspaper citations come from the Burney Newspaper Collection by Gale.

Calendar: Pre-1752 dates from the Julian calendar (old style) have been converted to their modern Gregorian (new style) equivalents.

Spelling: When directly quoting eighteenth-century records, I have retained the original spelling and grammar. The thorn letter form (þ), often rendered in a form resembling a "y," has been transcribed as "th" to facilitate reading.

Names: Three successive generations of Sharps have a Thomas and a John. There are two Elizabeth Sharps, who both marry men named Prowse. There are two Judiths, two Marys, and at one point, four Catherine Sharps. Uniquely identifying them without disrupting the narrative is challenging. Also, making the reader constantly refer to the family charts to decipher who is being discussed is cumbersome.

There is no perfect solution, particularly when it comes to talking about Catherine Sharp, who could be one of three sisters-in-law or a niece. Because most of them are the same generation, referring to them as junior or senior is inadequate. Referring to them by using their original surname, as opposed to Sharp, distances them from the Sharp interactions in a way that contradicts the records. Numbering them seems dehumanizing. Therefore, a variety of tactics have been employed to clarify which Catherine is under discussion. It was sometimes necessary to identify them as wife or widow of the brother they married. This is less than ideal, as it diminishes their individuality, but it reinforces their connections to the Sharps. Once a particular Catherine is identified she will generally be referred by her first name, as the Sharp siblings consistently are.

Introduction

"With colours flying & Musick playing"

Frances Sharp

"How different does the history of the family in early modern England look when we place the single person at its centre rather than the marital couple?"[1]

Amy Froide

In August 1777, the Thames was teeming with its usual combination of navy and merchant ships, prison hulks, docks, and pleasure barges. Near Richmond, boats of all types, including the Thames Navigation Board's yacht and sailing vessels with aristocrats, foreign diplomats, and other "well Dressed Company" jockeyed among smaller boats filled with similarly eager, though more modestly clothed, people. Hundreds gathered around a large and particularly well apportioned yacht, a mobile country house eighty feet long, with accommodations and provisions for two dozen and packed with musical instruments, including a harpsichord. A full-fledged concert was on offer, the yacht bedecked with sumptuous furnishings and an orchestra composed of the best performers in London, among whom the Sharp family, arrayed in their finery and at the height of their social prominence, played and sang. Youngest sister Frances described the moment: "The river was covered with boats of well Dressed company, our Party [was]...a charming band, & so with colours flying & Musick playing & all the company attending us, we went up."[2]

The Sharp siblings were exceptional. There is no rendering them an ordinary or average family. The eight siblings who lived to adulthood were musically and artistically gifted, ecclesiastically talented, reform-minded, and exceptionally good with money. They were, as a guest to one of their concerts noted, "a worthy family and musical."[3] Collectively, they wrote poetry, composed, and sketched. They published sermons, managed a large estate, provided for local poor,

---

[1] Amy Froide, *Never Married: Singlewomen in Early Modern England* (Oxford: Oxford University Press, 2005), 44.

[2] Frances Sharp to Judith Sharp, August 30, 1777, D3549/16/1/1, Lloyd-Baker Family of Hardwicke Court Collection, Gloucestershire Archives.

[3] Elizabeth Harris to James Harris Jr., April 7, 1772, transcription in Donald Burrows and Rosemary Dunhill, eds., *Music and Theatre in Handel's World: The Family Papers of James Harris 1732–1780* (Oxford: Oxford University Press, 2002), 670.

Being Single in Georgian England: Families, Households, and the Unmarried. Amy Harris, Oxford University Press.
© Amy Harris 2023. DOI: 10.1093/oso/9780192869494.003.0001

2 BEING SINGLE IN GEORGIAN ENGLAND

innovated medical treatments and communication networks, established a major regional charity, worked on parliamentary reform, and were early advocates of abolition. The family was also unusually well-connected. David Garrick came to their concerts; they corresponded with Benjamin Rush and Benjamin Franklin; they socialized with Samuel Johnson and Phyllis Wheatley, rubbed elbows with reformers, politicians, aristocrats, and high-ranking clergy. They were well-read, good conversationalists, and untiringly witty. They were not the most famous members of literary, musical, political, or religious circles, but they were well known in all those circles, and invitations to join the Sharps were highly valued. As one author remarked about the family, their "conduct [had]…rendered them, in different degrees, the objects of public estimation as well as private regard, and given to their very name a proverbial connexion with piety and beneficence."[4] Their piety was informed by a moderate, practical Anglicanism and rooted in sincere belief. What's more, they were friendly, warm, engaging, and consistently loving and supportive of one another. In other words, they were the best company. One observer even likened leaving a Sharp gathering to being removed from the Garden of Eden.[5]

The Sharps also had the resources to enjoy each other's company in style. The 1777 Thames spectacle was not anomalous; nearly every summer between 1750 and 1790 they enjoyed river cruises, often along the Thames, and long journeys together. Their self-styled "water schemes" took place on their own flotilla of yachts, barges, boats, and canoes where they dined, danced, and sang away summer evenings. Between them they could play the lute, organ, harpsichord, piano, clarinet, flageolets, kettle drums, violin, double flute, serpent, and cello. They also sang, danced, and composed. Prodigious musicians all, they enjoyed giving concerts to friends and, on more than one occasion, to the king and queen at Richmond.

One of their water schemes was captured in the family's portrait, painted by the famed Johann Zoffany between 1779 and 1781 (Plate 1). Zoffany composed the painting in stages as family members gathered in small groups to pose for the portrait. The painting's structure reveals important elements of Sharp family life. While three married brothers form the points of a triangle that frames the portrait, the overall composition pushes against simple patriarchal depictions of family relations. Elements of the portrait emphasize multiple connections between family members, no matter their marital and parental status: the flag billowing at the top was crafted by a sister and contained two brothers' intertwined standards. The two women holding hands were not Sharps by birth, but double

---

[4] John Owen, *A Discourse occasioned by the Death of Elizabeth Prowse, late of Wicken Park, Northamptonshire; Delivered in Substance at Fulham Church, on Sunday, March 4, 1810* (London: Printed for J. Hatchard by J. Tilling, 1810), 7–8, D3549/13/5/33.

[5] R.D.,"Visit to Mrs. Prowse at Wicken Park," extract of letter from a "Gentleman in Northumberlandshire to his Friend in London," October 2, 1777, D3549/14/1/6.

INTRODUCTION 3

sisters-in-law (in addition to being married to brothers, their siblings had married each other). One brother rests on the back of a sister's chair, another has his arm around a niece, and, by sight line or touch, every figure is connected to at least two other figures in the painting. If parent–child relations were the focus, there would be only the story of three separate families consisting of one child each, and the fact that the children were embedded in their parents' sibling network and within their own cousin network would disappear. In either of these scenarios, the heart of the painting—where a brother and sister, both unmarried and childless, share a glance and a piece of sheet music—would disappear entirely from the story.[6]

Like other conversation pieces, the portrait highlighted informality and sociability, but unlike many such pieces, the configuration of the sitters emphasized sociability that disrupted eighteenth-century notions of family power grounded in gender, age, and marital status: the eldest brother is depicted on the margins of the painting, the single siblings form the heart of the grouping, and the bonds between sisters-in-law and aunts and nieces are accentuated.[7] While patriarchy, hierarchy, and nuclear families are present in the portrait and Sharp family life, there are numerous other dynamics at play, particularly those involving the unmarried family members at the center. This book is about those dynamics. It is a story about the ways singleness and childlessness shaped family life.

So, what did family life look like from the vantage point of unmarried and childless family members? Many of the same concerns that occupied married people exercised the minds of their unmarried kin. They made decisions about living arrangements, social connections, and livelihoods in the absence of a spouse and children, but in conversation with siblings, aunts, uncles, and cousins. As adults, the unmarried Sharps negotiated with married family members over the distribution of property, the management of family resources, and the raising of children. Earlier generations' practices of courtship and marriage influenced how the Sharps understood family life, the relative importance their particular family placed on marriage, and the resources they could call upon should they not marry, which many of the Sharps realized or decided would not happen for them. This affected how they and their married kin thought of their legacy for future generations. In other words, placing an unmarried brother and a widowed sister at the center of the painting might have been purely for the sake of design, but it unwittingly underscored the centrality of single men and women to Sharp

---

[6] A twentieth-century art historian described the grouping in hierarchal terms centered on marriage and nuclear family units. He failed to point out, however, that other than the brother at the top with his wife and daughter seated in front of him, none of the siblings was grouped exclusively with a spouse and children. John Kerslake, "A Note on Zoffany's 'Sharp Family'," *The Burlington Magazine*, special issue devoted to Portraiture and Britain, 120 (908) (November 1978): 752–754.

[7] Kate Retford, "Sensibility and Genealogy in the Eighteenth-Century Family Portrait: The Collection at Kedleston Hall," *Historical Journal*, 46, no. 3 (2003): 533–560.

4   BEING SINGLE IN GEORGIAN ENGLAND

family life. Not only were the unmarried incorporated into family activities, but they influenced how married siblings worked within the family and were integral in shaping family culture.

Family Background

Though they inherited no land, the Sharp siblings inherited excellent social and ecclesiastic connections. They were grandchildren of an archbishop, their maternal grandfather and father were prebendaries of Durham Cathedral, and the family enjoyed "the charmed circle of ecclesiastical influence at Durham."[8] Eighteenth-century clergy came from the same families and social networks and patronage perpetuated this system.[9] Those patronage networks were especially important to the Sharps who did not have abundant finances. Their father, Thomas, the Archdeacon of Northumberland, and mother, Judith Wheler, used their limited finances to pay for Cambridge educations for the two eldest brothers, John (born 1723) and Thomas (born 1725). Both brothers enjoyed careers in the Church, John assuming his father's position as archdeacon when his father died. Charles (born 1728) was destined for an army career but died abroad in 1744. Three other children born between 1724 and 1727 died as infants or children.

The resultant age gap between John and Thomas and their younger siblings was eventually replicated by geographic distance. Initially, Thomas Jr.'s ecclesiastical appointment was in London, but by the 1760s he also had appointments in the north. His and John's church positions kept them in the north while the younger sons were apprenticed in the south. William (born 1729) and James (born 1731) completed their apprenticeships in the 1750s, established households, and became a surgeon and an ironmonger, respectively. Between 1731 and 1738 two additional siblings died as infants and the three surviving sisters joined the family: Elizabeth (born January 1733), Judith (born November 1733), and Frances (born 1738). Granville (born 1735) was the youngest son. Granville joined his brothers in 1750 when he was apprenticed to a London draper. When their parents died in 1757–58, the sisters moved south to join the London-based brothers, but regularly shuttled between London and their brothers and sister-in-law in Northumberland; Elizabeth eventually settled in Northamptonshire as a result of her 1762 marriage.

---

[8] 'Diary of Thomas Gyll' in *Six North Country Diaries*, volume 118 of *The Publications of the Surtees Society* (Durham: Surtees Society, 1910), 181. SoG Du/Per.

[9] W. M. Jacob, *The Clerical Profession in the Long Eighteenth Century* (Oxford: Oxford University Press, 2007); Brent S. Sirota, *The Christian Monitors: The Church of England and the Age of Benevolence, 1680–1730* (New Haven: Yale University Press, 2014).

INTRODUCTION 5

Demographically, the Sharp siblings were not entirely unrepresentative, though they had lower rates of marriage and higher ages at first marriage than most of their cohort. They perpetuated marriage patterns more like those found in the late seventeenth century or early eighteenth century than like their own cohort. In the late seventeenth century, as many as 20 percent of people had not married by their mid-forties, but in the 1750s and 1760s this percentage had fallen to below 7 percent. Similarly, the age at first marriage dropped from over 27 for men and over 26 for women in the early eighteenth century to over a year younger for men and nearly a year and a half younger for women in the Sharps' cohort.[10] Also, despite a decrease in age at first marriage in the eighteenth century, most men and women spent at least a decade as singles, moving from quasi-independence during apprenticeships and schooling to adult responsibilities and marriage. Paralleling the drop in age at first marriage was a drop in those who married later in life (after age 30).[11]

Though 29-year-old Elizabeth was not middle-aged when she married, as her eulogist claimed, the Sharp siblings did not follow their generation's typical marriage pattern. If they had, more of them would have married, and they would have married at considerably younger ages. Instead, of those fourteen children (eight of whom survived to adulthood), only five married and many married *very* late. The youngest at marriage was 29 and the oldest was 45. Only one of the siblings married before their parents died and it is telling that it was the youngest three siblings who did not marry at all and the sister just older than they who did not remarry after being widowed. The younger siblings grew up with a large group of older siblings, most of whom were not married and whose family energy, therefore, was focused on sibling relations. Also tellingly, the first two siblings to marry, married cousins, thus thickening the horizontal kinship ties at the same time they created new, more hierarchal ties. By the time the second sibling married in 1762, the family had already established a culture that was more about lateral connections with siblings and cousins than vertical connections to parents and children. The combination of late marriage ages and never-married siblings created a family culture where siblinghood offered the emotional, social, and economic comforts usually associated with marriage. Not marrying until their thirties or forties meant even the married siblings had had fifteen or twenty years'

[10] Amy Froide, "Hidden Women: Rediscovering the Singlewomen of Early Modern England," *Local Population Studies*, 68 (Spring 2002): 26–27; E. A. Wrigley and R. S. Schofield, *The Population History of England, 1541–1871* (Cambridge: Cambridge University Press, 1981), 255–265; Peter Laslett, *The World We Have Lost Further Explored: England Before the Industrial Age* (New York: Scribners, 1984), 113; John Gillis, *For Better, For Worse: British Marriages, 1600 to Present* (Oxford: Oxford University Press, 1985), 110–111.

[11] Steven King, "Chance Encounters? Paths to Household Formation in Early Modern England," *International Review of Social History*, 44 (1999): 42.

6 BEING SINGLE IN GEORGIAN ENGLAND

experience as single adults.[12] Similarly, widowhood returned some of them to singleness later in life.

The Sharp siblings were also influenced by their family's particular marriage pattern. Their parents had come of age at the turn of the eighteenth century and had experienced the mortality and marital demographics typical of that generation. Of their parents' combined thirty siblings, seventeen died in infancy or childhood—leaving thirteen who lived to adulthood. Of those thirteen, three never married. Of their mother's siblings who did marry, the brothers married in their mid-twenties, but only one sister married before turning 29. Of the three of their father's siblings who survived to adulthood, all married, but two of them not until their thirties. Therefore, the Sharp siblings inherited patterns of family life already colored by singleness. All families faced situations like those the Sharps encountered, even if they could not replicate the Sharps' social, and later financial, success. Families did not just adapt to or accommodate their single members; they were shaped by them.

Because their parents died relatively young when only one sibling was married, Sharp family power was more horizontal than we usually imagine of eighteenth-century families. The Sharps might have had an amplified version of this power structure, but when so many of their contemporaries entered adulthood with siblings but without parents or spouse, a more horizontal power structure would have been visible in other families as well, no matter their social standing.

Like families up and down the social scale, "their fortunes...frequently rested not on their parents but on all those...babies never born, children never matured, and adults never married."[13] The social mobility that put the Sharp siblings at a far more prosperous income level than their parents' partially rested on the infant mortality rates in their cohort as well as their own late marriages and low fertility. They outlived cousins, aunts, and uncles whose fortunes were funneled to surviving relatives, including the Sharp siblings. The siblings also benefited from their parents' social standing, something that ensured not just Cambridge educations for Thomas and John, but also patronage for a series of livings. Fortuitously, though somewhat counterintuitively, the siblings benefited from the combination of familial high social standing without an accompanying family estate. Without the pressures associated with primogeniture, even the Cambridge-educated brothers had to establish their own households and develop the skills to make them financially viable. It also meant that brotherly responsibility to house younger sisters in the event of parental death had to be shared among several

---

[12] Even for English women and men who married in their early to mid-twenties, they usually did so a decade after leaving home for schooling, apprenticeships, or service. Mary Hartman, *The Household and the Making of History: A Subversive View of the Western Past* (Cambridge: Cambridge University Press, 2004).

[13] Sheila Cooper, "Intergenerational Social Mobility in Late-Seventeenth- and Early-Eighteenth-Century England," *Continuity and Change*, 7, no. 3 (1992): 296.

brothers, an important factor in a family like the Sharps where the sisters clustered at the end of the birth order. William and James had the good fortune of inheriting flourishing businesses from their apprenticeship masters. They also had good relations with their masters, as evidenced by the long visits they paid to family in the north while still under apprenticeship contracts. Elizabeth benefited from her wealthy, landed in-laws/cousins, giving her a life interest in an estate after she was widowed.

The History of Telling the Sharps' Story

John (born 1723), Thomas (1725), William (1729), James (1731), Elizabeth (1733), Judith (1733), Granville (1735), and Frances (1738) did not anticipate the sparkling exhibit they would become in the 1780s, but ever since then they have been the subject of books and essays. Specifically Granville, often considered the grandfather of British anti-slavery, was the subject of various hagiographic treatments in the nineteenth and twentieth centuries. Other family members appeared in histories of musical performances or eighteenth-century professions and estate management. Histories of Anglican clergy also regularly commented on the siblings, due to their father and grandfather's high positions within the Church. Most recently the family has been the subject of a popular biography that emphasized their congeniality and the brothers' involvement in major social trends of late eighteenth-century England.[14]

---

[14] Prince Hoare, *Memoirs of Granville Sharp, Esq. Composed from his own manuscripts, and other authentic documents... With observations on Mr. Sharp's Biblical criticisms, by the...Bishop of St. Davids* (London: Henry Colburn, 1820); Charles Stuart, *A Memoir of Granville Sharp* (New York: American Anti-Slavery Society, 1836); Edward Charles Ponsonby Lascelles, *Granville Sharp and the Freedom of the Slaves in England* (London: Humphrey Milford, 1928); Ruth Anna Fisher, "Granville Sharp and Lord Mansfield," *The Journal of Negro History*, 28, no. 4 (October 1943): 381–389; Ernest Marshall Howse, *Saints in Politics: The 'Clapham Sect' and the Growth of Freedom* (Toronto: University of Toronto Press, 1952); Jeannette B. Holland and Jan LaRue, "The Sharp Manuscript, London 1759–c1793: A Uniquely Annotated Music Catalogue," *Bulletin of the New York Public Library*, 13, no. 3 (March 1969): 147–166; Gretchen Gerzina, *Black London: Life before Emancipation* (New Brunswick: Rutgers University Press, 1995); Brian Crosby, "Private Concerts on Land and Water: The Musical Activities of the Sharp Family, c.1750–1790," *Royal Musical Association Research Chronicle*, no. 34 (2001): 1–118; Adam Hochschild, *Bury the Chains: Prophets and Rebels in the Fight to Free an Empire's Slaves* (Boston: Houghton Mifflin Harcourt, 2006); Simon Schama, *Rough Crossings: Britain, the Slaves and the American Revolution* (New York: HarperCollins, 2006); Simon David Iain Fleming, "A Century of Music Production in Durham City 1711–1811: A Documentary Study" (PhD thesis, Durham University, 2009), http://etheses.dur.ac.uk/40; Briony McDonaagh, "Women, Enclosure and Estate Improvement in Eighteenth-Century Northamptonshire," *Rural History*, 20, no. 2 (2009): 143–162; Andrew Lyall, *Granville Sharp's Cases on Slavery* (Oxford: Hart Publishing, 2017); Michelle Faubert, *Granville Sharps' Uncovered Letter and the Zong Massacre* (London: Palgrave Macmillan, 2018); Hester Grant, *The Good Sharps: The Brothers and Sisters Who Remade Their World* (London: Chatto & Windus, 2020); Sean P. Hughes and G. Anne Davies, "Why is William Sharp's Name Forgotten When His Novel Method for Treating Fractures of the Ankle is Still Used Today?" *Journal of Medical Biography* (March 2022), https://doi.org/10.1177/09677720221082103.

8 BEING SINGLE IN GEORGIAN ENGLAND

In the first biography of Granville, written by a family acquaintance less than a decade after his death, the author mentioned Granville's brothers' work and personalities. Their wives were not mentioned and the sisters were described in one phrase: "the[ir] virtues were domestic and exemplary."[15] Similarly, a 1928 biography listed Granville's siblings but conflated Judith and Frances and claimed Elizabeth was not very involved with the Sharps because she was married.[16] A similar misrepresentation of Elizabeth was repeated in a 2009 account of the abolition movement.[17] A 2020 biography of the siblings dismisses much of the sisters' labor.[18] Dismissal or ignorance of women's activities, while disheartening, was not particularly unusual, at least for the nineteenth and early twentieth centuries. What is unusual is that sisters were mentioned at all in the early accounts meant to focus on Granville's singularly heroic anti-slavery work.

The siblings appear in Granville's biographies because anyone who encounters the Sharp family papers, no matter how focused they are on Granville's anti-slavery work, cannot avoid his siblings. It is impossible to tell his story without them. However, because the focus has so long been on Granville, with an inherited attitude about enlightened male action, the story of the Sharps' family life has become skewed and limited.

Intent on securing Granville on the heroic pedestal that earned him a monument in Westminster Abbey, accounts of his family life have rendered it solely as a support system and idyllic respite for the intrepid Granville. But family and domestic life were not merely beautiful backdrops for heroic men, they were a place of communal labor where families "routinized" their values through "unremarkable everyday rehearsal" in ways that made "imagined cultural ideals...tangible."[19] The Sharps' labor built and perpetuated households, provided for the material, social, and emotional support of each member, and yes, facilitated reform activities. Simultaneously, that labor inculcated family values and gendered expectations while shaping domestic power relationships.

A rich scholarly tradition has influenced how I approached the Sharp family. In particular, three strands of scholarship were essential to understanding the Sharps. First, understanding sibling relations is crucial. Though "ties of fraternal regard were drawn with unusual closeness" among the Sharps, siblinghood was a nearly universal experience in Georgian England.[20] Fortunately, scholarship on families, friendships, old age, and marital status have all touched on sibling

---

[15] Hoare, *Memoirs of Granville Sharp*, 22.   [16] Lascelles, *Granville Sharp*, 3.

[17] Schama, *Rough Crossings*, 22, 36.   [18] Grant, *The Good Sharps*.

[19] Henry French and Mark Rothery, "'Upon Your Entry into the World': Masculine Values and the Threshold of Adulthood among Landed Elites in England 1680–1800," *Social History*, 33, no. 4 (November 2008): 404.

[20] John Owen, "A Discourse Occasioned by the Death of William Sharp, Esq. late of Fulham House; Delivered in Substance at Fulham Church, on Sunday, March 25, 1810," *Gentleman's Magazine* (November 1810): 450–453.

relations.[21] Additionally, there has been a steady supply of sibling-based analyses, particularly in the last dozen years.[22] This scholarship has revealed siblings' importance to family financial, emotional, and social decisions. It has also shown how siblinghood—more resistant to legal and cultural changes than marriage—influenced conceptions of masculinity and domesticity.[23] Scholars have also highlighted how siblinghood's lifelong and horizontal nature make it unique among family relationships. Siblinghood was the most important family relationship for unmarried people in the eighteenth century; cousins, aunts and uncles, nieces and nephews all emerged from sibling relationships and were crucial to how unmarried people viewed and functioned within families. As historians of emotion have recently noted, "the emotional lives of couples are played out within the context of wider kin networks."[24] Siblings were also a principal source of friends.[25] Siblinghood offered not a surrogacy for marriage and parenthood, but its own unique qualities and intimacies.

Second, the twenty-first century has seen an increase in scholarship on marital status and the experience of singleness from the Middle Ages to the twentieth century and on both sides of the Atlantic.[26] This scholarship has highlighted not

[21] Susannah Ottaway, *The Decline of Life: Old Age in Eighteenth-Century England* (Cambridge: Cambridge University Press, 2004), 168–169; Ruth Perry, *Novel Relations: The Transformation of Kinship in English Literature and Culture, 1748–1818* (Cambridge: Cambridge University Press, 2004), 143–189; Naomi Tadmor, *Family and Friends in Eighteenth-Century England: Household, Kinship, and Patronage* (Cambridge: Cambridge University Press, 2001), 37, 120–122, 128, 137; Patricia Crawford, *Blood, Bodies and Family in Early Modern England* (New York: Routledge, 2004), 209–230; Froide, *Never Married*, 46–49, 52–64, 74–83, 107–110.

[22] Lori Glover, *All Our Relations: Blood Ties and Emotional Bonds among the Early South Carolina Gentry* (Baltimore: Johns Hopkins University Press, 2000); Lee Chambers, "Married to Each Other; Married to the Cause: Singlehood and Sibship in Antebellum Massachusetts," *Women's History Review*, 17, no. 3 (September 2008): 341–357; Leonore Davidoff, *Thicker than Water: Siblings and Their Relations, 1780–1920* (Oxford: Oxford University Press, 2011); Dallett Hemphill, *Siblings: Brothers and Sisters in American History* (Oxford: Oxford University Press, 2011); Christopher H. Johnson and David Warren Sabean, eds., *Sibling Relations and the Transformation of European Kinship* (New York: Berghahn, 2011); Amy Harris, *Siblinghood and Social Relations in Georgian England: Share and Share Alike* (Manchester: Manchester University Press, 2012); Jonathan R. Lyon, *Princely Brothers and Sisters: The Sibling Bond in German Politics, 1100–1250* (Ithaca: Cornell University Press, 2013); Bernard Capp, *The Ties that Bind: Siblings, Family, and Society in Early Modern England* (Oxford: Oxford University Press, 2018).

[23] Davidoff, *Thicker than Water*, 4–5, 260–262, 303–307.

[24] Katie Barclay, Jeffrey Meek, and Andrea Thomson, "Marriage and Emotion in Historical Context," in Katie Barclay, Jeffrey Meek, and Andrea Thomson, eds., *Courtship, Marriage and Marriage Breakdown: Approaches from the History of Emotion* (New York: Routledge, 2019), 4.

[25] Elizabeth Sharp Prowse's memoranda based on her diary sometimes show a distinction between friends and siblings. At other times she blurs those lines in a way described by Naomi Tadmor in *Family and Friends* (2001). See, for example, Elizabeth's notations on July 1759, September 28, 1769, August 22, 1794, October 10, 1795, and April 11, 1806.

[26] Lee Chambers-Schiller, *Liberty a Better Husband: Single Women in America: The Generations of 1780–1840* (New Haven and London: Yale University Press, 1984); Olwen Hufton, "Women without Men: Widows and Spinsters in Great Britain and France in the Eighteenth Century," *Journal of Family History*, 9 (1984): 355–376; Judith Bennett and Amy Froide, eds., *Singlewomen in the European Past, 1250–1800* (Philadelphia: University of Pennsylvania Press, 1999); Pamela Sharpe, "Dealing with Love: The Ambigous Independence of the Single Woman in Early Modern England," *Gender and History*, 11, no. 2 (July 1999): 209–232; Bridget Hill, *Women Alone: Spinsters in England, 1660–1850*

10 BEING SINGLE IN GEORGIAN ENGLAND

only the importance of those experiences, but also offered the corrective that despite the rhetorical force of marriage discussions, on any given day the majority of adults would have been unmarried.

My approach to singleness has been shaped by questions posed by Amy Froide in *Never Married* and Steven King in "Chance Encounters?" Froide asked what family life would look like if it began with single people instead of married couples; King called for micro-historical analyses of the process of getting married and forming households.[27] There are numerous family-based micro-histories. However, many of these have tended to employ family experiences as a means to discovering things about national or international concerns and not about internal family dynamics.[28] King, however, advocated for a micro-historical approach to families themselves. He argued that only a case-study approach could untangle the complex factors affecting marriage choices, such as personality, mortality rates, family negotiations, and economic considerations.[29] I employ King's approach, highlighting familial relationships and how they change over time. Perspectives of family life alter dramatically when the viewpoint of the unmarried becomes the starting point and a case-study approach is one of the best ways to see that perspective. Another advantage of using a single family as a case study is that it allows a close analysis of single women and single men simultaneously.[30]

Froide's answer to the question of how family life would look if it began with siblings drew from a variety of probate records and personal accounts to demonstrate several aspects of single women's lives: they had a broad, female-focused social network; they enjoyed meaningful connections with their family of origin, particularly sisters and especially single sisters; they maintained lasting connections with cousins, aunts, uncles, nieces, and nephews; and they played a vital role in the management of households and the perpetuation of property.

(New Haven: Yale University Press, 2001); Bella De Paulo, *Singled Out: How Singles are Stereotyped, Stigmatized, and Ignored, and Still Live Happily Ever After* (New York: St. Martin's Press, 2006); Cordelia Beattie, *Medieval Single Women: The Politics of Social Classification in Late Medieval England* (Oxford: Oxford University Press, 2007); Alison Duncan, "Power and the Old Maid: The never-Married Gentlewoman in Her Family, 1740–1835," *Women's History Magazine*, no. 63 (Summer 2010): 11–18; James Rosenheim, "The Pleasures of a Single Life: Envisioning Bachelorhood in Early Eighteenth-Century England," *Gender & History*, 27, no. 2 (August 2015): 307–328.

[27] Froide, *Never Married*; King, "Chance Encounters?" *International Review of Social History*, 44 (1999): 23–46. About the usefulness of case studies, see Karen Harvey and Alexandra Shepard, "What Have Historians Done with Masculinity? Reflections on Five Centuries of British History, c. 1500–1900," *Journal of British Studies*, 44, no. 2 (2005): 280.

[28] Emma Rothschild, *The Inner Life of Empires: An Eighteenth-Century History* (Princeton: Princeton University Press, 2011); *An Infinite History: The Story of a Family in France over Three Centuries* (Princeton: Princeton University Press, 2021); Reetta Eiranen, "Emotional and Social Ties in the Construction of Nationalism: A Group Biographical Approach to the Tengström Family in Nineteenth-Century Finland," *Studies on National Movements*, 4 (2019): 1–38.

[29] Steven King, "Chance, Choice and Calculation in the Process of 'Getting Married': A Reply to John R. Gillis and Richard Wall," *International Review of Social History*, 44, no. 1 (April 1999): 69–76.

[30] Froide, *Never Married*, 221.

The third strand of scholarship behind *Being Single in Georgian England* is the work on household management and gendered domestic authority. This scholarship is particularly rich for eighteenth-century England.[31] Scholars have discovered practices that reveal how ideas of "gender values were assimilated, enacted and reproduced within families."[32] Men, particularly elite and middle-class husbands and fathers, relied on kinship networks and households to establish their autonomy and independence. In what follows I echo much of what earlier scholars have discovered and demonstrate that in addition to the vertical axis of patriarchal authority there was a horizontal axis of sororal and fraternal authority upon which men and women negotiated domestic relations.

What the Sharps' Experiences Reveal

The Sharps' experiences underscore how domestic and marital decisions were shaped by a collective culture that had its own internal dynamics. Having multiple late-to-marry or never-married siblings meant that sibling ties continued to exert influence over family culture, even after some siblings married. The youngest three siblings never married and the sister just older than they never remarried after being widowed young, suggesting that, as family culture became more entrenched, finding an acceptable spouse became more difficult, and perhaps less desirable, for the younger siblings. In addition, the Sharp siblings influenced how the next generation approached marriage.[33] Pre-existing expectations and emotional bonds determined whether a Sharp married, even when there were possible suitors. Additionally, cousin marriage—systematically practiced by the Sharps—was a way to retain the existing family culture with a new marriage.

For the Sharps, couplehood was not central to household formation. The need for economic and material connections to others meant kin relations were inextricably bound with marital choices that went beyond individual emotional needs.[34] For both women and men, households granted status even without

---

[31] Amanda Vickery, *The Gentleman's Daughter: Women's Lives in Georgian England* (New Haven: Yale University Press, 1998); Philip Carter, *Men and the Emergence of Polite Society, Britain 1660–1800* (Routledge, 2001); Amanda Vickery, *Behind Closed Doors: At Home in Georgian England* (New Haven: Yale University Press, 2009); Jon Stobart and Mark Rothery, *Consumption and the Country House* (Oxford: Oxford University Press, 2016); Hannah Barker, *Family and Business During the Industrial Revolution* (Oxford: Oxford University Press, 2017); Margot Finn and Kate Smith, eds., *The East India Company at Home, 1757–1857* (London: University College London, 2018).

[32] French and Rothery, "'Upon Your Entry into the World'": 403. See also Karen Harvey, *The Little Republic: Masculinity and Domestic Authority in Eighteenth-Century Britain* (Oxford: Oxford University Press, 2012); Henry French and Mark Rothery, *Man's Estate: Landed Gentry Masculinities, 1660–1900* (Oxford: Oxford University Press, 2012).

[33] Amy Harris, "'She Never Inclined to It': Childhood, Family Relationships, and Marital Choice in Eighteenth-Century England," *Journal of the History of Childhood and Youth*, 12, no. 2 (Spring 2019): 179–198; Davidoff, *Thicker than Water*, 165–169.

[34] Barclay, Meek, and Thomson, "Marriage and Emotion," 4–5.

marriage. While some scholarly discussions of singleness focus on negative pressures (no one to marry, low wages, resistance from family members) or on prosperous women preferring singleness to unappealing spouses, the Sharps show how positive family relationships and successful household management could influence marital choices.

Advice literature cast marriage as the expected and preferred state, but eighteenth-century female critics pointed to marriage's inherent inequality as detrimental.[35] Though the Sharps did not advocate for reforming marriage's gendered hierarchy, their lived experience pushed against advice literature that saw marriage as a stabilizing force for both public and private behavior—as an institution that protected masculinity and femininity from "tainting" their primary spheres of action. For decades, most Sharps, male and female, successfully moved between public and domestic spheres without marriage's protective cloak, thereby blunting any social disapprobation the late-to-marry or never-married family members might have otherwise faced.[36]

The Sharp family is not representative of every eighteenth-century family, but it is representative of what was possible in the eighteenth century. The Sharps were exceptional, but they were not singular. In many ways the Sharps are a best-case scenario for married and unmarried kin working together.[37] This ground-level view of the Sharps exposes how families' internal dynamics shaped emotional and economic decisions across time and space; it highlights family as a process as much as a group of relationships.[38]

The Sharps' experience highlights that in the eighteenth century being unmarried did not render someone family-less. Despite the geographic distance between them, the Sharps were, as brother John once remarked, "remarkable for unanimity."[39] Their records show a family spread over Durham, Northumberland, Northamptonshire, and London, yet bound tightly together through correspondence, shared finances, extended visits, support for religious and social benevolence, care for nephew and nieces, and summer holidays spent together. To maintain connections between visits the siblings exchanged letters individually and as a group. During the 1750s their correspondence was dominated by what they termed "common letters." While a group audience was often assumed by

---

[35] Gillian Williamson, *British Masculinity in the Gentleman's Magazine, 1731 to 1815* (Basingstoke: Palgrave Macmillan, 2016), 98; Mary Astell, *Some Reflections on Marriage* (London: John Nutt, 1700).

[36] Chris Roulston, "Space and the Representation of Marriage in Eighteenth-Century Advice Literature," *Eighteenth Century: Theory and Interpretation*, 49, no. 1 (Spring 2008): 25–41.

[37] In other research I have found that similar patterns occurred, though with substantially less documentation, among families with small farm holdings; see Amy Harris, "The Longest Relationship: Analyzing Sibling Co-Residence," in Rosemary O'Day and Susan Cogan, eds., *Sibling Relationships in Early Modern England* (forthcoming).

[38] Carlfred B. Broderick, *Understanding Family Process: Basics of Family Systems Theory* (Thousand Oaks: Sage, 1993).

[39] John and Mary Sharp to Judith Sharp, May 14, 1770, D3549/16/1/1. It is telling that he used this term in the middle of the most contentious time in Sharp family relations.

INTRODUCTION 13

eighteenth-century letter writers, the Sharps explicitly wrote and read these letters as an ongoing fraternal conversation.[40] At the heart of these letters was a playful sense of puns and inside jokes—much of it completely incomprehensible to a modern reader. The Sharp siblings loved wordplay—as evidenced by their almost giddy use of the musical symbol # for their surname. The Sharps' pattern of inside jokes and witticisms formed a shared language that designated the siblings as the ultimate insiders.

While their family interactions were exclusive and intimate, other aspects of their social lives expanded far beyond their kin group. They cruised the rivers and canals between April and October and held musical evenings at one of their homes between November and March.[41] In essence, the Sharps created their own social season, overlapping the London social season but with a guest list entirely in their control. Communal and neighborhood social patterns became less public and increasingly domestic over the course of the early modern period.[42] The Sharps, like other wealthy Georgians, now had homes, dishes, and furnishings meant for hosting dinner parties and invitation-only social gatherings and they took advantage of those resources.[43] At William's first house they regularly hosted nearly one hundred guests and by the 1770s they offered occasional "glee evenings" with over four hundred attendees.[44]

Sharp family culture was educated, entertaining, and deeply religious. The sheer number of religious musical scores they possessed and regularly used highlights how religious belief and observance permeated all family activities.[45] Granville's personal daily musical devotional; John and Thomas's composing family prayers, hymns, and sermons; and Elizabeth's daily household prayers are among the most obvious examples of piety, but religious practice and belief were important to all the siblings.[46] While obviously influenced by the Enlightenment's "glorification of print culture, sociability, toleration, utility, and merit," the Sharps

---

[40] Letters had long been a way of constructing households and relationships: see Nancy Wright, Margaret W. Ferguson, and Andrew R. Buck, eds., *Women, Property, and Letters of the Law in Early Modern England* (Toronto: University of Toronto Press, 2004), 201–203; Sarah Pearsall, *Atlantic Families: Lives and Letters in the Later Eighteenth Century* (New York and Oxford: Oxford University Press, 2008); Eve Tavor Bannet, *Empire of Letters: Letter Manuals and Transatlantic Correspondence, 1688–1820* (Cambridge: Cambridge University Press, 2005).

[41] Crosby, "Private Concerts," 39.

[42] Keith Thomas, *Ends of Life: Roads to Fulfilment in Early Modern England* (Oxford: Oxford University Press, 2009), 224.

[43] Thomas, *Ends of Life*, 223–224.   [44] Crosby, "Private Concerts," 33–36, 101–107.

[45] Crosby, "Private Concerts," 68.

[46] John Sharp, sermon drafts, GB-0036-SHS, Durham Cathedral Library; John Sharp, family prayer, D3549/9/1/16; Thomas Sharp, hymn tunes, *c.*1750s–1760s, Bamburgh Manuscripts, Durham Cathedral Music Manuscripts, MS M89, MS M90, listed in Crosby, *Catalogue of Durham Cathedral Music Manuscripts*, 84–85; R. D., "Visit to Mrs. Prowse at Wicken Park," extract of letter from a "Gentleman in Northumberland to his Friend in London," October 2, 1777, D3549/14/1/6; James Sharp, scrapbook, 1772–1813, clipping account of visit to Wicken Park, October 1777, D3549/12/1/4.

14 BEING SINGLE IN GEORGIAN ENGLAND

resisted some of its secularizing aspects.[47] They combined religious practice with their desire for sociability and with what they considered common sense reforms.

Even with such familial abundance, the Sharps were not unfamiliar with the pressures families faced and how those pressures could lead to calamitous outcomes.[48] They witnessed family estrangements among their associates and were called upon to offer support or facilitate reconciliation. Among their relatives there were two disastrous marriages. Other relatives wrangled over property rights and a cousin, suffering from delusions, murdered his wife.[49]

The Sharps demonstrate ways domestic masculinity was enacted when it was not necessarily attached to the roles of husband and father and perhaps not even the role of householder. Though Samuel Richardson proclaimed that "A dutiful son, an affectionate brother, a faithful friend, must give a moral assurance of making an excellent husband," many men never became husbands.[50] Scholarship has considered male singleness, but often in opposition to or dependence on other men's domestic authority or constructed through public or intellectual endeavors. The Sharps' experience underscores ways single men were still essential and valued participants in the domestic economy. The brothers' experience leads to a reassessment of gendered domestic authority. Because all but one married and had households, it is easy to assume that was where their authority arose. However, they established households before marriage, most managed those houses as single men for many years, and most of them were not fathers until late in life. So, underneath their roles as married, householding fathers, there was a pre-existing experience as single brothers sharing household duties with sisters and other brothers.

Much about the Sharps will seem modern, but I have not attempted to trace roots of modernity or focus on elements of modern family life reflected in the Sharps' experiences. When I started this project, I thought the Sharps were unusual and interesting. And lucky. The more I have studied the records of their lives, the more I have noticed just how sincerely good they were. They were generous and kind to those with fewer resources while happily enjoying their own

---

[47] Margaret Jacob, *The First Knowledge Economy: Human Capital and the European Economy, 1750–1850* (Cambridge: Cambridge University Press, 2014), 53.

[48] Susan Broomhall, ed., *Emotions in the Household, 1200–1900* (Basingstoke: Palgrave Macmillan, 2008); Katie Barclay, Jeffrey Meek, and Andrea Thomson, "Marriage and Emotion in Historical Context," in Katie Barclay, Jeffrey Meek, and Andrea Thomson, eds., *Courtship, Marriage and Marriage Breakdown: Approaches from the History of Emotion* (New York: Palgrave Macmillan, 2019), 1–16.

[49] Elizabeth Sharp Prowse, memorandum and commonplace book, loose newspaper clipping after April 17, 1800, D3549/14/1/1; "Accounts in the matter of Granville William Wheler Medhurst, lunatic," Chancery Masters' Account Books, 1801–09, C 101/3800, TNA; "Petition for Maintenance of the Eldest Son of a Lunatic; and an Allowance of what the Committees have expended in discharge of his Debts [1806]," in *A Treatise on the Law Concerning Idiots, Lunatics, and Other Persons Non Compotes Mentis* (London: W. Reed, 1812), 2:564–573.

[50] Samuel Richardson, *A collection of the moral and instructive sentiments, maxims, cautions, and reflexions, contained in the histories of Pamela, Clarissa, and Sir Charles Grandison* (London, 1755), 228. *Eighteenth Century Collections Online*. Gale Group, accessed 2009.

abundance. They were capable of having a really good time, but never in a way that would harm the family's reputation and conviviality (no one developed gambling, drinking, sexual, or financial problems). I would be hard-pressed to discover an eighteenth-century family with better relationships and sense of social responsibility than the Sharps, but they were still thoroughly eighteenth-century people. The Sharps seemed completely unbothered by unequal investment in daughters' educations, or assumptions that relief efforts should be focused on the "worthy poor," or that Africans were axiomatically inferior, or that religious toleration did not include accepting Methodist enthusiasm. They saw injustice, but that did not lead to efforts to dismantle hierarchy, even as they argued for a more justly practiced hierarchy.

This acquiescence to many aspects of Georgian social hierarchy is starkly evident in the Sharps' seemingly unproblematic acceptance of a gendered hierarchy. While women had always had important social responsibilities, in the eighteenth century they had more publicly visible social roles.[51] However, the Sharp sisters did not join any debates on women's status or write on the topic and Granville's abstract ideas on marriage reflected a straightforward support for coverture. It is possible that the family's comparatively benign practice of patriarchy—one which afforded substantial independence for the sisters—buffered them from the more egregious experiences of gender inequality.

The Sharps' lived reality was more radical than any of their political or religious positions. Their daily experience was an implicit critique of hierarchal patriarchal household structures. While there were some hierarchies, particularly the unremarked upon one between husbands and wives, the most important Sharp power nexus was horizontal, not vertical. Unmarried and married, householders or not, parents or not, no sibling was cast as subordinate while others were cast as autonomous agents; no sibling held control over the purse-strings, thus constraining the others. Ultimately, the Sharps' experiences reveal how important lateral kin like siblings and cousins were to marital and household decisions, expose single sociability *not* centered on courtship, highlight the importance of aunting and uncling on their own terms, demonstrate how charitable acts and philanthropic endeavors could serve as outlets or partial replacements for parenthood, and uncover genealogical practices tied to values and identity instead of to biological descendants' possession of property.

*　*　*

Colors flying and music playing, from mid-August to early September 1777 the Sharps drew large crowds as they played away summer evenings on the Thames

---

[51] Anthony Fletcher, *Growing Up in England: The Experience of Childhood, 1600–1914* (New Haven: Yale University Press, 2008), 28–29; Bernard Capp, *When Gossips Meet: Women, Family, and Neighborhood in Early Modern England* (Oxford: Oxford University Press, 2003).

16 BEING SINGLE IN GEORGIAN ENGLAND

and canals. They traveled in William and James's new yacht, the *Union*, inviting anybody who followed them to tour the luxurious vessel; the yacht boasted eleven beds, could accommodate up to forty diners, and was furnished with "uncommon taste and magnificence [*sic*]."[52] What music they performed is not known, but given their fondness for Handel it is not too difficult to imagine them playing *Water Music*, consciously or unconsciously replicating its first performance, on board the royal barge sixty years previously.

The Sharps performed for the royal family in a similar fashion to a 1770 encounter—as they moved upriver and again on their return. In 1777, however, the king visited with the Sharps several times, arranging for performances and a tour of the yacht. During the Sharps' last night at Richmond, the royal family lingered after the music concluded. "To the great Entertainment of the King & Queen who stayed a great while as they could see what we were about," Frances told Judith. The monarchs followed along the shore where the boats made anchor and watched as the Sharps lit their candles, organized their supper, and prepared to retire for sleep.[53]

The yacht, the fluttering family colors, and the music were merely vehicles; the real entertainment was the Sharps themselves, a curiosity to see what they were about. And the Sharps knew it and enjoyed it. An account of the events was published in the newspaper, but it was not just outside observers who saw this encounter as a high point of Sharp sociality. One of the siblings transcribed the newspaper coverage and Frances's letter to Judith is one of only two documents of Frances's that were preserved and copied.[54]

As George III and Charlotte listened to the Sharps' music and observed their harmony, both musical and metaphorical, it is tempting to speculate about whether there was more than a touch of envy in the monarch's heart. Four of his siblings died between 1765 and 1775 and he struggled with his remaining siblings, particularly over their marital choices.[55] He might have been just a bit jealous of the Sharps' conviviality and tranquility as he watched them quietly snuffing out their candles and settling in for a peaceful night. The Sharps' encounter with the royal family was spectacular, but the Sharps' easy harmony came not from spectacular actions but from a lifetime of careful work. That work allowed the single and married Sharps to sail through life with enviable intimacy. Their journey reveals much about what it meant to live single in eighteenth-century families.

---

[52] "Extract from *General Evening Post*, 11–13 Sep 1777," copied and included with a copy letter from Frances to Judith describing the same events, D3549/16/1/1.

[53] Frances Sharp to Judith Sharp, August 30, 1777.

[54] For a detailed account of the 1770 and 1777 water schemes, including transcriptions of their accounts, see Crosby, "Private Concerts," 45–52.

[55] His siblings' marriages, sometimes done in secret, led to the Royal Marriages Act 1772. The act prohibited members of the royal family from marrying without the monarch's approval. It remained in force until its replacement by the Succession to the Crown Act 2013. For an account of George III's siblings, see Stella Tillyard, *A Royal Affair: George III and His Scandalous Siblings* (New York: Random House, 2006).

1

Prehistory

"At this period [1680s] the ArchB[isho]p of York, and his Brother Sir Joshua Sharpe, alter'd the spelling of the name, and the Armorial bearings... This Grant is now at Clare Hall 1825."[1]

Elizabeth Sharp Prowse, while preparing a family lineage chart

Introduction

In August of 1817, Andrew Bowlt, curate of Bamburgh, Northumberland, changed his surname and his family arms.[2] He became Andrew Sharp when he married Catherine Sharp, a long-time acquaintance. It was not uncommon practice for a man to change his surname to match a prominent, wealthy wife's name, especially if the woman was the last of a particular surname, as Catherine was. Additionally, Andrew's tying himself to the Sharps' ecclesiastical legacy was a wise career decision, given that for three generations the Sharps had held high ecclesiastical offices in the north. But there might have been an additional reason Andrew changed his surname. It might have been because Catherine and Jemima inherited a cabinet that had been in the family since 1687.

The cabinet was not particularly unusual or spectacular—it simply contained a coin collection begun in 1687 by their grandfather John Sharp as a diverting way to spend evenings, and around the time he and his brother altered the family arms referenced above. The coin collection had been passed to his eldest son, who then passed it to his brother Thomas. Thomas, in turn, passed it to one of his sons, also named John. And in 1792, the younger John bequeathed it to his daughter, Jemima. In his will, John described how the coins and their mahogany cabinet had "been in the Family for three Generations" and had "been collecting for above one hundred years," and he wanted them to continue in the family's possession. He then gave an unusual direction:

---

[1] Elizabeth Sharp Prowse, memorandum and commonplace book 1758, page 1, D3549/14/1/1.
[2] Andrew Bowlt, license to assume name of Sharp upon marriage with Catherine Sharp, with grant of arms, 1817, D3549/18/1/1.

Being Single in Georgian England: Families, Households, and the Unmarried. Amy Harris, Oxford University Press.
© Amy Harris 2023. DOI: 10.1093/oso/9780192869494.003.0002

18 BEING SINGLE IN GEORGIAN ENGLAND

my daughter should not part with my said cabinet out of her possession but still continue it down as far as in her lies in the Family and Name of Sharp but in case she should happen to Marry a person of the Name of Sharp or one who shall change his Name to Sharp in consequence of such Marriage cabinet and what belongs to it to be retained in her Family.[3]

Jemima never married, but she passed the cabinet and coins to her cousin Catherine in 1813. The coins had monetary value, but not enough to motivate Catherine's husband to change his surname. Instead, of greater value was what the coins represented: a family culture worth preserving. The coins' real value lay in their "Sharpness," their ability to transfer two centuries of family virtues and privileges to nineteenth-century descendants.

The coins, the cabinet, and their 130 years of history, were a manifestation of a central aspect of eighteenth-century family life: the generational transmission of family values. These values were sometimes associated with material objects, but they were often more subtly perpetuated in daily interactions. The Sharp familial culture that developed in the early eighteenth century—and the expectations surrounding it—is glimpsed in autobiographical writing or family correspondence and is valorized in later reminiscences.

The family culture Catherine and Jemima Sharp inherited had its roots in the mid-seventeenth century, when their great-grandparents were born. Those grandparents, Grace Higgons and Sir George Wheler, and Elizabeth Palmer and John Sharp, consciously cultivated certain behaviors, particularly those associated with Christian devotion and amiable family interactions. Simultaneously, infant and child mortality shaped family cultures and material inheritance. The Sharps' and Whelers' style of family governance and relationships influenced Sharp family culture throughout the eighteenth century.

The Whelers and Sharps

There are no existing firsthand records from the Sharp siblings' grandmothers, Grace Higgons or Elizabeth Palmer, but their grandfathers left records (Figure 1.1). From George Wheler's account of his upbringing and travels, as well as John Sharp's (later archbishop of York) prodigious ecclesiastical work, it is clear the Sharp siblings inherited a family culture that encouraged intellectual pursuits, prized spiritual and religious devotion, cultivated a love of books and art, and valued sociability. As was common for clerical families of the time, the Sharps and the Whelers ensured their children were taught to appreciate music, for both

---

[3] John Sharp, will, written April 17–May 21, 1792, proved May 2, 1793, Prerogative Court of Canterbury, PROB 11/1232, National Archives.

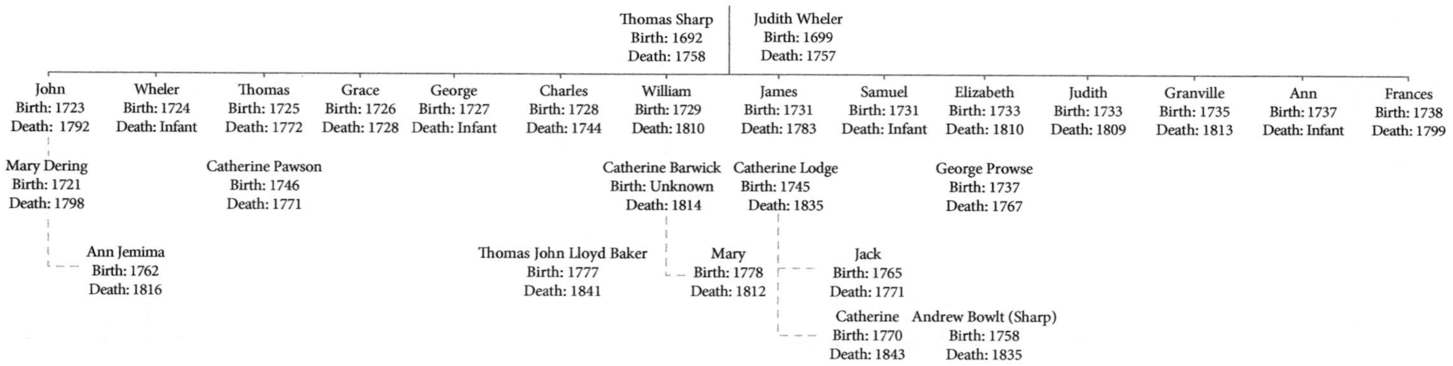

Thomas Sharp
Birth: 1692
Death: 1758

Judith Wheler
Birth: 1699
Death: 1757

John
Birth: 1723
Death: 1792

Mary Dering
Birth: 1721
Death: 1798

Ann Jemima
Birth: 1762
Death: 1816

Wheler
Birth: 1724
Death: Infant

Thomas
Birth: 1725
Death: 1772

Catherine Pawson
Birth: 1746
Death: 1771

Grace
Birth: 1726
Death: 1728

George
Birth: 1727
Death: Infant

Charles
Birth: 1728
Death: 1744

William
Birth: 1729
Death: 1810

Catherine Barwick
Birth: Unknown
Death: 1814

Thomas John Lloyd Baker
Birth: 1777
Death: 1841

Mary
Birth: 1778
Death: 1812

James
Birth: 1731
Death: 1783

Catherine Lodge
Birth: 1745
Death: 1835

Jack
Birth: 1765
Death: 1771

Catherine
Birth: 1770
Death: 1843

Andrew Bowlt (Sharp)
Birth: 1758
Death: 1835

Samuel
Birth: 1731
Death: Infant

Elizabeth
Birth: 1733
Death: 1810

George Prowse
Birth: 1737
Death: 1767

Judith
Birth: 1733
Death: 1809

Granville
Birth: 1735
Death: 1813

Ann
Birth: 1737
Death: Infant

Frances
Birth: 1738
Death: 1799

Figure 1.1 Sharp siblings with parents, spouses, and children

20 BEING SINGLE IN GEORGIAN ENGLAND

religious and recreational purposes.[4] Religious devotion and practice were at the center of family culture for both families.[5] Their descendants' descriptions of the Whelers and Sharps are unsurprisingly glowing. None of these records reveal much about day-to-day family life in the late seventeenth century, but they do touch on attributes and activities the families displayed and encouraged. In turn, those traditions and expectations influenced the Sharp siblings throughout their lives.

The Whelers

Sir George Wheler was born in Holland while his Royalist parents were in exile during the Interregnum. Though he had religious inclinations as a child, George initially pursued travel writing and antiquarianism.[6] As a young man he joined his father in a Chancery suit against other members of the extended Wheler family to claim a portion of a Spitalfields estate.[7] After his return from a journey to Venice, Greece, and Turkey, he was knighted in 1682 and then turned his attention to a clerical career.[8] With patronage and timely inheritances, he earned an MA at Oxford and was ordained in 1684. He held multiple livings as well as a prebendary in Durham.

In 1677, George married Grace Higgons (Figure 1.2).[9] Her father was a staunch defender of James II, and her brothers were fervent Jacobites who joined his exiled court in France.[10] They were arrested, though later released, for suspected involvement in the 1696 plot to assassinate William III.[11] Grace's Jacobite con-

---

[4] Elizabeth Chevill, "Clergy, Music Societies and the Development of a Musical Tradition: A Study of Music Societies in Hereford, 1690–1760," in Susan Wollenberg and Simon McVeigh, eds., *Concert Life in Eighteenth-Century Britain* (London: Routledge, 2016), 37–38; William Weber, "Musical Culture and the Capital City: The Epoch of the *beau monde* in London, 1700–1870," in *Concert Life in Eighteenth-Century Britain*, 74.

[5] Brent S. Sirota, *The Christian Monitors: The Church of England and the Age of Benevolence, 1680–1730* (New Haven: Yale University Press, 2014), 2.

[6] Sir George Wheler, autobiography, 1700, MS 3286, Lambeth Palace Archives (LPA).

[7] "The Estate of Sir Charles Wheler and the Wilkes family," in *Survey of London: Volume 27, Spitalfields and Mile End New Town*, ed. F. H. W. Sheppard (London: London County Council, 1957), 108–115.

[8] David Booy, *Personal Disclosures: An Anthology of Self-Writings from the Seventeenth-Century* (London: Routledge, 2016), 271–274.

[9] Joseph Lemuel Chester, comp., Joseph Foster, ed., *London Marriage Licenses and Allegations, 1521–1869* (London: Wyman and Sons, n.d.), Registry of the Vicar-General of Canterbury, George Wheler and Grace Higgons, marriage, August 31, 1677, St. Martin's in the Fields, digital image at https://www.findmypast.com/, accessed June 2, 2021.

[10] Leonard Naylor and Geoffrey Jaggar, "Higgons, Thomas (c.1624–1691), of Greywell, Hants," in B. D. Henning, ed., *The History of Parliament: The House of Commons 1660–1690* (Martlesham, Suffolk: Boydell and Brewer, 1983), http://www.historyofparliamentonline.org/volume/1660-1690/member/ higgons-thomas-1624-91, accessed June 17, 2021.

[11] W. P. Courtney and Eveline Cruickshanks, "Higgons, Bevil (1670–1736), historian and poet," *Oxford Dictionary of National Biography*, September 23, 2004, https://doi.org/10.1093/ref:odnb/13240, accessed June 17, 2021.

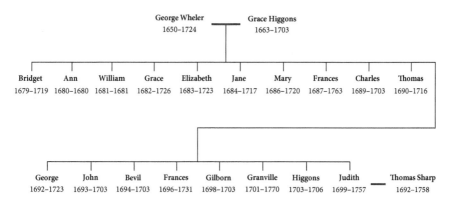

Figure 1.2 Wheler family chart

nections did not hinder George's ecclesiastical career, and Grace and George did not attempt to distance themselves from those connections. George purchased Grace's uncle Denis Granville's library when Denis, the dean of Durham, had his possessions seized to pay his substantial debts and following his flight to France after refusing to swear loyalty to William and Mary.[12] The Whelers also named multiple children after Grace's Jacobite relatives. The Whelers lived in London, until 1710, when George was made vicar of Houghton le Spring, Durham, and the family settled there.[13] They had eighteen children, ten of whom survived to adulthood.

George was creative and curious, with a passion for botany and science and he was elected a fellow of the Royal Society in 1677. As a young man he enjoyed mechanical work, music, and woodworking, and he even made his own musical instruments. As a religious leader he continued to enjoy dancing, music, good food, and drink. "Though austere in regard to himself," George was reportedly not "harsh or severe in his judgment of others...neither an enemy to innocent recreations nor to personal accomplishments, when consistent with the purity of the Christian character."[14] George was also glowingly described as one who "happily united the dignified manners and sentiments of birth and rank with the venerable simplicity and modesty of the Christian pastor."[15] Virtually nothing is known about Grace's interests; their household management and family culture prioritized patriarchal domestic authority, colored by piety and a relaxed style of socializing. Books, reading, and education were important

---

[12] David Pearson, "English Book Owners in the Seventeenth Century" (working paper, The Bibliographic Society, 2007, revised version 2010), 50, https://sas-space.sas.ac.uk/2592/2/English_book_owners_in_the_seventeenth_century_2010_-_revised.pdf.
[13] "Sir George Wheler (CCEd Person ID: 96735)," *The Clergy of the Church of England Database 1540–1835*, http://www.theclergydatabase.org.uk, accessed February 3, 2021.
[14] Robert Surtees, *The History and Antiquities of the County Palatine of Durham* (London: Nichols, Son, and Bentley, 1816), 1:172.
[15] Wheler, autobiography; Surtees, *History and Antiquities*, 172–173.

aspects of Wheler family life, and they endowed a charity school for girls at Houghton le Spring.[16]

The Sharps

Elizabeth Palmer married John Sharp in 1676, when she was 20 and he 30 (Figure 1.3).[17] The Palmers were landed gentry from Lincolnshire, but they also had ties to London and were owners of High Easter Manor in Essex.[18] Elizabeth and John were introduced to each other by her brother-in-law.

John Sharp was from a line of Yorkshire trade families, but he was educated at Bradford Grammar School and then obtained a BA and MA from Christ's College, Cambridge.[19] He was ordained in 1667 and quickly advanced in the Church, becoming increasingly powerful and influential in the years leading up to the Glorious Revolution. His mother had been a loyalist while his father had been more puritanical and parliamentarian during the civil war. He was part of the second reformation to improve clerical training and he staunchly defended conformity against both Catholic and Presbyterian influences. Despite becoming archbishop of York in 1691, he did not always agree with William and Mary's

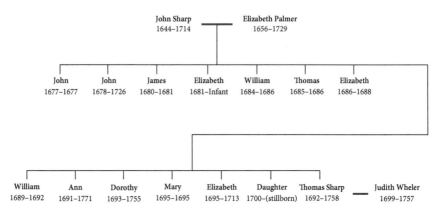

Figure 1.3 Sharp family chart

[16] Frank H. Rushford, *Houghton Le Spring: A History* (Durham: Durham County Press, c.1950), 69.
[17] Church of England, Diocese of London, marriage bonds and allegations, Elizabeth Palmer and John Sharp, marriage allegation, May 10, 1676, LMA MS 10091/28, digital image at "London and Surrey, England, Marriage Bonds and Allegations, 1597–1921," https://www.ancestry.co.uk/, accessed May 10, 2013.
[18] William Palmer, will, written September 17, 1655, proved August 5, 1657, Prerogative Court of Canterbury, TNA PROB 11/267, digital image at https://www.ancestry.co.uk/; A. R. Maddison, ed., *Lincolnshire Pedigrees* (London: Surtees Society, 1904), 3:752.
[19] Barry Till, "Sharp, John (1645?–1714), archbishop of York," *Oxford Dictionary of National Biography*, September 23, 2004, https://doi.org/10.1093/ref:odnb/25213, accessed February 24, 2021.

policies, such as their support for societies for the reformation of manners. John's success skyrocketed with Anne's succession to the throne. He became a key ecclesiastical and spiritual advisor to the queen and an avid supporter of the crown.

In addition to collecting coins, John also dabbled in botany, despite his tendency to turn such pastimes into tasks to be performed, "too apt to make a business of that which should only be recreation," he wrote.[20] His intellectual curiosity and talents—and his interest in cultivating these qualities in his family members— were appreciated by his son Thomas, who did the same for his children. John was also described as "a man of deep personal piety," an attribute much admired and commented on by his descendants.[21] He was credited with being hospitable and kind to subordinates, distant kin, the poor, and even animals.[22] Additionally, one of his sons later described him as an affectionate parent.[23]

Elizabeth Palmer Sharp was held up as a model of proper femininity, one of the "virtuous ladies of her generation."[24] Men at the turn of the eighteenth century (particularly married householders) were expected to oversee the household economy, and their wives were expected to be competent managers of household financial obligations.[25] Though femininity was often conflated with ideas of private domesticity, eighteenth-century women were also increasingly expected to govern public-facing social obligations as well.[26] Elizabeth fit this pattern since she was credited as the one who "in private... pulled many of the wires that determined [her husband's] actions, particularly his charities."[27]

Though his political ecclesiastical work was conservative, in his personal dealings he showed pastoral concern for his clergymen. It was uncommon at the time for church leaders to socialize with their ecclesiastical inferiors. However, Elizabeth and John frequently invited clergymen and their wives for dinner, establishing broad sociability as part of their family culture.[28]

---

[20] A. Tindall Hart, *Life and Times of John Sharp, Archbishop of York* (London: Society for the Propagation of Christian Knowledge, 1949), 308, BX 5199 H3, William Andrews Clark Memorial Library (WACML).

[21] Till, "Sharp, John"; Thomas Sharp, *The Life of Dr. John Sharp: Archbishop Sharp*, n.d., handwritten copy, COLL 1891/9/2, York Minster Archives (YMA).

[22] Hart, *Life and Times of John Sharp*, 295, 298; Granville Sharp, memorandum about Archbishop Sharp copied from book of anecdotes by Thomas Furnis, n.d., D3549/9/1/8.

[23] Thomas Sharp to John Sharp, c.1748–1754, 00452/C/3/2/1, Northumberland Archives (NAW).

[24] Hart, *Life and Times of John Sharp*, 292.

[25] Karen Harvey, *The Little Republic: Masculinity and Domestic Authority in Eighteenth-Century Britain* (Oxford: Oxford University Press, 2012), 24, 32, 43.

[26] Anthony Fletcher, *Growing Up in England: The Experience of Childhood 1600–1914* (New Haven: Yale University Press, 2008), 28–29; Ingrid Tague, "Aristocratic Women and Ideas of Family in the Early Eighteenth Century," in Helen Berry and Elizabeth Foyster, eds., *The Family in Early Modern England* (Cambridge: Cambridge University Press, 2007), 184–208.

[27] Hart, *Life and Times of John Sharp*, 292.

[28] W.M. Jacob, *The Clerical Profession in the Long Eighteenth Century* (Oxford: Oxford University Press, 2007), 15–17, 272.

Family Values and Siblings

Elizabeth and John's son Thomas Sharp once remarked that the family enjoyed "an easy and pleasant way of living."[29] As with the Whelers, recreation, hobbies, and entertainment were incorporated into family life and seen as necessary to good living. In this way, both families participated in the familial and friendly socialization that became progressively important to early eighteenth-century households. Instead of shunning casual conversation and relaxing socialization as distractions from ecclesiastical and scholarly endeavors, as was more common in the sixteenth and seventeenth centuries, they invested in the time and material goods it took to host dinner guests, visitors, and those seeking patronage.[30]

George Wheler, like other late Stuart and early Georgian authors, unapologetically described household governance as patriarchal, but he also saw "gradations of power in the home."[31]

Something similar could have been said about the Sharps, who seem to have managed those gradations well enough to provide a sociable and tranquil domestic life. Both families recognized and worked to conform to the expectations of an orderly household in which comfort and peace grew from clear gender, age, and status hierarchies governed by a benevolent patriarch.[32] Such household governance was simultaneously the manifestation of and support for a political organization built on paternalism. George, for example, explicitly linked the "Publick Father" of the nation and the "Private Father" of the family.[33]

In ecclesiastical and domestic affairs, the Whelers and the Sharps believed in social hierarchy and loyalty to the monarch; however, they also emphasized their commitment to the Church as being above jockeying for political position.[34] Deeply devout in their Christian beliefs, they also shared a deep commitment to the Church and were part of the growing importance of charity to professional clerical identity. Both families navigated the choppy waters of late seventeenth-century religious–political conflicts well enough to enjoy increased prominence and wealth in the eighteenth century.

Despite the comfortable atmosphere of their homes, Wheler and Sharp children were encouraged to be serious and diligent. Thomas, the youngest Sharp

---

[29] Thomas Sharp to John Sharp, October 23, 1712, Add.MS. 956/1, Palace Green Library, Durham University (PGL).

[30] Keith Thomas, *The Ends of Life: Roads to Fulfillment in Early Modern England* (Oxford: Oxford University Press, 2008), 220–225.

[31] Harvey, *Little Republic*, 4.

[32] Susan Dwyer Amussen, *An Ordered Society: Gender and Class in Early Modern England* (Oxford: Basil Blackwell, 1988), 96, 134; Richard Grassby, *Kinship and Capitalism: Marriage, Family, and Business in the English-Speaking World, 1580–1740* (Cambridge: Cambridge University Press, 2001), 85–116.

[33] George Wheler, *Protestant Monastery: Or, Christian Oeconomicks* (London, 1698), qtd. in Harvey, *Little Republic*, 45.

[34] Sirota, *Christian Monitors*, 40–44.

PREHISTORY 25

son's undergraduate commonplace book, for example, contains 361 pages in Latin, roughly organized alphabetically, and shows an orderly and studious undergraduate.[35] However, while it appears that the Whelers and Sharps conformed to societal expectations of household governance, they were also on the leading edge of a softer, sometimes more indulgent family life and parenting typically associated with the mid-eighteenth century instead of the late seventeenth.[36] George Wheler credited his parents with being ever "indulgent yet carefull" in raising him.[37] Though there is no direct record account of George and Grace's parenting style, it is possible that their daughter Judith was raised in a similarly indulgent yet careful manner.

During a break from his studies at Cambridge, Thomas Sharp suggested that life at home with his parents was so relaxed that he overate and was less than industrious.[38] Thomas later described his father "with all his Piety [he was] one of the most cheerful men alive, the most free and easy in his temper... He never let his Devotions put any business to a stand, or any man to an inconvenience: but would break, when interrupted... and entertain the addresses of such as applied to him with the utmost candour and good humour."[39] In an era when the justification of divine right to rule was constantly pitted against parliamentary approval to rule, the Whelers' and the Sharps' domestic lives seem to negotiate a similar tension between asserting assumed hierarchies and a enjoying a more relaxed, almost child-centered home life.[40]

Both families relied on professional and kinship networks to further their children's fortunes. Archbishop Sharp's close relationship with Queen Anne positioned him perfectly to help his sons in their chosen careers. His son John entered politics when his father, whose ecclesiastical holdings included Ripon Manor in Yorkshire, put his son forward as the Tory representative for Ripon. Despite his death in 1714, during Thomas's university education, the archbishop's patronage assured Thomas's career from the moment he set himself on an ecclesiastical vocation.[41]

The relaxed atmosphere and comfortable homes of the Whelers and Sharps might have set them apart from other families. But in another respect, they shared with all their contemporaries the one inescapable truth of family life: infant and

---

[35] Thomas Sharp, commonplace book, c.1715, D3549/7/1/9.

[36] Joanne Bailey, *Parenting in England, 1760–1830* (Oxford: Oxford University Press, 2012), 30–37; Hugh Cunningham, *The Invention of Childhood* (London: BBC Books, 2006), 115–116, 121.

[37] Sir George Wheler, autobiography, 5.

[38] Thomas Sharp to John Sharp, October 23, 1712, PGL.

[39] Thomas Sharp, *Life of Dr. John Sharp*, 87–88.

[40] Joseph Hone, *Literature and Party Politics at the Accession of Queen Anne* (Oxford: Oxford University Press, 2017).

[41] Thomas was ordained a deacon on June 16, 1717 in London and a priest in February 1718 in York. His first published sermon was *A Charity-Sermon for the Relief of Poor Widows and Children of Clergymen* (1721), a cause he supported throughout his life and that inspired his long involvement with the Corporation of the Sons of the Clergy.

26 BEING SINGLE IN GEORGIAN ENGLAND

child mortality. Thomas Sharp and Judith Wheler came from large families, but high infant and child mortality rates reduced their sibling cohorts, especially Thomas's. In the late seventeenth century, parents might lose as many as 12 percent of their children in the first year of life and the same percentage in the subsequent decade.[42] Nine of Thomas's thirteen siblings died in infancy or childhood. Another of his sisters, Elizabeth, died when she was 17 and he was 20. Judith Wheler was the sixteenth of eighteen children, ten of whom survived to adulthood. One of her brothers died when he was 26 and she was 17. Two additional Wheler siblings died in their early thirties when Judith was 25 and 32, respectively.

Losing siblings was a common feature of early modern childhood and adolescence. However, while much has been written about parents experiencing the loss of a child, less is known about how young people were affected when a sibling passed away. Siblings often visited and cared for ailing and dying siblings.[43] When teenaged Elizabeth Sharp died, a letter from her father expressed common, sincere sentiments about sorrow and hopes for her salvation.[44] Thomas and his siblings' response to her death is not known. Similarly, we have no record of Judith's response to her siblings' deaths. Most likely, Thomas and Judith felt deep sorrow at these passings, participating in prayers for their siblings as well as discussions about them being in heaven, embraced by a loving Christ.[45]

Family members, particularly siblings, normalized class and gender behavior for one another.[46] Because Judith lost both of her parents before her twenty-fifth birthday and Thomas lost his father when he was only 21, Judith's and Thomas's siblings were probably as important, if not more, to perpetuating family expectations than their parents were. Thomas Sharp's 1712 letter to his older brother John provides a glimpse of such sibling labor (see Interlude 1). In fewer than two hundred words the letter reveals how Thomas maintained functional and supportive relationships with his brother and sister. He expressed love and affection, as well as apologetic deference to John; reported on family health; referenced their parents' ability to provide a comfortable home; and described traveling with their sister Ann, visiting her home, helping her with a household task, and spending time with her young son. Thomas told of how he and Ann drank to John's health, and then Thomas expressed love to John's wife and daughter and a hope that John would not have to travel to Ireland in the winter.[47] Though this content is

---

[42] Chris Galley and Nicola Shelton, "Bridging the Gap: Determining Long-Term Changes in Infant Mortality in Pre-Registration England and Wales," *Population Studies*, 55, no. 1 (March 2001): 65–77.

[43] Hannah Newton, *The Sick Child in Early Modern England, 1580–1720* (Oxford: Oxford University Press, 2012).

[44] Hart, *Life and Times of John Sharp*, 294–295.   [45] Newton, *Sick Child*, 101, 141, 153.

[46] Henry French and Mark Rothery, "'Upon Your Entry into the World': Masculine Values and the Threshold of Adulthood among Landed Elites in England 1680–1800," *Social History*, 33, no. 4 (November 2008): 402–422; Amy Harris, *Siblinghood and Social Relations in Georgian England: Share and Share Alike* (Manchester: Manchester University Press, 2012).

[47] Thomas Sharp, Cambridge, to John Sharp, October 23, 1712, PGL.

unremarkable, it reveals the sinews that made functional and supportive relationships possible, and it demonstrates these were well-established aspects of Sharp family life.

Two of Thomas's surviving siblings were close in age to him (one a year older and one a year younger). The three of them were more than twelve years younger than their oldest surviving brother, John, but Thomas remained close and connected to all his siblings throughout his life. He regularly corresponded with John and often visited his sister Ann and her husband, Heneage Dering, whom Thomas was also close with. The similarities of their gendered experience kept John and Thomas connected across age and professional distances. They were both "taught well" by a Mr. Ellis, despite his status as a nonjuror who had not sworn loyalty to William and Mary. Thomas followed his brother to Leeds School, then to St. Paul's school in London, and eventually to Cambridge. John, however, pursued a political career, entering Inner Temple and then being elected to the Commons. Thomas described his brother as "a polite scholar, an accomplished gentleman, a most affectionate husband and father, a true friend and desirable companion, beloved and esteemed by all who knew him."[48] John was the Tory MP for Ripon until 1714, when the accession of George I changed the political winds. He retired to the Northamptonshire estate settled on him by his father-in-law and never entered politics again. Therefore, just as Thomas was coming of age (he was 22 in 1714) and preparing for a clerical career, his brother John was leaving public life.

Thomas also maintained meaningful relationships with extended kin. He, his brother John, and their brother-in-law Heneage Dering were supportive and lifelong friends. Thomas kept accounts for both, Heneage loaned £1800 pounds to John, and Thomas was executor for Heneage's will.[49] Thomas and Heneage regularly corresponded and encouraged their children to build relationships. Heneage's autobiography shows he also modeled family sociability with in-laws, cousins, and more distant kin.[50] Parents were essential transmitters of family values, but they were not alone in creating and disseminating family values. Sharp and Dering aunts, uncles, and cousins were equally invested. Unmarried kin could be particularly focused on perpetuating family culture as they did not have to incorporate in-laws' familial values.

Scholars have noted that "the successful transmission of…[family] values was as vital for survival, honour and authority of gentry families as the strict

---

[48] Leonard W. Cowie, "Sharp, John (1678–1727), politician," *Oxford Dictionary of National Biography*, September 23, 2004, https://doi.org/10.1093/ref:odnb/47277, accessed February 19, 2021.

[49] John Sharp, memorandum about debt to Heneage Dering, July 29, 1716, D3549/7/2/3; Heneage Dering, will, written April 12, 1745, proved May 11, 1750, Prerogative Court of Canterbury, PROB 11/779, TNA, digital image at "England and Wales, Prerogative Court of Canterbury Wills, 1384–1858," https://www.ancestry.co.uk/, accessed July 20, 2018.

[50] Heneage Dering, "Autobiographical Memoranda," in *Publications of the Surtees Society*, vol. 65, *Yorkshire Diaries and Autobiographies in the Seventeenth and Eighteenth Centuries* (Durham: Surtees Society, 1877): 338–347.

28   BEING SINGLE IN GEORGIAN ENGLAND

settlement system or prudential marriage."[51] This is highlighted for the Sharps, and particularly Thomas, whose houses and property belonged to the Church, and for Judith Wheler, who as a youngest daughter did not stand to inherit any real estate. Thomas and Judith lacked a physical estate in which family values were enshrined and perpetuated; their efforts to perpetuate their families' social standing were instead channeled through values and virtues.[52] This lack of an estate also meant that Judith and Thomas would avoid the uncertainty of broken promises and disputes over property that had occurred earlier in the extended Wheler family.

While there is some record of Thomas Sharp's upbringing and education, there is little information about Judith Wheler's early life. Judith was raised in Houghton le Spring and likely received the standard education for girls of the time, including music, household accounting, home remedies, and recipes. She seems to have had more than basic artistic and musical training. After she married, she kept a children's songbook and maintained a family recipe book.[53] Considering her father fondly remembered his own somewhat indulgent upbringing, it is possible he and her mother were like other educated and prosperous parents who "paid attention to, and enjoyed, displays of individuality and creativity in children."[54] Given her parents' endowment of a charity school for girls, it is probable they also invested in their daughters' educations, most likely with private tutors. Like other girls of her social standing, Judith would have received religious instruction, both catechetical and behavioral, with an expectation that "social training" would "add polish to a girl's essential inner purity."[55] Her son later recalled her as "amiable," but beyond that, there are few references to her character or activities within the family circle.[56] This is undoubtedly at least partially due to the fact that any personal writing of hers did not survive. The lack of information about her (whether at the time or in the surviving record) has its roots in eighteenth-century expectations that women's activities, important as they were, were built on women's "self-abnegation and self-sacrifice."[57]

---

[51]   French and Rothery, "'Upon Your Entry,'" 422.

[52]   French and Rothery, "'Upon Your Entry,'" 413–414.

[53]   Judith Sharp, songbook, 1756, D3549/8/1/3; Sharp family, recipe book, eighteenth century, D3549/8/1/5. The bookplate on the inside cover of the songbook is for Judith Sharp, daughter of mother Judith Sharp. However, the content had older components, written in multiple hands. The Gloucestershire Archives groups this with the older Judith's papers, suggesting they were informed by family knowledge of who originally owned the book.

[54]   Adriana Benzaquén, "'Pary lett none see this impertinent Epistle': Children's Letters and Children in Letters at the Turn of the Eighteenth Century," in Rachel Conrad and L. Brown Kennedy, eds., *Literary Cultures and Eighteenth-Century Childhoods* (Basingstoke: Palgrave Macmillan, 2020), 81–82.

[55]   Fletcher, *Growing Up in England*, 29.

[56]   Granville made the remark about his mother in the 1790s while annotating one of his father's catalogs. Granville Sharp, annotations of Thomas Sharp's "Catalog of Clergy of Durham," c.1790s, 175, COLL1891/9/1, YMA.

[57]   Fletcher, *Growing Up in England*, 29; see also 32–33.

Courtship of Judith Wheler and Thomas Sharp

At 23 and 28, respectively, Judith and Thomas married at the typical age for their class and cohort.[58] While Judith was younger than the average first-time bride in eighteenth-century England, it was not unusual for gentry women to marry in their early twenties. Judith's siblings who survived to adulthood had widely dispersed marriage ages. Like Judith's siblings, Thomas's brother and sisters married at very different ages. Therefore, neither family precisely matched typical late-marriage patterns, for England overall or for elite families.

Judith and Thomas met via their parents' efforts to bring them together, a perfect social match for the youngest daughter of Sir George Wheler, prebendary of Durham, and the youngest son of the late archbishop of York. The Sharp and Wheler families enjoyed what one observer termed a "charmed circle of ecclesiastical influence at Durham."[59] Thomas and Judith benefited from a network of clerical patronage, augmented by marital ties, that typified the eighteenth-century Church.[60] Thomas sought his brother's advice about the match (see Interlude 1), but there is no firsthand account from Judith about her thoughts on the marriage. It is still possible to see glimpses of her personality and their approach to marriage from descriptions of her from a contemporary diarist: John Thomlinson. Thomlinson described Judith when he surveyed socially appropriate families with eligible daughters and calculated who would be the best catch for his personal and professional ambitions.

Thomlinson's namesake uncle was the rector of Rothbury before Thomas assumed the position in 1720. The younger Thomlinson hoped that his uncle would help him get into orders and pass the Rothbury living to him. Wrapped up with concerns over the younger Thomlinson's career were his marriage prospects. In the late 1710s, he sought his childless uncles' advice on the timing of marriage and the choice of a bride. In November 1717, he first considered John Ord's eldest daughter, who was in his estimation, a "religious, good natured woman, not so handsome as the second who is a proud, conceiting herself to be a witt, etc." He comforted himself that the elder daughter and her mother were "women of parts, or extraordinary sense," with enough capacity to "manage a house, etc." With such ambivalence it is no wonder that just eleven days after penning those words

---

[58] E. A. Wrigley and R. S. Schofield, *The Population History of England 1541–1871* (Cambridge: Cambridge University Press, 1989).

[59] "Diary of Thomas Gyll," in *Publications of the Surtees Society*, vol. 118, *Six North Country Diaries* (Durham: Surtees Society, 1910), 181.

[60] Thomas's aunt had a sister-in-law who married Judith's uncle: Dering, "Autobiographical Memoranda," 337. Thomas and Judith's familial patronage networks continued to influence them after their marriage. Lord Crewe, Bishop of Durham, was George Wheler's patron who gave him the prebendary stall and the parish of Houghton le Spring. Lord Crewe was also the bishop that approved Thomas Sharp for his initial clerical positions. Though Lord Crewe died in 1721, those connections eventually brought Thomas the trusteeship of Bamburgh Castle in 1737.

30 BEING SINGLE IN GEORGIAN ENGLAND

he considered a second option: Judith Wheler. "Some thoughts of Sir G. Wheler's youngest daughter an very managing woman, keeps account of all matters of house and husbandry, etc." Thomlinson, his uncles, and his brother debated the merits of these women and a selection of others spread across northern England, but by February 1718, Thomlinson hit upon a surefire way of deciding between Miss Ord and Miss Wheler: he put their "names on peice[s] of paper in a hatt" and drew out Miss Ord's name. One would never accuse Thomlinson of being overly sentimental.[61]

While Thomlinson was mulling over his marriage prospects—often baldly discussing his preference for wealth and position—he was also concerned that his uncle was not giving him enough preference as rector for Rothbury and that he seemed to be losing out to Thomas Sharp for the position. This despite Thomlinson acting as his uncle's curate and despite assurances from his brother and the Bishop of London that Thomas "was a melancholy man" whose friends were trying to dissuade him from taking the living.[62] It must have stung to discover that not only did Thomas Sharp get the living at Rothbury in July 1720 but also that he and Judith were courting by the end of 1721 and they married in June 1722 in the private chapel at Houghton le Spring.[63] However, Thomlinson was sanguine about both disappointments, soon moving on to consider other marital and professional prospects, ideally at the same time.[64]

John Thomlinson's difficulties illustrate how marital prospects could be beyond one's control, even for men who had greater autonomy in the marriage market than women did. Early in 1722, he was considering marrying, or perhaps was even engaged to, a woman of Amington, Staffordshire. He also considered courting a woman from London, who came with some £900 a year, as well as a promise of the living of Glenfield, Leicestershire (a far better financial match than if he had married Judith Wheler, who had only the total sum of £1000). The lady of Amington had a "better fortune," but the lady from London could have an augmented inheritance because "other sisters may die." A search of parish registers reveals that the lady from London had at least four younger sisters between the ages of 6 and 18, making Thomlinson's statement a rather cold assessment of childhood mortality. The rather brutal calculations Thomlinson made settled him on marrying the woman from London, 16-year-old Catherine Winstanley, in May

---

[61] "Diary of John Thomlinson," in *Publications of the Surtees Society*, vol. 118, *Six North Country Diaries* (Durham: Surtees Society, 1910), 91–92, 105, 112; Thomas Seccombe, "Thomlinson, Robert (*bap.* 1668, *d.* 1748)," rev. Philip Carter, *Oxford Dictionary of National Biography*, Oxford University Press, 2004, https://www.oxforddnb.com.erl.lib.byu.edu/view/article/27254, accessed March 26, 2016).

[62] "Diary of John Thomlinson," 162.

[63] Surtees, *History and Antiquities*, 176.

[64] "Diary of John Thomlinson," 167. Church of England, St. Mary at Hill, London parish registers, John Tomlinson and Catherine Winstanly, marriage, May 20, 1722, P69/MRY4/A/001/MS04546, LMA, digital image at *London, England Church of England Baptisms, Marriages and Burials, 1538–1812*, https://www.ancestry.co.uk/, accessed November 2, 2019.

1722.[65] His diary does not indicate why he chose her, but her father's patronage and the promise of being rector of Glenfield were the likely motivations, given his blunt calculations about monetary and social benefits of marriage. These hard-nosed considerations were quite different from Thomas Sharp's deliberations about Judith. However, Thomas, like most contemporaries, was not beyond property and financial considerations (there was a reason he made sure to mention Judith's £1000 in the letter to his brother John). No matter how the Thomlinsons' marriage matured after their wedding, while selecting a bride in the 1710s and early 1720s, Thomlinson's mind was focused on securing a position and financial security, not on finding a companionate partner. Thomas and Judith were fortunate to have had both position and security along with compatibility in their union.

Conclusion

All families leave a legacy of expectations and values for the next generation, whether consciously or not. The Whelers and Sharps acted in accordance with typical family practices of the time.[66] From that foundation, social and religious values developed and material possessions were endowed with significance beyond their monetary value. In addition to the coins in the Sharp family cabinet, the Sharp siblings later possessed books written by their grandfather Wheler, their grandfather Sharp's extensive library, and a family recipe book begun probably in their grandparents' generation.

As was common in the eighteenth century, the Sharps did not have relationships with their grandparents. Two of the grandparents died many years before the siblings were born. Of the two remaining grandparents, their grandfather Wheler died when John, the oldest grandson, was a few months old; their grandmother Sharp died in 1729 when John and Thomas were 6 and 4, respectively. More than property, the siblings inherited from their grandparents the family patterns and expectations they had learned from their parents, aunts and uncles, and older cousins, thus inheriting the religious and social values inculcated in earlier generations. Archbishop Sharp's seemingly mundane decision from 1687 to collect coins symbolized the important, but not always discussed, values and expectations that shaped Sharp family culture well into the nineteenth century. In the 1760s, Granville Sharp, at the beginning of his anti-slavery and reforming

---

[65] "Diary of John Thomlinson," 66; Church of England, St. James Piccadilly Westminster, parish registers, baptism of Catherine Winstanley, February 1, 1706 (NS), STG/PR/7/57, City of Westminster Archives Centre, digital image at *Westminster Church of England Parish Registers*, https://www.ancestry.co.uk/, accessed June 3, 2021.

[66] Patricia Crawford, "Katherine and Philip Henry and Their Children: A Case Study in Family Ideology," *Transactions of the Historic Society of Lancashire and Cheshire*, 134 (1984): 39–73; French and Rothery, "'Upon Your Entry,'" 402–422.

career, remarked that he was not very familiar with the details of his grandfather Sharp's life. Though he did not know much biographical information about him, he clearly had learned the values of spiritual devotion, Anglican practice, family socializing, and an impulse to improve the conditions of the oppressed valued by his grandparents. The Sharp siblings' notations and labels on the documents left by their grandparents and parents show that the earlier generations were largely successful in transmitting their values. The Sharp siblings, born in the 1720s and 1730s, entered a family culture already shaped by relatively congenial parenting practices, a culture grounded in Christian ideals, and day-to-day domestic entertainments, such as books, music, and amiable sociality.

Interlude 1
Meeting of the Minds

In fall 1721 Thomas Sharp made a trip to Durham to visit his sister and new brother-in-law (Dorothy and Thomas Mangey). While there he learned that George Wheler had approached Thomas's mother, the widowed Elizabeth Sharp, to propose a marriage between his youngest daughter, 22-year-old Judith, and Thomas. Despite knowing what his mother and Judith's father were discussing, Thomas was at pains to make sure neither parent, nor Judith herself, knew that he both understood and "approved of...[the] proposal."[1] Though he did not say it, it is apparent that he and Judith had interacted during that Durham visit, and he made it clear that marrying her was attractive to him.

Before making his personal desires known, however, Thomas, like most early eighteenth-century men, wanted advice from a trusted source. Considering it "a matter of such consequence" he determined he "ought both to consider well myself, & also have the advice of my best friends." In late November 1721, he wrote his brother John to learn his opinion of the match. John, fourteen years Thomas's senior, had married over a decade earlier and would have been a natural choice for marital advice.

Given the permanent nature of marriage and its long-lasting impact on one's social and financial standing, many people took an entirely practical approach to marriage. Thomas Sharp was not immune to the same reflections, though Judith's money mattered less to him than other aspects of the match—her dowry was "a point of no consideration" because he was "little disposed" to matters of "worldly interest." Of course, Thomas could be more accommodating than others, as he already possessed Rothbury, Northumberland, one of the wealthiest parish livings in England. Even if Thomas's intentions were unalloyed with financial concerns, he was keenly aware of needing the approval of his friends and family and assumed they would need to know Judith would come to the marriage with £1000.

Thomas also clearly understood the practical and professional implications of his marital choice. Knowing his mother and Judith's father were already supportive of the match, he sought to counsel with the archbishop of York for professional advice, in addition to seeking his brother John's personal advice. Understandably, the archbishop encouraged him to marry at the first appropriate opportunity. Thomas told John that as far as he could judge "both from the

---

[1] Thomas Sharp to John Sharp, November 28, 1721, Add.MS. 956/2, PGL.

Being Single in Georgian England: Families, Households, and the Unmarried. Amy Harris, Oxford University Press.
© Amy Harris 2023. DOI: 10.1093/oso/9780192869494.003.0003

character & person" of Judith, she would be "the most usefull & agreeable wife" of any woman he had ever encountered. The combination of good character, agreeableness, and useful training—"a very managing woman [who] keeps account of all matters of house and husbandry," as a rival suitor had described her—made Judith the ideal spouse for a prosperous eighteenth-century clergyman. Presumably John also approved, for Thomas and Judith married the following June. This letter, and an earlier letter Thomas wrote to John, are the only firsthand accounts from either Thomas or Judith before their marriage.

Dear Brother   Rothbury- Nov.[ber] 28th 1721.

When I was at Durham wth Bro. Mangey, S[r] G[eorge] W[heler] made some proposals to my Mother, wth w[ch] she seemed not to be displeased, & wth w[ch] she acquainted me; You will easily guess upon me mentioning this, that one of y[e] Knights Daughters was proposed to me for a Wife. While I staid as Durham, I purposely avoided given S[r] George or any of his family any suspicions that I understood, or approved of his proposal. thinking that in a matter of such consequence, I ought

both to consider well my self, & also have y[e] advice of my best friends. I have since wrote to y[e] Archb[isho]p of York, who being one of my best friends, I thought could give me y[e] properest advice what to do in this case as a clergyman, & thus situated in y[e] way of my profession. He advises me to take y[e] opportunity I meet with, agreeable to my Relations, & likely to answer y[e] ends I propose in marriage; & approves of this, as such.

I can yet determine nothing till I have consulted so near a Relation & so dear a friend, as you are.

So far as I can Judge both from y[e] character & person of y[e] daughter, She will make me y[e] most usefull & agreeable wife, of any Lady, that I have yet heard of, or seen.

I was told that a 1000[lb] is all that S[r] Ge. give to any of them. with me, this is a point of no consideration, nor ever will be, if it be none to my Relations. Were I as little disposed to any sort of Love, as I am to that of money, & could rule all my desires, as well as that of worldy interest, I should be a better and happier Man. I have very freely told you my thoughts & beg you will as freely tell yours to you affectionate Brother

My Love and best wishes to Sister and Children. Tho: Sharp

2

Growing Up Sharp

"More affectionate Parents could not be or more worthy."[1]

Elizabeth Sharp Prowse describing her parents

"With great learning & indefatigable labour."[2]

Granville Sharp describing his father's efforts

Introduction

"Indefatigable" and "affectionate," the Sharp siblings described Thomas and Judith Sharp as ideal eighteenth-century parents and themselves as recipients of the best of eighteenth-century childhoods. Family is the first culture and society a child encounters, and the Sharp children encountered a comfortable, nurturing, and creative society. They also inhabited a family that had clear ideas about which values and behaviors they wanted to inculcate in their children. As the previous chapter outlined, the older generations of Sharps and Whelers consciously cultivated family life around particular social, religious, and relational values. The Sharp siblings' grandparents had left them traditions of uprightness flavored by sociability, creativity, and music—traditions their parents proved particularly adept at perpetuating.

Throughout their lives, the siblings attempted to comport themselves according to the traditions and expectations they had inherited. Because the siblings produced no contemporary accounts in the 1720s and 1730s, or at least none that survive, their later views of their parents were undoubtedly colored by the passage of time. Writing as adults, often many years after their parents' deaths, the Sharp siblings remarkably mentioned very little disappointment, let alone grievance, in their descriptions of their parents or their upbringing, providing only small glimpses here or there that their parents did not always perfectly fulfill all their children's expectations.

Records of childhood are often ephemeral, but it is possible Elizabeth began keeping a diary as early as 1743 when she was 10 years old, as that is when the

---

[1] Elizabeth Sharp Prowse, memorandum and commonplace book March 16, 1758, page 19, D3549/14/1/1.

[2] Granville Sharp, annotations of Thomas Sharp's "Catalog of Clergy of Durham," c.1790s, page 139, COLL1891/9/1, YMA.

Being Single in Georgian England: Families, Households, and the Unmarried. Amy Harris, Oxford University Press.
© Amy Harris 2023. DOI: 10.1093/oso/9780192869494.003.0004

family chronicle she compiled late in the century begins to have details and personal recollections likely recorded at the time. Her chronicle—along with later observations from the siblings, firsthand accounts of Sharp family life from contemporaries, three letters from their father, and a songbook begun by their mother—constitute the contemporary accounts of the siblings' childhood.

Many scholars locate the roots of modern childhood in the eighteenth century. Aspects of modern childhood experience—age as a universal social category more essential than social class; childhood as a stage of innocence; and children as tabula rasa, upon which cultural expectations were imprinted—are all visible in the Sharps' upbringing.[3] Locke's 1693 *Some Thoughts Concerning Education* is often credited with radically reimagining childhood in positive terms. Children came, not colored by sin or corruption, but as clean slates upon which their elders would inscribe habits of thought and behavior suited to their gender and class roles.[4] Such an approach to childrearing was not shared by all families, especially if they adhered to the more strict aspects of Puritan or Quaker beliefs, but for most Anglicans and even some dissenters, eighteenth-century childhood was a time of both relative freedom and careful instruction.[5] There are even hints of it in earlier Sharp and Wheler generations, where words like "indulgent," "easy," and "pleasant" were used to describe their parenting.

No matter how pleasant the Sharps' childhood was, for them, as for families across Protestant Europe, religion shored up parents', and particularly the father's, domestic power. Additionally, religious practice was essential to the young Sharps' understanding of ethics and what we would now call prosocial behavior.[6] Simultaneously, children were taught to value British exceptionalism.[7] The expanding corpus of children's literature as well as increasing literacy rates among the young facilitated these instructions and also provided entertainment for young people.

---

[3] The Sharps' social class and moderate approach to Anglicanism put them in the middle of these changes in ways not enjoyed until much later by other groups. Miriam Slater, *Family Life in the Seventeenth Century: The Verneys of Claydon House* (London: Routledge, 1984); Steven Mintz, *Huck's Raft: A History of American Childhood* (Cambridge: Harvard University Press, 2004).

[4] The text was radical in many ways, but the fact that Locke's ideas developed through regular interaction with children, instead of from axiomatic statements, he followed a tradition of other seventeenth-century authors, though none of them with Locke's clout and influence. Adriana Silvia Benzaquén, "Locke's Children," *Journal of the History of Childhood and Youth*, 4, no. 3 (Fall 2011): 382–402; Barbara Ritter Dailey, "Youth and the New Jerusalem: The English Catechistical Tradition and Henry Jessey's 'Catechisme for Babes' (1652)," *Harvard Library Bulletin*, 31, no. 1 (1982): 34–35.

[5] John C. Sommerville, "Puritan Humor, or Entertainment, for Children," *Albion*, 21, no. 2 (1989): 227–247; Steven Mintz, *Huck's Raft: A History of American Childhood* (Cambridge: Harvard University Press, 2004), 11; David J. Hall, "What Should Eighteenth Century Quakers Have Read?" *Journal of the Friends' Historical Society*, 62, no. 2 (2011): 103–110.

[6] Mary Hartman, *The Household and the Making of History: A Subversive View of the Western Past* (Cambridge: Cambridge University Press, 2004); Lyndal Roper, *The Holy Household: Women and Morals in Reformation Augsburg* (Oxford: Clarendon Press, 1989).

[7] Troy Bickham, "Preparing for an Imperial Inheritance: Children, Play, and Empire in Eighteenth-Century Britain," *Journal of British Studies*, 60, no. 3 (July 2021): 658–688.

What emerges from a discussion of the Sharps' childhood and youth is the importance of a collective identity and the self-conscious way their family created it. Youngest brother Granville once compared his siblings to a band, which comparison, beyond the musical connection, was emblematic: each played their own instrument, but did so in a way that enhanced the group's work (see Interlude 2). Grandparents, aunts, uncles, and parents may have fostered an environment of shared values, but the siblings and their cousins took those materials and built their own collective identity that combined individual expression and a sense of permanent belonging. The siblings were their own inner circle; their cousins inhabited a second, slightly distanced circle. As the siblings aged, they added further circles of social and emotional bonds, but the core circle of association created in their younger years proved remarkably durable and meaningful.

Infancy and Early Childhood in the 1720s and 1730s

Rothbury, Northumberland, where Thomas and Judith raised their children, would not have sprung to mind as the ideal place to raise elite children in the early eighteenth century. The parish was nestled in the Coquet Valley at the base of the stark Cheviot Hills and in the 1720s was not far separated from Jacobite attempts to restore the Stuarts to the throne.[8] Despite lingering Jacobite support, this did not seem to cause problems for Thomas and Judith.[9] The Sharp siblings were little affected by the political and religious upheavals of the late Stuart and early Hanoverian era, benefiting from the previous generations' fortunate navigation of those times. The Sharps also benefited from an increasing prosperity for clerical families.[10] Despite its rugged isolation, Rothbury was the second most valuable living in the country.

Thomas's ability to navigate religious differences was attributed to his practical and pastoral emphasis, an approach to religious practice he and Judith taught their children. In the late seventeenth and early eighteenth centuries the Church "was engaged in a multifaceted program of confessional revitalization" emphasizing reform, personal devotion, and pastoral care over dogmatic enforcement of

[8] Jacobite supporters had spent a night in Rothbury in October 1715 while gathering support, and even after the defeat, the area continued to have many Jacobite sympathizers.

[9] Thomas Sharp, declaration of conformity, 1720, EP 59/46, NAW. The lack of disruption was despite Judith having Jacobite uncles, including one who served as James II's secretary of state. Undoubtedly, Thomas and Judith enjoyed the lingering influence of their fathers' ecclesiastical prominence and loyalty to the crown. Alternatively, given that Thomas's predecessor at Rothbury had Stuart sympathies, it might have been Judith's Jacobite connections that proved helpful with Thomas's parishioners. Kathleen Wilson, *The Sense of the People: Politics, Culture and Imperialism in England, 1715–1785* (Cambridge: Cambridge University Press, 1995), 320.

[10] Ian Green, "The First Years of Queen Anne's Bounty," in Rosemary O'Day and Felicity Heal, eds., *Princes and Paupers in the English Church 1500–1800* (Leicester: Leicester University Press, 1981), 231–254.

38 BEING SINGLE IN GEORGIAN ENGLAND

religious rules.[11] Thomas adopted these views, once remarking it was not necessary to "pay obedience" to all legal canons, particularly those which were impractical.[12] Those views, apparently shared by Judith, colored their approach to childrearing, inculcating their children "with wholesome instruction" meant to encourage a personal belief and sincere concern for others.[13] As Granville noted in the 1790s, their father had followed the archbishop's advice about "always endeavouring in reality to be what he would wish to appear."[14]

As Thomas and Judith settled into domestic life in Rothbury and into "unsullied nuptial love," as one observer described it, Thomas's career continued its stellar rise.[15] He was a conscientious parish administrator, keeping careful accounts of estate rentals and parish charities.[16] He was only 30 when he was made archdeacon of Northumberland in February 1723. His professional success was immediately followed by familial success: the couple's first child, John, was born on March 16. John was followed in rapid succession by a brother, Wheler, who was born the following spring but lived only a few weeks. Another brother, Thomas, was born in March 1725 just five days after John's second birthday and christened on the second anniversary of John's christening. Whether their parents purposely chose the anniversary or whether it was mere coincidence, being christened on the same day linked John and Thomas in a way that foreshadowed their lifelong connection.

A sister, Grace, was born in the spring of 1726, followed by George in 1727, and Charles in February 1728. But George did not survive past infancy and Grace died in May 1728 while their father was in York, engaged in a "perplexity of affairs." When he heard the "very afflicting news," Thomas immediately wrote Judith, who was home at Rothbury with 5-year-old John, 3-year-old Thomas, and 3-month-old Charles: "My real concern," he wrote, was, "to relieve and comfort you under the sorrow w[hi]ch I am sure you labour under for the removal of your daughter." Thomas comforted his wife by reminding her that Grace's "innocence will make her very happy, w[hi]ch is more than it could do, during her little stay in this world," comments that suggest Grace had suffered and been unhealthy most of her life. He considered himself "unfortunate" to be away at the time when he "could earnestly wish" to be with his wife, but he was grateful that God had

---

[11] Sirota, *The Christian Monitors*, 2.

[12] J.C. Shuler, "The Pastoral and Ecclesiastical Administration of the Diocese of Durham 1721–1771; with Particular Reference to the Archdeaconry of Northumberland" (PhD thesis, Durham University, 1975), 185, http://etheses.dur.ac.uk/1316/1/1316.pdf.

[13] Owen, *A Discourse occasioned by the Death of Elizabeth Prowse*, 7–8.

[14] Granville Sharp, annotations of Thomas Sharp's "Catalog of Clergy of Durham," 175. Emphasis in original.

[15] William Dolben to Thomas Sharp, July 16, 1757, D3549/7/2/16.

[16] Rents for the estates of Sharperton, Harbottle, and Wester Todhills, Rothbury, Northumberland, parish chest materials, 1720–48, microfilm 2,193,200, items 2–3, DGS 4024477, images 30–148, FHL; E. Mackenzie, *An Historical, Topographical, and Descriptive View of the County of Northumberland*, 2nd edition (Newcastle upon Tyne: Mackenzie and Dent, 1825), 2:55–60.

preserved half of their children. If Thomas had suspected Grace was mortally ill, it is possible that he, like many early modern fathers, would have remained home to help nurse her and pray for her.[17] Thomas also expressed thankfulness that Judith continued to live, emphasizing her goodness, faith, and ability to "improve her self upon ye loss of [her children]" and he hoped she would eventually resign herself cheerfully to God's pleasure. He concluded the letter with assurances that he would pray that everything that happened would be for Judith's own good, in which he had "so great an interest."[18]

The Sharps lost a third of their children before their fourth birthdays, a difficult, but common experience for early modern parents.[19] Caring for an ill child was labor intensive for everyone in the household. Grace's illness might have happened suddenly, as fathers would have usually been important participants in caring for ill children. If he had known of the illness, Thomas might have chosen to remain at home.[20] Regardless, Judith's role would have been central, perhaps emphasized by Thomas calling Grace "your daughter," reflecting that girls remained their mother's children more than their brothers, whose gender-segregated education in older childhood reduced the time they spent with their mothers.[21] Judith would have directed the production and administration of medicine and treatments during times of sickness. The family recipe book, like most early modern recipe books, contained both food and medicinal recipes, including for common ailments such as colic, kidney stones, rickets, and colds. Having a sick, and possibly dying, child was agony for parents, but Thomas's expression of grief combined with religious resignation to the loss of young children, was a common parental response during a time of high infant and child mortality.[22] As Thomas did, Christian ministers, no matter the denomination, emphasized the happiness awaiting deceased children. This teaching, in turn, was meant to provide parents not just consolation but eventual joy.[23]

After the death of Grace, Thomas and Judith had eight additional children, six of whom survived to adulthood. No letters remain that recount the experience of losing the other two children, or the two who preceded Grace in death. Perhaps

[17] Hannah Newton, *The Sick Child in Early Modern England, 1580–1720* (Oxford: Oxford University Press, 2012), 102–103, 224.

[18] Thomas Sharp, York, to Judith Sharp, Rothbury, May 25, 1728, D3549/8/1/1.

[19] Robert Woods, *Children Remembered: Responses to Untimely Death in the Past* (Liverpool: Liverpool University Press, 2007), 44–46.

[20] Newton, *Sick Child*, 110–120.

[21] Anthony Fletcher, *Growing Up in England: The Experience of Childhood 1600–1914* (New Haven: Yale University Press, 2008).

[22] Newton, *Sick Child*, 121–157; Joanne Bailey, *Parenting in England* (Oxford: Oxford University Press, 2012), 29–32. Fatherly concern for ailing children was common throughout Western Europe. Benjamin Roberts, "Fatherhood in Eighteenth-Century Holland: The Van Der Muelen Brothers," *Journal of Family History*, 21, no. 2 (1996): 218–228.

[23] Katie Barclay, "Grief, Faith and Eighteenth-Century Childhood," in Katie Barclay and Kimberley Reynolds, eds., *Death, Emotion and Childhood in Premodern Europe* (London: Palgrave Macmillan, 2016), 173–190.

40 BEING SINGLE IN GEORGIAN ENGLAND

Judith and Thomas were together on those other occasions, for the careful preservation of the letter about Grace suggests their young children's deaths were long remembered, no matter how much consolation and happiness the family received from their faith. And Thomas and Judith must have kept a record of those children because seven decades later, as she worked on constructing a family lineage chart, their daughter Elizabeth listed all her siblings by name, including those who died before Elizabeth was born. The blue circles on the chart representing the Sharp siblings were spaced to allow Elizabeth to easily include the spouses and children for those who married (Plate 2 and (upper image) Plate 3). This required putting some siblings out of order, but Elizabeth compensated by numbering each of them to indicate their birth order. The effect of this was to show the Sharps who died young nestled between their siblings who lived longer. Formal, public lineage records between the seventeenth and nineteenth centuries usually placed those who died as infants in a nameless cluster on the edge of heraldic visitation records or published genealogies, labeling them merely as "others died young." Elizabeth's record of her deceased siblings and Judith and Thomas's preservation of Grace's letter indicate the ways grief and love were memorialized within English families, in contrast to how heraldic or published records displayed family lines.[24]

Thomas concluded his letter about Grace's death with "your most affectionate husband," a typical epistolary phrase, but one that appears to have been accurate. Later recollections from their children and contemporary observers consistently focused on the Sharps' devoted affection for their children. Granville described their father as engaging and gentle, and especially adept at interacting with children and putting them at ease, "for he had a peculiar expression of sincerity & kindness in his whole address." He described their mother as "faithful and amiable."[25]

Ten months after the death of Grace, the Sharps had their seventh child, William. A month later, Thomas Sr.'s mother died, leaving the children without any grandparents. William was followed by James in 1731 while the family was spending time in Durham and then by Elizabeth and Judith, ten months apart in 1733. Granville was born near the end of 1735 and Ann in the spring of 1737. Ann died just a few days past her first birthday, a couple of weeks before the birth of the last sibling, Frances, in May 1738.

---

[24] For examples of children who died young being marginalized in published heraldry and genealogical records, see Thomas May and Gregory King, *The Visitation of the County of Warwick, 1682*, in *Publications of the Harleian Society*, ed. W. Harry Rylands (London: Harleian Society, 1911), 62:31. At times, heraldic visitations did not name anyone besides the heir or children who married other prominent families. H. Sydney Grazebrook, *The Heraldry of Worcestershire* (London: John Russell Smith, 1873). See also Patricia Crawford, "Katherine and Philip Henry and Their Children: A Case Study in Family Ideology," *Transactions of the Historic Society of Lancashire and Cheshire*, 134 (1984): 39–73.

[25] Granville Sharp, annotations of Thomas Sharp's "Catalog of Clergy of Durham," 175.

The Sharp children were baptized in either Rothbury church or, after their father became prebendary at Durham, in Durham Cathedral. Baptism symbolically incorporated the baby into the Christian community. In the eighteenth century the ritual also came to symbolize a family, rather than a public, religious rite of passage.[26] For the Sharp siblings a baptism ceremony did both, given the number of their relatives and friends among the powerful and wealthy Church leaders in the north.

In total, Judith had fourteen children in fifteen years, six of whom died as infants or young children. Women of Judith's social standing often had more children than women of lower socioeconomic groups, largely due to employing wet nurses and forgoing the contraceptive effects of breastfeeding.[27] Considering how often Judith was pregnant, it is unlikely she breastfed her children for more than a brief period, if at all. She would have regularly employed wet nurses, potentially more than one, as there were times when there could have been three children not yet weaned. Other servants would have also been employed to care for the young children and perform household tasks. Clerical families, with their connection to charity schools and poor relief, often employed more servants than households of similar size.[28] The Sharps likely had a handful of full-time servants and an unknown number of temporary or part-time servants, such as wet nurses or day laborers, supplemented by tutors and instructors. But even with servants and nurses, Judith bore the physical and emotional brunt of frequent childbirth and child death. In the first sixteen years of her marriage, in addition to the death of her father six months after she gave birth to John, Judith did not go eighteen months without birthing or burying a child. On average she bore or buried a child every ten months. The month Grace died represented the conclusion of a grueling fourteen months in which Judith and Thomas welcomed two children and lost two children. While the Sharp siblings later described their mother as affectionate, they list few details about her impact on their upbringing. It is possible the unrelenting pattern of pregnancy, childbirth, and grief necessarily constrained Judith's early relationships with her children.

Disease and accidents led to many childhood deaths in the early eighteenth century. Though no diaries survive that expose Judith's or Thomas's thoughts about their children's accidents and illnesses, the surviving evidence suggests they were likely similar to other parents who carefully noted the many hazards children faced. Like other parents of the time, the Sharps also likely expressed

---

[26] Will Coster, *Baptism and Spiritual Kinship in Early Modern England* (Aldershot: Ashgate, 2002), 45–74.

[27] Dorothy McLaren, "Marital Fertility and Lactation 1570–1720," in Mary Prior, ed., *Women in English Society 1500–1800* (New York: Methuen and Co., 1985), 22–53.

[28] Bridget Hill, *Servants: English Domestics in the Eighteenth Century* (Oxford: Clarendon Press, 1996), 172–175.

gratitude for every accident or illness that did not end in serious injury or death, thanking God for his mercy in preserving their children's lives.[29]

When one of the Sharp children died, their siblings, like other children of this era, "were not expected to grieve like adults;" they often encountered death and were encouraged to learn Christian doctrines of salvation and consolation to prepare for their own good death and help their siblings and friends face death with resignation, if not joy.[30] Less is known about the impact of sibling death on eighteenth-century children and no records survive to detail the Sharp siblings' experiences with the loss of their cohort when they were young. Sibling loss would not have been the same across the sibling group. The children on the older end of the birth order would have remembered siblings who died young, sometimes remembering relationships that ceased before younger siblings were born or capable of remembering (Figure 2.1). When George (d. 1727) and Grace (d. 1728) died, John and Thomas were 5 and 3, respectively. The young brothers would have recognized the loss of siblings they had shared the nursery with, and John likely had memories of George and Grace that lingered to adulthood. But he would have been the only one with those memories. Things were different when the next sibling, Samuel, died in September 1734. Samuel was not quite 3 years

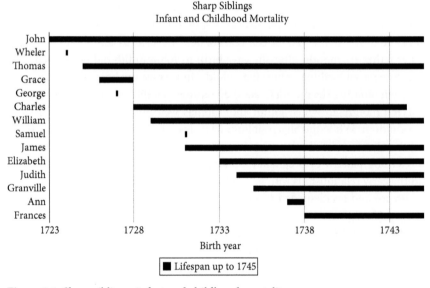

Figure 2.1 Sharp siblings: infant and childhood mortality

---

[29] Ralph Houlbrooke, ed., *English Family Life, 1576–1716: An Anthology from Diaries* (Oxford: Basil Blackwell, 1989), 167–169.

[30] Barclay, "Grief, Faith and Eighteenth-Century Childhood," 187; Hannah Newton, "'Rapt Up with Joy': Children's Emotional Responses to Death in Early Modern England," in Katie Barclay and Kimberley Reynolds, eds., *Death, Emotion and Childhood in Premodern Europe* (London: Palgrave Macmillan, 2016), 92–100.

old, and all of his older brothers would have felt his loss. Additionally, those brothers were all old enough to hold memories of Samuel for the rest of their lives: John was 11, Thomas 9, Charles 6, William 5, and James not quite 4. John was living eighty miles away at school in Yorkshire at the time and must have felt grief compounded by separation. Similarly, when 1-year-old Ann died in April 1738, it is possible that most of her older brothers were enrolled in schools far from home. At the time of Ann's death, John and Thomas were teenagers, and Charles was 10. The other siblings were likely still at home: William was 9, James 7, Elizabeth 5, Judith 4, and Granville two and a half; Frances was born a few weeks after Ann's death.

It is possible the Sharps did as other children and said prayers for each other, acted as pallbearers, and participated in the funeral procession. If away from home, they also might have returned home to care for ill or dying siblings.[31] Due to the timing of their siblings' deaths, the older group of siblings—the five older brothers—experienced two or three sibling deaths when they were old enough to grieve the loss and remember whom they lost. The younger siblings—the sisters and Granville—experienced only one sibling death, that of a new infant when most of them were not old enough to appreciate the loss or to remember it later in life. Even though the younger siblings were less directly affected by the loss of their sisters and brothers than the older boys were, they still would have experienced the second-hand grief of their parents and their older brothers.

Loss and death did not dictate all aspects of the Sharp siblings' childhood. They had a lively and abundant experience. Like other professional and clerical families, the Sharps grew up in a home that valued "gentility, fun, moderation, and good company."[32] In particular, music was central to the Sharp children's education and socializing. Their parents were remarkable for their commitment to their children's musical training and performance. Judith and Thomas Sr. were "skilled both in the theory and practice of Music."[33] Judith kept a book of song lyrics and nursery rhymes. Some of the songs were children's songs but others contained political and religious satire, indicating that wit and humor were taught alongside or through music.[34] Lyrics about rejected suitors were mixed with songs about the shifting political and religious loyalties clergymen had to navigate between the reigns of Charles II and George I and also with songs celebrating British and Irish unity at the coronation of George I.[35]

---

[31] Newton, *Sick Child*, 100, 103.

[32] Janet E. Mullin, "'We Had Carding': Hospitable Card Play and Police Domestic Sociability among the Middling Sort in Eighteenth-Century England," *Journal of Social History*, 42, no. 4 (Summer 2009): 1001.

[33] Granville Sharp, annotations of Thomas Sharp's "Catalog of Clergy of Durham," 175.

[34] Judith Sharp, songbook, 1753, D3549/8/1/3.

[35] Judith Sharp did not list titles in her songbook, but many of the songs can be traced using *Eighteenth Century Collections Online* (https://www.gale.com/primary-sources/eighteenth-century-collections-online). "Young Roger Came Tapping at Dolly's Window" was published in various collections between the 1730s and 1790s. It first appeared in *The Vocal Miscellany* in 1738. "Welch Morgan,

44 BEING SINGLE IN GEORGIAN ENGLAND

Sharp musical instruction was not the basic musical education late eighteenth- and nineteenth-century girls received in order to improve their marital prospects.[36] The training was a serious commitment of time and resources to ensure their children learned musical performance (both instrumental and vocal) as well as composition. Simultaneously, music and religious practices were intertwined as the Sharp children learned sacred music both at home and through choral services and concerts. Handel's *Messiah* was performed at their parents' Durham house in September 1751 and there were other small concerts at their homes in Rothbury and Durham, as well as attendance at concerts in Durham Cathedral.[37] Durham enjoyed a varied and lively musical scene; Thomas Sr. consistently joined choral services at Durham Cathedral, where their uncle James Hasletine was organist and choir director.[38] Hasletine had married their maternal aunt, suggesting the Wheler family was also musically educated and inclined.

Music was worship and learning, but it was also exciting and encouraged informality. By the time they were 10 years old, the children learned to play various wind and string instruments, and some of the sisters were taught to play the harpsichord. Instruction began when they were young, and they shared music between them, each signing their names in their music books.[39] The children regularly performed together; on a published score of "The Cuckoo Concerto," four or five of the brothers signed their names and edited the score to increase the parts from five to seven, suggesting they adapted it to include more sibling participants.[40]

The Sharp home also provided space for plays, concerts, and exploration. Granville later recounted that he would take books with him into the Rothbury orchards, where, after climbing a tree, he would read. It is unlikely he was the only child allowed time to explore and read on their own.[41] At Rothbury the family lived in the rectory, which was a repurposed fourteenth-century defensive tower—Whitton Tower in the eponymous hamlet on a hill above Rothbury. Thomas and Judith expanded the rectory and built "Sharp's Folly" nearby to make

---

Young Teague, and Brisk Sawney the Scot" was published a handful of times in the first half of the century. Similarly, versions of "The Vicar of Bray" were published throughout the eighteenth century, the oldest one in 1716.

[36] Brianna E. Robertson-Kirkland, "Music-Making: A Fundamental or a Vain Accomplishment?" *Women's History*, 2, no. 10 (Spring 2018): 30–34.

[37] Crosby, "Private Concerts," 3.

[38] Roz Southey, "Competition and Collaboration: Concert Promotion in Newcastle and Durham, 1752–1772," in Susan Wollenberg and Simon McVeigh, eds., *Concert Life in Eighteenth-Century Britain* (Aldershot: Ashgate, 2004), 55–70; Simon David Iain Fleming, "A Century of Music Production in Durham City 1711–1811: A Documentary Study" (PhD thesis, Durham University, 2009), http://etheses.dur.ac.uk/40.

[39] Brian Crosby, *A Catalogue of Durham Cathedral Music Manuscripts* (Oxford: Oxford University Press for Dean and Chapter of Durham, 1986), 88. Crosby describes cathedral manuscript MSS M183-M189, which contained part-books owned by the Sharp children.

[40] John Frederick Lampe, "The Cuckoo Concerto," score, music owned by John Sharp while at Trinity College, Cambridge, Music MS 185, Durham Cathedral Library.

[41] Hoare, *Memoirs of Granville Sharp*, 498–499.

astronomical observations and to employ the local masons.[42] Undoubtedly, Thomas also taught his children in the astronomical tower since he was always "attentive...not to lose any proper opportunity of instructing others."[43] During a visit home, teenaged Granville sketched the Whitton home (lower image, Plate 3). His sketch shows the tower/house and the folly rising above fields and orchards, the sketch decorated with the family crest and arms at the bottom. Later in life various siblings journeyed to Rothbury, fondly remembering their childhood there; Rothbury long held an important place in their collective family identity.[44]

During their childhood, the Sharp siblings benefited from changing attitudes toward children, from one of assumed wickedness due to original sin to one of assumed innocence.[45] Parents were expected to pass crucial values to their children, including piety, virtue, industriousness, filial duty, and domesticity.[46] The Sharp parents passed these values on and coupled them with a love of music and wit (informed by extensive reading). And they granted an unusual measure of independence, if more than Granville had the leisure to roam the orchards with large books. It was not possible, Granville once wrote, to adequately describe his father to someone who did not know his "engaging and affectionate deportment" and his "happy influence on the minds of others." Granville also described his father as having "a peculiar expression of sincerity and kindness...indicat[ing] that all his communications came from his heart."[47] Both Thomas and Judith were described as "truly affectionate" parents who practiced and taught integrity and honesty.[48] Outsiders praised them for raising "virtuous," "amiable," and "steady" children.

They also raised their children to be witty and funny among their friends and family. Sadly no letters from Judith to her children survive, but the few surviving letters from Thomas are informal and friendly. He usually called them by their nicknames and recounted daily details he thought would amuse them. In letters, the siblings also addressed each other by their nicknames—Jack, Tommy, Billy, Jimmy, Betsy/Bessie, Jud/Judy, Greeny, and Fanny—well into adulthood, even as they increasingly used more formal modes of address in letters.[49] Even in their

---

[42] Madeleine Hope Dodds, ed., *A History of Northumberland* (Newcastle upon Tyne: Andrew Reid, 1940), 15:317, 15:342.

[43] Granville Sharp, annotations of Thomas Sharp's "Catalog of Clergy of Durham," 175.

[44] Granville Sharp, sketch of Whitton Tower near Rothbury, 1754, in "Scrapbook of cuttings and photographs regarding Whitton Tower, Rothbury parish church, etc.," EP 103/117, NAW.

[45] Will Coster, "Tokens of Innocence: Infant Baptism, Death and Burial in Early Modern England," in Bruce Gordon and Peter Marshall, eds., *The Place of the Dead: Death and Remembrance in Late Medieval and Early Modern Europe* (Cambridge: Cambridge University Press, 2000), 266–287.

[46] Bailey, *Parenting in England*, 174–198.

[47] Granville Sharp, annotations of Thomas Sharp's "Catalog of Clergy of Durham," 140.

[48] Granville Sharp, annotations of Thomas Sharp's "Catalog of Clergy of Durham," 139.

[49] Sharp sibling common letters, c.1756–1763, D3549/7/2/15; Thomas Sharp to Betty (Elizabeth) Sharp, April 26, 1750, D3549/10/1/1; Thomas Sharp, rough notes and books given to children, 1750s, D3549/7/2/17.

46 BEING SINGLE IN GEORGIAN ENGLAND

later letters, the adult sibling might reference an absent sibling by a nickname. This seemed to be especially true for Jim and Jud, but the practice suggests other nicknames were used in face-to-face interactions.[50] Nicknames and inside jokes furthered a sense of collective identity among the siblings. Additionally, their adult correspondence shows a willingness to share first-draft letters, a sign of intimacy. Corrections, cross-outs, and sloppy handwriting appear in their personal letters with a frequency not seen in correspondence with outsiders.

Even in playful exchanges, the Sharp parents consistently emphasized diligence and study were part of family culture. In a 1734 letter to his 11-year-old son John, who was at school, Thomas Sr. reported on recent events from home. After referring to his son by his nickname, Jack, Thomas described a visit from the Dering cousins, which meant "the more the merrier" for dinner and dancing. He reminded John that studying might not always be an enjoyable task, but it was the correct thing to do. Thomas also included details of domestic entertainments, humorous story and jokes, and greetings from John's cousin Mary. Thomas recounted an elaborate joke that included calling himself, Judith, and John's younger siblings buffoons and loafers, a joke that ended in smiles and great laughter. Thomas used a mixture of fatherly advice and amusing stories in his letter without sacrificing a reminder on the importance of studying: the letter was written entirely in Latin. Thomas told young Jack that he debated whether to write in Latin or English and decided that writing in Latin would be good practice for his son.[51] The letter shows that Thomas was subject to contemporary conventions about fatherhood that emphasized a father's duty to prepare his children, particularly his sons, for future employment and responsibilities, but he did it with the typical Sharp penchant for mixing work with humor and entertainment.

As the 1734 letter suggests, whether for schooling or apprenticeships, the Sharps left the family *house* but not family relationships or even the family economy. While some have described children's education or training as "the move from the family into independent employment," this description does not accurately depict how the Sharps, and most eighteenth-century people, transitioned into employment.[52] When John departed for Cambridge, he packed musical scores, many inscribed with notations by his siblings. Any time he played from his music, he would have had physical reminders of his childhood and his siblings. The Sharps engaged in a variety of activities that maintained their connections to one another even as they pursued independent professions. Their father's

---

[50] Harris, *Siblinghood and Social Relations*, 60–66, 97–98.

[51] Thomas Sharp to John Sharp, December 27, 1734, D3549/9/1/1. For childhood epistolary conventions, see Adriana Benzaquén, "'Pray let none see this impertinent epistle': Children's Letters and Children in Letters at the Turn of the Eighteenth Century," in Andrew O'Malley, ed., *Literary Cultures and Eighteenth-Century Childhoods* (London: Palgrave Macmillan, 2018), 75–96.

[52] Patrick Wallis, Cliff Webb, and Chris Minns, "Leaving Home and Entering Service: The Age of Apprenticeship in Early Modern London," *Continuity and Change*, 25, no. 3 (December 2010): 377, 388.

careful report to their mother when he took Granville to London, the common letters between the sisters at home and the brothers at Cambridge or London, the fact that John and Thomas shared rooms and reading materials at Cambridge, the extended visits the parents initiated for the girls to visit their brothers, and the gatherings for musical evenings at William's house all neatly extended the Sharps' childhood interactions into adulthood closeness. For families with the means of maintaining regular correspondence and visits, their boys leaving for school or apprenticeships did not sever or even necessarily weaken family ties. Letters tied the Sharps together even as distance separated them. Those ties would prove durable and needed in the coming years.

At the moments the brothers took steps toward independence, their parents reminded them of their ties to siblings and cousins. Though the Sharps later had a second home in Durham and regularly visited Ripon, Durham and Ripon were not London. Visits to Ripon, where their uncle was dean of the cathedral, reinforced ties to extended family as much as it expanded their social circle. Even as the older boys went to grammar school, visits and letters kept them connected to home and their cousins and younger siblings. Being far removed from cities helped their efforts. Rothbury was not full of social equals for the Sharp children to associate with. While the Sharps shared some characteristics with rural middling families—enough resources to enjoy consumer goods, but minimal property holding, and a "belief in the virtues of work and economic independence,"—the Sharps were differentiated from their neighbors by education, social standing, and familial connections.[53]

The Sharp siblings knew the Sharp cousins: the two surviving daughters (ten to twenty years older than the Sharps) of their uncle John; their one Mangey cousin, John, who was the son of their aunt Dorothy Sharp Mangey; and their seven surviving Dering cousins, who were closer in age to the Sharp siblings (Figure 2.2). The Sharp siblings were less close with their cousins on the Wheler side. Their mother had seventeen siblings, twelve of whom made it to adulthood, but of those only seven married, and not all of them had children who survived them. Some of the Wheler cousins lived in Kent and Cornwall, making regular visits with them impractical and infrequent, but Thomas and Judith used letters to keep their children informed of their various cousins.[54] The same letter reveals a closeness between the Sharp and Dering cousins. While the reports of the Huttons and Middletons reveal no such closeness, the letter demonstrates one way the Sharps maintained even minor connections to extended kin through conversation and correspondence.

---

[53] Joan Kent, "The Rural 'Middling Sort' in Early Modern England, c.1640–1740: Some Economic, Political and Sociocultural Characteristics," *Rural History*, 10, no. 1 (April 1999): 34.

[54] For example, in his 1734 letter to John referenced above, Thomas Sr. reported on a difficulty between George Hutton and Aunt Middleton. George Hutton was Judith Sharp's nephew (through her sister Elizabeth) and therefore John's cousin. Aunt (Frances) Middleton was another sister of Judith's: Thomas Sharp to John Sharp, December 27, 1734.

48   BEING SINGLE IN GEORGIAN ENGLAND

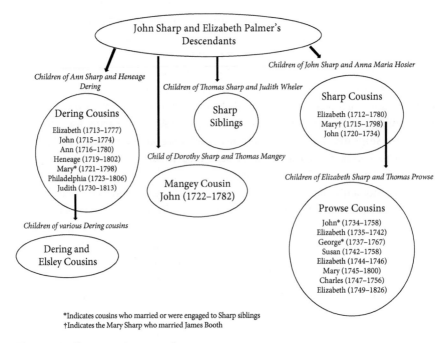

*Indicates cousins who married or were engaged to Sharp siblings
†Indicates the Mary Sharp who married James Booth

Figure 2.2 Sharp cousin network

The cousin network the Sharp siblings inherited was smaller than might be expected, given that Judith and Thomas had eleven siblings between them who married. The Sharp children had some cousins who were substantially older than they and, as a result, often maintained relationships with their cousins' children. Their cousin Elizabeth Sharp Prowse, for example, was twenty years older than John, and she acted more as an aunt for the siblings, particularly those who later lived in London, which was closer to her estate in Northamptonshire. The Dering cousins, children of Anne Sharp and Heneage Dering, were the Sharp siblings' closest cousins on their father's side, and they maintained lifelong relationships with them, particularly the youngest three Dering sisters, who were close in age to the Sharps. Because Thomas's brother-in-law Heneage was dean of Ripon, making regular connections with that side of the family was easier than it would have been with the Wheler cousins, who lived mostly in Kent. The Sharps still maintained relationships with the Wheler cousins, as the siblings' adult correspondence demonstrates, but these relationships do not appear to be as close as the Derings' relationships when they were children. Financial and social embeddedness with extended family was part of daily life during the siblings' childhood. Material objects such as books, music, and toys likely circulated among the Sharps and their various cousins.[55]

---

[55] For example, the Sharp children might have played with a dollhouse owned by their aunt Ann Sharp Dering and later owned by her daughter (their cousin) Elizabeth Dering Elsley. See C. Reginald

Formal and Informal Education in the 1740s

For two years—from the birth of Frances in 1738 to the departure of John for Cambridge in 1740—the Sharp sisters and the younger brothers lived with their parents, primarily in Rothbury. After their father was appointed a prebendary in 1732, they also had a home in Durham and likely visited Bamburgh Castle after their father became a trustee of Lord Crewe's trust and assumed management of the castle in 1737. As they entered their early teens, all the brothers spent long stretches away from home. John attended school in Northallerton, Yorkshire, as early as 1734. Letters and visits kept the siblings connected even as the older ones began preparing for their adult lives. By the mid-1740s, the older brothers had entered grammar schools, and then started apprenticeships or advanced education at Cambridge. In 1743 alone, Thomas entered Cambridge, Charles entered an academy in preparation for service in the East India Company, and William began an apprenticeship with a London surgeon. Their parents and 10-year-old Judith traveled with the boys, installing them in their various locations as they went. Eleven-year-old Elizabeth did not join them, but spent the time with the Derings in Ripon. By traveling together and placing sons in close geographic proximity (except Charles), the move from home was executed in a manner likely to strengthen family ties and underscore their importance, rather than rupture or sever them in an effort to make the sons completely independent.

Judith and Thomas would have been well aware of the risks of sending their sons so far from home, even with the best of placements. Particularly for Charles, who was destined for a career in the empire—a part of British life Thomas and Judith had no experience with—they must have felt some trepidation at sending their son abroad. Tragically Charles's career ended before it began; he died in Jakarta en route to India in 1744. Though it is unlikely his younger siblings fully understood the risks Charles faced by traveling abroad, they must have felt his loss, even 6-year-old Frances. Without the normal trappings of funeral and burial, the role the siblings played in mourning or memorializing their 16-year-old brother is not known.

Just one year after Charles's death, the 1745 Jacobite rebellion came close to disrupting the Sharps' childhood. In November 1745, Thomas Sr. wrote John at Cambridge about the "fresh fears" in Durham when the soldiers left.[56] Some feared areas in Durham and Northumberland would support Charles Stewart in his struggle for the English throne as they had his father. The Sharps had left Rothbury for Durham, at least in part, to find greater safety there.[57] Though the

---

Grundy, *The Connoisseur: An Illustrated Magazine for Collectors*, 52 (September–December 1918): 216–17, https://archive.org/stream/connoisseur52londuoft/connoisseur52londuoft_djvu.txt.

[56] Thomas Sharp to John Sharp, November 22, 1745, D3549/9/1/1.

[57] Bishop Edward Chandler of Durham to Mr. Archdeacon [Thomas Sharp], October 15, 1745, Add. MSS. 6482, fol. 125, British Library, quoted in R. Barry Levis, "The Jacobite Uprising of 1745 and

50 BEING SINGLE IN GEORGIAN ENGLAND

rebel Jacobite forces did not reach Durham, or Rothbury as they had in 1715, there were still disruptions in the Sharp household during the winter of 1745–46; one captain quartered with the Sharps and military horses filled the Sharp stables. Everyone waited for news from Carlisle about the state of affairs there, and Thomas reported the Sharp homelife was like living "in the midst of the army" while rumors swirled.[58]

As the rebellion proved unsuccessful and as successive Hanoverians assumed the throne with less Jacobite resistance, the Sharps never experienced the same momentary nervousness of 1745–46 again. Instead, for most of the siblings, the 1740s were a decade in which gender increasingly differentiated their experiences. Over that decade, through both informal and formal education they began the gradual process of leaving their childhood home, as the brothers, followed later by the sisters, moved south. Even as gender and distance differentiated the siblings' experiences, they maintained close connections to each other and to their sense of collective identity.

Informal Education

Judith and Thomas Sr. had grown up in homes containing elements of flexible, even indulgent, childrearing practices. Lockean ideas about the malleability of children also likely influenced them just as they did many English parents. While the Sharp home was full of music, games, and diversions, these activities were used to teach skills children would require as adults. From analyzing Judith's handwriting in her songbook it appears that she had a hand in teaching the children to write. Her daughters' adult handwriting looks more like hers than her sons' handwriting. Though the boys likely had the help of their mother's writing instruction when they were young, their more formal education away from home influenced their penmanship. Perhaps they enjoyed learning games with colorful, hand-drawn alphabet and lesson cards similar to those Jane Johnson invented in the 1740s.[59] Undoubtedly, they benefited from the growing body of literature for children and books describing child development.[60] Educated families of the eighteenth century invested in books, notebooks, pen, ink, and paper, as well as the time to teach children the proper way to handle all those objects, training

the Ecclesiastical Province of York: 'Quenching the Flame of Bold Rebellion,'" *Northern History*, 51, no. 1 (March 2014): 55n93.

[58] Thomas Sharp to John Sharp, November 22, 1745.

[59] Jane Johnson manuscripts, c.1740–1759, LMC 1649, Indiana University Archives, http://webapp1.dlib.indiana.edu/findingaids/view?doc.view=entire_text&docId=InU-Li-VAA1275.

[60] Mary Hilton, Morag Styles, and Victor Watson, eds., *Opening the Nursery Door: Reading, Writing and Childhood 1600–1900* (London: Routledge, 1997).

their bodies and minds for the serious work of life.[61] Any doodles, games, and letters Sharp siblings may have produced prepared them for the intellectual and physical labor of keeping household accounts, conducting extra-household financial transactions, and corresponding with social and professional networks. Letter-writing was a particularly important skill for both girls and boys to learn, and the Sharp children learned not just the mechanics of writing but also the epistolary conventions they would rely on throughout their lives.[62]

Playing on the hillside above Rothbury, reading in the orchard, climbing the astronomical tower, spending time in Durham (with perhaps trips to Bamburgh Castle), and living within a refurbished tower themselves, the siblings enjoyed an exceptional eighteenth-century childhood. Few details survive about what the children were taught at home or what the girls were taught separate from their brothers who left home at young ages for formal education and training. However, their father's will suggests that all the siblings could read French and Italian and that the older two brothers also received additional training in Latin, Greek, and Hebrew.[63] All were taught music, both its theory and performance—and all could play multiple instruments. Many of them also sang, composed, and danced. Most of them were taught the basics of sketching and drawing, with sister Judith perhaps receiving more training.

Despite Thomas and Judith's relatively progressive parenting, gender and age eventually combined to put girls and boys on different trajectories. In the eighteenth century, childhood was becoming a universal category that began to surpass social position in determining one's legal standing or capacity, but social position and gender persisted as key determinants for children's fortunes.[64] With no property to be inherited by the eldest son, the impact of birth order was more diffused for the Sharps. Additionally, because the girls were at the younger end of the birth order, the difference between their education and the greater investment in the boys' formal education may have made gender's impact less apparent. Primarily, the lack of an estate meant the family avoided some of the worst consequences sometimes faced by others due to gendered imbalances.

While the Sharp sisters did not receive training meant to prepare them for professions, they were still trained in literature, music, bookkeeping, and household management (as their later activities attest). The ultimate goal of education for elite girls like the Sharps was to help them make suitable matches and to prepare them to manage households and raise children. Moreover, in the eighteenth

---

[61] Matthew Daniel Eddy, "The Nature of Notebooks: How Enlightenment Schoolchildren Transformed the *Tabula Rasa*," *Journal of British Studies*, 57, no. 2 (April 2018): 275–307.

[62] Susan Whyman, *The Pen and the People: English Letter Writers 1660–1800* (Oxford: Oxford University Press, 2009).

[63] Thomas Sharp, will, written March 1, 1758, proved May 30, 1758, Prerogative Court of Canterbury, PROB 11/838, National Archives (TNA).

[64] Holly Brewer, *By Birth or Consent: Children, Law, and the Anglo-American Revolution in Authority* (Chapel Hill: University of North Carolina Press, 2005).

century, wealthy girls and women were increasingly "out and about," expected to be heavily involved in social, recreational, literary, and public engagements.[65] The sisters benefited not only from private instruction, but also from regular correspondence and communication with their brothers when the brothers engaged in formal education away from home. The Sharp brothers were given opportunities their sisters did not have to build on their young training by departing for university, India, or apprenticeships. However, given the literary and musical content of their adult correspondence, it is clear that both sisters and brothers were taught from a young age to read and write, to be clever while doing it, and to draw, paint, or compose.

From the pieces of surviving contemporary evidence, the Sharp children likely received advice most eighteenth-century parents gave their children: younger siblings should follow the example of worthy elder siblings. This advice was most often followed when it reflected "consensus between parents and children," a situation that seemed to prevail in the Sharp home.[66] The Sharp brothers, for example, seemingly never pushed against their parents' advice; undoubtedly distance from home allowed them autonomy or flexibility while connections to one another also helped maintain overall compliance with parental expectations. They avoided the "distractions and temptations" of Cambridge and London.[67] Their practice of writing common letters to each other maintained the connection between the sisters in the north and the brothers in the south (see Interlude 2). And as soon as they had resources, the siblings used them to facilitate socializing with each other. John and Thomas shared lodgings in Cambridge; William and James invested in sailing barges and households that would allow regular family concerts and meals. By staying connected to each other, the siblings avoided the dangers and vices many parents feared could upend their children's prospects once they left the sphere of parental supervision.

Elizabeth later recounted that their father "had a generous mind and open Heart and notwithstanding his large Family never overspent his Income…and often in making up his yearly account had a balance which he always immediately gave away in Charities never laying up any cash from any of his Preferments for his Family in future." There is more than a hint of ambivalence in her account— made some forty years after her father's death. She coupled the observation with a note that it was their mother's fortune that was divided between the three sisters, implying the girls were particularly shorted by their father's generosity to strangers.[68]

---

[65] Fletcher, *Growing Up in England*, 29–30.

[66] Henry French and Mark Rothery, "'Upon your entry into the world': Masculine Values and the Threshold of Adulthood among Landed Elites in England, 1680–1800," *Social History*, 33, no. 4 (November 2008): 413–414, 418, 421.

[67] Fletcher, *Growing Up in England*, 212.

[68] Elizabeth Sharp Prowse, memorandum and commonplace book, 1758, D3549/14/1/1.

Finding a balance between generosity to others and comfort for themselves became an important aspect of the siblings' adult lives.

Elsewhere, Elizabeth emphasized their father's worthiness and affection, but her comment expressing disappointment in how family resources were allocated indicates that the Sharps, despite all their gifts and abundance, could not avoid the common pitfalls of sibling tension and even rivalry. While children owed their parents filial duty, differences in treatment, or even perceived differences in treatment, could engender conflict between siblings and between children and parents.[69] Like most eighteenth-century sisters, Elizabeth did not seem to object to the built-in gendered differences in how she and her brothers were raised; her critique was centered on one of her father's behaviors that damaged his children's prospects—a serious charge of parental failure in the eighteenth century. In the surviving documents from the Sharp siblings, this critique was the only less-than-glowing description of Thomas and Judith as parents. Balancing expectations to love children equally within existing gender, birth order, and marital status hierarchies could make for tricky family dynamics. Undoubtedly, Elizabeth's criticism was not the only time the Sharp siblings experienced disappointments in their childhood. But such occasions appear to have been the exception, not the rule in the Sharp household.

The Sharp children had access to an enormous variety of books. In addition to his own books, Thomas Sr. inherited half of his father's library in 1714; the remaining half was initially inherited by his brother John, but rejoined Thomas's half after John's death in 1727. Thomas and John worked together to catalog and organize their father's collection.[70] The combined libraries, comprising hundreds of volumes, contained information on an expansive array of topics that the children would have had access to either directly through reading or indirectly from their parents', tutors', and relatives' opinions that appeared in those books, as some were written by family members. There were books in French, Latin, Greek, and a smattering of other European languages. As the children grew, Thomas gave some of the books to them, including a first edition of Newton's *Principia* to John, medical books to William, and seventeenth-century philosophical and religious texts to Elizabeth and Judith.[71]

Thomas and Judith encouraged their children to keep a careful accounting of what they read. John, following his father's example, began to keep a book list and a commonplace book when he went to Cambridge in 1740. Elizabeth may have

---

[69] Richard Grassby, *Kinship and Capitalism: Marriage, Family, and Business in the English-Speaking World, 1580–1740* (Cambridge: Cambridge University Press and Woodrow Wilson Center Press, 2001), 208–210; Amy Harris, "'That Fierce Edge': Sibling Conflict and Politics in Georgian England," *Journal of Family History*, 37, no. 2 (April 2012): 155–174.

[70] "Catalogue of tracts belonging to John Sharp (1677–1727), Thomas Sharp (1693–1758), and Archbishop John Sharp (1645–1714)," Bamburgh MS A12, PGL, http://reed.dur.ac.uk/xtf/view?docId=ark:/32150_s1w0892b02q.xml.

[71] Thomas Sharp, rough notes and books given to children, 1750s, D3549/7/2/17.

54 BEING SINGLE IN GEORGIAN ENGLAND

begun a commonplace book in the 1740s and eventually Granville also started and kept a commonplace book. Though Elizabeth's book does not survive, the family chronology she later compiled hints such a book once existed. John's book list is the oldest surviving and most complete list of reading materials from the Sharps' childhood or youth. He kept the list intermittently until the 1760s, and it contains not only expected classics, natural philosophy, music, and history, but also popular novels such as *Tom Jones*, *Clarissa*, and *Amelia*, with the date he read them.[72] The inclination and training to write their thoughts, let alone the material resources and quiet time to oneself such training required, offered the siblings time to develop a sense of personal identity. Simultaneously, participating in the same activities, perhaps even at the same time, the siblings reinforced their collective identity.

The Sharps' informal training included lessons in family identity. Granville later remembered Charles sketching their family arms and inscribing on it the motto "Fortes Fortuna juvat."[73] Other siblings engaged in capturing and preserving markers of family identity. In addition to Granville's sketch of their childhood home, Elizabeth's late eighteenth-century family chronicle suggests that in addition to her commonplace book, she began a diary to record important family events.

Outside observers agreed that Judith and Thomas succeeded in raising "virtuous and amiable" children who demonstrated "piety and beneficence."[74] They expected and modeled that piety should be expressed not just in personal devotions but in public charitable work and pastoral care for others. Granville recalled that their father "retained at his own expense five, if not more, different schools in the villages, at convenient distances, for the instruction of poor children." Children of Catholics and dissenting parents "were equally admitted to the benefit of the schools," in which "very strict care was taken not to give any offense to them, or their parents, about the difference of religious opinions."[75] Additionally, after 1737 the Sharps' charitable endeavors expanded to include Bamburgh Castle refurbishment. Judith and Thomas also engaged in smaller acts of charity, recommending, for example, an old Wheler family servant who had become indigent to the care of officials in Houghton le Spring.[76]

---

[72] Bamburgh Library manuscripts catalog, descriptions for Bamburgh MS C4 and Bamburgh MS R.7, PGL, http://reed.dur.ac.uk/xtf/view?docId=ark/32150_s1w0892b02q.xml.

[73] The motto translates as "fortune favors the brave," a motto that was sadly ironic in light of his parents' bravery in sending Charles to India, an act that resulted in his untimely death. Granville Sharp to John Sharp, July 7, 1786, D3549/13/1/S8.

[74] William Dolben to Thomas Sharp, July 16, 1757, D3549/7/2/16; Owen, *A Discourse Occasioned by the Death of Elizabeth Prowse*, 7–8.

[75] Hoare, *Memoirs of Granville Sharp, Esq.*, 15.

[76] Thomas Sharp, to Ralph Robinson, December 10, 1750, Houghton le Spring, EP/HO 689, Durham Record Office (DRO).

Formal Education and Training

As in other educated and prosperous families, formal education away from home was reserved for the boys. Young girls and boys were usually taught at home by parents and private tutors, but once the boys reached 10 or 11 years, they attend residential or day grammar schools. As teenagers the boys either attended university or began apprenticeships. Families used apprenticeships to improve their children's social standing, but the system largely perpetuated social hierarchies.[77] Parents throughout the early modern period sent older sons to university or the Inns at Court and younger sons to apprenticeships.[78] Apprenticeships were less expensive than university training, but placement in an apprenticeship associated with a prestigious London livery company provided requisite opportunities for sons of the gentry and prosperous clerical families.[79] Like many of their contemporaries, the younger Sharp brothers' move to London for apprenticeships gave them access to financial and social networks provided by wealthy masters.[80] Completed London apprenticeships also would grant the boys entrance into the freedom of the city, with its attendant business and political rights.

Profits from rectory property they held in Doncaster allowed Judith and Thomas Sr. to send their sons to grammar schools—most of them attended Durham Grammar School for at least a part of their primary education—and to send the oldest two sons, John and Thomas, to university.[81] Though the Sharp brothers could have attended the school in Ripon where their uncle, the dean, was among the school's governors, Durham Grammar School was more prestigious than Ripon, and their parents regularly visited or resided in Durham.[82] It is probable that the opportunity to regularly see their sons influenced Thomas and Judith's decision to choose the school at Durham. Like other parents of their social standing, the Sharps worked to strike a balance between preparing their boys to be leaders in society and the nation, and ensuring that they did not succumb to the pitfalls of independence.[83] Even the younger sons' apprenticeships, instead of university educations, were matters of serious and careful consideration. There are no records detailing how Judith and Thomas chose masters for their sons, but given the variety of the specialties they were trained in—the East

---

[77] Helen Barry, *Orphans of Empire* (Oxford: Oxford University Press, 2019), 147–202.

[78] Patrick Wallis and Cliff Webb, "The Education and Training of Gentry Sons in Early Modern England," *Social History*, 36, no. 1 (February 2011): 36–53.

[79] Wallis and Webb, "Education and Training of Gentry Sons," 44.

[80] Jacob, *Clerical Profession*, 3–6.

[81] Hoare, *Memoirs of Granville Sharp*, 27; Charles S. Earle and Lawrence A. Body, eds., *Durham School Register*, 2nd edn. (London: Bradbury, Agnew, & Co., 1912), 100–101; John Edward Jackson, *The History and Description of St. George's Church at Doncaster* (London: J. B. Nichols and Sons, 1855), lv–lvii.

[82] Ripon Grammar School Minute Book, 1764–69, RGS/B/1/2, Borthwick Institute, University of York (BIY).

[83] French and Rothery, "'Upon your entry,'" 403.

56 BEING SINGLE IN GEORGIAN ENGLAND

India Company, medicine, ironmongering, drapery—the boys' preferences were likely considered.[84] Undoubtedly, the Sharps also drew on social networks to learn about appropriate masters who could be trusted with their sons. The Sharps seemed motivated by the reputation of a master's household and his ability to provide training meant to give a boy employment and financial security for the future. Interestingly, religious denomination was less important to them. Granville's first master was a Quaker. Granville always seemed quite pleased that he went from a Quaker to a Presbyterian master and later lived with a Catholic and a non-believer.[85]

Judith and Thomas took pains to launch their sons' professional training, and in return they received (and probably expected) the sons' dutiful attention to their studies and work. A 1748 letter from John at Cambridge to his father reveals how John's efforts to conform to his parents' expectations colored his experience. No similar letters from the other sons survive, so it is tempting to see John's position as eldest son as making him particularly keen to perpetuate the family's scholarly and clerical prominence. He was ordained a deacon on October 23 that year and wrote his father two days later about his preparations. He dutifully noted that he had done all in his power to prepare for his exams on liturgy, canons, and "every thing that is in the prayer book." He reported he had read most of the Greek New Testament and Septuagint Old Testament. He also described spending nine hours reading aloud in order to be a more natural reader and then assessed how well he read in recent chapel and ordaining services. "I can't easily describe to you the anxiety & flutter I was in on Sunday night having engaged to read in the Chapel the ^next^ morning," he wrote. His need to fulfill his father's expectations are clear, but recognizing he might sound self-centered, he ended with an apology for such a "tedious account" that might make it look as if he was "fond of talking of myself."[86] The anxious and somewhat insecure John succeeded; he was ordained a priest the following spring and appointed vicar of Hartburn by the end of 1749.

William was schooled at home and at a nearby day school until he was 14, at which age he was sent to London to begin an apprenticeship to a surgeon.[87] James, at 15 years old, followed William to London in 1746 and began his apprenticeship to a Leadenhall Street ironmonger and the Company of Drapers.[88]

---

[84] Adriana Benzaquén, "Educational Designs: The Education and Training of Younger Sons at the Turn of the Eighteenth Century," *Journal of Family History*, 40, no. 4 (2015): 462–484; Ilana Krausman Ben-Amos, *Adolescence and Youth in Early Modern England* (New Haven: Yale University Press, 1994), 62–67.

[85] Hoare, *Memoirs of Granville Sharp*, 28. Elizabeth Sharp Prowse, memorandum and commonplace book, 1758, pages 13–14, D3549/14/1/1.

[86] John Sharp to Thomas Sharp, October 25, 1748, D3549/7/2/9.

[87] John Owen, "A Discourse Occasioned by the Death of William Sharp, Esq.," excerpted in *Gentleman's Magazine*, 80, no. 2 (1810): 450–453.

[88] James Sharp, apprenticeship bond, August 22, 1746, father Thomas Sharp, master Samuel Southouse, Drapers' Company, Records of London's Livery Companies Online, https://londonroll. org/, accessed August 18, 2019. James became a freeman of London through completing the apprenticeship in March 1755.

Similarly, Granville, not quite 15, was escorted to London in 1750 to begin his apprenticeship with a member of the Fishmongers' Company.[89] Granville did not complete his schooling at Durham; he was withdrawn and enrolled in a smaller school focused on writing and arithmetic to prepare him for an apprenticeship and a trade.[90]

The Sharp boys were slightly younger than most of their contemporaries when they began their apprenticeships. In the 1740s most apprentices in London started their training when they were between 15 and 16 years old, and apprentices from the north tended to be even older, usually between 17 and 18. Prosperous families tended to send their sons to London apprenticeships later than the average age because they were not as dependent on the boys' earnings, allowing them the luxury of staying home longer.[91] Interestingly, the Sharp sons began their apprenticeships when they were between 14 and 15, younger than the northern cohort and younger than boys of their social class. This decision was perhaps prompted by financial considerations. With the family homes being connected to clerical appointments, Judith and Thomas did not have an estate their eldest son could inherit or their children share. Also, their marriage settlement provided only £1000 for each child. They had sufficient resources to send the two oldest boys to university (as pensioners), but with four additional sons to educate, they may have determined it was better to launch the boys into apprenticeships as soon as possible so that they would sooner have financial independence.[92]

The siblings must have recognized how finances influenced each other's prospects. Elizabeth remarked upon it decades later, and John proposed sharing rooms with Thomas when Thomas joined him at Cambridge—a suggestion their father approved of on financial grounds.[93] James's 1746 apprenticeship bond cost £200, Granville's 1750 bond cost £150, and William's likely cost at least £100, if

---

[89] Granville Sharp, apprenticeship indenture, May 31, 1750, father Thomas Sharp, master John Halsey; transfer of apprenticeship upon Halsey's death, to another freeman, May 9, 1755, COL/CHD/FR/02/0826-0-34, LMA, digital image at *Freedom of the City Admission Papers, 1681–1930*, https://www.ancestry.co.uk/, accessed July 3, 2018.

[90] Earle and Body, *Durham School Register*, 100–101. The student registers do not survive for the eighteenth century, but the school compiled lists from other sources in the early twentieth century, and these sources list Thomas, William, James, and Granville among their alumni. It is probable that Charles also attended school there. John first attended school in Northallerton, but he later moved to Durham.

[91] Wallis, Webb, and Minns, "Leaving Home," 387, 389–390.

[92] John Sharp was admitted a pensioner of Trinity College on May 12, 1740. He became a scholar in 1741 and a fellow in 1746. He received his BA in 1744, his MA in 1747, and his DD in 1759. He was ordained a deacon at Ely on October 23, 1748, appointed rector of Hartburn, Northumberland, in 1749, and became archdeacon of Northumberland upon his father's death in 1758. He held at least five additional ecclesiastical appointments throughout his life. Thomas Sharp Jr. was admitted a pensioner of Trinity College on May 3, 1743. He became a scholar in 1744, received his BA in 1747, was made a fellow in 1749, and received his MA in 1750. He was ordained a deacon at Ely on June 4, 1750 and a priest in London on February 28, 1755. He became perpetual curate of Bamburgh in 1757 and vicar of Bartholomew the Less in 1765.

[93] Thomas Sharp Sr. to John Sharp, November 22, 1748, NRO 00452/C/3/2/1, Northumberland Archives.

58 BEING SINGLE IN GEORGIAN ENGLAND

not more due to the surgeon's reputation.[94] All of these costs were less expensive than university training with its attendant housing and food costs or the £200 a year it could cost to keep a son at the bar.[95] Because of Thomas Sr.'s involvement with the Corporation of the Sons of the Clergy, a group that helped the widows and children of poor clergy, he must have known that many livings provided inadequate incomes.[96] Knowing the limitations of the number of sufficiently prosperous clerical appointments might have become an additional motivation for Thomas and Judith to find apprenticeships, rather than clerical training, for their younger sons.

Conclusion

The Sharp siblings were born into a world built on hierarchies, but the family culture they inherited had a more nuanced approach to childrearing. As part of their family culture, they inherited religious and charitable ideals and valued the labor it took to maintain relationships with kin across space and time. In the process, they established their own committed relationships and collective identity. Childhood closeness had long-term effects. Their shared childhood and family culture influenced how they imagined domestic life in later years, laying the foundation for how they would negotiate relationships and household governance in the future. The household contained "gradations of power," as their grandfather Wheler described, and as they aged the siblings had to both mediate and maintain hierarchies based on age and birth order.[97]

A variety of educational avenues for children formed a patchwork of options that differed in length, content, and quality based on a combination of social position and gender. The Sharp children enjoyed the best of eighteenth-century educational options, both informal and formal. Private tutors, a father who built an astronomical observation tower, a highly educated mother, books and music (with the attendant activities of reading, performance, and practice) were essential elements to the Sharps' shared childhood.

The boys could have transitioned into peer groups at school and university and as clerics. Many eighteenth-century children connected more to nonrelated peers and those they met once they moved away from childhood homes, creating social and domestic lives somewhat distanced and independent from their families of

---

[94] Granville Sharp, apprenticeship indenture to John Halsey, Fishmongers Company, May 31, 1750, COL/CHD/FR/02/0826-0 834, LMA, digital image at *London, England, Freedom of the City Admission Papers, 1681–1930*, https://www.ancestry.co.uk/, accessed February 3, 2018.
[95] Jacob, *Clerical Profession*, 47.   [96] Jacob, *Clerical Profession*, 41–47.
[97] Karen Harvey, *Little Republic*, 3–4.

origin.[98] But the Sharp parents facilitated the boys' maintaining connections to each other, their sisters, and their cousins through visits and correspondence. Similarly, Judith and Thomas held their daughters close; shuttling between Durham and Rothbury meant the girls' associations, too, were centered on siblings and cousins. The Sharps' resources and encouragement reinforced the siblings' connections to each other and to the collective experience of being a Sharp, to "Sharpness," one might say. Our understanding of this era often emphasizes the independence of adolescents, which seems so different from our time. The experience of the Sharp family counterbalances that emphasis with the simultaneous fact that families of origin remained important connections for those who left home.[99] The Sharp siblings reached young adulthood with entrenched familial patterns that would shape their social interactions, marital choices, and household arrangements for the next three decades.

[98] John R. Gillis, *Youth and History: Tradition and Change in European Age Relations 1770–Present* (New York: Academic Press, 1974), 9.

[99] Harris, *Siblinghood and Social Relations*, 44; Marc Klemp, Chris Minns, Patrick Wallis, and Jacob Weisdorf, "Picking Winners? The Effect of Birth Order and Migration on Parental Human Capital Investments in Pre-Modern England," *European Review of Economic History*, 17, no. 2 (2013): 210–232.

Interlude 2
Common Letters

The 1750s could have been a time of transition that created or widened a gap between the siblings as geographic distances exaggerated the differences birth order and gender already had created, but their parents worked to prevent any such gap from developing. In 1743, when their parents took Charles and William to London for training, 9-year-old Judith joined them. In 1750, when 21-year-old William completed his apprenticeship, he and 19-year-old James spent two weeks in Durham, constantly lobbying their parents to let 17-year-old Elizabeth join them in London. Though their petition, something they continued to discuss throughout the spring, proved unsuccessful, their mother promised them she would bring Elizabeth for a visit the following year. She kept that promise and in 1751 she and Elizabeth first went to Cambridge to see John, being joined there by Thomas and William. They then stayed six weeks at William's house on Mincing Lane in the heart of the city. When their father was appointed to Southwell Minster in Nottinghamshire in 1753 and gained a residence there, family visits became easier due to Southwell being halfway between Durham and London. Connections with John, who married in 1752 and resided in Hartburn, Northumberland, did not suffer because Hartburn was only fifteen miles from Rothbury and forty miles from Durham (where John also had duties assisting his father in his archidiaconal duties).

Buttressed by their parents' efforts, the siblings developed their own customs in order to maintain their relationships despite geographic distance. In 1754, they began their common letters—a joint correspondence built on light-hearted content, witty stories, and full of puns in the highest style of eighteenth-century humor. Elizabeth later noted their parents' support for the correspondence:

> My Father and Mother on their death Beds expected the satisfaction this weekly correspondence had given them, being thereby assured that their Daughters would be protected by their Brothers, and happy with them.[1]

Though encouraged and appreciated by their parents, the correspondence was self-contained within the sibling circle. Elizabeth noted the practice ended after their parents died and the sisters dispersed into their brothers' households.

---

[1] Elizabeth Sharp Prowse, memorandum and commonplace book, 1754, page 17, D3549/14/1/1.

Being Single in Georgian England: Families, Households, and the Unmarried. Amy Harris, Oxford University Press.
© Amy Harris 2023. DOI: 10.1093/oso/9780192869494.003.0005

INTERLUDE 2: COMMON LETTERS   61

However, a couple of letters from the early 1760s suggest the practice lingered beyond their parents' deaths. It is hard to say who enjoyed the common letters the most because only the brothers' half of the correspondence survives and even that is clearly incomplete. But Thomas and Granville seemed to particularly revel in the practice—both its content and its style.

It is not clear who started the tradition. It was common for letters to be shared and read aloud to a group or family members in eighteenth-century England.[2] The Sharps put their particular stamp on the practice by establishing their own epistolary rules. The letters were informal, full of sketches and jokes, in varying degrees of propriety and bawdiness, and clearly a delightful entertainment for the siblings. The Sharps also wrote about concerts and religious music and engaged in the musical version of the common-letter jokes by writing and singing "catches"— songs sung in rounds meant to be humorous and full of puns. Banter between the siblings was *de rigueur*, so no matter who the author was, everyone was sure to find themselves discussed and teased, and to have their own rejoinders reported and joked upon. Thomas even chastised his sisters for writing a pun in a similar style to one he and another brother had already used, meaning the sisters' joke was not nearly as clever as it could have been "had you proceeded upon another Plan." Instead "the Design was discovered before we had read 3 Lines."[3] Taking puns to their full, preposterous, extent was usually expected as long as high standards of creativity and wittiness were followed. To pun properly, required repetition so to "never let a pun be lost, but repeat and comment upon it."[4]

The siblings engaged in innuendo and ridicule though perhaps not to the extremes of cruel humor often on display in the second half of the eighteenth century by the so-called polite classes.[5] One common letter had an elaborate pun about the new organ William purchased in 1754. Calling the organ "Miss Morgan" he went on to describe "her" attributes in mildly bawdy language. Granville sketched a man and mocked his Yorkshire dialect.

The letters connected the siblings at a crucial moment. Just as their age, gender, and birth order could have diminished their sense of shared identity, the letters served to bridge those gaps. In 1759, sober-minded archdeacon John, who was 37, wrote a lengthy letter on "common letter day" to his London siblings, including 21-year-old Frances. He began the letter with uncertainty about his ability to "continue to write a common letter by myself, but however I'll do the best I can." His best was to write each sibling individually in the same letter. Even for the eldest brother, the rules of Sharp correspondence had to be carefully followed or

---

[2] Clare Brant, *Eighteenth-Century Letters and British Culture* (London: Palgrave Macmillan, 2006).
[3] Thomas Sharp to Sharp Sisters, November 20, 1757, D3549/7/2/15.
[4] Thomas Sheridan and Jonathan Swift, *Ars pun-ica, sive flos linguaraum: The Art of Punning* (Dublin: 1719), 9. My thanks to Kate Retford for alerting me to this text.
[5] Simon Dickie, "Hilarity and Pitilessness in the Mid-Eighteenth Century: English Jestbook Humor," *Eighteenth-Century Studies*, 37, no. 1 (Fall 2003): 1–22.

62 BEING SINGLE IN GEORGIAN ENGLAND

deviation properly explained. He wrote Tom, Will, Jim, Granville, Bessy, and Fan, using their informal youthful nicknames and employing Italian musical terms— there was a separate section for Tom and Fanny labeled "Duetto." The content of the letter was serious, largely about distributing bequests of property and cash from their father's will, but the style was playful, using musical terms to set apart various sections and closing with both an "air" and a "chorus." In the air, John congratulated himself "for this extraordinary scheme of a common Letter," perhaps hoping to cut off any criticism that the practical content did not comply with humorous expectations. The chorus for all "Brothers & Sisters Tutti" concluded with the following remark employing the typical common letters' dual-meaning prose.

> I make no Doubt but you will all of you take care, to play your respective Parts duly as I have laid them before you, to do them Justice in the Execution, & above things not to be out of Time, for they must be play'd Allegro, tho' not quicker than you can property manage them. I shall then have good reason to cry Bravissimo, & if there sh[oul]d be occasion, to Encore you too, against another time. J.S.[6]

The Sharps decided the letters were worth preserving. That letters from the brothers, but not the sisters, survive suggests the sisters, or their parents initially, were the first to recognize the importance of saving the letters. Later, however, it appears Thomas might have made copies and Granville certainly made copies of many letters and sketches, indicating they too came to understand the letters' value in transmitting the family's values and history. Forty-eight unique letters survive, mostly from 1756 and 1757, and several of them with at least two copies. The copies were later bound in high-quality leather book whose spine was inscribed "Common Letters MSS" and entitled inside as "Some Extracts from the Common Letters or Family Correspondence of the #s between 1755 and 1763." There are sketches (mostly by Granville) as well as a drawing of William's pipe organ (see upper image, Plate 4).[7]

Sampled below are two brief letters. They were chosen because they show the typical style but are shorter than letters that covered pages or those centered on inside jokes spread across multiple letters. The explanatory notations in the first letter were made by Granville when he copied the letter. In the second letter, a paragraph break has been inserted to facilitate reading.

---

[6] John Sharp to Sharp siblings, February 6 and 8, 1759, D3549/7/2/15.
[7] For an analysis of the musical world revealed in some of the common letters, see Crosby, "Private Concerts," 26–31.

INTERLUDE 2: COMMON LETTERS   63

[18 November 1757][8]

Who commands in the Van?

<u>Brother Tom</u> He's the Man.

As he leads with his feet,

He will certainly <u>beat</u>.

A few Taps with his Bow

will keep Order you know.

<u>Lovey Jones</u>, who is reckon'd

To play a Staunch Second,

As he Fiddles with Flee,

<u>Aid de Camp</u> let him be,

Charlie's not so quick,[9]

yet he Play's a good Stick,

Make him Captain — Agreed:

His own* <u>Crowd</u> he may lead,   *Crowd is a West Country name for a Fiddle

And if he himself stay,

His <u>Crowd</u> won't run away.

<u>Paxton</u> Rules in the Rear,

<u>Cox</u> is Chief Engineer,

<u>Bill's</u> a Caterer trim,

Then there's <u>Corporal Jim</u>.

And besides those 2 Brothers,

There's <u>Eales</u>, <u>Lewis</u>, and others.

But now I shall quote

Our alliance of <u>Note</u>.

<u>Great Savage</u> Commands

His own Regular Bands,+   +The Choristers of St. Paul's Cathedral

O what strength he can bring,

---

[8] Thomas wrote a letter to the sisters on this date using similar military language to describe a family concert. He then included this poem by Granville and added his own postscript to the poem. "The Muster Roll," two bound copies, pages 59–60, 74–77, D3549/7/2/15. An additional, loose copy is stored with James's papers. It has several small differences, indicating the poem was later revised by Granville. See D3549/12/1/6.

[9] This is not a reference to brother Charles who died in 1744, but to James's butler, Charles Colehouse. See Crosby, "Private Concerts," 49, 53, 58.

64 BEING SINGLE IN GEORGIAN ENGLAND

All his <u>Infantry</u> sing.

And as <u>Simpson</u> is made[10]

Our All'y, <u>who's afraid?</u>

Now good Reader excuse

All the Faults of my muse,

Let no Critics be hard

When a Drummer turns Bard

Tho the Verses run <u>rough</u>⁺ ⁺a Rough is a particular <u>Beat</u> in Drumming

For this story of fighting

Is the <u>Drummers</u> own Writing.

G.S.

I'm by no means a <u>Poet</u>,

(You very well know it)

But, when <u>Rhyme's</u> on <u>the Anvil</u>

Call <u>Drum-Major Granville</u>"

T.S.

[November 1757]

Be it known to all whom it may concern, that We, TS, WS, JS, & GS of the Parish of St. Dunstans in the County of Middlesex, do Attest, protest, and declare against the proceedings or manner of conducting or Frameing of the Last common Letter recd by us the aforesaid TS &c &c &c For as much as the said Letter (contrary to the Express Laws, & Fundamental Rules of common Letters recd by us aforetime) hath, or doth contain, or set forth 3 whole sides, or Pages out of 5 of the same (wch, tho you shou'd have for an Advocate the most Judicious Lawyer, he must acknowledge it with^out^ further Quirk or Quibble to be the better half) filled up with Divers Paragraphs, Sentences, or Epistles, severally addressed, appointed, or directed, to, & for the only proper use & behoof of one Brother Fletcher, alias, William, alias Billy, the Brother of Mordecai! & Forasmuch as the above paragraphs &c &c doth consist of, or doth contain, Sundry, or Divers Answers to Quarys, Questions, & Inquirys written or inscribed on in, or upon a several, or separate pieces of Paper unread by us the abovemention'd TS, W & &c &c & wraped up in a common Letter destined Northward, by the said Bror. Fletcher, alias &c &c—All wch proceedings (whatsoever they may be in Civil Law) are Deemed refractory to the Customary Laws, & Nature of Letters common to a Body Politick, wch, do not admit of private addresses to any one who^m^soever.

---

[10] The Simpsons and Savages were regularly among the performers listed in the "Visiting Books" covering 1773–83, D3549/12/1/5.

INTERLUDE 2: COMMON LETTERS   65

We do therefore hereby admonish & advise the above Delinquents to avoid any further trespasses of the like kind on pain of further Cognizance being taken, & strict enquirys made into their true reasons for so Doing. We likewise gather from the said Letter that the Offending Partys are preparing to try this matter with us the said T.S. WS. &c &c for we can produce the hand writing of on of the Partys, testifying that F# (likewise one the Partys) hath already taken into her Service, a neibouring Emminent Counsellour, who as the said writing doth witness, hath lately been employed in making a Survey, preparatory to the commencement of a Suit in wch he, the s[ai]d Counsellor, must be Plaintiffve as such case doth require, & now forasmuch as we are apprehensive that the forcable pleadings, & Singular Address, of the said Civilian may gain a great asseendancy in this Court, insomuch that on Terms being ended, he may be in a fair way of carrying away the Cause from us, by an Action of Covenant Individaull, wch hath neither release, nor repeal. Therefore We, (Divers good Causes, & considerations as hereunto Especially moving) do resolve to stop all further proceedings against eth said Delinquents on their future good behaviour, being unwilling to hazard the uncertainty of a Lawsuit.

—& in plain English—

Be it known to you that we never read that Letter inclosed in a late common Letter form Billy Fletcher, that we shall not for the future suffer any words to pass unread by us in the common Letter.

3

To Marry or Not to Marry

"[N]egotiations for our new Family Alliance go on prosperously."[1]
Granville Sharp describing preparations
for brother William's wedding in 1765

Introduction

The year 1750 represented the Sharp siblings' entrance into young adulthood—that vaguely defined span of time between the mid-teens and mid-twenties when early modern English girls and boys became early modern English women and men.[2] Typically, the gradual process of becoming an adult brought with it employment, household governance, marriage, and children. Both women and men found financial and social credit in running households. The foundation of that ideal household was most often a good marriage to someone who was socially and emotionally compatible. Theoretically, such households were headed by a married man with his wife as a junior partner and the servants and children under his strict, but rational, control.

If the Sharps had followed the marriage pattern of their cohort, most of them should have married in the 1750s, but only John married in that span.[3] In the first half of the 1750s, the brothers began establishing their own households and launching their careers. Simultaneously, the sisters' circle began to expand as their father's professional appointments expanded. In 1750 only the teenaged sisters, Elizabeth, Judith, and Frances, remained in their parents' homes in Rothbury and Durham. John was settling in at Hartburn, Thomas was ordained a deacon, William finished his apprenticeship and set up his own household, James was in the middle of his training, and Granville was about to join his brothers in London to begin his apprenticeship. By 1760 all the Sharp siblings had launched their adult lives and by 1770 all who would marry had done so. During the 1750s and 1760s the Sharps crafted their adult identities and social patterns. And they decided—or let the moment to decide slide past—whether to marry or not.

---

[1] Granville Sharp to John Sharp, August 16, 1765, COLL 1891/3/5, YMA.
[2] Ilana Krausman Ben-Amos, *Adolescence and Youth in Early Modern England* (London: Yale University Press, 1994); Keith Thomas, "Age and Authority in Early Modern England," *Proceedings of the British Academy*, 62 (1976): 205–458.
[3] Wrigley and Schofield, *Population History*, 255, 263; King, "Chance Encounters?," 42.

Being Single in Georgian England: Families, Households, and the Unmarried. Amy Harris, Oxford University Press.
© Amy Harris 2023. DOI: 10.1093/oso/9780192869494.003.0006

The Sharps and their contemporaries married or not due to a complex mixture of personality, chance, economic pressures, and class and family expectations. Agency and decision-making are always constrained or colored by these factors.[4] The Sharps' experiences with courtship and marriage demonstrate all these aspects and the relative weight they were granted at different moments in the family's history. They also reveal that while the Sharps often avoided the conflicts most sibling cohorts experienced, marital choices and household arrangements could spark difficulties. The Sharps' marital choices were varied; they had opportunities to marry at young ages, or to delay or avoid marriage and remarriage. These choices were bound up with their potential for financial and household independence and continuing connection to their siblings. As James later put it, marital choices depended on whether the prospective spouse was a "person that will continue to keep us in the present happiness we now enjoy."[5] Additionally, the Sharps sought companions who were both personally and publicly beneficial to the whole family. As James also explained, marriage was desirable as long as it "continued those Blessings to us as well in Publick as amongst ourselves."[6]

The Sharps' approach to household formation did not assume marriage's centrality to households or emotional intimacy. Single people's importance to household affairs and all family members' involvement in courtship negotiations are well understood and documented.[7] However, they are often described only from the perspective of a married householder or the courting couple. The Sharps' experience reveals another layer of family interaction undergirding those better-understood aspects of family life: the dynamic processes within the family of origin which produced both a set of relationships and a process by which individuals made decisions. Ultimately, this diminished the importance of marriage in crafting Sharp adult identities. Their experience also highlights siblinghood's powerful emotional bonds and its capacity to encourage communal decision-making. In the process, they created a shared, almost egalitarian decision-making process, running counter to hierarchical understandings of domestic and familial relationships. Their years of experience balancing individual desires with communal decision-making meant to marry or not to marry was a communal decision as much as it was an individual choice.

While the unmarried sisters—all clustered at the younger end of the family group—followed typical genteel patterns of living with their parents or brothers when they were young, as they aged some of them became householders in their

---

[4] Emma Griffin, "A Conundrum Resolved? Rethinking Courtship, Marriage and Population Growth in the Eighteenth-Century England," *Past and Present*, 215, no. 1 (May 2012): 125–164; Steven King, "Chance, Choice and Calculation in the Process of 'Getting Married': A Reply to John R. Gillis and Richard Wall," *International Review of Social History*, 44, no. 1 (April 1999): 69–76.

[5] James Sharp to John Sharp, February 23, 1764, D3549/9/1/4.

[6] James Sharp to John Sharp, February 23, 1764.

[7] Froide, *Never Married*, 44–86; Hill, *Women Alone*, 67–80; Ottaway, *The Decline of Life*, 141–172; Sally Holloway, *The Game of Love in Georgian England: Courtship, Emotions, and Material Culture* (Oxford: Oxford University, 2019), 9–10.

68 BEING SINGLE IN GEORGIAN ENGLAND

own right. Elizabeth, for example, first acted as housekeeper for James, then married and took up housekeeping with her husband. When she was widowed five years later, she assumed householding and housekeeping of Wicken Park. Judith, on the other hand, eventually acquired a home in Durham with a niece, perhaps after years of being a surrogate householder for John's house there, without ever marrying. Frances never had her own household but moved between (and helped manage) her siblings' homes.[8] Thomas had accommodations associated with his ecclesiastical appointments, but not ones large enough to become a site of Sharp socialization. Similarly, Granville rented rooms in London, but he too never had a separate household. Participation in shared sibling households, however, provided Thomas and Granville access to domestic aspects of masculinity even without wives or children.[9]

Having independent households instead of one family home led to the Sharp siblings entering adulthood by leaving their childhood home not for a home with their spouse but as a member of three sibling-based households among which the Sharps rotated. The shared management of these homes meant that the siblings did not require marriage to enjoy the benefits of shared household governance. At first glance, Judith, Frances, Granville, and Thomas might appear as domestic dependents in their siblings' households, but their letters and account books show how embedded all siblings were in each other's household management. The ostensibly dependent siblings managed accounts, facilitated the flow of goods and services to and from the households, purchased and transported household items, and loaned and borrowed money. All those actions were undertaken at their own discretion or in collaboration with other siblings, but rarely, if ever, were they dictated by the house-owning siblings or under the control of a married couple. Alongside any individual desire that inclined or disinclined one to marriage; there might have been subtle or overt discouragement from siblings when they incorporated single siblings as household partners, not dependents.

Household governance, and the gendered authority of housekeeper or householder that came with it, was usually connected to marriage for women and men. The Sharps' late marriages, or lack of marriage, reveal other ways gendered domestic power was enacted and enjoyed. Things described as husbandly or wifely in household manuals were performed by Sharp siblings.[10] Sharing household duties with siblings might have also diminished, or at least diffused, the hierarchal tensions in household management where, despite neatly gendered categories, women and men's daily activities blurred the distinctions between them.[11]

---

[8] Widows headed nearly 13 percent of households in early modern England, but single women only 1.1 percent, though they were more likely to if they were older and wealthier, as Judith eventually became. Froide, *Never Married*, 19.

[9] Anthony Fletcher, "Manhood, the Male Body, Courtship and the Household in Early Modern England," *History*, 84, no. 275 (July 1999): 431.

[10] Harvey, *Little Republic*, 30.   [11] Harvey, *Little Republic*, 34, 115.

Establishing Households in the 1750s

In 1750 William completed his London apprenticeship and on April 23 that year he proudly set up his own household on Mincing Lane (Figures 3.1 and 3.2). Earlier in the year, he and James had traveled to Durham to visit their family. They then returned with their father and Granville, whom Thomas Sr. was placing in an apprenticeship with a linen draper. During Thomas Sr.'s time in London, William visited his father each day, recounting his housekeeping skills. His father's description of this momentous change in William's life, in a letter to Elizabeth, captures William's enthusiastic, if not always skilled, assumption of householding responsibilities. "On Tuesday morning," Thomas Sr. reported, William "bought a shoulder of Mutton for dinner. and says his Maid roasted it extreamly well, only Mrs. Reed scolds because he used his new pewter: without scowring it first." Despite this mistake, William earned Mrs. Reed's approbation for the manner in which he provided adequate food for himself and his lodger. William had clearly been trained to think carefully and frugally about household tasks and to negotiate with and learn from servants. Thomas Sr.'s letter continued to detail how William carefully made the shoulder of mutton last: "I must not forget his frugality in making the drippings of ye shoulder [of] Mutton on Tuesday serve to fry the batter of the pancakes on Wednesday." The mutton and pancakes were important details for William, who clearly enjoyed recounting his successes to his father, pleased with attaining this marker of adult masculinity. Thomas Sr. seemed a bit amused by William's eagerness, but also pleased by William's daily reports: "What he has had to day I cannot tell now but shall know by and by when he comes in to sit with me as he does every night."[12]

Thomas Sr. recognized that his children were undergoing a transformation and standing at a precarious juncture. He wrote principally to report about placing Granville in his new apprenticeship and was clearly concerned about leaving the 15-year-old alone in a new master's house in sprawling London. He comforted himself, and presumably Judith, with the fact that he and the master had provided Granville with furniture, and more importantly that he had placed his son equidistant between 19-year-old James and 21-year-old William's residences, so "that the three stand in a triangle." Eighteenth-century parents wished to see their children develop sibling bonds of mutual support; Thomas and Judith seemed particularly dedicated to that goal.[13] Using their childhood nicknames, Thomas Sr. reported that "Jemmy" and "Billy" also seemed concerned that Greeny (Granville) not feel isolated or lonely during his first few days in London; on the morning of Granville's second day in his new place James, himself in the latter stages of an apprenticeship with an ironmonger, brought Granville a new apron

---

[12] Thomas Sharp to Betty (Elizabeth) Sharp, April 26, 1750, D3549/10/1/1.
[13] Heal and Holmes, *Gentry in England and Wales*, 86.

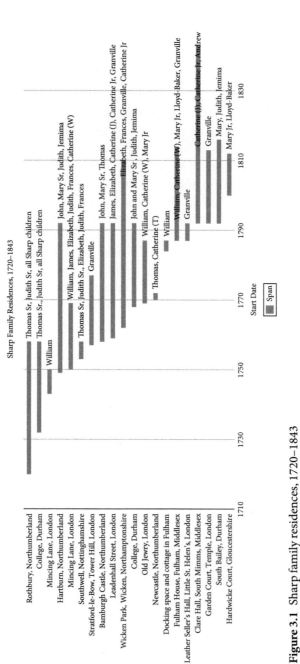

Figure 3.1 Sharp family residences, 1720–1843

TO MARRY OR NOT TO MARRY 71

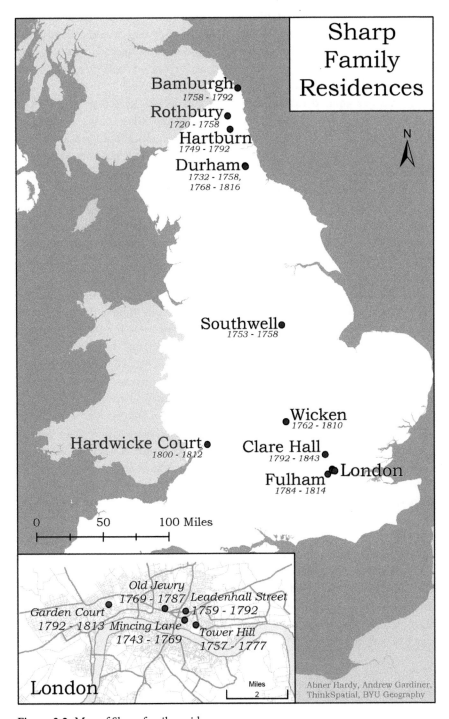

Figure 3.2 Map of Sharp family residences

72 BEING SINGLE IN GEORGIAN ENGLAND

that "tho' it cost but a shilling, pleased Greeny much." Later that same morning William also came for a visit and their father came by in the evening. Their father reassured himself, saying that Granville "seem'd in good spirits all that day, and has continued so ever since." The letter also reported William's desire that 17-year-old Elizabeth come to London to be his housekeeper.

Thomas Sr.'s amused tone at this suggestion foreshadows that he and their mother would ultimately refuse this plan, but the letter still succeeds in capturing the moment when most of the Sharp children were launched toward independence. Thomas Sr. would return north and had to trust that his three sons, augmented by Thomas Jr., who had an ecclesiastical position in the city, would sustain and support one another. The trepidation Thomas Sr. felt was not unfounded. The last time he and Judith delivered sons to London—William and Charles seven years earlier—it was the last time they saw Charles, who died en route to India. The possibility that leaving Granville might mean never seeing him again combined with the certainty of seldom seeing him for years to come explains the anxiety that colored Thomas Sr.'s letter.

Had the Sharp parents known what was to come for their children during the 1750s and beyond, they would have been comforted. Thomas Sr. and Judith helped establish two networks for their children—one revolving around John and Thomas Jr.'s clerical appointments (mostly in the North) and another centered in London with the three younger brothers. The sisters remained with their parents (they were all under the age of 18 at the time), but would later join those two sibling centers. Thomas Jr. acted as a sinew between the two networks in the 1750s because of his ecclesiastical appointments in London and his long association with John, first being close in age and then overlapping during their time at Cambridge. By placing the brothers within easy distance of one another and encouraging the boys' inclinations to support one another across households, the Sharp parents helped establish a pattern of socialization that would sustain and support their children for another six decades. Unwittingly, they might have also dampened their children's motivation for marriage.

At the age of 21, William, now a practicing and inventive surgeon, settled happily into his domestic role.[14] Though possessed of good social connections and an open, cheerful temperament, he was not eager to marry. The presence of three of his brothers made for a comfortable social and emotional life. He hoped Elizabeth would soon be a part of their circle and he undoubtedly would have devised a means to bring the two younger sisters—Judith (age 16) and Frances (age 12)—if they had been older. He was thrilled to contemplate his home as a gathering place

---

[14] In 1767 William published a letter he had read before the Royal Society the previous year about treating broken bones. In a footnote he explained he had been working with the idea as early as 1748, while still an apprentice. William Sharp, *An Account of a New Method for Treating Fractured Legs* (London, 1767), 15.

for musical performances and socializing with his siblings (and presumably eventually learning to scour new pewter before using it).

These social patterns continued through the 1750s as the brothers settled into their professional roles in London. James was inventing and refining the production of stoves, carriages, and wheels; William was experimenting with splints for broken legs and acquiring a larger house; both brothers were becoming freeman of the city and taking on apprentices.[15] By 1757 Thomas Jr. had the living at St. James, Duke's Place (in addition to his appointment as curate to Bamburgh the same year) and Granville completed his apprenticeship.

However, two years, 1757 and 1758, permanently altered the Sharps' lives. In the spring of 1757 the sisters and their parents traveled south to visit the brothers. Even decades later Elizabeth fondly remembered the long visit. While in London they met with their Prowse cousins (the children of their first cousin, another Elizabeth Sharp) and romance blossomed between John Prowse and Judith Sharp. But that was last enjoyable family event for some time. When the family returned to Rothbury that spring, their mother fell seriously ill and died on July 2. John and Thomas joined their father at her funeral services at Durham Cathedral and she was buried there, near her parents. The remaining brothers traveled north to join their sisters and father and the family retreated to Rothbury. They spent two weeks together there, sharing grief and consolation. After those weeks, the brothers returned to their homes and the sisters and their father returned to Durham. Their grief was compounded when a 16-year-old Prowse cousin died of bowel inflammation, only to be followed ten days later by the death of her brother John (Judith's fiancé) of smallpox. Less than three weeks later they suffered another staggering loss when their father died on March 16.

John, Thomas, and Granville journeyed to attend the funeral in Durham, afterwards assisting their sisters in "preparing to leave Durham as soon after as possible" and traveling to Rothbury to "settle our affairs and pack up and take leave of the two happy Homes we had been blessed with," Elizabeth wrote.[16] Though they had a lifestyle similar to gentry families, their father's death threw into stark relief that the sisters' housing was entirely dependent on their father's employment. They had to vacate both homes quickly for the new rector of Rothbury and the new prebendary of Durham Cathedral were installed within two weeks of Thomas's death. After packing up the two houses, the six siblings went to Hartburn to spend time at John's home. Judith remained there with John,

[15] William Sharp, master, Charles Granville, apprentice, May 6, 1758, apprenticeship indenture duty, Board of Stamps: Apprenticeship Books, Series IR 1, piece 21, TNA, digital image at *UK, Register of Duties Paid for Apprentices' Indentures, 1710–1811*, https://www.ancestry.co.uk, accessed April 2, 2021; *Records of London's Livery Companies Online*, Freedom of James Sharp, son of Thomas Sharp of Durham, March 26, 1755, Company of Drapers; *Records of London's Livery Companies Online*, apprenticeship of William Watts to James Sharp, 1759, Company of Drapers, http://www.londonroll.org, accessed April 2, 2021.

[16] Elizabeth Sharp Prowse, memorandum and commonplace book, page 20, 1757–58, D3549/14/1/1.

74 BEING SINGLE IN GEORGIAN ENGLAND

but Elizabeth, Judith, Granville, and Frances traveled toward London. In Islington they encountered James and William riding up from London to meet them. While moving their possessions to their brothers' carriages they happened to see the Prowses' carriage. In the previous nine months the Sharps had lost both of their parents and the Prowses had lost two children. The grieving Sharps and "Mr. Prowse...with the remaining part of his Family" had an "unexpected Meeting and a very affecting one on all Sides."[17]

The loss of parents was not unusual for young adults; most people had lost at least one parent by the time they were 30.[18] While the death of parents could lead to less financial and domestic cooperation between siblings, the Sharps drew closer together and further intertwined their fortunes.[19] The Sharps were fortunate that the sisters had a respectable cash inheritance and that the brothers were settled and had the resources to comfortably house their sisters.

Courtship Decisions and Negotiating Household Relations

The Sharps approached courtship and marriage decisions from a family culture built on lateral connections and centered in communal decisions due to the combination of the loss of their parents and the strength of their sibling and cousin ties. In 1750 John, the oldest, was 27 and by 1760 Frances, the youngest, was 22. This period should have been a decade with numerous marriages among the eight siblings, but it was not. And it raises the question why.

The 1750s

It is not particularly surprising that John, the eldest son, married first. Since he left for Cambridge in 1740 at age 17 he had shown a determined sense of duty to his family, to his studies, and to his ecclesiastical obligations. John was, in his own words, "indefatigable" once he knew his responsibility. Though he had no responsibilities associated with being heir of an estate, he was like such men whose obligations to brothers and sisters could influence their marital choices.[20] In the absence of direct evidence of his decision to court and to marry, it is tempting to ascribe the same indefatigable approach to his efforts to marry the right person at the right time and with parental approval. Because marriage was an important marker of adulthood and clerical uprightness, it is also not surprising that John

---

[17] Elizabeth Sharp Prowse, memorandum and commonplace book, page 21, 1757–58.
[18] Laslett, *Family Life and Illicit Love*, 162–163.
[19] Heal and Holmes, *The Gentry in England and Wales*, 87.
[20] Heal and Holmes, *The Gentry in England and Wales*, 62.

married just three years after settling at Hartburn. No letters survive to explain his social activities between when he arrived in Hartburn in 1749 and when he married in December 1752, but the circumstances of his changing family relationships might have had just as much impact as his new ecclesiastical responsibilities. Brother Thomas, who had followed John's footsteps to Trinity College, Cambridge, had obtained his MA in 1750 and been ordained a deacon that same year. Thomas subsequently settled in London, where he had clerical duties at St. James, Duke's Place in Aldgate.[21] By settling in London, he joined William, James, and Granville. While John was at Cambridge, he would have had daily contact with Thomas and the ability to regularly visit his younger brothers in London. By 1750, however, John was in a rural parish in Northumberland, far from the sibling he was closest to and the other siblings in London. Also, though John always enjoyed association with his parents and his younger sisters, when he returned to the North in 1749, the girls ranged in age from 11 to 16—hardly the ideal social group for a 26-year-old man on the threshold of adult employment and responsibility. It is no wonder that he turned his indefatigable energy to finding a bride.

It might have been at this junction that John first read his grandfather Wheler's *The Protestant Monastery: or, Christian Oeconomicks*. Grandfather Wheler died in 1724, when John was less than a year old, so John's possession of the book came either via his mother or by purchase. He eventually claimed it as his own, inscribing it with "John Sharp Hartburn." It seems reasonable that he used this book in the early 1750s to help him prepare for marriage. It contained the typical late seventeenth- and early eighteenth-century advice about what to look for in a wife: that "she love to be at home, and not gadding abroad from House to House, ever tatling with the Gossips of the Town; telling and hearing, if not making Stories."[22] It also contained advice meant to prepare a young man to become a householder: how he should prepare for fatherhood, lead a household, decorate a home, spend his time, and pray during family worship. How much John followed the advice is unknown, but he soon found someone to marry—someone he had known his entire life: his first cousin, Mary Dering.

Mary Dering was the daughter of Heneage Dering and Ann Sharp (John's paternal aunt). Since childhood the Derings and Sharps had visited in each other's homes and, though no letters between the young cousins survive, likely participated in correspondence. The Derings were also bound to the Sharps by professional and personal ties. Heneage was named after his father's patron, Heneage Finch, Earl of Nottingham, whose chaplain in the early 1690s was none other than John Sharp, the eventual archbishop, Thomas's Sr.'s father.

---

[21] Brian Crosby, *Private Concerts on Land and Water*, 4–5.

[22] Sir George Wheler, *The Protestant Monastery: or, Christian Oeconomicks. Containing Directions for the Religious Conduct of a Family* (London, 1698), 45–46. Personal copy of John Sharp, Bamburgh D.3.70, PGL.

76 BEING SINGLE IN GEORGIAN ENGLAND

The archbishop employed the younger Dering as his secretary in the 1680s and 1690s, but then Dering took holy orders when he was 47 and eventually became the Dean of Ripon. Dean Dering married the archbishop's 21-year-old daughter, Ann, in 1712.[23]

Mary Dering (the sixth of the eight Dering children) was 28 when she and John courted. It is not clear when that courtship began, if it started as soon as John returned north, or perhaps they were reacquainted after her father's death in 1750, or perhaps they had maintained a personal correspondence that does not survive. In any event, their courtship would have necessitated communication and perhaps even undertaking the hundred-mile journey from Hartburn to Ripon. Given his closeness to Thomas Jr., it is also likely that John was like many of his contemporaries who sought out a brother's advice on courtship and marriage—much like their father had done thirty years earlier.[24] In the weeks leading up to the wedding the Sharps and Derings drafted a marriage settlement involving several cousins in the financial and property details.[25] At the same time, John penned a five-stanza prayer for their marriage. He pleaded for God's care to keep them bound to him and to each other, "that in all Changes and Alterations of our Condition we may religiously preserve an immutable Love unto & Delight in each other, to the End of our Days."[26] On December 4, 1752, the couple married in Ripon; Mary was given away by her mother, John's aunt.[27] After the wedding, the couple journeyed to Durham to visit John's parents. His siblings did not seem to be in attendance, which was not unusual considering the great distances they would have had to travel in the middle of winter.

John and Mary were a socially superb match and their marriage was a steady source of support and enjoyment for forty years. However, John's siblings did not immediately follow his example; he was the only Sharp to marry for a decade. There were many reasons early modern English men and women did not marry or delayed marriage. Among the obstacles to marriage that the other Sharp siblings shared with their cohort were the ambiguous place of women's social and property status related to their marital status; the high expectations of finding someone socially, emotionally, and economically compatible; and concerns about the future since marriage was practically indissoluble.[28] A bad

---

[23] Thomas Sharp correspondence with brother-in-law Heneage Dering, D3549/7/2/3; Thomas Sharp to John Sharp, December 27, 1734, D3549/9/1/1.

[24] Grassby, *Kinship and Capitalism*, 42, 66–68.

[25] John Sharp and Mary Dering, marriage settlement, November 25, 1752, D3549/9/1/2.

[26] John Sharp, prayer for his marriage, *c*.1752, D3549/9/1/2.

[27] Elizabeth Sharp Prowse, memorandum and commonplace book, 1752, page 17; Church of England, Ripon Cathedral parish registers, marriage of John Sharp and Mary Dering, December 4, 1752, PR/RI 1, North Yorkshire County Record Office, digital image 51 of 52, "Yorkshire Marriages," http://findmypast.com, accessed April 7, 2021.

[28] Holloway, *The Game of Love*, 143–165; Froide, *Never Married*, 182–221.

match or a match gone sour could not easily be exited and shoddy in-laws could not be easily jettisoned.

Eighteenth-century courtship and marriage were not devoid of affection and the desire for a pleasant companion, but they were also governed by clear-eyed practicality. John Thomlinson, for example, when attempting to court the Sharps' mother, had listed her common sense and ability to keep household accounts as factors in her favor. Additionally, conduct literature recommending sober instead of passionate men as potential husbands highlights the importance of rationality in marital decisions. Finding someone who was not only temperate, rational, and skilled at account-keeping, but also acceptable to one's family was not an easy task. Marrying beneath one's social status was widely remarked upon, and it could generate financial as well as social trouble for the couple.[29] When he was a governor of Ripon Grammar School, Heneage Dering, Mary's father, once presided over the removal of a school usher when it was discovered that a 15-year-old student had clandestinely married the usher's sister-in-law, a "woman of unsuitable age & ffortune" for a grammar-school student.[30] For families across the socioeconomic scale, the best way to find a suitable partner was through endogamy—marriage with a near relative or a close associate with professional ties to the family.[31] This was the pattern among the Sharps' extended family; spouses were found among those who had generational, ecclesiastical, or familial connections. These relationships were key not only in meeting potential spouses but in making those potential mates acceptable to the family and its social circle. John Sharp's marriage to first cousin Mary Dering, the daughter of a close friend and advisor of John's grandfather, was the perfect scenario.

Marriage was strongly encouraged for both men and women, but while it brought socially accepted roles and markers of adulthood, it was not without its difficulties, particularly for women.[32] Men's greater autonomy in courtship and marriage was openly acknowledged in advice literature. As one author put the question: "Why do Men often marry for Beauty, women seldom?" and then provided the answer: "Because men have often the Freedom of Choice, Women seldom."[33] Even if women had had equal freedom of choice, coverture influenced their considerations, especially for women with property. The biblical injunction that a husband and wife should be "one flesh" was seen as a legal and economic absolute: "since the masculine comprises the feminine, the whole flesh thus made

---

[29] King, "Chance Encounters," 23–46.

[30] Ripon Grammar School minute book, 1704–69, RGS/B/1/2, BIY.

[31] Polly Morris, "Incest or Survival Strategy? Plebeian Marriage within the Prohibited Degrees in Somerset, 1730–1835," *Journal of the History of Sexuality*, 2, no. 2 (October 1991): 235–265; Stone and Stone, *An Open Elite?*, 36–40.

[32] Bridget Hill, "The Course of the Marriage of Elizabeth Montagu: An Ambitious and Talented Woman without Means," *Journal of Family History*, 26, no. 1 (January 2001): 3–17.

[33] "The Ladies Oracle," quoted in Daniel Renaud's commonplace book, 1751–63, [page 57] MS 1977.007, WACML.

78 BEING SINGLE IN GEORGIAN ENGLAND

one out to be referred to the masculine, which is more worthy." That it was Granville who wrote that line, shows that even in a family so colored by sibling egalitarianism, assumptions about women's subordinate role within marriage remained pervasive.[34]

Early modern English women recognized that the office of wife brought them household authority, but it was built on a model of submission to male authority.[35] As Mary Astell starkly put it, a man courting a potential wife was looking for someone to manage his household, his children, and his own emotional needs while having no expectations of him. He wanted "one whom he can intirely Govern and consequently may form her to his will and liking, who must be his for Life and therefore cannot quit his Service let him treat her how he will."[36] Unmarried women from wealthy families, however, could potentially govern their own households outside marriage because they often inherited more household goods and money than their married sisters. Grandfather Wheler's will was explicit on this matter. Recognizing that not all families had elder brothers upon whom younger, unmarried sisters could rely on for a "convenient place to inhabit" he left his unmarried daughters a house with gardens and orchards for as long as they were single, thereby reducing any "inconvenience and hazard of honor."[37]

Singleness was not without its potential pitfalls, but for genteel women with some prospect of financial independence, the social recognition, companionship, and potential for motherhood and household governance had to be weighed against the loss of autonomy, authority, and female friendships, which were often deep and rich.[38] Additionally, women like the Sharp sisters who occupied elite social spaces, but did not have elite financial resources, might find suitable marriage options limited by monetary constraints. The sisters' inheritance of £700 each, granted in their parents' marriage settlement, even supplemented by material goods they inherited, would have limited potential suitors to those already well provided for. Furthermore, certain benefits of marriage faded over

---

[34] Prince, *Memoirs of Granville Sharp*, appendix II:iv, quoted in Katherine Paugh, *Politics of Reproduction: Race, Medicine, and Fertility in the Age of Abolition* (Oxford: Oxford University Press, 2017), 60.

[35] Katie Barclay, "Intimacy and the Life Cycle in the Marital Relationships of the Scottish Elite during the Long Eighteenth Century," *Women's History Review* 20, no. 2 (April 2011): 189; Natasha Korda, "Marriage, Identity, and the Pursuit of Property in Seventeenth-Century England: The Cases of Anne Clifford and Elizabeth Wiseman," in Nancy Wright, Margaret W. Ferguson, and A. R. Buck, eds., *Women, Property and the Letters of the Law in Early Modern England* (Toronto: University of Toronto Press, 2004), 179.

[36] Mary Astell, *Some Reflections on Marriage* (London: John Nutt, 1700), 36–37.

[37] Sir George Wheler, will, written 1719, codicils written 1721–23, proved 1724, Prerogative Court of Canterbury, TNA PROB 11/597, digital image at *England and Wales, Prerogative Court of Canterbury Wills, 1384-1858*, https://www.ancestry.co.uk, accessed February 3, 2020.

[38] Froide, *Never Married*, 44–86; Pamela Sharpe, "Dealing with Love: The Ambiguous Independence of the Single Woman in Early Modern England," *Gender and History*, 11 (1999): 209–232; Christine Peters, "Single Women in Early Modern England: Attitudes and Expectations," *Continuity and Change*, 12 (1997): 235–245.

time; as the biological chance for children declined, so did some of marriage's social and personal advantages for prosperous women. Simultaneously, inheritance from older relatives, returns on investments, and the possibility of sharing a household with sisters decreased the financial imperatives. In addition, age could bring a type of social respect for genteel women, no matter their marital status, as they were often referred to as "Mrs." especially if they managed a household or their own property.[39]

For both women and men a choice to marry was also a choice to wed one's fortunes to a range of kin for decades to come. If a couple was fortunate, the attachments that came with marriage could provide a lifetime of support, but an unfortunate in its choice of partner, the disastrous marriage could send destructive waves through other relationships. The Sharp siblings, thanks to their childhood observations, were aware of marriage's potentially disruptive impact on existing family dynamics. In 1742 their aunt Dorothy Sharp Mangey brought a Chancery case against her husband for his failure to comply with their 1721 marriage settlement. At stake was £2400 meant to purchase an estate for their son.[40] Though Thomas Sharp Sr. was not involved in his sister's initial marriage settlement, the rancor between the Mangeys and the souring of the relationship between the sisters-in-law affected him as well. In 1743 he was summoned to the Mangeys' marriage separation trial. Though Mangey was unable to obtain a separation, he sent Dorothy to Durham. In the meantime, he made a point of quickly journeying to Southwell to see the Sharps, who were understandably surprised to see the man who had summoned their father and his other sister to testify against Dorothy. Aunt Dorothy had considered coming to Southwell as well, "not knowing her Husbands intention of calling as soon there, after his Tryal against her." Elizabeth reported that "happly she did not" and she and the Sharps avoided "firther distress."[41] While distressing, most of the Sharp siblings were too young at the time to have been aware of the details, but their continued association with their aunt and cousin throughout their lives undoubtedly exposed them to conversations and correspondence about the topic.

As adults the siblings were involved in the fallout from another unsuccessful marriage among their cousins. Mary Sharp, daughter of their uncle John, married

---

[39] Amy Louise Erickson, "Mistresses and Marriage: or, a Short History the Mrs," *History Workshop Journal*, 78 (2004): 39–57. The parish register entry for John and Mary's marriage refers to Mary, who was 28, as "Mrs. Mary Dering." By the time she was 27, letters to Judith regularly came addressed to Mrs. Sharp. And strikingly, in their burial records some Prowse siblings who died as children were referred to as "Mrs" or "Mr"—signifying their social status as children of a man styled esquire.

[40] Dorothy also targeted her brother John's widow, Anna Maria. John had been part of the marriage settlement and had been tasked with getting the money to the Mangeys. After his death, in 1726, Anna Maria completed his task. However, Dorothy claimed that neither of them should have given the money directly to her husband; they should have purchased a freehold estate for her son instead. *Sharp vs. Mangey* (1742), Court of Chancery Pleadings, 1701–69, C11/1069/42, TNA.

[41] Elizabeth Sharp Prowse, memorandum and commonplace book, typescript, page 4, D3549/14/1/2.

80 BEING SINGLE IN GEORGIAN ENGLAND

James Booth in 1748.[42] As James was styled esquire and was "an Eminent Conveyancer of London," this should have been a good match. However, James was Catholic, "much to the greef" of the Sharps and other relations, especially considering their grandfather's distaste for dissenters and Catholics.[43] Such a match led Mary Sharp's maternal grandfather to leave Mary a legacy, but not any interest in his property (Wicken Park, Northamptonshire). Instead, he left it to Mary's younger sister. Some years later, Elizabeth Sharp was granted a life interest in Wicken Park, meaning her cousin's poor match economically benefited Elizabeth for decades to come.

That unintended benefit, however, was not without costs for the Sharps. The Booth match was not only disapproved of, but it also proved calamitous. From the beginning Booth was "a Most cruel bad Husband." The Booths lived together for nineteen years, none of them happy, and eventually Booth agreed to a separation. That separation, however, was negotiated with near relatives: Elizabeth, her sister-in-law, her brother William, and her mother-in-law (Mr. Booth's sister-in-law). The negotiations were held at James Sharp's house on Leadenhall Street, within a few weeks of Elizabeth herself becoming a widow in 1767. Not arriving until 10 p.m. and staying until midnight "in great anger at times," James Booth finally agreed to a complete separation and to provide £200 per annum to his estranged wife, "at his or her death to repay it to her Family"—an arrangement that remained in place until his death in 1778.[44] As Katie Barclay has noted, "marital breakdown was challenging not just for couples but also to a social order that built upon the household."[45] The Booth debacle was just one example; there was plenty of evidence of bad marriages and unsatisfactory in-laws for the Sharps to observe.

Given the difficulties within the marriages the Sharps saw around them and the restrictions of their membership in such a small, charmed circle, it is perhaps not surprising that there was a decade between John's marriage in 1752 and Elizabeth's in 1762. Additionally, many among their extended kin were slow to marry—if they married at all. Several of the Sharps' aunts and uncles on both

---

[42] Church of England, St. Anne and St. Agnes, London parish registers, marriage of James Charles Booth and Mary Sharp, July 2, 1748, P69/ANA/A/006/MSO6766/001 LMA, digital image at *London, England, Church of England Baptisms, Marriages and Burials, 1538–1812*, https://www.ancestry.co.uk, accessed August 1, 2016.

[43] Elizabeth Sharp Prowse, memorandum and commonplace book, page 13, July 2, 1748, D3549/14/1/1; J.M. Rigg, "Booth, James Charles (*bap.* 1703, *d.* 1778)," rev. Andrew D. E. Lewis, *Oxford Dictionary of National Biography*, Oxford University Press, 2004; online edn., January 2010 [https://www.oxforddnb.com/display/10.1093/ref:odnb/9780198614128.001.0001/odnb-9780198614128-e-2882, accessed March 29, 2016].

[44] Elizabeth Sharp Prowse, memorandum and commonplace book, September 9, 1767.

[45] Katie Barclay, Jeffrey Meek, and Andrea Thomson, "Marriage and Emotion in Historical Context," in Barclay, Meek, and Thomson, eds., *Courtship, Marriage and Marriage Breakdown: Approaches from the History of Emotion* (London: Routledge, 2021), 5; Joanne Bailey and Jessica L. Malay, "Constructing Families," *Journal of Family History*, 40, no. 4 (October 2015): 448–461.

sides married later in their lives. Many relatives never married, including half of the Dering cousins. The longer the siblings went without marrying and without incorporating a new in-law, the more entrenched their social patterns became, and the harder it became to find a suitable partner. The common letters the siblings exchanged, their family concerts, and the long visits they made to one another's homes further strengthened their ties to siblings and cousins, especially after their parents' deaths in 1757 and 1758. For 24-year-old Judith in particular, those losses plus the loss of her fiancé in 1758 completely altered her future household, marital, and financial choices.

The Sharp siblings were not ignorant of the social expectations surrounding marriage, but any pressure they felt about courtship and marriage was channeled into joking or punning in the common letters. The letters reference the foibles of courtship, bad marriages as cautionary tales, and the silliness of marriage plots— but usually indirectly, as a pun about something else. In addition to the long letter detailing the sensual beauties of "Miss Morgan"—William's new pipe organ— Granville once described his brother's new horse in a similar style, punning on a potential wife's physical and financial attributes when applied to a horse. It is possible the occasional joke using courtship or marriage as a humorous vehicle for another topic was a way of relieving any pressure to marry or perhaps a way of masking discomfort with how disruptive marriage could be. Simultaneously, while prescriptive literature strongly encouraged marriage and warned women of the dangers of becoming "old maids," during the 1750s the Sharps' sparkling charm seems to have made them nearly immune to such suggestions and they evoked only envy, not pity, from their peers.[46]

The 1760s

By the summer of 1759, the sisters had joined the brothers in London, and James had acquired his own home on Leadenhall Street, purchased with a £1000 loan from their cousin who would have been Judith's mother-in-law if death had not intervened. Elizabeth joined James while Judith and Frances continued living with William on Mincing Lane. There the siblings created an enviable pattern of social, musical, and emotional support that must have excluded all but the bravest of possible suitors. Elizabeth described their life in the late 1750s and early 1760s with great fondness. The siblings' geographic proximity allowed them to replace their common letters with daily gatherings. Mincing Lane was the central gathering place; Elizabeth noted, "we all met every evening when My Brothers businesses

---

[46] Susan S. Lanser, "Singular Politics: The Rise of the British Nation and the Production of the Old Maid," in Judith M. Bennett and Amy M. Froide, eds., *Singlewomen in the European Past, 1250-1800* (Philadelphia: University of Pennsylvania Press, 1999), 304–305.

were over to a little music amongst ourselves & to supper. Brother Thomas when in Town was there & Brother Granville from the Tower and ourselves." She and James would sometimes host the evening gatherings at their Leadenhall Street home, "but whatever other engagements took place it was all our Party together" either at home or at public concerts.[47]

Occasionally others were invited: "Sunday evenings sacred music at Mincing Lane and both our Rooms well filled one with our particular Friends, the other with the best performers who join'd our own Band."[48] The scene of five or sometimes seven single Sharp siblings bedecked in their finery and possessed of keen musical sensibility and talent attending London concerts must have been a spectacle—and not one likely to convince strangers that they would be welcome to assume intimacy within that circle. The favor of joining the Sharps at home was reserved for "our particular Friends" and one has the distinct impression that finding spouses among those friends was not an especially high priority for the 20- and 30-something Sharps. For example, Thomas, busy shuttling between London and his new appointment as curate of Bamburgh, always behind in his correspondence with his siblings, and taxed by his numerous ecclesiastical duties, seemed too preoccupied to bother with marriage plans for the bulk of the 1750s and 1760s.[49] Similarly, at the end of 1762, Frances, accompanied only by two servants, traveled from London to visit John and his family, a journey of three hundred miles on horseback, "for her health." Traveling thus also allowed her to visit friends along the way and she "was quite recovered to health by the time she arrived at Hartburn"—a remarkable example of Sharp independence.[50]

By 1760 a collective Sharp identity was in full bloom. Adding new members might have decreased the social capital that this identity brought the siblings, particularly the sisters who would assume a new surname and be expected to expend more of their social and emotional labor on their husband's kin. John's marriage had not required this sacrifice; it came before the siblings' social patterns were fully entrenched, incorporated a cousin, and attended his relocation to the North where sibling social activities were not as frequent. The 1760s were different, however. Four siblings married between 1762 and 1770. Who married, when, and why underscores the continued importance of pre-existing relationships and expectations. Elizabeth was the first—and only—sister to marry, reflecting women's more limited courtship options.

---

[47] Elizabeth Sharp Prowse, memorandum and commonplace book, July 21, 1759.

[48] Elizabeth Sharp Prowse, memorandum and commonplace book, July 21, 1759.

[49] Bamburgh, Northumberland parish registers, May 15, 1757, EP 59/1, NAW; Thomas Sharp, Bamburgh, to Judith Sharp, Mincing Lane, London, April 10, 1761, D3549/16/1/1.

[50] Elizabeth Sharp Prowse, memorandum and commonplace book, January 2, 1763. On women's outdoor activities, see Rose Alexandra McCormack, "Roaming, Riding and Racing: Leisured Women's Exercise, Sport and Al Fresco Entertainment at the Eighteenth-Century Spa," in John Hinks and Catherine Armstrong, eds., *The English Urban Renaissance Revisited* (Newcastle upon Tyne: Cambridge Scholars Publishing, 2018), 96–115.

TO MARRY OR NOT TO MARRY   83

Like John's a decade before her, Elizabeth's path to marriage wound through very near kin; endogamy provided an easy answer. However, Elizabeth's decision to marry, even when a perfect match presented itself, was a gradual process. George Prowse, four years Elizabeth's junior, turned 21 in 1758, the summer after his brother and Elizabeth's father had both died. He was then heir to Wicken Park, but he was still young and new to his role. Elizabeth and George slowly built a relationship over several years, and their families strengthened their own ties to one other. George's mother, the Sharps' cousin, took on a maternal role toward the Sharp siblings after the death of their parents. She loaned money to James and acted as advisor and confidante to the London siblings. Perhaps this watchful care of the newly orphaned cousins put George and Elizabeth in more regular contact, allowing their relationship to grow.

Unlike the quiet affair of John's marriage in 1752, Elizabeth's wedding was an occasion for a grand family gathering. John and his wife, Mary, traveled from Northumberland to London, and John performed the marriage ceremony at St. James Church on the morning of April 27, 1762. William gave Elizabeth away, and all the remaining siblings were in attendance, as well as Elizabeth's new parents-in-law and two sisters-in-law. Like others of their social standing, George and Elizabeth's visits and familial celebrations continued long after the wedding ceremony.[51] "When the service was over the whole Party went down to Edmonton & Breakfasted with Lady Lake," and then they all journeyed to Wicken Park, Northamptonshire together.[52] Elizabeth's marriage, and her parents-in-law bestowal of Wicken Park on the new couple, meant that Elizabeth Sharp Prowse was now part of the landed gentry and Wicken Park became an additional center of Sharp socializing.[53]

George and Elizabeth did not immediately settle into domestic life at Wicken. Instead, they spent a few weeks there, then traveled to London with George and his family for his father's health. Eventually, they decided to journey to southern France in the hopes that it would help his father's condition. They spent the next fifteen months in France (thereby missing James's 1764 wedding). Further traveling to Devonshire and Bath filled several additional months, so it was October 1764 before Elizabeth permanently settled at Wicken Park, her mind "filled with the care of commencing Housekeeping again," and she and George having "no small pleasure...in forming our Plans for living there."[54]

---

[51] John R. Gillis, *For Better, for Worse: British Marriages 1600 to Present* (Oxford: Oxford University Press, 1985), 138.

[52] Elizabeth Sharp Prowse, memorandum and commonplace book, April 27, 1763. Lady Lake had been a regular attendee at the Sharp family concerts. See Crosby, *Private Concerts on Land and Water*, 100.

[53] The Prowses owned other homes, one in Axbridge, Somerset and a home on Argyle Street in London.

[54] Elizabeth Sharp Prowse, memorandum and commonplace book, October 1–5, 1764.

84 BEING SINGLE IN GEORGIAN ENGLAND

Within days of their arrival, Elizabeth's London-based siblings joined them at Wicken Park, and within weeks Elizabeth and George returned the favor by visiting the Sharp and Prowse siblings in London. Elizabeth had managed to transition from single to married without causing a ripple in her social and familial relations. Her home became an additional residence for her remaining single siblings and a site for long visits from the married siblings and the Prowse cousins. She thereby further fortified a household network built on sibling and cousin relationships. Like John's, Elizabeth's marriage did not require a drastic restructuring of family dynamics.

The inclusion of Mary Dering and George Prowse brought spouses into the family while simultaneously buttressing cousin relationships, which seems to have inadvertently raised the bar even further for those who would wish to join the Sharp circle. John, Elizabeth, and Judith had found compatible spouses within their cousin network, but while the Sharp siblings were close with their other cousins, most of these relatives were already married or were only young children in the 1750s. Because the sisters had fewer ways to find suitable partners outside their established family and social networks and due to men's greater autonomy in marital matters, it is not surprising that it was three male Sharps who married in the eight years following Elizabeth's marriage. But even for them, finding someone suitable to the existing family patterns required careful work.

Elizabeth's marriage triggered a recalculation on James's part. He and Elizabeth had shared a household and its governance for three years and she had been a constant visitor in his home for two or three years before that.[55] When Elizabeth married in 1762, James was 31, had a comfortable home, and was economically prosperous. He was busy designing and patenting various components of carriages, carts, and wheels, and he was suddenly without a housekeeping companion. Simultaneously, James's business in wheels and carts was becoming highly profitable. These altered circumstances made James reconsider his marital prospects.

James probably met Catherine Lodge, a woman some fourteen years his junior, via business and neighborhood connections with her family. The Lodges were prosperous packagers and exporters who lived in Little St. Helen's, a neighborhood immediately to the north of Leadenhall Street.[56] By the end of 1763, the Lodges were invited to Sharp musical evenings, and by early 1764 James was accompanying his sister Frances to her daily riding lessons as a means of interacting with Catherine, who attended the same riding school.

---

[55] James began to appear in the poor rate books immediately after acquiring the house on Leadenhall Street in 1759. Because only heads of household were listed, Elizabeth's presence in and contribution to the household goes unrecorded. St. Andrew Undershaft, poor rate assessment, 1744–71, P69/AND4/C/003/MS04122/001, LMA.

[56] *Kent's Directory for the Year 1740: Containing an Alphabetical List of the Names and Places of Abode of the Directors of Companies, Persons in Publick Business, Merchants, and other Eminent Traders in the Cities of London and Westminster, and the Borough of Southwark of London* (London: Henry Kent, 1740), 51; *Kent's Directory for the Year 1763* (London: Henry Kent, 1763), 77.

In addition to his attraction to Catherine, central to James's courtship was the approval of his siblings and the need to marry a "person that will continue to keep us in the present happiness we now enjoy." In a February 1764 letter to John, James noted that while "Miss Lodge has ever appear'd amiable to me, and very desirable from her Person, Behaviour, and Connections," and while his feelings for Catherine were strong and had "troubled" him for some time, he was most concerned that his relationship with his sisters and brothers not suffer by an addition of a wife. Though his siblings seemed "very desirous" for him to marry, James proceeded cautiously. "The thoughts of this has occasiond me to look more narrowly into my Circumstances," he wrote.[57] The letter reveals two common eighteenth-century courtship patterns: the need to balance marrying appropriately and affectionately combined with the involvement of a sister as an intermediary. But James's letter reveals that his existing sibling relationships were the circumstances that occupied him the most and the factors that would dictate whether he married or not.

To his delight, James determined that he would be able to marry Catherine and retain the happiness he found with his siblings. "I have the happiness to find there such that I need not be afraid to sett out…and live in such a manner as will be agreeable to me," he wrote to John. James's primary goal, his "grand point in View," was to assure "the Continuation of our present happiness in one another, for what do we now enjoy that has not been the Effects of our natural Affections and Assistance of each other!" James concludes by saying, "while this [happiness] continues amongst us what can hurt us?"[58]

James was thrilled and relieved to discover for himself that "Miss Lodge seems to be a person that will continue those Blessings to us as well in Publick as amongst ourselves." He rightly noted that finding a potential spouse who augmented his already exceptional family relations was something to be grateful for. "Should I meet with success," he wrote, "I think I bid fair for being made the happiest man living." James's letter to John meant that all the Sharps knew of his deep affection for Catherine Lodge before she did, though James thought she might have suspected it. However, his siblings and Catherine's "friends" (perhaps a group that included her family) urged him not to make his regard known until "frequent partys and further acquaintance may give her some Inclination to be amongst us." The general fondness of the Sharps, including John and Mary, for Catherine gave James "great hopes" that a "little time may give me some advantages with her."[59] All of James's careful attention to incorporate Catherine into the Sharp circle made it so that very little additional time was required to convince Catherine; she and James were married two months later on May 3, 1764 in James's parish

---

[57] James Sharp to John Sharp, February 23, 1764, D3549/9/1/4.
[58] James Sharp to John Sharp, February 23, 1764.
[59] James Sharp to John Sharp, February 23, 1764.

86   BEING SINGLE IN GEORGIAN ENGLAND

church.[60] Three weeks later, upon their return from France, George and Elizabeth met with Catherine and the other Sharp siblings "with much satisfaction to us all" and were pleased with the new "acquisition to our Family."[61] James's personal decision, like those of his siblings before him, was not entirely personal; it was familial.

James's marriage was instrumental in spurring William's marriage. James married, after years of sharing a household with William and after acquiring his own home, had kept his household tightly connected with William's. Thus, James's decision to marry seemingly increased William's desire to marry. As with James, William's financial success was likely an additional motivation. Elizabeth described both as "increasing in Business beyond their Expectation" in 1762.[62] Not accidentally, William found someone to marry among James's new relations. James's wife's sister, Elizabeth Barwick, lived near William's home on Mincing Lane. Her husband, John Barwick, belonged to a family of wealthy linen drapers and his sister, Catherine Barwick, was in the social circle that developed among the Sharps, Lodges, and Barwicks.[63] Catherine's eligibility was likely improved by one of her brothers being a clergyman and that she brought £3500 in stock to the marriage.[64]

When William first began to think of Catherine Barwick as a potential wife is unknown, but most likely immediately following his introduction to the Lodges because by the following summer (1765), Lodge and Barwick siblings were regularly socializing with the Sharps. By July of that year, William determined to marry Catherine and immediately began preparing for her addition to his household by making renovations to the home that had been the linchpin in the Sharp household universe since 1757. William was fortunate, as James was before him: the remainder of the family saw Catherine as an addition to their company, not just as a companion for William. "The Negotiations for our new Family Alliance go on prosperously," Granville wrote to John that August, adding that he hoped William would "be made happy very soon."[65]

William and Catherine married on September 5, 1765 in London, though many of the Sharp siblings were absent. The fact that families did not necessarily gather for weddings underscores that wedding ceremonies of the eighteenth century were just the last in a series of steps that constituted early modern English courtship. The ceremony was relatively unimportant compared to the stability of the match and the approbation of friends and family—in this case, the new

---

[60] Church of England, St. Andrew Undershaft, London, parish registers, James Sharp and Catherine Lodge, marriage May 3, 1764, LMA P69/AND4/A/01/MS 4109/1, digital image at https://www.ancestry.co.uk, accessed May 14, 2013.

[61] Elizabeth Sharp Prowse, memorandum and commonplace book, May 27, 1764.

[62] Elizabeth Sharp Prowse, memorandum and commonplace book, July 1759 and April 27, 1762.

[63] St. Matthew Friday Street, London, church and poor rate, 1723–66, P69/MTW/C/003/MS 07775, LMA.

[64] William Sharp and Catherine Barwick marriage settlement, 1765, D3549/11/1/2.

[65] Granville Sharp to John Sharp, August 16, 1765, COLL 1891/3/5, YMA.

in-law's fit with Sharp family expectations. The ritual was less important than the interaction, visits, and letters that cemented ties between the newcomer and the family unit.[66] It is telling that, not long after the wedding, William and Catherine (along with Catherine's sister) journeyed to Wicken Park to spend time with Elizabeth, showing the strength of the ties that had been created.

James and William were 33 and 36, respectively, when they married. This is notable because they had been independent and ever-more-prosperous house-holders for nearly fifteen years beforehand. They were embedded in the best of London social circles. They invited large gatherings of friends and musicians on their flotilla and they regularly hosted friends for musical evenings at home. In other words, they had been exposed to plenty of opportunities to meet and court potential spouses. But it was only after Elizabeth married and subsequently altered James's domestic arrangements that the brothers became serious about finding women to marry.

Sadly, the unalloyed enjoyment of the three in-laws the Sharps acquired between 1762 and 1765 did not last long. Unfortunately for Elizabeth, her ideal domestic situation disintegrated just two years after William's marriage. First, her father-in-law died in January 1767, drawing all the Sharps into shared mourning for their cousin, particularly Thomas who traveled to Dover to meet the Prowses and then accompanied the body to Axbridge, Somerset for burial.[67] Then, just eight months later, Elizabeth's husband, George, was "seized with a dreadful Fever." Her mother-in-law and two sisters-in-law attended to Elizabeth and her husband, and they were shortly joined by William and his wife, "but all was in vain." George died on August 25, 1767, "the very greates[t] shock and affliction."[68] Elizabeth's grief at the loss of her husband, her mother-in-law's decision in 1772 to settle Wicken Park on Elizabeth for life (should she remain unmarried), and the excellent relationship Elizabeth had with her in-laws disinclined her to remarry. Women, especially those like Elizabeth who enjoyed social and financial security, were much less likely to remarry than their male contemporaries.[69] Once the painful grief lessened, Elizabeth seemed content with her situation and disinclined to disrupt all that she enjoyed.

Despite these losses, by 1768 the Sharp family had grown to include John and Mary's daughter, Ann Jemima, and James and Catherine's son, Jack. These children were joined by Jack's little sister, Catherine, in June 1770, and by that point it appeared that the Sharps would enter the stage of family life that most of their cohort had already experienced: the diminishment of sibling ties as the demands

---

[66] Eve Tavor Bannet, *Empire of Letters: Letter Manuals and Transatlantic Correspondence, 1680–1820* (Cambridge: Cambridge University Press, 2005); Sarah Pearsall, *Atlantic Families*; Holloway, *The Game of Love*, 45–68.

[67] Elizabeth Sharp Prowse, memorandum and commonplace book, January 3, 1767.

[68] Elizabeth Sharp Prowse, memorandum and commonplace book, August 20–25, 1767.

[69] Joanne Bailey, *Unquiet Lives*, 192.

88 BEING SINGLE IN GEORGIAN ENGLAND

of marriage and childrearing took precedence. Perhaps this change in family patterns would have influenced how Thomas and the youngest three siblings (Judith, Granville, and Frances) approached courtship and marriage decisions. And perhaps that is what would have happened, if difficulties, and ultimately tragedy, had not overcome them during the next four years.

The 1770s

Initially, 1770 held great promise. In addition to the anticipation of Catherine's birth, 45-year-old Thomas decided to marry 24-year-old Catherine Pawson. The Sharp siblings were not bothered by Thomas's choice; Catherine came from a prosperous merchant family from Newcastle with solid connections to local gentry and she was, in John's estimation, an "amiable Good Creature"—they had no objections to her suitability.[70] How Thomas met Catherine is not known, but when he proposed marriage in December 1769, the family was pleased; Elizabeth even noted the progress in his courtship. In the early months of 1770, Thomas, John, and the Stephensons (Catherine's mother and step-father) began to work out the details of the marriage settlement.[71]

Despite the positive beginning, and unlike the previous sibling marriages, Thomas's decision was ultimately met with consternation. When it came time for Thomas to decide on a living situation, the London siblings were dismayed to find that John and Mary would not move from Bamburgh Castle and surrender it to Thomas and his new wife. John was the trustee of the castle, but he, Mary, and Thomas had shared it for many years. Because John was vicar of Hartburn and had a house there, the southern siblings reasoned that he should surrender the castle's living quarters to Catherine and Thomas, who was the perpetual curate of Bamburgh (which did not have a rectory or vicarage for his quartering). In what would be the deepest, and apparently only moment of serious Sharp acrimony, it was insinuated that John and Mary loved Thomas less than the rest of the siblings loved him, an accusation that bitterly hurt the couple. The tension between spousal relations, siblinghood, and household governance that had so fortuitously been negotiated four previous times was not so easily resolved in Thomas's case. The Sharps suddenly found themselves in a situation common among their contemporaries: difficulties in navigating competing loyalties between family of origin and spouse, particularly over household arrangements.[72] The letters that

[70] John and Mary Sharp to Judith Sharp, May 14, 1770.
[71] Elizabeth Sharp Prowse, memorandum and commonplace book, December 22, 1769, January 6, 1770, D3549/14/1/2; Thomas Sharp and Catherine Pawson, marriage settlement, July 4, 1770, D3549/9/1/5.
[72] Heal and Holmes, *The Gentry in England and Wales*, 52; Amy Harris, " 'That Fierce Edge': Sibling Conflict and Politics in Georgian England," *Journal of Family History*, 37, no. 2 (April 2012): 155–174.

flew north to south and the spirited conversations held in the sitting rooms in Hartburn, London, and Wicken Park during this time were the only indication of family rancor to have survived in the thousands of pages of surviving family documents. It was by all measures anomalous. But in a family so accustomed to harmonious relationships, the contention had the potential to strike a catastrophic blow.

In April and May 1770, a letter from John and then letters from John and Mary together described at length how the northern Sharps had already devised a means to perpetuate the domestic tranquility that they had enjoyed for nearly fifteen years, at one point even using an elaborate metaphor about two children sharing a hobby horse.[73] They explained to Judith and the others that since John and Mary only lived at the castle during the summer months, Mary would retain her household leadership at those times, while Catherine could assume the household reins any time Mary chose to retreat to the country the other nine months.[74] Beyond the content of the letter, the employment of a detailed metaphor echoes the epistolary style of the common letters the siblings exchanged in the 1750s and 1760s. John and Mary might have hoped memories of those lighthearted letters would sway the southern siblings.

The southern siblings' response does not survive, but apparently John's letter did not calm all of their concerns, for John and Mary wrote again in May, this time far more hurt and troubled that their siblings had misunderstood their designs. John first explained that he and Mary could not just quit the castle and leave it in Thomas's control because John was the trustee appointed by the owner of the castle's trust, and it was not up to John to alter that arrangement; indeed it was "a very tender point" for him because he considered the castle, upon which he had poured his talents, money, and industry for twelve years, "a child of my own." John then assured his siblings that he, Mary, Thomas, Catherine, and Catherine's family were all in complete harmony on the matter. As he wrote Judith:

> Dear Sister, how should it be likely that my Bro. & I who have always lived in the utmost Harmony and never have had any little Bickerings or Quarrels or so much as Disputes, not even about the point in Question, _for in this our sentiments are exactly alike_; I say, how then is it likely that either we or our wives sh[ould]d find any inconvenience in living together under the same Roof, especially when it will be our mutual Interest as well as constant endeavour to make each other as Happy as we can?[75]

---

[73] The full text of these letters appeared in Rachel Cope, ed., *Managing Families, II*, vol. 4 of Rachel Cope, Amy Harris, and Jane Hinckley, eds., *Family Life in England and America, 1690–1820* (London: Routledge, 2015), 47–54.

[74] John Sharp to Judith Sharp, April 21, 1770, D3549/16/1/1.

[75] John and Mary Sharp to Judith Sharp, May 14, 1770, D3549/16/1/1.

90   BEING SINGLE IN GEORGIAN ENGLAND

John and Thomas had been close throughout their lives; they were two years apart in age and were baptized on the same day two years apart, were educated together at Cambridge, and had shared clerical duties and household felicity in Northumberland since the mid-1750s.

Stung by such an unprecedented misjudgment by his siblings, John addressed the deeper issue: the potential threat to Sharp family harmony. "I think I know my Brother so well & he me," John asserted, "that there will never be any misunderstanding between us. Our Family has always been remarkable for unanimity—May it never be interrupted!" He desperately continued to explain the disagreement and plead for understanding. "Dear Brothers & Sisters," he wrote, "suffer us to make a fair trial here in the North how happily we can go on together." He then emphasized how important family harmony was to him: "I am not happy…unless I think I can make every body happy about me or endeavour to do so, shall I not then particularly labour this point with respect to Two Persons whom I sincerely Love & Esteem."[76] John recognized that the tension over this marriage could perhaps doom Thomas and Catherine's match and, more troublingly, canker Sharp sibling bonds. He and Mary worked diligently to assure the others that no such thing was intended, nor likely to happen, as everyone involved was equally concerned with each other's happiness. All were determined that marriage and siblinghood could peacefully co-exist in the same household as it had done so far.

Though no letters or diary entries survive to explain just how the conflict was resolved, it appears that John and Mary's letters accomplished their goal. Thomas and Catherine married in July in Newcastle, and the disagreement was not mentioned again. While the northern siblings did not join the southern siblings' river sailing trip that summer (probably coincidentally since they did not join every year), normal correspondence resumed, and Elizabeth and others journeyed north early in 1771 to visit Thomas and his new bride.

While the conflict was resolved, the high emotions it engendered were compounded by a series of other crises in the latter half of 1770 and throughout 1771 and 1772. William's wife Catherine suffered a miscarriage in 1770, a press gang abducted four men from James's iron works in January 1771, and then in a shattering string of weeks between late January and early March Jack, James, and Catherine's 6-year-old son died, then Thomas's wife fell ill and gave birth, prematurely, to a stillborn son, dying herself a few hours later. Judith and Elizabeth were in attendance, and they quickly wrote Thomas to join them in Newcastle so that he was there when his wife of less than nine months died. Immediately following those searing griefs was the loss of two cousins in the spring and summer of 1771, Thomas's mistreatment at the hand of his in-laws regarding the marriage

---

[76] John and Mary Sharp to Judith Sharp, May 14, 1770.

settlement in the autumn of 1771, and Aunt Dering's death in November. The next year did not begin any better, when a cousin died in March.

Letters and diary entries from this time often betray a heightened fear for family members' health. Little Catherine's smallpox inoculation in April 1771 was monitored with trepidation and everything the Sharps did was shadowed by grief, "all their spirits were much depressed, by their late loss."[77] In June 1772, John wrote to Thomas using the customary black wax seal indicating his family's observance of mourning for the death of the elderly Aunt Dering (who was also John's mother-in-law). Seeing the black wax terrified Thomas. The letter "put me into such a Panic," he wrote, "before I opened it, th[a]t I have scarce recovered it yet; for, not recollecting th[a]t you were in mourning...y[ou]r black wax alarmed me, lest any Accident sh[oul]d have happen'd to my Sister or Jimima." Before he finished opening the letter, no doubt trembling with fear, he remembered Aunt Dering's death, which "set my Heart at ease, wch before was not...less alarmed than if I had seen a spectre."[78]

If 1772 began badly, it ended even worse; Thomas died at the end of November at Hartburn from a "fit of the cholick."[79] He was buried in Newcastle beside his wife and son.[80] Other than Elizabeth's recording the death of such "an affect[ionate] Husband & Bro[the]r" in the chronicle she compiled decades later, no accounts survive about the devastation Thomas's death must have caused, particularly for John and Mary who likely cared for him in his last illness. Open-hearted, good-natured, and humorous, in many ways, Thomas had been at the heart of the Sharps' carefully crafted world, and now he was gone. He was the first sibling to die in nearly thirty years and the last of the siblings to marry; perhaps the thought of doing anything else to disrupt family relations, which now must have felt very brittle, was more than the remaining siblings could bear to face.

Grief once again may have colored Judith's rejection of a marriage proposal that same year. Elizabeth remained hopeful that her younger siblings might marry, even if she was not inclined to do so herself. In 1770, Elizabeth's mother-in-law granted the living at Berkeley, Somerset to a Dr. Kent, a long-time friend of the Prowses.[81] This change in Dr. Kent's financial status seems to have triggered his and Elizabeth's consideration of his marriage possibilities. Forty-five-year-old Dr. Kent, a long-time friend and an author and clergyman, appeared a natural fit for 38-year-old Judith. In March 1772, Elizabeth acted as a go-between for

---

[77] Elizabeth Sharp Prowse, memorandum and commonplace book, April 1771.

[78] Thomas Sharp to John Sharp, June 30, 1772, NRO 452/C/3/2/4/9, NAW.

[79] "Diary of Thomas Gyll," in *Six North Country Diaries*, vol. 118 of *The Publications of the Surtees Society* (Durham: Surtees Society, 1910), 225, SoG Du/Per.

[80] Elizabeth Sharp Prowse, memorandum and commonplace book, November 25, 1772.

[81] Elizabeth's account does not give Dr. Kent's first name, but he must have been the Ambrose Kent Jr. (*c.*1727–1793) who earned his DD in 1768 and became rector of Berkeley in March 1770. "Ambrose Kent (CCEd Person ID 34586)," *The Clergy of the Church of England Database 1540–1835*, http://www.theclergydatabase.org.uk, accessed April 1, 2016.

92 BEING SINGLE IN GEORGIAN ENGLAND

Dr. Kent's marriage proposal—a proposal Judith apparently declined, because no mention of any connection between her and Dr. Kent was ever made again. Judith may have declined because she simply did not find Dr. Kent appealing or perhaps because he did not compare well with the budding relationship she had had with her cousin John Prowse before his untimely death cut it short. Or perhaps she calculated, as James had done nearly a decade before, that the material support and emotional bonds she enjoyed with her siblings and nieces were not worth disrupting. Furthermore, marriage would likely have curtailed her independence to travel between Northumberland, London, and Northamptonshire to visit siblings as much as she liked, often with Jemima accompanying her.

Judith and the other sisters might have also encountered expectations enjoined in prescriptive literature that women be "cautious in displaying your good sense," and that if they "happen to have any learning, keep it a profound secret, especially from men, who generally look with a jealous and malignant eye on a woman of great parts, and a cultivated understanding."[82] If Judith encountered such attitudes from a man it is easy to imagine she would have been disinclined to consider any advances from him. Whatever her reasoning may have been, Judith determined that marriage would disturb the pleasant waters of Sharp sociability, particularly in the wake of so many griefs that year.[83]

Granville and Frances, the youngest brother and sister, also never married, a fact partially attributable to viable alternatives they found in sibling relationships and shared households. Very little of Frances's writing survives, so her thoughts about courtship are more obscure, but Granville's hesitancy to marry seems to have been influenced by his preference for study and quiet. His brothers William and Thomas were more demonstrative and expressive with others than Granville was with outsiders.[84] In contrast, Granville's emotional energy and light-hearted moments seem to have been reserved entirely for his existing family and their children. In his domestic situation, he preferred quiet, solitude, time to study and write, and the company of like-minded family members. As he completed his apprenticeship and went to work for the Ordnance Office in the 1750s and 1760s, Granville taught himself Greek and Hebrew. During his brothers' courtships and weddings during the mid-1760s, he was studying law to help Jonathan Strong, a former slave, retain his freedom. He published a pamphlet against the slave trade in 1769 and refused his uncle's offer of a prosperous living the same year.[85] With a family overflowing with clergy, his refusal of such an offer seems puzzling at first.

[82] John Gregory, *A Father's Legacy to his Daughters* (London: W. Strahan, T.Cadell, 1774), 31–32.
[83] Ambrose Kent settled in Berkeley and acquired additional ecclesiastical appointments. He married a few months after Judith rejected his proposal. Church of England, Fulham, Middlesex, July 11, 1772 marriage Ambrose Kent and Mary Barrow, *Greater London Marriage Index*, http://www.findmypast.co.uk, accessed March 23, 2021; Ambrose Kent, will, proved June 10, 1793, Prerogative Court of Canterbury, TNA PROB 11/1233.
[84] Hoare, *Memoirs of Granville Sharp*, 19–22.
[85] Hoare, *Memoirs of Granville Sharp*, 44–45.

He reported that he envisioned a broader field for himself, beyond the confines of ecclesiastical appointment. Given his father's and brothers' occupations, he was in a good position to judge the demands of such work.

Granville may not have wanted the confines and obligations of a parish and potentially the pressure of a wife and children who could have limited the scope of his influence and activities, which included writing and reforming efforts. Even bachelor clerics had demanding domestic duties as they cared for tenants, servants, and parishioners.[86] Moreover, Granville expended time, emotions, and energy building relationships with his siblings and nieces, which made it difficult for outsiders to get to know him well. For Granville, time spent with family was time well-spent, and he was unbegrudgingly supported and housed by his siblings. Due to this situation, Granville may have considered parish and possible domestic responsibilities as a limitation not just on his intellectual and reform endeavors but on the familial abundance he already enjoyed. Though he later maintained rooms near the Inns of Court, Granville spent most of his time at the homes of William, James, and Elizabeth. He was fully embedded in the joint Sharp households as a caretaker for the ill, the young, and the dying and as a financial manager, but he was never an independent householder. The lack of household and marriage responsibilities gave Granville an intellectual and social freedom; siblings, nieces, and meaningful work satisfied his emotional and relational needs.

Granville also benefited from the social acceptance of intellectual pursuits instead of sexual and marital pursuits for men. In certain intellectual and religious circles, such as at Cambridge and Oxford, male virginity and celibacy could be encouraged or even required.[87] For both men and women a decision to remain single usually signaled a decision to remain celibate because sexuality was tightly bound to courtship and marriage.[88] Associated with courtship and marriage, approved sexual expressions usually came along with adulthood.[89] While pre- and extra-marital sex was not unusual, true promiscuity was not generally practiced, especially in the social and ecclesiastical circles the Sharps inhabited.[90] Another sexual option for eighteenth-century English young adults was celibacy, although since at least the sixteenth century there had been much debate about whether long-term celibacy was socially, physiologically, or morally acceptable.[91] Celibacy did

---

[86] Hill, *Servants*, 175.

[87] William Gibson and Joanne Begiato, *Sex and the Church in the Long Eighteenth Century* (London: I.B. Tauris, 2017), 174–194.

[88] Judith Spicksley, "The Early Modern Demographic Dynamic: Celibates and Celibacy in Seventeenth-century England" (doctoral thesis, University of Hull, 2001), 153–168, https://core.ac.uk/download/pdf/5222469.pdf.

[89] Tim Hitchcock, *English Sexualities, 1700–1800* (New York: St. Martin's Press, 1997), 24–41.

[90] Rosemary O'Day, *Women's Agency in Early Modern Britain and the American Colonies* (Harlow: Pearson, 2007), 114–116.

[91] Froide, *Never Married*, 157–159.

not automatically carry today's assumptions of loneliness and lack of close or intimate relationships because sexuality did not have a monopoly on intimacy and because many people "lived outside heterosexual dyads for all or part of their adult lives."[92] In a context where various forms of intimacy were available via a variety of relationships, for much of the century sexual celibacy was not categorically disparaged, and in some situations was particularly valued. There were even debates about whether men should prioritize marriage or singleness as the most moral or Christian way of living.[93]

In certain circumstances, celibacy could be socially understood sexual decision or circumstance, especially for women. For genteel and aristocratic women, celibacy was not exactly a choice since the value of "chastity was thoroughly internalized," but it was also true that female virginity "cease[d] to be aberrant" as it had been in the seventeenth century and became a recognized "stage of a woman's life that [was] properly protracted."[94] For the Sharp sisters, eighteenth-century assumptions that unmarried, genteel women were virginal was axiomatic, but celibate men inclined to clerical or intellectual pursuits were also acceptable—perhaps more than among their European or American counterparts or their contemporaries in commercial or laboring occupations.[95]

Identifying sexuality before the modern period is an analytical slippery slope. Perhaps Granville and Frances were not sexually attracted to the opposite sex or not particularly sexually inclined at all. Or perhaps they were—it is impossible to know. But in their social and familial circles, celibacy was an acceptable and expected sexual behavior for the unmarried. By the end of the century this was becoming less the case for men, but by that point Granville's age and social prominence protected him from the sometimes harsh criticism of single or celibate men.[96] The line between intense intimacy and sexuality are not easily discernible by modern eyes, but the Sharps' suggest that sisterhood and brotherhood, devoid of a sexual component, offered satisfying emotional intimacy, as close relationships did for other single women.[97] For the unmarried Sharps, celibacy was a way of expressing loyalty and intimacy to their siblings, showing that they would not jeopardize those relationships for sexual dalliance.

Another explanation for the chosen singleness and celibacy of the youngest Sharp siblings is the impact of birth order. By 1772 Judith, Granville, and Frances

---

[92] Susan Lanser, "Of Closed Doors and Open Hatches: Heteronormative Plots in Eighteenth-Century (Women's) Studies," in Ana de Freitas Boe and Abby Coykendall, eds., *Heteronormativity in Eighteenth-Century Literature and Culture* (Farnham: Ashgate, 2014), 25.

[93] William Van Reyk, "Christian Ideals of Manliness in the Eighteenth and Early Nineteenth Centuries," *The Historical Journal*, 52, no. 4 (December 2009): 1056–1057.

[94] Fletcher, *Growing Up in England*, 26; Corrine Harol, *Enlightened Virginity in Eighteenth-Century Literature* (New York: Palgrave Macmillan, 2006), 65–66.

[95] Erik R. Seeman, "'It is Better to Marry than to Burn': Anglo-American Attitudes towards Celibacy, 1600–1800," *Journal of Family History*, 24, no. 4 (October 1999): 397–419.

[96] Gibson and Begiato, *Sex and the Church*, 189–190.   [97] Froide, *Never Married*, 70–74.

were 39, 37, and 34, respectively. They had enjoyed tightly woven, socially dynamic, and emotionally supportive family relationships their entire lives, and they had the examples of older siblings who had lived singly even longer. They had financial independence due to a combination of inheritances and investments. Additionally, the bar that had been high for spousal entrance into the Sharp family in the 1750s had been continually raised in the 1760s. Each subsequent in-law who smoothly slid into the flow of Sharp family relationships without causing a ripple increased the pressure on the next potential spouse. Eventually, the Sharp siblings might have set the bar just a bit too high to be practical for those who were still unmarried to consider adding a spouse. It was better to preserve their existing ties than risk disrupting them for the uncertain potential satisfactions of marriage.

Conclusion

For eighteenth-century women and men, there were a variety of reasons for remaining single. Whether they married young, married late, did not remarry after widowhood, or did not marry at all, people's marital choices were shaped by opportunities, missed chances, obstacles, death, and disinclination. For the Sharps, their own family circumstances interacted dynamically with gendered, economic, and social expectations. These circumstances made about half the siblings choose marriage, but even those who did marry spent many years as single adults. Being unmarried or having unmarried siblings was, for them, not lamentable. It was just normal. The Sharp siblings' relationships were sustained by years of shared household governance without the conflicts such household arrangements often generated in other families. The only exception was the months leading up to Thomas's marriage and the change in sibling households it heralded. It is worth remembering that John, Mary, and Thomas were older than all the London siblings and had been managing their household affairs for fifteen years. Apparently, the well-oiled machine of Sharp relationships had erased many of the hierarchies of age and birth order. The difference in Thomas's experience compared to the four previous sibling marriages is as striking as it is illustrative of the Sharps' need to have "remarkable unanimity" in all things.

Even though the Sharps did not marry at the age most in their cohort did, this delay was not necessarily a social disadvantage, particularly because it was ameliorated by their many social advantages. For the Sharps, adulthood did not necessarily come with marriage, nor its associated sexual activity, or its economic activity governed by a conjugal couple. For the Sharps, getting married required not just managing personal desires, but negotiating the group's desires. The Sharps' family of origin did not just facilitate or intervene in courtship decisions and negotiations. It established patterns that, in turn, dictated the channels

96 BEING SINGLE IN GEORGIAN ENGLAND

those decisions could follow. The established family culture subtly or explicitly generated the possibilities and limitations of the Sharp siblings' courtship and marital decisions. Granville's repeated refusals of his uncle's offer of a living and Judith's refusal of Dr. Kent's proposal likely sprang from the same source—contentment with their family situation and connections, contentment perhaps shadowed by the cascading family deaths at the time. Granville's and Judith's experience with domestic tranquility and enjoyment was lifelong; they were not about to jeopardize it for marriage. Especially after the 1760s it would have taken a deep romantic interest from a Sharp and a colossal effort by a potential spouse to persuade a sibling to change their circumstances. No wonder so few outsiders succeeded in adding themselves to this tight-knit group.

Not every family could do what the Sharps did, but the Sharps' experience reveals the long-lasting and powerful nature of lateral relationships and communal decision-making possible in many families. The Sharp relationships also show the power of internal family patterns and culture, some decades in the making. They also highlight how changes within the family of origin shifted collective thought about marriage and courtship decisions beyond the emotional and material concerns of a single individual.

Socializing and shared households were the backbone of the Sharp family for nearly sixty years. They built the foundations of their family group in the 1750s, and by 1770 they had incorporated all the in-laws they ever would. Additionally, because there were not numerous children to add to this dynamic (in 1771 only 9-year-old Ann Jemima and 1-year-old Catherine remained), the adult Sharps continued to enjoy the household, travel, and social patterns they had established in their twenties when they were all single. Marriage, especially with their mostly endogamous partners, had not diminished their lateral ties or excluded the unmarried siblings. On the contrary, the marriages had fortified horizontal ties and kept the unmarried and childless at the center of the family culture.

4
Living Single

"We continued...together most comfortably."[1]

Elizabeth Sharp Prowse about a months' long family visit

"I am...left here all alone, which is very dull, after spending so much time in a large & most agreeable society."[2]

Granville Sharp to John Sharp after parting from a family visit to the north

"How merrily we live."[3]

Song sung at a family gathering

Introduction

In December 1760, Thomas was overseeing repairs on Bamburgh Castle when workmen, who were digging out a dilapidated turret in preparation for installing a staircase, found a weathered tin box. Upon opening it, they discovered an old document written in "old Roman Characters" illegible to most of them. Thomas, however, giddily recognized it as an ancient prophecy about the castle that predicted John's efforts to restore it. Full of pagan imagery, the document rhapsodized about the time when the ruins of Bamburgh would rise again, restored by a new, "generous, wise, & just" founder, "firm to his purpose, faithfull to his trust, Keen as his Parts, unblunted as his Name." The parallels to unblunted Sharps being faithful as trustees of the castle were too obvious to miss. Thomas excitedly wrote both John and Judith about his findings, marveling at a prophecy equal in importance and timeframe, in his mind, to the twelfth-century Prophecy of Merlin.[4]

Thomas's excitement about the purported prophecy highlights the Sharps' view of their domestic arrangements. They were not only capable and talented in their household improvements and governance, they were literally fulfilling prophecy. Thomas was not troubled in the least that it was John and not he who fulfilled this prophecy; the document merely confirmed everything he already thought about

---

[1] Elizabeth Sharp Prowse, memorandum and commonplace book, typescript, December 1793, D3549/14/1/2.

[2] Granville Sharp to John Sharp, August 30, 1785, D3549/13/1/S8.

[3] Granville Sharp, undated note in his commonplace book, D3549/13/4/1.

[4] Thomas Sharp to John Sharp, December 6, 1760, D3549/9/1/4; Thomas Sharp to Judith Sharp, December 9, 1760, D3549/16/1/1.

Being Single in Georgian England: Families, Households, and the Unmarried. Amy Harris, Oxford University Press.
© Amy Harris 2023. DOI: 10.1093/oso/9780192869494.003.0007

98 BEING SINGLE IN GEORGIAN ENGLAND

his brother's place in the world and, by extension, his own role in supporting that place.[5] Though the prophecy was likely Thomas's creation, in a period when many contemporaries believed in the power of visions and prophecy, especially when such things were connected to personal and familial forms of identity, the document does reflect the Sharps' perception of providence working in their lives.[6] Perhaps more remarkable than trusting that one's domestic efforts were prophetically ordained, even if only in the imagination, was the Sharps' penchant for seeing their successes as shared, for believing a sibling's happy household arrangements were one's own happiness. As with marital choices, Sharp household management simultaneously reinforced individual and communal identities.

Eighteenth-century genteel homes had more demarcated private spaces designed around comfort and sociality. Instead of medieval and early modern great halls where prosperous families offered hospitality to neighbors, friends, and subordinates, wealthy urban Georgian houses focused more on "elegant entertainment of a select group of social equals."[7] Rounds of visiting, with their attendant drinking of tea, were formalized and expected among wealthy classes by the end of the century, leading to architectural and furniture rearrangements. Certain spaces allowed various forms of intimacy, depending on the relationship between those using the room, for which purpose, and at which time of day.[8]

The Sharps fully participated in these changes, organizing not just their individual homes, but the configuration of their collective homes that combined practical skills with the enjoyment of comfortable home life (see Figures 3.1 and 3.2). Bamburgh Castle was under almost constant renovations and was geared for the relief of the poor. As much as John, Mary, and Thomas invested in Bamburgh, Hartburn vicarage acted as a place for smaller parties and family intimacy. James's Leadenhall Street house retained many trappings of early modern homes that combined private and social spaces with workspaces. His house never saw large parties but was reserved for small-scale concerts and family dinners. William's London homes, especially the later one at Old Jewry, were for the large social gatherings and public activities. Elizabeth's Wicken Park estate acted as a collective private retreat for all the southern Sharps, no matter their regular residence. The configuration of their homes reflected, on a large scale, middling or genteel

---

[5] This was not the only prophetic reference to their family. A 1768 letter from Dr. Dodd to Granville mentions an acquaintance of Grandfather Sharp's who had dreamed he would be archbishop, thirty-five years before he became such. The story of this dream had circulated widely at the time, and Dr. Dodd wondered if Granville's generation knew of it. Dr. Dodd to Granville Sharp, January 11, 1768, D3549/13/1/D12.

[6] Ann Plane, *Dreams and the Invisible World in Colonial New England: Indians, Colonists, and the Seventeenth Century* (Philadelphia: University of Pennsylvania Press, 2014), 97. The improbability of a twelfth-century document perfectly rhyming in eighteenth-century pronunciation hints at the author. Thomas was a key participant in the common letters and though prophecy's tone lacks the humor of those letters, it was likely an exaggerated version of that genre.

[7] Amanda Vickery, *Behind Closed Doors: At Home in Georgian England* (New Haven: Yale University Press, 2010), 292.

[8] Benjamin Heller, "Leisure and the Use of Domestic Space in Georgian London," *The Historical Journal*, 53, no. 3 (September 2010): 623–645.

household configurations: spaces for work, for public socializing, and for intimate family interactions.

No sibling began householding at the time they married; all who managed households did so, at least initially, as a single person. Running a household as a single person or in conjunction with married kin could be complicated. Single sisters often lived with married kin, or each other, and often acted as housekeepers for brothers with varying degrees of harmony and success.[9] Thomas Sr. and Judith had tried to prevent such difficulties, encouraging social and domestic closeness among their children, even after they left home. The marriages of Elizabeth, James, and William and the turmoil over Thomas's marriage and the attendant household reshuffling signals that even a family so exceptionally friendly and affectionate as the Sharps recognized how power structures of household governance could be tricky. Ultimately, the Sharps not only successfully navigated those tricky waters, but they flourished, expanding their households and social networks to encompass the highest members of London society.

Sharp households were never truly independent and were not axiomatically hierarchical. The Sharps laid the foundation for their extraordinary domestic felicity in the 1750s, when all but John were single, and when they first began establishing households and buying sailing vessels as conveyances for river music-making. In some ways the sailing vessels were the siblings' first collective home. In the 1750s, while aboard their boats, the siblings established socializing patterns, which were echoed in the witty common letters they exchanged. Both sailing and the common letters were recreational, but they also required careful management of resources and, in the case of the sailing vessels, servants. Those management patterns transferred to their permanent households in the later 1750s and 1760s. Because the siblings were not married when they established households they acted as if they inhabited joint households instead of households managed by a married couple with a dependent sibling residing there. The connections they shared—financial, social, and material—made a flexible and durable family structure that could respond to illness, loss, and death without collapsing or disintegrating. The Sharps who were unmarried and childless not only participated fully with their married kin but were also essential to how married family members constructed their domestic and social lives.

1750s: Common Letters and Music on the Water

Before most of the siblings had established their permanent households, they built an imagined shared household via the common letters they exchanged and

---

[9] Ruth Perry, *Novel Relations: The Transformation of Kinship in English Literature and Culture 1748–1818* (Cambridge: Cambridge University Press, 2004), 168–170; Bridget Hill, *Servants: English Domestics in the Eighteenth Century* (Oxford: Clarendon Press, 1996), 119–122.

100 BEING SINGLE IN GEORGIAN ENGLAND

the sailing trips they took in the 1750s. Letter writing, the eighteen-century genre par excellence, was essential to family, business, and patronage networks as well as national and imperial ambitions.[10] Letters, the most ubiquitous and accessible household material objects, circulated between households, bringing together private domestic concerns and public social connections. As one historian put it, letters "mapp[ed] relationships that extend[ed] outward into broader social and textual networks."[11] The Sharps influenced other relatives to follow their epistolary custom. In January 1768 when Elizabeth received word from her cousin/ sister-in-law about a marriage proposal she had declined, Elizabeth also noted that her sister-in-law "begun to write to us at Wicken as common Letters, very agreeable to us."[12]

In 1750 John and William were the only siblings with independent households, though John's was tied to his position as vicar of Hartburn. As Thomas, William, James, and Granville established themselves in apprenticeships or appointments in London, it would not have been surprising if they had developed a sibling social circle separate from John and the sisters in the North, especially if more siblings had married in the 1750s. Even with Thomas traveling between and the sisters visiting the South with their parents, without concerted effort to maintain epistolary ties, infrequent visits were not likely to be strong enough to perpetuate the sibling culture they enjoyed as children. After their parents died, the siblings supplemented their correspondence with shared travels and shared households.

William's house on Mincing Lane was not the only place to host gatherings; William and James hit upon a unique supplemental social space: boats. In 1753 William purchased a barge and a skiff (the *Apollo* and the *Griffin*, respectively) and began holding weekly musical gatherings on board. On an August Saturday that year, William, James, and Granville, with seven other friends, including three single women, climbed on board the two boats. Bustling around them, servants loaded the things they would need for a two-day voyage. In addition to sailing equipment, dishes, and furniture, were oils, salt, bread, butter, tea, and sugar. Those were joined by roast beef, veal, ham, pickles, cheese, a fruit pie, small beer, and multiple bottles of cider and wine. The Sharps fully enjoyed the variety and abundance of foreign foods supplied to the English by a thriving import market. Recipe books written in both William and Granville's hands give directions for everything from buttered potatoes to almond tarts, and from lemon wine to

---

[10] Sarah Pearsall, *Atlantic Families: Lives and Letters in the Later Eighteenth Century* (New York: Oxford University Press, 2008); Kate Smith, "Imperial Families: Women Writing Home in Georgian Britain," *Women's History Review*, 24, no. 6 (2015): 843–860.

[11] Jennifer Summit, "Writing Home: Hannah Wolley, the Oxinden Letters, and Household Epistolary Practice," in Nancy E. Wright, Margaret W. Ferguson, and A.R. Buck, eds., *Women, Property, and Letters of the Law in Early Modern England* (Toronto: University of Toronto Press, 2004): 202.

[12] Elizabeth Sharp Prowse, memorandum and commonplace book, January 12, 1768, typescript, D3549/14/1/2.

orange biscuits.[13] Expenses for the weekly gatherings on the *Apollo* also included strawberries, raspberries, chocolate, and on more than one occasion, repairing broken windows.[14]

The onboard gatherings were not only for sailing and dining. Servants also brought on board horns, various woodwinds, five books, and three desks (most likely music stands).[15] On a nearly weekly basis during the summer, the brothers repeated this pattern, gathering onboard for dinner and music. And undoubtedly for witty conversation; jokes, witticism, puns were essential to conversation and social gatherings like dinner parties "in this age when dullness was the worst of social vices."[16] When the young Sharp brothers sailed, they cultivated the best in sociability by bringing good company who would guarantee good conversation, food, music, and books.

For other young men in their late teens and early twenties, these musical gatherings would not have been a standard weekly diversion. There were many more commercialized leisure opportunities for men.[17] Clubs, sporting events, coffee houses, and taverns offered a variety of male social interactions, but other than later membership in musical clubs, the Sharp brothers did not regularly engage in any of those typical diversions. They neither hunted nor participated in other displays of honor and masculinity; for example, Granville famously declined, in 1767, to duel with the former owner of Jonathan Strong, the enslaved man Granville and his brothers had helped.[18] William was known to credit providence for keeping him (and presumably his brothers) from the "seductive tendency of fashionable amusements" in London, especially when contrasted with their childhood in the "comparative solitude and sobriety of the North."[19]

That the brothers refrained from the city's most seductive offerings can be credited to the fact that most of their social interaction was production based as much as it was consumption based. They drew in patronage networks instead of seeking them out. Household hospitality extended "strands of mutual obligation and the return of hospitality formed and bound social circles together, keeping

---

[13] Sharp family recipes, D3549/8/1/5; William Sharp, recipes and notes on wine-making, *c.*1762–*c.*1803, D3549/10/1/2. This latter collection is catalogued with William's papers, but the various hands indicate he was not the sole contributor.

[14] Sharp brothers, boat books, 1753–55, 1773–76, D3549/12/1/1.

[15] Sharp family boat books, 1753–55, D3549/12/1/1.

[16] Dickie, "Hilarity and Pitilessness," 8.

[17] Angela Schattner, "'For the Recreation of Gentlemen and Other Fit Persons of the Better Sort': Tennis Courts and Bowling Greens as Early Leisure Venues in Sixteenth- to Eighteenth-Century London and Bath," *Sport in History*, 4, no. 2 (2014): 198–222; Holger Hoock, "From Beesteak to Turtle: Artists' Dinner Culture in Eighteenth-Century London," *Huntington Library Quarterly*, 66, no. 1/2 (2003): 27–54.

[18] Robert Shoemaker, "Male Honour and the Decline of Public Violence in Eighteenth-Century London," *Social History*, 26, no. 2 (May 2001): 190–208.

[19] John Owen, "A Discourse Occasioned by the Death of William Sharp, Esq. Late of Fulham House; Delivered in Substance at Fulham Church, on Sunday, March 25, 1810," reviewed in *Gentleman's Magazine*, 80, no. 2 (1810): 451, http://www.HathiTrust.org, accessed July 1, 2019.

102   BEING SINGLE IN GEORGIAN ENGLAND

local relations running smoothly."[20] The Sharp siblings were perfectly, even in their minds providentially, situated at the nexus between early eighteenth-century social connections built on nepotistic patronage and later patterns of social position based on the ability to participate in the "enlightened knowledge economy."[21] They easily straddled inherited privilege and the beginnings of meritocracy. Their approach meant they did not have to navigate the rules of a pre-existing institution to build such social networks. While they had always benefited from ecclesiastical networks, when it came to their music, boats, and homes, their confidence in their ability to build their own networks was almost boundless.

Musical training also encouraged a shared identity anchored in the consumption and production of music. Perhaps it was their parents who inspired the siblings' love of signing their surname with the musical symbol for sharp ($\sharp$). On one occasion, Granville even wrote his entire signature with musical notation of a G-sharp on a treble clef.[22] John played cello, Thomas the violin, and William the organ, horn, and clarinet. James played the bassoon and serpent. Granville played the kettledrums, flute, double-flute, oboe, clarinet, and harp. Elizabeth played the harpsichord and later the piano. Judith played the lute and the *angélique*. Thomas, James, Granville, and Frances all sang, as did niece Catherine; the brothers sang in trio, Frances and Catherine as soloists. William and James hired servants who played instruments and Elizabeth paid for two servants to be taught how to play French horn. Granville wrote a "Short Intro to Vocal Music," and John and Thomas composed hymns.[23] That abundant musical experience could make them a bit snobbish about performances they found wanting; they were dismissive of mediocre music. St. Paul's organist, as Thomas wrote, did not excel at keeping time and supplied the cathedral music only "very thinly."[24]

Following a pattern of home musical evenings from their youth, John's home in Hartburn and William's in London were the first centers for Sharp family gatherings and musical evenings with friends. The frequent "water schemes" evolved and expanded over time and persisted for over three decades. More than sailing vessels, the *Apollo* and the *Griffin* were the Sharps' first joint effort to host social gatherings, manage servants' labor, budget, and plan household logistics. In small notebooks labeled "boat books," William kept a record of who would be invited

---

[20] Janet E. Mullin, "'We Had Carding': Hospitable Card Play and Police Domestic Sociability among the Middling Sort in Eighteenth-Century England," *Journal of Social History*, 42, no. 4 (Summer 2009): 992–993. Mullin is summarizing Susan Whyman's argument; Whyman, *Sociability and Power in Late-Stuart England: The Cultural Worlds of the Verneys 1660–1720* (Oxford: Oxford University Press, 1999), 18.

[21] Margaret Jacob, *The First Knowledge Economy: Human Capital and the European Economy, 1750–1850* (Cambridge: Cambridge University Press, 2014).

[22] Granville Sharp, invitation to Uncle James Hasletine, December 12, 1757, D3549/13/1/H13; the invitation was also copied into the bound common letters, D3549/7/2/15, bound copy, 85–86.

[23] Crosby, "Private Concerts," 74–75.

[24] Thomas, William, James, and Granville Sharp to sisters, *c.*1756, D3549/7/2/15.

and hired and what food and instruments would be packed (upper image, Plate 5). The Sharps were not alone in seeing the Thames as a place of entertainment, particularly upriver.[25] It was popular to conduct river races and celebrations on the Thames; the Sharps were not the only ones who traveled the river "with colours flying," but few managed it so long and so sumptuously. For the early weekly sailing trips the cost was split between William, James, Granville, and occasionally a friend. Granville usually contributed much less because he was still an apprentice in the mid-1750s.[26] Even then his contribution of 2s. 6d. made participation in the water schemes a moderately expensive entertainment. A visit to Vauxhall Gardens or second gallery seats at a play, for example, cost only 1s.[27]

That the young Sharp brothers could afford not only to purchase the sailing vessels but to regularly stock them and pay for boatmen and servants demonstrates how their collective financial prosperity began to position them among London's elite. William had the good luck to inherit his master's business upon the master's retirement. As soon as he and other siblings had independent households their financial status began to expand on their pre-existing social abundance. Only a "tiny percentage of families...could spend more than a few pounds per annum on 'cultural' products...indeed, precious few families could spend more than a few shillings a month, if that."[28] Over time, the combination of their wealth and status made the Sharp homes among the most comfortable and safe in eighteenth-century London.[29]

In addition to dining and playing music on the barges and yachts in the mid-1750s, the London-based siblings gathered most evenings at William's house. These evenings often had forty or fifty in attendance. Informal concerts and "glee evenings" were a nearly weekly occurrence in the winter months. Understandably, water concerts were confined to the warmer months.[30] The lighthearted concerts on the barge and during glee evenings were paralleled by sacred and solemn music every other Sunday evening. Sacred music was part of daily life as well. Granville, for example, with his homemade harp accompanied himself singing psalms in Hebrew each morning.[31]

The boats grew in size and luxury as their homes did after the 1750s. William's first attempt at cooking mutton in 1750 heralded a lifelong enjoyment hosting

---

[25] Margarette Lincoln, *Trading in War: London's Maritime World in the Age of Cook and Nelson* (New Haven: Yale, 2018), 162, 177.

[26] Crosby, "Private Concerts," 1–118.

[27] Robert D. Hume, "The Value of Money in Eighteenth-Century England: Incomes, Prices, Buying Power—and Some Problems in Cultural Economics," *Huntington Library Quarterly*, 77, no. 4 (2015): 383.

[28] Hume, "Value of Money in Eighteenth-Century England," 378.

[29] Amanda Vickery, "An Englishman's Home Is His Castle? Thresholds, Boundaries and Privacies in the Eighteenth-Century London House," *Past and Present*, 199 (May 2008): 147–173.

[30] Hoare, *Memoirs of Granville Sharp*, 59, 146, appendix, ixx–xiii; Crosby, "Private Concerts," 33.

[31] Crosby, "Private Concerts," 78.

104   BEING SINGLE IN GEORGIAN ENGLAND

guests. He purchased a series of homes between the 1750s and the 1780s, each grander than the last, eventually allowing him to host nearly four hundred guests at a time. One historian's description of eighteenth-century sociability could have been written with William in mind: "In planning house parties, even for small numbers of guests, hosts and hostesses poured time and effort into planning every detail for the comfort of their company, close neighbours and rarely-seen visitors alike."[32] The Sharps prioritized cultural consumption and production as essential to their domestic arrangements. It is striking that prosperous, socially well-positioned young men such as the Sharps centered their social energy in their own domestic sphere. Though they attended public concerts and entertainments, they spent far more time and resources on providing entertainment for themselves and others on their boats and at their homes.

William and James's efforts highlight how single men managed domestic arrangements. They were not passive participants in public performances or in domestic gatherings arranged by women; they were agents. Men's household account management and its importance to eighteenth-century masculinity are well documented, but William went far beyond managing accounts.[33] He managed all the details of who was invited, how much food and wine should be ordered, and which instruments and musicians needed to be brought on board, and he kept a careful record—part accounts, part to-do list, and part celebration of all the details a successful social event required. Analysis of married men's involvement in planning for social events or visits has demonstrated that despite their involvement, it was usually the women who had a "greater hands-on role in the actual mechanics of hospitality."[34] Men often reaped the "dividend[s] accruing from unequal shares of the products of social labour."[35] The single Sharp brothers' actions, however, suggest that women's greater hands-on involvement might have had as much to do with marital status as with gender. The Sharps' singleness meant the brothers had to be involved in the mechanics if they wanted to reap the benefits of social gatherings. By establishing such social patterns during the ten to fifteen years after they acquired a house and the boats but before they married, William and James never completely surrendered the mechanics of hospitality to their wives. In fact, even after they married, the planning of sailing journeys and concerts in London remained largely the brothers' doing.

From surviving records, it is evident that William's wife eventually assumed the responsibility of keeping a record of the planning for social gatherings, but William, James, and later Granville remained consistently involved in the details. The brothers had spent 1750–51 lobbying their parents to allow Elizabeth to move

[32] Mullin, "'We Had Carding,'" 992–993.
[33] Amanda Vickery, "His and Hers: Gender, Consumption and Household Accounting in Eighteenth-century England," *Past and Present* supplement (2006): 12–38.
[34] Mullin, "'We Had Carding,'" 994.
[35] R.W. Connell, *Gender and Power* (Stanford: Stanford University Press, 1987), 75.

south and act as William's housekeeper. Perhaps if they had been successful, Elizabeth would have managed more of the hospitality responsibilities, but it seems unlikely that the brothers would have lost interest in the logistics of hospitality. While servants of both sexes and of various ranks did the physical labor, neither William nor James depended on a woman organizing and planning these events. Though there is less documentary evidence, it appears that John, and perhaps Thomas, established similar habits between the time John obtained the living of Hartburn in 1750 and when he married in 1752. In any event, Elizabeth and the other sisters did not join their brothers' households until 1758, by which point the brothers had had nearly a decade's experience with household and hospitality management; they had never viewed this labor as unmasculine.

1760s and 1770s: Flourishing Households, Expanding Circles

After their parents' deaths the sisters' domestic arrangements had to be reconfigured. Parental death was always a major factor in children's financial and social standing in early modern England.[36] For the Sharps, their parents' deaths in 1757 and 1758 altered the sisters' household organization, and by doing so, completely remapped the geography of family interaction. The following year, 1759, became a turning point for the Sharps. In addition to the sisters joining their London-based brothers in 1758, John was appointed a trustee of Bamburgh Castle, in his father's stead. In June 1759 he completed his doctorate of divinity and visited Thomas while in Cambridge (Thomas was in residence working on his BD), where they were joined by Elizabeth for a week's visit. Mary and Judith, who had been visiting a Dering cousin (Mary's brother), then arrived in Cambridge and the entire group joined the remaining Sharps at William's house on Mincing Lane. The only one missing was Frances, who had been with their Prowse cousins. On July 14, Judith and William met Frances at Turnham Green and "brought her on board the Apollo Barge in the River where we were all ready to receive her 5 Brothers & 4 Sisters to her great surprise."[37] They spent a week visiting Greenwich, Vauxhall, the top of St. Paul's, and enjoying "an agreeable Day" on the *Apollo*. On the 21st, James and Elizabeth moved to James's new house on Leadenhall Street and began housekeeping there. Granville returned to his rooms at the Tower (where he worked for the Ordnance Office). Frances and Judith remained at Mincing Lane, where all the siblings, including Thomas when he was in town, gathered every evening for supper and music "amongst ourselves."[38] The events of

[36] Sheila Cooper, "Intergenerational Social Mobility in Late-Seventeenth- and Early-Eighteenth-Century England," *Continuity and Change*, 7, no. 3 (1992): 296.

[37] Elizabeth Sharp Prowse, memorandum and commonplace book, June–July 1759, page 24, D3549/14/1/1.

[38] Elizabeth Sharp Prowse, memorandum and commonplace book, June–July 1759, page 24.

the summer of 1759 forecast what was to come. They did not know it, but as the 1760s dawned, the Sharps embarked on what would be an era of unmitigated domestic, social, financial, and philanthropic success.

Beyond the weekly sailing concerts, groups of Sharps traveled between their homes many times a year (Figure 4.1). Occasionally, a smaller group of siblings traveled together, as William, his wife Catherine, and Judith did when they spent three weeks in France in 1776. Additionally, the southern siblings had "water schemes" several times a summer, and the entire group gathered at one of their homes or for a longer journey every two or three years in between the 1750s and 1770s.[39] And for many years they had had prominent guests among their visitors; for example, they hosted several aristocratic visitors for a water scheme in 1763.[40]

Northern Homes at Hartburn, Bamburgh, and Durham

The first Sharp sibling household was John's in Hartburn, when he became vicar at the end of 1749.[41] Hartburn was a lucrative appointment for the young vicar; the vicarage consisted of a kitchen, hall, parlor, cellar, three upper chambers, and two grain lofts. It was also accompanied by various outbuildings, a barn, orchards, over a hundred acres of glebe land, and various tithes, rents, and common rights. It was worth over £1100.[42] On the glebe lands, John built a tower (perhaps echoing his father's similar effort in Rothbury), established a pleasure garden, and expanded a grotto.[43] After his marriage to cousin Mary Dering in 1752 the two of them hosted family members on a regular basis. There were at least two occasions, one in 1765 and one in 1785, when the southern siblings traveled north to spend extended time with John and Mary. Unlike the more sober performances of sacred music John hosted when at Durham, the Hartburn concerts were more relaxed and John eagerly joined in the performance. Among the additions he made to the vicarage, were "two very large rooms, a dining and drawing-room in which his delight was to entertain his neighbours with musical performances."[44] An observer noted that when John was "in the ecstasy of enjoyment he would throw off his coat, and fiddle among baronets and squires, and their lady wives and daughters, in his shirt sleeves, till...he was black in the face."[45]

---

[39] Elizabeth Sharp Prowse, memorandum and commonplace book, August 20, 1772; August 31–September 9, 1773; August 15–30, 1774; July 12–29, 1776, 42, 44–45, 47–49, 52, typescript, D3549/14/1/2.

[40] Granville Sharp to John Sharp, August 30, 1763, D3549/1/4.

[41] "John Sharp (CCEd Person ID 20289)," *The Clergy of the Church of England Database 1540–1835*, http://www.theclergydatabase.org.uk, accessed July 2, 2017.

[42] John Hodgson, *A History of Northumberland*, part 2 (Newcastle upon Tyne: Edward Walker for J. B. Nichols, 1827), 1:297–300.

[43] Hodgson, *History of Northumberland*, 1:298.

[44] Crosby, "Concerts on Land and Water," 60.   [45] Crosby, "Concerts on Land and Water," 60.

Plate 1. Family portrait by Johan Zoffany, on loan to The National Gallery, London; © Lloyd-Baker Estate, used with permission

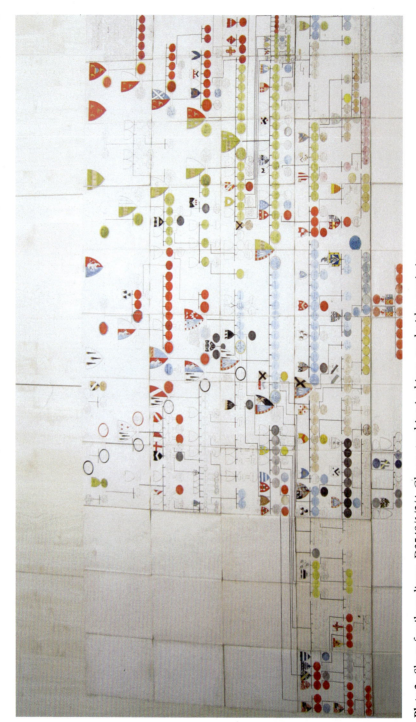

Plate 2. Sharp family pedigree, D3549/1/2/4, Gloucestershire Archives, used with permission

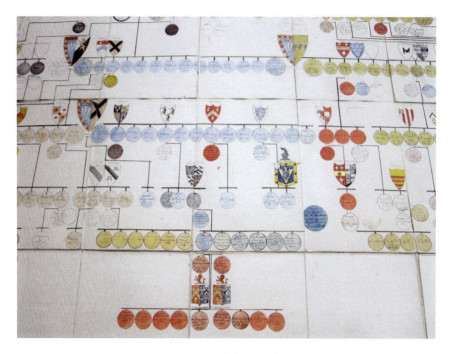

Plate 3. (Upper image) Sharp family pedigree (detail), Gloucestershire Archives, used with permission; (lower image) Whitton Tower sketched by Granville Sharp, 1754, Northumberland Archives, used with permission

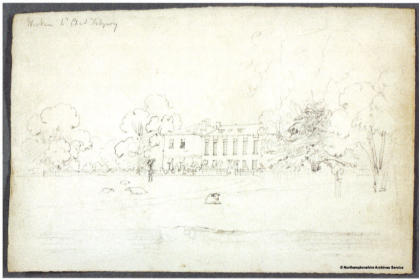

Plate 4. (Upper image) sketch of William Sharp's organ, "Miss Morgan," by a Sharp sibling, *c*.1750s, D3549/7/2/15, Gloucestershire Archives, used with permission; (lower image) pencil sketch of Wicken Park by Charles Fitzroy, *c*.1818–27, Northamptonshire Archives, used with permission

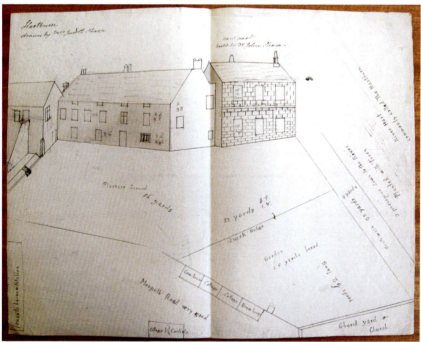

Plate 5. (Upper image) first entry in the Sharp boat books, 1753, D3549/12/1/1, Gloucestershire Archives, used with permission; (lower image) drawing of Hartburn vicarage and grounds, Northumberland by Judith Sharp, D3549/8/1/6, Gloucestershire Archives, used with permission

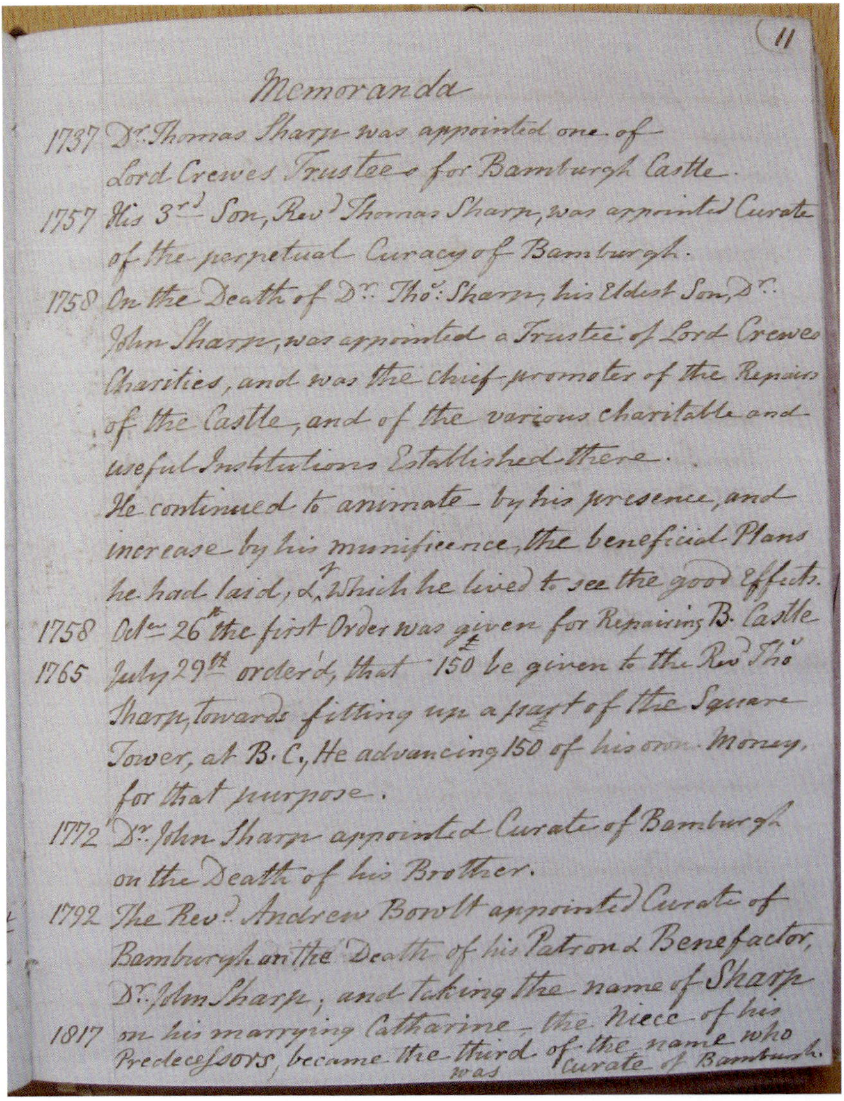

Memoranda

1737 Dr. Thomas Sharp was appointed one of Lord Crewes Trustees for Bamburgh Castle.

1757 His 3rd Son, Revd Thomas Sharp, was appointed Curate of the perpetual Curacy of Bamburgh.

1758 On the Death of Dr. Tho: Sharp, his Eldest Son, Dr. John Sharp, was appointed a Trustee of Lord Crewes Charities, and was the chief promoter of the Repairs of the Castle, and of the various charitable and useful Institutions Established there.
He continued to animate – by his presence, and increase – by his munificence, the beneficial Plans he had laid, & which he lived to see the good Effects.

1758 Octr 26th the first Order was given for Repairing B. Castle

1765 July 29th order'd, that £150 be given to the Revd Tho" Sharp, towards fitting up a part of the Square Tower, at B. C, He advancing 150 of his own Money, for that purpose.

1772 Dr. John Sharp appointed Curate of Bamburgh on the Death of his Brother.

1792 The Revd Andrew Bowlt appointed Curate of Bamburgh on the Death of his Patron & Benefactor, Dr. John Sharp; and taking the name of Sharp

1817 on his marrying Catharine – the Niece of his Predecessors, became the third of the name who was Curate of Bamburgh.

Plate 6. Elizabeth Sharp Prowse, memorandum and commonplace book, D3549/14/1/1, Gloucestershire Archives, used with permission

Plate 7. (Upper image) miniature of Judith Sharp (1733–1809), Lord Crewe's Charity, used with permission; (lower image) miniature of Thomas Sharp (1725–1772), Lord Crewe's Charity, used with permission. [The Charity indicated that the miniature of Thomas was not labeled and they determined it was of James. However, the collection of miniatures, other than the one of Granville, are exclusive to the family members who lived together in Northumberland: John, Mary, Judith, and Jemima. Thomas would be the obvious brother to include in the group and the miniature depicts a man wearing a clerical style wig.]

Plate 8. (Upper image) Sharp family monument, Bamburgh parish church, photograph © Susan Barwood, 2022; (lower image) portrait of Catherine Sharp by Margaret Carpenter, Bamburgh Castle, used with permission, photograph © Susan Barwood, 2022

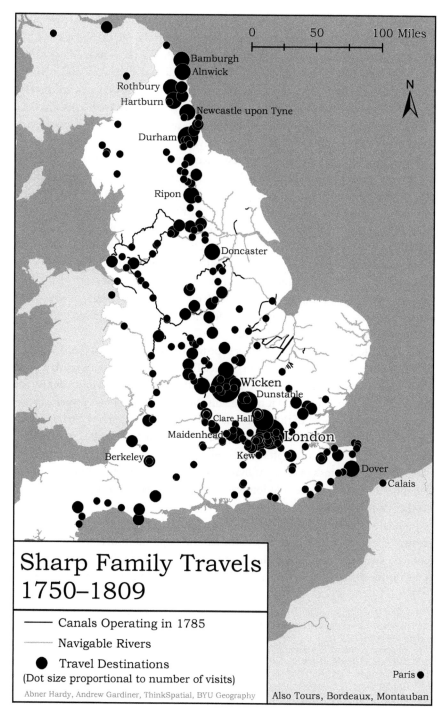

Figure 4.1 Map of Sharp family travels, 1750–1809

108   BEING SINGLE IN GEORGIAN ENGLAND

Judith, after her initial residence with William in London, split her time between Northumberland, Durham, and long visits to the South. She was central to improvements John made at Hartburn. She sketched the house and grounds and, with the skill of an architect, helped John design doorways and mantels (lower image, Plate 5).[46] She was also connected to her southern siblings' households. She once gifted four sheep to Elizabeth at Wicken.[47] It is also possible she helped maintain John's college house at Durham or Hartburn, since he and Mary spent only three months at each home every year.[48]

Throughout his life, even with ecclesiastical positions spread from Northumberland to London, Thomas preferred to reside with John and Mary and he did so most of the time. Busy shuttling between London and, after his 1757 appointment as vicar of Bamburgh, Thomas may have spent time at various lodgings associated with Church positions, but other than the brief time from his marriage in 1770 to his death in 1772, he never managed his own household.[49] From the time he left home for Cambridge in 1743 until his death, Thomas usually resided with John and helped in managing household affairs for him. Near the end of his life, Thomas told John he always preferred to live with him, and tellingly, several of the hymn tunes he composed were named after the homes he shared with John: Hartburn, Bamburgh, and Cambridge.[50]

In 1758, John assumed his father's position as a trustee of Lord Crewe's Charity's and caretaker of Bamburgh Castle. Their father had been a trustee since 1737, so the brothers had long been familiar with the castle. John immediately set out to refurbish the castle and it became his, Mary's, and Thomas's principal residence for the remainder of their lives. At a bit over £55 per annum, the curacy of Bamburgh was not particularly lucrative, even after an early eighteenth-century augmentation. It also had no attached residence, so his appointment as curate did not interrupt Thomas's practice of living with John; instead, the situation solidified it because the obvious solution was to share the castle's living space with his brother and sister-in-law.[51]

John later described the improvements he made to the castle once he became a trustee. The scale of his endeavor and the labor it required from skilled craftsmen, laborers, and servants is staggering. Renovations included schools, accommodations for teachers, an infirmary, and a library. In addition, he enlarged windows,

---

[46] Judith Sharp, drawings of Hartburn house and grounds, D3549/8/1/6.

[47] Elizabeth Sharp Prowse, memorandum and commonplace book, 19 December 1787, 73, typescript, D3549/14/1/2.

[48] John Sharp, visitation answers, 1782, NRO 452/C/3/2/12, NAW.

[49] Bamburgh, Northumberland parish registers, May 15, 1757, EP 59/1, NAW; Thomas Sharp to Judith Sharp, April 10, 1761, D3549/16/1/1.

[50] Crosby, comp., *A Catalogue of Durham Cathedral Music Manuscripts* (Oxford: Oxford University Press for the Dean and Chapter of Durham, 1986), 82–84. Hymns were often named after the places where they were composed, but Thomas's lack of London-place names in his hymns highlights his connection to John's residences.

[51] Extracts from Thomas Sharp Sr.'s visitation record for Bamburgh, 1723, EP 59/76, NAW.

LIVING SINGLE   109

rebuilt the walls, and made other repairs, about which he wrote: "with a proper degree of Castle Enthusiasm in which you will perhaps think I am far gone."[52]

On another occasion, John passionately described the castle and its associated charities as his child. He was clearly the most connected to Bamburgh, but other siblings were highly invested in the renovations and daily functioning of the castle. Thomas maintained a lifelong connection to Bamburgh because it brought him close to John. As much as Thomas enjoyed London, he preferred Bamburgh. "You know I like to reside Bambrough above all other Places," he wrote. Continuing, he emphasized it was not just the place he missed, but John's presence: "[I] more particularly regret the being absent from it when you are there."[53]

Thomas's letter to Judith about the Bamburgh prophecy was the most sensational exchange with the southern siblings, but there were years of more mundane discussions. In the early 1770s, James provided expert advice on paving stones intended for the castle and then provided for their purchase in London and transport to Northumberland.[54] Later that decade, Granville offered advice on a potential steward and about a plan to keep joint accounts.[55] Judith acted as messenger between John and William when John sought suggestions for a potential surgeon for Bamburgh.[56] She might have also helped with other interior design elements as she had in Hartburn. At the very least, she helped John choose suitable picture frames.[57]

Beyond Bamburgh and Hartburn, the northern Sharps also had homes in Durham. When their father died in 1758, the sisters sadly bid farewell to their childhood homes in Rothbury and Durham. However, a decade later, John established an additional residence in the city because of his new appointment as a prebend of Durham Cathedral.[58] It is possible Judith acted as housekeeper for John's Durham residence. Therefore, by 1770 Durham reclaimed its importance to Sharp domestic and social arrangements the early nineteenth century. While in residence in Durham, John hosted regular concerts of sacred music and presumably Judith also hosted musical gatherings.[59] John's daughter Jemima was often in her aunt Judith's company, and after John's death, Jemima, her mother Mary, and Judith began sharing a home on South Bailey, Durham. Perched on the point, overlooking the river, and in the shadow of the cathedral it was "a most pleasant

[52] John Sharp to Edward King, Esq., March 5, 1786, Add MS 1014, PGL.

[53] Thomas Sharp to John Sharp, June 30, 1772, NRO 452/C/3/2/3/37, NAW.

[54] Assorted letters about managing Bamburgh Castle; principal Sharp correspondents were John, Thomas, James, and Granville, NRO 0452/C/3/2/4, NAW.

[55] Granville Sharp to John Sharp, May 8, 1779, NRO 0452/C/3/2/18/24, NAW.

[56] William Sharp to Judith Sharp, September 14, 1774, NRO 0452/C/3/2/5/69, NAW.

[57] Judith Sharp to John Sharp, October 22, 1776, NRO 0452/C/3/2/6/43, NAW.

[58] James Sharp to John Sharp, January 12, 1769, D3549/9/1/4; "John Sharp (CCEd Person ID 20289)," *The Clergy of the Church of England Database 1540–1835*, http://www.theclergydatabase.org.uk, accessed July 2, 2017.

[59] Hoare, *Memoirs of Granville Sharp*, Appendix VI, page xii; Crosby, "Private Concerts," 60.

110 BEING SINGLE IN GEORGIAN ENGLAND

one & a most sweet situation as any in Durham."[60] While comfortable, the South Bailey home could not boast the size of the London Sharps' parties and musical evenings. Though the scale of interaction was smaller in Durham than in London or Wicken, it maintained expected Sharp standards of social and musical events. When Granville, William, and William's wife, Catherine, visited Durham in 1796, for example, they regularly played music together in the evenings—in addition to attending plays and concerts.[61] Tellingly, Granville consistently referred to his sisters' and niece's house as "home," when he visited, signifying how shared Sharp houses offered the comforts of home to all siblings.

London Homes at Mincing Lane, Leadenhall Street, and Old Jewry

While John and Thomas settled into homes in Northumberland, William and James began to establish their household routines in London. The Sharp brothers were like thousands of other young people who had come to London for employment. Mid-century London was loud, noisy, and crowded, humming with trade, activity, and entertainments. Poverty and crime abounded and the social distance between poor neighborhoods and the comfortable Sharp social gatherings could not have been greater. For example, in William and Catherine's late eighteenth-century household inventory just one bed chamber's linen and furniture, including 108.5 yards of green worsted damask, was worth over £78. Meanwhile, a widowed or single mother of three children might receive from the parish overseers of the poor, 6s. a week, perhaps augmented by food and clothing subsidies. In other words, a poor family's total annual support might be worth less than one-quarter the cost of a single room in a wealthy household.[62]

After their parents' deaths, Elizabeth and Frances initially joined James in living with William at Mincing Lane. Granville, who had rooms near the Tower, and Thomas both regularly visited. In 1759 Judith also joined them, though she would later split her time between visits to the South and permanent residence in Durham. Even with William's larger home on Mincing Lane, it could be a bit crowded. Acquiring a new house, however, was an expense no one was able to assume in the late 1750s, unless they had help. James was fortunate that just as his former master prepared to leave the business, his cousin Elizabeth Prowse was able and willing to loan him £1000 so he could buy the building and business on

---

[60] Elizabeth Sharp Prowse, memorandum and commonplace book, April 28, 1792, typescript, D3549/14/1/2.

[61] Catherine Sharp (niece), annotations of Granville Sharp's diaries, February 19–April 6, 1796, book 2, pages 122–125, D3549/13/4/2.

[62] St. Paul Covent Garden, overseers of the poor account for Elizabeth Crosbie, 1796–97, DGS 5135114, image 640 of 790, FHL.

Leadenhall Street.[63] James "commenced Housekeeping in Leadenhall Street" in July 1759.[64] Judith and Frances remained at Mincing Lane, but Elizabeth joined James at his house, thus finally fulfilling his and William's wishes from years earlier that Elizabeth would join in householding with them. Even after James and Elizabeth's departure, the siblings continued to meet each evening. Occasionally the three from Mincing Lane, plus Thomas and Granville, would spend the evening at Leadenhall Street, "but whatever other engagements took place it was all our Party together," Elizabeth noted.[65]

The Sharps gathered at Leadenhall Street and at their Prowse cousins' home at affluent Argyll Place in west London. It was at Mincing Lane, however, where the London-based Sharps first grounded their domestic and social lives. William moved from his first home to a larger one on the same street in April 1757, coinciding with his mother and sisters' long visit that spring. William's youthful enjoyment of householding continued unabated. In preparation for his 1765 marriage he refurnished the house, hurrying to finish before Catherine joined him.[66]

William's move to his second Mincing Lane home in 1757 and James's acquiring of the Leadenhall Street home in 1759 signaled the brothers' increasing prosperity. That their sisters joined them in housekeeping was instrumental to both houses' early success. But none of the sisters long remained housekeeper to a brother. Elizabeth had her own household after 1762, Frances and Judith rotated between sibling households, and Judith later shared a home with her sister-in-law and niece. Elizabeth later recalled the late 1750s and early 1760s with much fondness, noting that her siblings were the kindest and most affectionate siblings possible and that it brought her happiness to see William and James "increasing in Business beyond their Expectation."[67] Brothers cooperating in or supporting one another's domestic and business affairs was not unusual, but as with so many things, the Sharps were particularly skilled and particularly lucky in those ventures.[68]

Unlike the Mincing Lane house, even with its onsite surgeries, the house at 15 Leadenhall Street was as much a manufacturing site as it was a home.[69] James produced carriage wheels and parts (earning a patent for one design) as well as a

---

[63] St. Andrew Undershaft, London, poor rate assessments, 1759–60, P69/AND4/C/003/MS04122/001, LMA; Elizabeth Sharp Prowse, memorandum and commonplace book, July 21, 1759, 25, D3549/14/1/1.

[64] Elizabeth Sharp Prowse, memorandum and commonplace book, July 21, 1759, 25, D3549/14/1/1.

[65] Elizabeth Sharp Prowse, memorandum and commonplace book, July 21, 1759, 25, D3549/14/1/1.

[66] Granville Sharp to John Sharp, August 16, 1765, Papers of Archbishop John Sharp Collection, COLL 1891/3/5, YMA.

[67] Elizabeth Sharp Prowse, memorandum and commonplace book, July 1759, page 26, D3549/14/1/1.

[68] Heal and Holmes, *The Gentry in England and Wales*, 114, 170, 269, 306; Hannah Barker, *Family and Business During the Industrial Revolution* (Oxford: Oxford University Press, 2017), 97–102.

[69] Plans of Leadenhall Street home of James Sharp, c.1760s, D3549/12/2/8; *The London Directory for the Year 1780*, 15th edn. (London: T. Lowndes, 1780), 146, entry for James Sharpe, ironmonger, 15 Leadenhall Street, digital image at *London, England, City Directories, 1736–1943*, https://www.ancestry.co.uk, accessed November 2, 2020; St. Andrew Undershaft, poor rates, 1772–1808, P69/AND4/C/003/MS 04122/002, LMA.

112   BEING SINGLE IN GEORGIAN ENGLAND

variety of farming implements and stoves.[70] In addition, James had another factory on Tooley Street, a mile away on the south side of the Thames.[71] Workshops and warehouses sprouted up across London in the latter half of the eighteenth century, many of their owners experimenting and inventing much like James did.[72] Leadenhall Street was near the East India House and put James's household in the heart of Britain's imperial and industrial activities. He also spread his influence via writing and advertising; in the 1770s and 1780s he published items promoting his mechanical inventions and his ideas for improving the nation's canal system.[73] He also rented space near Elizabeth's home in Wicken where he could demonstrate and refine his carriage and cart designs after experimenting with them in the estate's fields and roads.[74]

Unsurprisingly, James multitasked by enjoying musical events on the water and developing his professional interests in improving transportation and communication. Canal building and expansion was booming in the 1760s, but London's canal system lagged behind that of other regions in James's estimation.[75] He wrote reports of critiquing the awful state of the Thames and suggested improvements for it and the surrounding canals.[76]

James and Catherine remained at their Leadenhall Street house the rest of his life. Their growing prosperity paralleled William and Catherine's in the 1760s and 1770s. The cost of premiums that James charged for apprenticeships indicates his increased wealth and social prominence. In 1759 and 1760, just after he acquired the Leadenhall Street house and manufactory, he charged £5 for a seven-year apprenticeship bond. By 1763 a similar bond cost £300, and by 1770 it cost £735—more than three times the cost of his own apprenticeship twenty-four years earlier. His apprentice from 1770 was the son of a man styled as "esquire"— thus hinting at the value of James's reputation and connections as much as his

---

[70] James Sharp, *An Account of the Principle and Effects of the Air Stove-Grates...Together with a Description of the Late Additions and Improvements Made to Them by James Sharp...No. 15 Leadenhall Street, London...N.B. The Manufactory is at No. 133, Tooley Street, Southwark*, 10th edn. (London, 1781), TS 425.S451, New York Historical Society.

[71] Executors of James Sharp, lease, Sharp's Iron Manufactory on Tooley Street, June 17, 1784, O/086/069, LMA.

[72] Lincoln, *Trading in War*, 159.

[73] James Sharp, "Fire Grates for Warm Fresh Air," advertisement in *Morning Herald and Daily Advertiser*, 3; "Patent for Fire Grates," advertisement in *Morning Herald and Daily Advertiser*, August 19, 1782, 4; August 27, 1782, 1, digital images at https://newspaperarchive.com, accessed June 4, 2020.

[74] Briony McDonagh, "'All Towards the Improvements of the Estate': Mrs Elizabeth Prowse at Wicken, 1764–1810," in R.W. Hoyle, ed., *Custom, Improvement and the Landscape in Early Modern Britain* (Farnham: Ashgate, 2011): 276.

[75] Leslie Tomory, *The History of the London Water Industry 1580–1820* (Baltimore: Johns Hopkins University Press, 2017).

[76] "New River Company: Report on Proposed Canal from Waltham Abbey to Moorfields by Robert Whitworth and Address on Canals by James Sharp to the Lord Mayor," 1773, ACC/2558/MW/C/15/150, LMA.

LIVING SINGLE   113

mechanical skills.[77] William and Catherine's financial fortunes also continued to rise; by the end of the century their annual income put them among the wealthiest Londoners.[78]

In January 1769, William and Catherine, with James's help, sold Mincing Lane and moved a mile northwest to a large, grand home on Old Jewry. With a typical Sharp approach, immediately after the move William embedded himself in local concerns; he was regularly present for vestry meetings and was seriously engaged in the parish's discussion about installation of a new organ and new stoves, the latter to be installed by James.[79] It does not appear that Catherine, nor James's wife (also Catherine), had musical ability, for they never appear in the names of performers. However, both sisters-in-law were engaged in the social events held in their homes; Catherine, William's wife, kept a "visiting book" from 1773 to 1783.[80]

The move to Old Jewry represented a major shift in Sharp social ambitions in London. No other European city "had as much musical entrepreneurism" as London did and the Sharps fully joined in the musical abundance.[81] James was sad to see the Mincing Lane house go ("no more jolly doings there") given its importance to their shared domestic happiness, but he remained hopeful that their musical evenings would not cease with the move. His ambivalence about the larger scale of social gatherings did not prevent him from performing at them. Perhaps he was concerned particularly with the more intimate family and friends' musical evenings, for Number 8 Old Jewry was capacious and described as "the Noblest house in the City of London," its multiple gathering spaces allowing William and Catherine to host nearly four hundred guests.[82] And unlike gatherings at the Mincing Lane houses, only rarely were there fewer than sixty guests at the Old Jewry assemblies.[83]

The house was clearly purchased with large social gatherings in mind. The entrance measured fifty by thirty feet, with a "Grand painted stair case...lofty dining room 40 by 20...a parlour 20 by 15" and three smaller rooms on the ground floor alone.[84] It was not just the size of Old Jewry nor the size of the guest

[77] *Records of London's Livery Companies Online*, apprenticeship of James Hitchins, 1760; apprenticeship of Joseph Matthews Beachcroft, 1763; apprenticeship of William Page, 1770; apprentices to James Sharp, Company of Drapers; http://www.londonroll.org, accessed April 2, 2021.

[78] William Sharp, statements of income made for tax purposes, 1797, D3549/23/1/10; L.D. Schwarz, "Social Class and Social Geography: The Middle Classes in London at the End of the Eighteenth Century," *Social History*, 7, no. 2 (May 1982): 167–185.

[79] St. Olave, Old Jewry, London, parish accounts, June 6, 1771; January 27, 1774; December 20, 1780; April 12, 1786; P69/OLA2/B/002/MS04412/002, LMA.

[80] Catherine Barwick Sharp, visiting book, 1773–83, D3549/12/1/5.

[81] William Weber, "Musical Culture and the Capital City: The Epoch of the *beau monde* in London, 1700–1870," in Susan Wollenberg and Simon McVeigh, eds., *Concert Life in Eighteenth-Century Britain* (Aldershot: Ashgate, 2004), 77.

[82] James Sharp to John Sharp, January 12, 1769, D3549/9/1/4.

[83] Crosby, "Private Concerts," 35.

[84] James Sharp to John Sharp, January 12, 1769, D3549/9/1/4; Plans of William Sharp's house in Old Jewry, 1769, D3549/10/1/4 (8 Old Jewry was previously owned by Sir Matthew Blakiston,

114 BEING SINGLE IN GEORGIAN ENGLAND

list that indicated the increased prosperity of William and Catherine's household or the shared Sharp households. The social status of their guests was decidedly elite. The Sharps supplemented their own performances by hiring eminent professional musicians and by inviting those prominent in the theater, music, and government; David Garrick, the Sheridans, the Duke of Cumberland, and Lord North were among the guests invited to Old Jewry concerts.

The Sharps had enormous competition for elite guests; eighteenth-century London was bursting with concerts and plays, including those associated with charitable fund-raising—all vying for the attention of wealthy patrons.[85] There were also numerous musical societies, to which at least William and Granville belonged.[86] These entertainments collapsed categorical boundaries between diversion, philanthropy, consumerism, religion, and social networking. It is difficult to imagine a social and cultural milieu better suited to Sharp inclinations and talents. That the Sharps were able to draw such large crowds amid countless other entertainments highlights their rise to the pinnacle of London society. For example, Elizabeth Harris, from the musical family who supported Handel's career, attended a "Concerto Spirituale" at the Old Jewry in April 1772, despite knowing only one other guest.[87] The Sharps were not the only family to hire professional musicians and to host concerts, but few families could afford to replicate the scale or frequency of the Sharps' concerts. In 1779, Harris remarked that there were perhaps "too many concerts, and people begin now to think [it] necessary to retrench their expences."[88] The Sharps did not require retrenchment; they once hired a gunner for a musical performance, perhaps to accompany a performance of Handel's *Music for Royal Fireworks*.[89]

Who was invited and to which level of intimacy signaled much about the relations between host and guest, since "inviting or being invited by the right people could yield substantial rewards…entertaining was often an effective means of consolidating or advancing one's social standing."[90] David and Eva Marie Garrick, for example, once breakfasted with the Sharps on board the *Apollo*—a more intimate interaction than attendance at a large party would have afforded. James Crainston first joined them for a musical evening on the water, but then he was invited to

---

alderman and one-time lord mayor of London). John Noorthouck, "Book 2, Chp. 15: Cheap Ward," in *A New History of London Including Westminster and Southwark* (London: R. Baldwin, 1773), 587–593, *British History Online*, https://www.british-history.ac.uk/no-series/new-history-london/pp587-593, accessed July 28, 2021.

[85] Sarah Lloyd, "Pleasing Spectacles and Elegant Dinners: Conviviality, Benevolence, and Charity Anniversaries in Eighteenth-Century London," *Journal of British Studies*, 41, no. 1 (January 2002): 23–57.

[86] Crosby, "Private Concerts," 21–30.

[87] Elizabeth Harris to James Harris Jr., April 7, 1772, transcription in Donald Burrows and Rosemary Dunhill, eds., *Music and Theatre in Handel's World: The Family Papers of James Harris 1732–1780* (Oxford: Oxford University Press, 2002), 670.

[88] Elizabeth Harris to Gertrude Harris, February 6–8, 1779, transcription in Burrows and Dunhill, *Music and Theatre in Handel's World*, 1008.

[89] Crosby, "Private Concerts," 23.   [90] Mullin, "'We Had Carding,'" 993.

return the next day with his flute so he could perform with them.[91] Catherine Talbot, a bluestocking who was also the archbishop of Canterbury's protégé and secretary, was friendly enough with the Sharps to remind them of "their kind promise to bring themselves & their Music to Lambeth" in the summer of 1761.[92] In the late 1760s, William and James hosted Dugald Clarke, a mixed-race wealthy Jamaican, at their homes and on board the barge—an expression of "most sincere hospitality and friendship" he remembered for twenty years.[93] Beyond invitations, such social connections were essential to personal and household financial and professional success.[94]

The social standing of the Harrises, the Garricks, Clarke, and Talbot was typical of Sharp guests, but for the Sharps it was perhaps less about who was invited— as that list was very long—and more about who was not invited. The most obvious example is the wealthy Beckford family. At first glance, the Beckfords and Sharps should have been close associates. Both families had a passion for music— the Beckfords invested in an organ for their country house a year before William had his organ installed at his home—and both hosted many of the same guests (see upper image, Plate 4). But despite those overlapping musical interests and guest lists, there is no evidence they visited or even corresponded with each other. Since the Beckfords' wealth and social position came from their Jamaican sugar plantations, where they collectively enslaved thousands of people, it is no surprise the anti-slavery Sharps were not inclined to socialize with the Beckfords, or vice versa.[95] The Sharps were not entirely removed from the slave economy, however. Their culinary and gastronomic pleasures were built on international influences from trade networks and colonial holdings. Despite their anti-slavery proclivities, slave-produced sugar, tea, chocolate, and coffee joined citrus, spices, potatoes, and melons on the Sharps' tables.[96] But the Beckford's direct connection to slavery may have been more than the Sharps were willing to include in their social patterns. Granville was happy when political opponents were still able to enjoy the concerts with them, but the Beckfords' direct involvement with slavery made for an unbridgeable social gap.[97]

---

[91] Sharp family boat books, April 13, [1759], D3549/12/1/1.

[92] Catherine Talbot to Sharp family, June 1761, D3549/12/1/3.

[93] Dugald Clarke to Granville Sharp, May 15, 1790, D3549/13/1/c12. Clarke was in London in 1770 to petition the Privy Council to grant him exemptions from laws that limited people of color's property rights. See Daniel Livesay, *Children of Uncertain Fortune: Mixed-Race Jamaicans in Britain and the Atlantic Family, 1733–1833* (Chapel Hill: University of North Carolina Press, 2018), 21, 95.

[94] Craig Muldrew, *The Economy of Obligation: The Culture of Credit and Social Relations in Early Modern England* (Basingstoke: Palgrave, 1998).

[95] David Hunter, "The Beckfords in England and Italy: A Case Study in the Musical Uses of the Profits of Slavery," *Early Music*, 46, no. 2 (2018): 285–298.

[96] Jillian Azevedo, *Tastes of the Empire: Foreign Foods in Seventeenth Century England* (Jefferson: McFarland and Co., 2017).

[97] Granville Sharp to General Oglethorpe, August 12, 1777, quoted in Crosby, "Private Concerts," 47.

116 BEING SINGLE IN GEORGIAN ENGLAND

Two journeys, one in 1770 and the other in 1777 (discussed in the Introduction), highlight the Sharps' shared domestic labor, their enjoyable social connections, and their social prominence. In 1770, the London siblings "were very pressing" that Elizabeth and Frances would join them for a water party. The sisters left infant Catherine with her nurse at Wicken and joined their brothers on August 5. Playing music as they sailed past Kew, they drew the attention of the royal family, so they stopped to provide a half hour's concert for the young princes and their attendants, obligingly performing song requests. William's position among royal surgeons undoubtedly facilitated the exchange. The Sharps journeyed on, above Richmond, and dined there. On their return they caught the ear of the king and queen, who came to the shore to listen to the spontaneous concert. On August 8, the Sharps presented an even greater spectacle when, while rehearsing on board a bit above London Bridge, they were joined by "a great Number of boats with Companey" greater than any crowd the Sharps had previously drawn. The Sharps hoped to quietly sail past Kew, but "there had been notis given" to the young royals (three princes aged 5, 7, and 8 and the 4-year-old princess royal) who came "skiping to the water side" eager to hear another concert. The Sharps once again continued up river where they not only drank tea but distributed it to all the "Companey in the Boats near us, which appeared very acceptable." They then learned the king and queen were in the gardens. So, they struck up a song and sailed closer to where the royals were seated on a shaded bench. The Sharps anchored opposite them and began a full concert, including two renditions of *God Save the King.* Not even a sudden rainstorm and the rush to shelter for both the monarchs and the instruments could spoil the moment. The Sharps performed for an hour and a half, and the large crowd which had gathered on other boats joined in on the last verse of *God Save the King.* The Sharps rowed away as the monarchs departed in their carriage; "they seemed pleased, and much entertained at the hurry when the rain came on."[98] George III particularly enjoyed the concert—a month later, during an interview with James about Thames improvements, the king preferred discussing the Sharps and their music instead of practical matters.[99]

Southern Retreat at Wicken Park

Like her brothers and their growing prominence and wealth in the 1760s and 1770s, Elizabeth too showed a talent for household and estate management at

[98] Elizabeth Sharp Prowse, memorandum and commonplace book, August 5–8, 1770, 34–36, typescript, D3549/14/1/2.

[99] J.A. Woods, "James Sharp: Common Coucillor of London in the Time of Wilkes," in Anne Whiteman, J.S. Bromley, and P.G.M. Dickson, eds., *Statesmen, Scholars and Merchants: Essays in Eighteenth-Century History Presented to Dame Lucy Sutherland* (Oxford: Clarendon Press, 1973), 281–282.

LIVING SINGLE 117

Wicken Park, Northamptonshire (lower image, Plate 4). As her skills expanded, so too did the land and condition of the estate, eventually making her one of the most important landowners in Northamptonshire. Wicken Park was the home of her in-laws/cousins, the Prowses. They had inherited the estate from Charles Hosier, the older Elizabeth Sharp Prowse's maternal grandfather. The Hosiers, and then the Prowses, were the most prominent family in the region. Wicken was a small parish, having fewer than three hundred inhabitants in the mid-1760s. In addition to Wicken Park a mile south of the village, the Prowses owned the manor which included the village and were involved in local improvements. Thomas Prowse, Elizabeth's father-in-law, an amateur architect, had rebuilt the church tower and made substantial renovations to Wicken Park.[100] If death had not intervened, Jack Prowse and Judith Sharp would have benefited from the generosity Elizabeth and her husband George enjoyed, but Jack's death in early 1758 ended both the marital and property arrangements that had been made.[101]

After Elizabeth and George's 1762 marriage, his parents gave the newlyweds Wicken Park for their primary residence. For the first two years of their marriage, Elizabeth and her husband had traveled with his family across much of southern England and into France as they sought places suited to improve her father-in-law's health. In the fall of 1764, as Elizabeth and George traveled toward Wicken, she anticipated the enjoyment and labor of housekeeping. "My mind," she wrote, "was filled with the care of commencing Housekeeping again." She and George spent much of their journey from Bath to Wicken "having had no small pleasure," she wrote "in forming our plans for living [at Wicken]." Within weeks of arriving, they hosted both Prowse and Sharp family members.[102]

After her father-in-law's and husband's deaths in 1767, Elizabeth's mother-in-law (and first cousin) granted Elizabeth a life interest in the estate.[103] Her mother-in-law reaffirmed Elizabeth's interest in 1772, even though by that time her daughter had married and had a son who would be the eventual male heir. Elizabeth's retention of Wicken Park provided for her needs in what appeared would be a long widowhood (in 1772 Elizabeth was only 39), and it left the estate in the hands of a skilled manager. It also incentivized her remaining a widow, as remarrying would have meant surrendering the life interest in Wicken Park.

---

[100] Francis Whellan, *History, Topography and Directory of Northamptonshire*, 2nd edn. (London: Whittaker and Co.; Northampton: Abel and Sons, 1874), 584–585; "Wicken" in *A History of the County of Northampton*, vol. 5: *The Hundred of Cleley*, ed. Philip Riden and Charles Insley (London, 2002), 413–38, http://www.british-history.ac.uk/vch/northants/vol5/pp413-438, accessed February 23, 2016; Elizabeth Sharp Prowse, memorandum and commonplace book, 1750, 15, D3549/14/1/1.

[101] Wicken manor, enclosure agreement, 1757, 364P/014, NRO.

[102] Elizabeth Sharp Prowse, memorandum and commonplace book, October 1 and October 5, 1764, 38, D3549/14/1/1.

[103] Demise of Wicken Park, from Mrs. Prowse of Berkeley to Mrs. Prowse of Wicken, May 20, 1772, D3549/14/1/5; Elizabeth Sharp Prowse, memorandum and commonplace book, May 20,1772, D3549/14/1/1.

118   BEING SINGLE IN GEORGIAN ENGLAND

As with many women from landed families, widowhood brought a level of household and economic autonomy for Elizabeth.[104] She thrived in her new role and proved herself a dedicated and talented manager of the house and estate. She also continued her deceased father-in-law's efforts to improve the estate, house, and parish church by retaining the well-respected architect John Sanderson to complete the church renovations.[105]

The life interest in Wicken made Elizabeth a manager of one of the largest estates in Northamptonshire. She actively continued the previous generation's effort to expand the estate until it included most of the village among its 2200 acres.[106] Initially James helped her keep the estate account books, but within two years, she was fully in charge of both household and estate management, working with her steward to scrupulously track personal, household, and estate income and expenses.[107] Elizabeth, in turn, reciprocated James's assistance by purchasing his rolling carts and having him install his stoves at Wicken Park. She also helped him acquire Northamptonshire timber for use in his workshop.[108] Additionally, she demonstrated the typical Sharp penchant for innovation and improvement. She read broadly about new techniques for improving estates and implemented a variety of changes to make the farms more profitable and the cottages more comfortable.[109] She moved tenants from one-year agreements to longer leases, continued to enclose pasture, gave generously to parish poor relief, sponsored day schools, improved the gardens, roads, and outbuildings, and experimented with new crops. Elizabeth's innovation and her combined efforts with James were long appreciated, as niece Mary's long poem extoling the comforts and virtues of Wicken attests.

> Methinks I see those gates, low sunken, wide
> Which open flew with hospitable haste
> To hale the coming visitor's approach
> Still readier when of some long-absent friend
> The chariot rolling o'er the terrace smooth

---

[104] Amy Louise Erickson, *Women and Property in Early Modern England* (London: Routledge, 2002), 187–203.

[105] Elizabeth Sharp Prowse, memorandum and commonplace book, April 19, July 2, and October 20, 1770; October 3, 1776, 32, 34, 36, 53, typescript, D3549/14/1/2.

[106] Briony A.K. McDonagh, "Women, Enclosure and Estate Improvement in Eighteenth-Century Northamptonshire," *Rural History*, 20, no. 2 (2009): 143–162; "Wicken," in *A History of the County of Northampton*, 413–438.

[107] Elizabeth Sharp Prowse, personal ledger and estate ledger, 1768–71, 1774–79, and 1779–84, 364P/067, 364P/068, and 364P/069, NRO; Elizabeth Sharp Prowse, cash book, 1774–91, 364P/070, NRO; Elizabeth Sharp Prowse, household accounts and recipes, 1783–1814, 364P/071, NRO.

[108] McDonagh, "Women, Enclosure and Estate Improvement," 155; McDonagh, "'All Towards the Improvements of the Estate,'" 268.

[109] Julie Day, "Household Management as a Method of Authority for Three Eighteenth-Century Elite Yorkshire Women," *Women's History Magazine*, no. 66 (Summer 2011): 30–37.

   ...
What happy faces crowded to the door!
What joyful expectations flushed each cheek,
While the pleased menials ran with smiling looks
To aid the guest that brought their mistress joy.[110]

Paralleling her brothers' London homes, Wicken Park became a principal location of Sharp sociability in the South. For nearly fifty years it was a site of long family visits and residence by the sisters and nieces. Niece Mary once waxed poetic for several pages about Wicken's virtues.[111] She described Wicken as a place "consecrate[d] to social happiness," where she and her cousins wiled away winter evenings in needlework, cozily ensconced in the drawing room, "delightful scene / Of man a pleasure, social or alone."[112]

Anglican religious observance was an important element of Wicken life. Elizabeth had a bell installed to call for household-wide daily prayer. Niece Mary later described that daily ritual as something informed by deep devotion and as deeply embedded in the household routine:

Here too at morn and eve with pious mien,
While all her house's inmates high and low
Assembled, knelt in humble awe around,
Would the dear mistress raise her gentle voice.
In meet confession, prayer, and grateful praise
To Him, whose care preserved them night and day.[113]

While Elizabeth did not insist all estate employees be Anglican, she did not tolerate nonconformist evangelizing. She had no qualms about firing a Methodist dairy maid who invited Methodist preachers to visit her at Wicken Park and otherwise spent her time attempting to convince villagers to join her at Methodist meetings.[114]

Wicken was also a site for musical gatherings and a launching spot for canal voyages. In August 1774 the Sharps undertook a two-week canal voyage, first gathering at Wicken, then driving to Braunston, nearly ninety miles west, where they, servants, instruments, food, and accoutrements were transferred to their barges at what would later become the Grand Junction Canal. A local newspaper reported the spectacle of James's rolling carts arriving, accompanied by the brothers on horseback and the sisters ("smart ladies") in chariots. Villagers gathered to

---

[110] Mary Sharp Lloyd Baker, "Wicken," 9, typescript, D6919/2/4.
[111] Mary Sharp Baker, "Wicken," c.1810, typescript, D6919/2/4.
[112] Mary Sharp Lloyd Baker, "Wicken," 4, 7, typescript, D6919/2/4.
[113] Mary Sharp Lloyd Baker, "Wicken," 7, typescript, D6919/2/4.
[114] Elizabeth Sharp Prowse, memorandum and commonplace book, July 29, 1801, 98, typescript, D3549/14/1/2.

120 BEING SINGLE IN GEORGIAN ENGLAND

watch liveried servants carrying instruments and hampers of wine and food onto a barge bedecked with James's arms, mahogany furniture, and silk streamers. As the crowd gathered, James had the band play for them. Not bad, as the author put it, "for an ironmonger."[115]

Wicken was also the site of a spontaneous concert and harvest celebration one evening. On September 26, 1777, the Sharps had gathered for a musical celebration among themselves, but when they heard Wicken laborers were also hosting their own harvest celebration, the Sharps decided to combine the two celebrations. While everyone apparently had a very good time, the laborers' enjoyment of a "harvest home" and the Sharps' description of a "fête champêtre" underscored social hierarchies. The social divisions were replicated in the spontaneous procession that developed: first the liveried servants, then the ladies, then the band (with the brothers playing their instruments and Elizabeth's servants playing the French horns), then the harvest wagon with children on top, and then the adult laborers. Niece Catherine began singing "Harvest Home," and the rest of the group joined in, but when she started dancing, the laborers did not think it appropriate to join her. With much "huzzaing," the tenants, servants, and "the happiest set of peasants in England" continued drinking and celebrating as they dispersed from the house into the twilight.[116]

The Sharps continued to incorporate cousins in their musical and social activities. Their Hosier and Booth cousins joined them for a boat journey on May 13, 1753, and on May 24 a Dering cousin joined them on board.[117] The Sharps were particularly close to their Dering cousins; they included them in humorous letters and had extended visits with them as they had done as children when they shuttled between Durham, York, and Ripon.[118] Undoubtedly the marriage of cousin Mary Dering and John facilitated continuing connections, though it is noteworthy that Dering–Sharp interactions persisted in the South and were not dependent on John and Mary's Northumberland or Durham households. The Dering and Sharp cousins shared numerous long visits, with music an important element of their visits. In the fifty-six years between 1753 and 1809, Elizabeth recorded forty-two separate Dering cousin visits. While there were occasional gaps of more than five years, typically every two or three years, the Sharps and Derings had extended or multiple visits within a year.

Given how little survives of Frances's writing, it is not clear how much she might have participated in the improvement activities at Wicken. Elizabeth's ledgers suggest Frances kept her own accounts and she clearly traveled and visited

---

[115] Crosby, "Private Concerts," 56–57.

[116] Elizabeth Sharp Prowse, memorandum and commonplace book, September 26, 1777, 56, typescript, D3549/14/1/2; Crosby, "Private Concerts," 57–58.

[117] Sharp brothers, boat books, May 13 and 24, 1753, D3549/12/1/1.

[118] Heneage Dering, "Autobiographical Memoranda," in *Yorkshire Diaries and Autobiographies in the Seventeenth and Eighteenth Centuries, Publications of the Surtees Society*, 65 (1877): 346.

independent of Elizabeth. It is possible she engaged in actions like Judith's giving four sheep to Wicken. She was definitely essential to the social and musical gatherings. Like Judith and Granville, Frances's rotation among sibling households meant she was an important component of each household, but not fully responsible or encumbered by household management. Some of these arose merely from the circumstances of earlier deaths and marriages among family members, but it was likely influenced by Judith, Frances, and Granville's life-long singleness as well as their position as the youngest three siblings. Frances, in particular, was only in her early teens when her brothers began establishing households. No one would have expected her to establish her own household or assume housekeeping duties instead of an older sister or sister-in-law. As she aged, she became more directly involved in household management, but by the time she was 20 there were several flourishing, well-governed Sharp households to choose from. There was no need for her to establish her own home or to take on more household leadership.

Granville

Granville's domestic arrangements were unusual among the siblings. Like Frances he never acquired his own household, but unlike Frances he simultaneously maintained residence with his siblings and rented rooms for study and proximity to the Inns at Court. Upon completing his apprenticeship in 1757, he found employment in the Ordnance Office, and by the late 1760s, he was renting a modest home near the Tower, paying £20 in annual rent.[119] When he disagreed with the government's handling of the American colonists' demands, he left his position with the Ordnance Office. In 1764, he became passionate about the abolition of the slave trade and slavery through his involvement with Jonathan Strong's efforts to gain his freedom. From that point forward Granville's interests were in social reform far more than in work as a civil servant. Once he left the Ordnance Office he never had regular employment, with his siblings' support and agreement. Perhaps with more than a measure of confidence of a doted-upon younger sibling, he once wrote that he knew for his siblings: "Everything…concerning me is equally interesting."[120] Supporting this claim, James and William assured Granville that they would financially support him when he left the Ordnance Office in 1777.[121]

Granville maintained private rooms in various locations while principally residing with his siblings. He first lived with William at Old Jewry, then in 1787 he moved to Leadenhall Street when William moved to Fulham, though he rented

[119] Granville Sharp, land tax assessments, 1766–68, St. Mary Stratford-le-Bow, London, London Metropolitan Archives, digital image at *London, England, Land Tax Records, 1692–1932*, https://www.ancestry.co.uk, accessed January 11, 2021.

[120] Granville Sharp to John Sharp, October 31, 1787, D3549/13/1/S8.

[121] Hoare, *Memoirs of Granville Sharp*, 126–127.

an additional room for study near Guildhall and near a house once occupied by James's in-laws.[122] The room was affordable (costing only £5 in annual rent) and gave him, he wrote, the "privilege of walking in a more noble & spacious Gothic Hall & Parlour, as well as in the Garden belonging to the Company; all which are perfectly retired & quiet, & convenient for reading, which is a great satisfaction to me."[123] He also benefited from his siblings' dedication to his studies. When William and Catherine retired to Fulham in 1787, Granville had a study above a cottage that William built on the grounds, and Elizabeth built a library for Granville's books at Wicken.

Maintaining Material and Emotional Needs

As this chronology of Sharp households between the 1750s and the 1780s demonstrates, none was truly independent. People, goods, services, and financial support flowed between the homes, even as locations and marital statuses changed. Subsets of siblings and the group as a whole worked together on a variety of household and material concerns. Their embedded financial connections replicated the mental and emotional labor they performed for one another. And of course, none of the Sharps' labor was possible without the labor of dozens of servants.

The Sharps kept accounts across households and by various siblings who may or may not have lived in that household. The most obvious example was the way Elizabeth and James co-managed different households for large portions of the 1760s. The Leadenhall Street house and manufactory were in James's hands mainly because of Elizabeth's intervention on his behalf. While she recognized that the "kind offer" of the £1000 loan from their Prowse cousins enabled James to buy the property, it was, Elizabeth noted, "through me" (emphasis in original).[124] Granville and John also maintained consistent support of each other's financial accounting. Granville often sought John's advice about his writing and publication plans; he mixed those requests in letters that recounted how he settled John's London accounts or purchased and shipped items for John's household.[125] Granville admitted that he was a "very irregular Accomptant" compared to John's careful bookkeeping, sometimes being unable to specifically account for £15 to £20 a year. He flattered John about John's greater skill—perhaps hoping John

---

[122] Granville Sharp to John Sharp, March 24, 1787, D3549/13/1/S8.

[123] Granville Sharp to John Sharp, March 24, 1787. Like many Londoners, Granville recognized the difficulty of finding space—indoors or outdoors—that allowed for solitude and quiet. See Vickery, "An Englishman's Home Is His Castle?," 158–159.

[124] Elizabeth Sharp Prowse, memorandum and commonplace book, July 21, 1759, 9, typescript, D3549/14/1/2.

[125] Granville Sharp to John Sharp, 1765–92, D3549/13/1/S8.

would offer to manage them for him—but also reminded John that since he was "frequently employed in your Commissions," John would be "very ready to execute" Granville's in return.[126]

Like the partnership of Elizabeth and James and the cooperation of John and Granville, Sharp household arrangements often strengthened or created dyads and triads among the siblings. Many groupings were formed in relation to birth order and gender, but households perpetuated the closeness. The oldest dyad was John and Thomas. Other than the gap of a year or two between when John began school or university and when Thomas did, the brothers shared a residence for more than four decades. Similarly, their closeness in age and geographic proximity in London put William and James in constant contact. They lived in the same house or within easy walking distance of each other for all of James's life, lasting more than sixty years. Granville's presence in London also created a triad with William and James. Elizabeth and James formed a dyad when they shared a household together and when James helped Elizabeth establish herself as mistress of Wicken. The sisters' closeness in age made a natural triad of them, especially while Judith lived in London with Elizabeth and Frances. Once Judith established a home in Durham, Elizabeth and Frances formed a subset dyad since Frances principally resided at Wicken. After James died, Granville's partnership with James's widow, Catherine, made another relational dyad. Other examples could be given, but this list is sufficient to highlight how shared household responsibilities brought the entire family together and created additional bonds among smaller groups of the siblings.

Beyond household expenses, the siblings completed errands, exchanged remedies and recipes, bought lottery tickets and group gifts, read each other's writing and made suggestions for its improvement, purchased lace and fabric, executed wills, participated in marriage settlements, paid bills and took receipt of payments, purchased and read books on topics interesting to a sibling, and in many ways acted as banking services for each other, keeping accounts of money received from and expended for each other.[127] In fact, in 1779, John suggested they set up a banking fund between them that would further facilitate the financial and household transactions they undertook on one another's behalf.[128] Their labor was constant; it was the warp and woof of households, threads of letters and gifts and money that tied together households and relationships.

In addition to financial and accounting embeddedness, the Sharp households and boats were overflowing with objects that underscored their family identity

---

[126] Granville Sharp to John Sharp, January 3, 1766, D3549/13/1/S8.

[127] Thomas Sharp to John Sharp, February 2, 1761, D3549/9/1/4; James Sharp to John Sharp, November 30, 1768, D3549/9/1/4; William Sharp, recipes and notes on wine-making, c.1762–c.1813, D3549/10/1/2; Granville Sharp to John Sharp, December 14, 1784, D3549/13/1/S8; Elizabeth Prowse, estate and personal ledger, May 5, 1768, 364P/067, NRO.

[128] Granville Sharp to John Sharp, May 1779, NRO 0452/C/3/2/18/24, NAW.

124   BEING SINGLE IN GEORGIAN ENGLAND

and connections. As with Judith's sketches of Hartburn, the siblings sought family members' input on landscaping, architecture, and interior design. Anyone not immediately and energetically engaging in such activities might experience pressure from other siblings to share his or her opinion on their projects. In 1767, Judith, John, and James, for example, had lengthy conversations about paving stones meant for Bamburgh, but these stones were to be acquired by James and shipped from the South. Thomas was caught up in the endeavor because his siblings "talked so much & set so hard at me," and pestered him so long that, he told John, "there will not be Peace" until he gave an immediate and full report of the stone's availability, condition, and requirements.[129] Everyone was equally involved in providing materials for one another's domestic, professional, and artistic pursuits. Granville's commonplace books had recipes for paint and ink, including one for "colouring plans," as well as recipes from Judith and from the Fulham House recipe book kept by William and his wife.[130]

Sharp homes were full of reminders of their connections to each other. Thomas once insisted John have a good portrait painted of himself so that Thomas could have a way to remember John in his absence. A catalog of the paintings in Fulham House and Clare Hall offers a glimpse of how much Sharp interior decoration was designed or produced by a member of the family or depicted a member of the family.[131] Paintings and chalk drawings by Judith were accompanied by artwork from nieces Mary and Catherine's childhood drawings and augmented with work by cousins. Judith's sketch of John and paintings or miniatures of Granville, William, cousins, grandfathers, and in-laws brought family members to mind regularly. Their childhood home in Rothbury and John's Hartburn home were drawn or painted by both Granville and Judith. Shared family events were also memorialized: Granville's drawing of a "glee evening," framed family arms, and paintings of the *Union* and the *Apollo* adorned additional walls. Family values and interests were underscored by portraits of clergymen and composers. While there were paintings of London or country scenes and a Gainsborough, the bulk of the 129 pictures depicted family members or were created by them.

As important as artwork was to creating and perpetuating Sharp family cohesion, most central to Sharp material culture and family identity was the possession and sharing of books and music.[132] Some books, like Thomas's red-leather, gilded display copy of the *Book of Common Prayer* or books inherited from their grandparents, were meant as decorative items signaling the family's values or virtues.[133] Other books and scores fulfilled the same purpose but were also

---

[129] Thomas Sharp to John Sharp, April 7, 1767, NRO 00452/C/3/2/4/9, NAW.

[130] Granville Sharp, commonplace books, 14, 94, D3549/13/4/1.

[131] Catalogue of Fulham House pictures, early nineteenth century, D3549/23/1/30.

[132] Abigail Williams, *The Social Life of Books: Reading Together in the Eighteenth-Century Home* (New Haven: Yale University Press, 2017), 36–63.

[133] *The Book of Common Prayer* (1758), owned by Thomas Sharp (1771), Bamburgh Q.2/42, PGL.

intended for practical use. Constant musical practice and performance required the siblings consistently maintain their instruments and purchase music. Amid other occupational and household details, their letters reveal the labor involved in their musical activities. James purchased strings for John's double bass and had them shipped to Newcastle; Judith reported on her sisters' progress in musical ability; Granville purchased cathedral music for John; and the nieces' musical training was carefully observed.[134] Dozens of musical manuscripts and books survive from the Sharp collections. They show a fondness for Handel, but there were also works by William Boyce and other prominent composers, as well as pieces of their own composition.[135] It is also clear the musical scores circulated among the siblings. Some manuscripts and scores were passed from sibling to sibling, each writing his or her name when the piece came to his or her possession; other scores were jointly owned. This practice started in their childhood, and the scores were reused and carefully preserved. One piece, "The Cuckoo Concerto," was signed by Thomas, Charles, and James in 1741, when they were aged 16, 13, and 10 , respectively. Eventually the piece was collected with other music John kept with him at Cambridge.[136]

Financial and material concerns could not be separated from emotional support. The exchange between Granville and John about account-keeping demonstrates the careful emotional work that buttressed the financial details. The younger brother's partial apology for not being as skilled as his older brother, the gentle reminder that he was occupied with his own concerns while also performing tasks for his brother, the expression of implicit trust that Granville's somewhat laissez-faire bookkeeping and John's assiduous checking of accounts were honest and based in a shared desire to help one another. It might also reflect birth order's impact on their relationship: John, the eldest and dutiful one, Granville the younger and protected one. Additionally, John might have had their father's tendency to spend more on charitable activities than his household budget could sustain and Granville's help with accounts might have served as a gentle additional check. Advice literature enjoined that "generosity wrong placed becometh a vice," and it is possible that their father's generosity, almost to a fault, made some of them cautious.[137] Mary once remarked that earlier in their marriage, when she and John's "circumstances were rather strait," she begrudged his spending money

---

[134] James Sharp to John Sharp, February 10, 1769, D3549/9/1/4; Thomas Sharp to Judith Sharp, April 10, 1761, D3549/16/1/1; Granville Sharp to John Sharp, March 2, 1769, COLL 1891/3/24, YMA; Judith Sharp to John Sharp, October 22, 1776, NRO 00452/C/3/2/6/43, NAW.

[135] Crosby, *Catalogue of Durham Cathedral Music*, xxii.

[136] John Frederick Lampe, "The Cuckoo Concert," in John Sharp's music collection, Music MS 185, 81, Durham Cathedral Library.

[137] Thomas Fuller, *Introductio ad Prudentiam: Or, Directions, Counsels, and Cautions, Tending to Prudent Management of Affairs in Common Life* (London: Stephen Austen, 1727), 122. The advice was published in various forms and under various authors and publishers throughout the eighteenth century.

126   BEING SINGLE IN GEORGIAN ENGLAND

on improving Bamburgh Castle. After she explained to him that he had to "limit his expences to a yearly sum," Mary's concerns lessened.

The Sharps thought they were remarkable for always getting along, but what really made them remarkable was a consistent willingness to do the emotional labor to understand one another and to work through disappointments and conflict. The most obvious case of conflict among the siblings (described in Chapter 3) was the lead up to Thomas's marriage and Judith's labor as go-between about the matter. In addition, jokes Thomas made about sending a common letter late as a way of apologizing for minor infractions or Granville's continued questioning for clarification from John when something John said about elections seemed a paradox to Granville, show how attuned the siblings were to potential emotional reverberations from seemingly simple or pragmatic interactions.[138] Surviving letters also expose a tendency to reassure one another they were always willing to change behavior or ideas that might cause discord among them.

Such effort to prevent even the smallest misunderstanding or conflict did not mean the siblings avoided discussing contrary opinions. Thomas was always concerned that John knew how much he supported and respected him. However, those feelings did not prevent him from differing with John's perspective on Church doctrines, nor from expressing those thoughts at length. Thomas once wrote John about the practice of fasting, telling him he had wrestled with the topic from "all sides and comparing it with scripture & reason." He concluded that they do not "observe a Fast with any Degree of Propriety," seemingly disagreeing with an assertion John, and their father, had previously made. Thomas concluded with apologies for the length of the letter, written over many days, but asserted doing so was "only in compliance with yr desire, to tell you my reall Thoughts of the Matter." The apology was clearly meant to soften the blow of Thomas's refusal to "assent even to my Dear Father's opinion, till I thought I c[oul]d find some Grounds to go upon."[139]

In addition to careful management of emotional connections, managing members' physical health was an important part of household life. The siblings, like their contemporaries, regularly reported on each other's health to absent relatives and they regularly tended and nursed ailing family members. For example, during Elizabeth's absence from Wicken, she spent the majority of three weeks in London caring for her mother-in-law/cousin, who was confined with a leg complaint. Elizabeth was with her every day "by 10 in the morning" and did not leave until 10 in the evening while William, daily attended her.[140] Letters are full of queries about and reports on family members' health. If one's illness appeared potentially

---

[138] Granville Sharp to John Sharp, October 13, 1767, COLL 1891/3/15, YMA.

[139] Thomas Sharp to John Sharp, November 23, 1761, NRO 00452/C/3/2/2, NAW.

[140] Elizabeth Sharp Prowse, memorandum and commonplace book, February 23 and 26, 1776, 52, typescript, D3549/14/1/2.

fatal, letters between the siblings combined reports on the treatments and status in the middle of reports on the person's household and financial health. In this way, the letter writer assured the rest of the family that he or she had sufficient resources, and sufficient knowledge of those resources, to care for any remaining family members, debts, and medical expenses should the person pass away. Being so entwined in one another's financial and household affairs meant that incapacity or death of a sibling was not compounded by the stress of caring for a household one had no familiarity with. Also, because the household, financial, and emotional labor was distributed across the siblings, they were able to deploy family members if several siblings were ill or suffering at the same time but in different locations. For example, in October 1786, when Judith had an operation and William had difficulty with his eyes, the remaining sisters and brothers dispersed to their households to care for both ailing siblings.[141]

Servants

The Sharps' intertwined households and social calendars were impossible to maintain without the labor of paid servants. The Sharps were assiduous household managers and took great pride in being such—writing recipes, keeping accounts, paying for supplies or doctors, holding household prayer—but by the 1770s the days when William scoured his own pewter were long gone. With the Sharps' busy visiting calendar, it was impossible to maintain a household and its attendant agricultural or manufacturing labor without dedicated and skilled housekeepers, stewards, maids, nurses, tutors, butlers, and foremen, as well as temporary laborers hired for harvest and for construction or manufacturing projects. For example, when Elizabeth had rooms at Wicken Park painted in February 1776, she did not preside over the project. After several months' absence, she returned to the painting completed, purposely in preparation for her return. She would have known about the painting, determined its need and arranged payment, but it was her steward and servants who remained onsite to cover or move the furniture, manage disruptions in household routines, and resolve any unexpected problems or delays.

In addition, the clergymen brothers had multiple parish livings and relied on curates and clerks to manage day-to-day business and to provide pastoral care in the Sharps' absences. Thomas, for example, once excused himself for remaining in London instead of joining John in the North because his parishioners did occasionally like to see their vicar, especially at Easter.[142] He also once complained

---

[141] Elizabeth Sharp Prowse, memorandum and commonplace book, October 1786, 513, typescript, D3549/14/1/2.

[142] Thomas Sharp to John Sharp, June 30, 1772, NRO 00452/C/3/2/3/37, NAW.

128   BEING SINGLE IN GEORGIAN ENGLAND

to Judith about the need to compete with other clergy in order to maintain his positions. "I am under a cruel necessity," he wrote, "of all this Trouble & a great Expence...& am besides steward for the sons of the Clergy in this Part, have a Curate to provide &c."[143] Though Thomas complained to John and Judith, it was servants and clerks who maintained the day-to-day operations during his long absences.

In most respects the Sharps were generous, but not entirely atypical eighteenth-century employers, despite the hagiographic accounts of how they treated servants. They paid competitive wages, covered food and travel expenses, and improved housing conditions.[144] A book of servants' wages kept by niece Catherine in the early nineteenth century shows annual wages ranging from £4–£5 to £12 12s.[145] The higher range was roughly the equivalent of a skilled tradesman's income for three or four months' labor. Beyond wages, Sharp householders, especially Elizabeth, were regularly involved with their servants' familial and domestic arrangements. Elizabeth's account of her long-time coachman's departure from her employ in 1784 illustrates the intertwined relationship of householder and servant, beyond payment for labor. That May, Elizabeth was disappointed to discover her coachman of twenty years, Thomas Walton, was "detected in making money in what he had no right to do." On May 21 he drove her to London, and on May 24, she recorded that he "left me suddenly, his wife has dead, but he left 7 children at Wicken and left a 20£ in my hands in part for their maintenance." With that £20 and her own resources, Elizabeth "got them all out in time to do for themselves" with "some satisfaction to my self." The only boy, age 12, was eventually apprenticed to a nearby shoemaker, and the older girls, all in their later teens, were placed presumably in domestic service. What Elizabeth arranged for the youngest girl, 6-year-old Susanna, is not known.[146]

While servants' figurative fingerprints are all over the Sharps' domestic and social arrangements, their names and personalities are not always visible. In an elegy, niece Mary wrote about Wicken, servants were mentioned many times, but often only in terms of expressing Elizabeth's noble treatment of them: "She rul'd her happy village" in such a way that the local peasants adored her, "even babes

---

[143] Thomas Sharp to Judith Sharp, April 10, 1761, D3549/16/1/1.

[144] Elizabeth Sharp Prowse, personal ledger and estate ledger, 1768–71, 364P/067, NRO; Jacob F. Field, "Domestic Service, Gender, and Wages in Rural England, c.1700–1860," *Economic History Review*, 66, no. 1 (February 2013): 249–272.

[145] Catherine Sharp, servants' wages book, 1807–11, D3549/17/2/1.

[146] Church of England, Wicken, Northamptonshire parish registers, Walton children's baptisms, 1766–79, 364P/3, NRO, digital images at "Northamptonshire, England, Church of England Baptisms, Marriages and Burials, 1732–1812," https://www.ancestry.co.uk, accessed March 5, 2021; Elizabeth Sharp Prowse, personal ledger and estate ledger, 1779–84, 364P/069, NRO; John Tidman, apprenticeship indenture tax for Thomas Walton, September 5, 1786, *Board of Stamps: Apprenticeship Books*, IR1, piece 33, TNA, digital image at *UK Register for Duties Paid for Apprentices' Indentures, 1710–1811*, https://www.ancestry.co.uk, accessed March 5, 2021.

LIVING SINGLE   129

looked up with reverential awe."[147] Elizabeth's account and memorandum books offer a less hagiographic account, showing how she and her steward, Joseph Foxley, worked with common purpose and dedication. In one way the Sharps were very unusual employers: they required or facilitated musical training in select servants. William and James hired butlers with musical abilities so they might augment the orchestra at Sharp musical gatherings and water schemes. Similarly, Elizabeth paid for two servants to be taught how to play the horn.

Like their contemporaries, the Sharps also left bequests to long-term retainers and servants. Personal maids, butlers, and stewards often received £30–£50 in addition to any wages due to them. Other servants were left £5–£10, wages due, and perhaps a request that executors and family members provide recommendations for the servants seeking new employment. Given that similar amounts were delineated in multiple wills between the 1790s and the 1830s, they were likely in line with the "proper" amounts the genteel classes were expected to leave to servants. Slightly more generous was John's bequest of six-months' wages, in addition to wages already due to all the servants. Some wills also attempted to incentivize or express gratitude for others' servants. Judith left £20 to Jemima's maid and butler and £7 to three additional servants of Jemima; Catherine (James's widow) left £100 to her daughter and son-in-law's servant.

Sibling Support in Illness, Death, and Retirement, 1783–87

In the spring of 1783, Frances fell ill while staying with William and Catherine in Fulham. The sickness was alarming enough that they determined she needed to travel to Bristol and "strongly requested" that Elizabeth go with her. Elizabeth rushed to Fulham to fetch Frances and they arrived in Bristol on June 2. As Frances recovered, they visited with William and his family at Bath. Elizabeth recorded that Frances was "quite recovered" by early July.[148] The sisters returned to Wicken July 10 and learned that James had become suddenly and seriously ill from a "Paralytic Disorder." Over the coming months, the siblings tried various locations to improve James's health. He and his family spent a month at Wicken, then in September they traveled to Weymouth for the waters, then on to various Devon and Dorset towns before returning to Weymouth in mid-October. Judith, William, and his family had initially been in the group but had returned to Fulham in early October. Granville traveled between Wicken, Fulham, and

[147] Mary Sharp Lloyd Baker, "Wicken," 2.
[148] Elizabeth Sharp Prowse, memorandum and commonplace book, May 15–November 5, 1783, 66–67, typescript, D3549/14/1/2. This account of James's decline is drawn from Elizabeth's account, Granville's extracted diaries, and letters Granville wrote John. Catherine Sharp (niece), annotations of Granville Sharp's diaries, August 22–November 12, 1783, book 2, 8–15, D3549/13/4/2; Granville Sharp to John Sharp, November 3 and 6, 1783, D3549/9/1/4.

130   BEING SINGLE IN GEORGIAN ENGLAND

Leadenhall Street as needed. James began contemplating that this might be his last illness, for at the end of August he sent Granville to his house with keys to the safe, and in early September he gave Granville his personal ledger and account book. As James continued to decline throughout October, the siblings determined they should return to London "by slow journeys," which James "seemed more particularly to desire." Near the end of October Elizabeth "despaired the getting him home." Meanwhile, in London, Granville and James's brother-in-law were reviewing James's business accounts to assess what would happen to his widow and their daughter should James pass.

On October 31 William and Granville set out to meet James and the others and assist in getting James back to Leadenhall Street. James was so weak and ill it was a struggle to get him in and out of carriages, a difficulty further exacerbated by an "accident of vicious Horse," which further delayed their journey. They had to move James to another chaise. The entire group was "in the most horrible dilemma that can be conceived" as they struggled to help James, "my poor Brother being then a Dying Man!" Granville wrote. They finally arrived at five in the evening on November 2, with James "in extremis." Granville carefully lifted him out of the carriage and "carried him myself into his own Home." The struggle to get James home before he died was followed by two days of James growing "weaker and weaker," requiring around-the-clock care. His wife Catherine and the sisters took turns, two at a time, "continually with him with unremitted attention." On the third day, Granville wrote John of the sad news: "Human care I fear will be in vain for there seems to be no hopes of his life at present. I can only say that he is still alive."

Granville had previously written John for a loan for the Leadenhall enterprise because several merchants owed James substantial sums but were unable to pay them. In his November 3 letter, Granville noted that the "most part" of his and the southern siblings' fortunes were intertwined with James's. Much of the letter is about making financial arrangements "at this scarce time for money," a topic that seems out of place given James's condition. However, there is a sense that Granville took comfort from managing financial details, not only for James's household but for the siblings' shared fortunes. A sense that when the inevitable happened, they would grieve the loss of their brother while simultaneously being comforted that their shared households would continue, that they would not also have to grieve the loss of place. On November 4 neither Elizabeth nor Granville wrote in their diaries and no one wrote a letter to John. In that textual silence, the gathered siblings watched over James and Catherine and contemplated the inevitable loss.

At about three in the morning on November 5, a fire broke out in Aldersgate Street. Alarmed that it was a neighboring house on fire, Granville rushed into the street to determine whether they would have to move "my poor dying Brother," he wrote John. He told John that it was the "greatest relief of oppression I felt in

LIVING SINGLE 131

my life, when I ran into the Street, & found that the fire was at some distance." Granville returned to James's room. He, Catherine, and Judith convinced Elizabeth and Frances to take a rest, and the remaining three stayed with James as he, "patient... & resigned... died without any apparent sign of pain, no convulsions, or even the least struggle." To Judith fell the task of writing John and Mary about what Elizabeth described as "very great greef, from so great a loss." A week later Granville acted as chief mourner as James was buried in the vault at St. Mary Ax beside his son, Jack.

After the staggering loss of James, the first sibling or sibling-in-law death in over a decade, the family eventually returned to their routine visits. In 1785 they determined to take what would become their last long family journey together. In July the southern siblings first gathered at Wicken and Southwell (where they had spent some of their childhood) and then moved north to visit with cousins and friends, eventually arriving in Durham. Between Durham, Hartburn, and Bamburgh, they spent nearly a month with John, Mary, and Jemima. "We were then 9 Bro[the]rs & Sis[te]rs & 3 Nieces, our No 12," Elizabeth wrote.[149] While in Northumberland the twelve Sharps climbed to the top of Breseley Tower "to see the Becaon made at the Manufactory of James Sharp... in 1781." Niece Catherine carefully also added up the number of Sharps (twelve), emphasizing their small group, the group most touched by the loss of James, and the one most likely to find meaning in remembering him via viewing the product of his work.[150]

The southern group journeyed on to the Lake District and into Scotland before returning to Wicken in early September. Like their 1770s canal journeys, the Sharps made quite a spectacle, traveling in three of their own carriages, each carriage assigned a driver and an outrider. While they dined with friends and cousins and enjoyed large public concerts along the way, all accounts of the journey emphasized their sibling–niece-based circle. Niece Catherine's mathematics and Elizabeth's note of "our No 12" included the sisters-in-law, despite the two Catherines not joining in singing a catch during one evening's visit with friends. Even after decades of marriage and closeness with their in-laws, their lack of musical ability perpetuated the slightest distinction between those born Sharp, including the nieces, and those who were not. The itinerary also underscored the siblings' shared childhood connections. In addition to Southwell, they visited Bradford but were "much disappointed" when the current occupant of their grandfather Sharp's childhood home would not allow them to tour it. They also

---

[149] Elizabeth, Frances, and Granville kept diary accounts of the journey, and William and Granville wrote letters to John about the portion of the trip John and his family did not join. Elizabeth Sharp Prowse, memorandum and commonplace book, June 17–September 3, 1785, 69–71, typescript, D3549/14/1/2; Frances Sharp, travel diary, 1785, D3549/15/1/1; Catherine Sharp (niece), annotations of Granville Sharp's diaries, July 1–August 31, 1785, book 2, 21–32, D3549/13/4/2; Granville Sharp to John Sharp, August 30, 1785, D3549/13/1/S8; William Sharp to John Sharp, September 12, 1785, D3549/9/1/4.

[150] Catherine Sharp, note on 1785 family outing, D3549/17/5/2.

132 BEING SINGLE IN GEORGIAN ENGLAND

dined with the archbishop of York at Bishopthorpe; as Frances wrote, it was "very agreeable" to the Sharps to see the place where their grandfather lived and their father was born. And they were happy to visit Rothbury, their "native home."[151]

Despite the small distinction between original and in-law Sharps and despite John's health precluding him from joining them in the Lake District, unlike the sorrowful journeys of late summer and fall 1783, the extended 1785 experience was a "a most delightful happy journey." As the party broke up—first, John, Mary, and Jemima remained behind in Northumberland, and later, Granville left the returning group before they arrived at Wicken—they expressed the difficulty of doing so. It is easy to interpret those partings were felt more keenly in the shadow of James's death and in the recognition that age and circumstances would probably prevent any such lengthy family journeys in the future. "The pleasure of happy meetings of Relations and friends," Granville wrote John, "must generally be attend with the disagreeable alloy of parting." Even Granville, who enjoyed his solitude, found being alone in London "very dull, after spending so much time in a large & most agreeable society."[152]

By September the southern siblings had traveled nearly 1300 miles and visited one Welsh, seven Scottish, and twenty-three English counties. It is striking the journey took them to every home they lived in as children and included long stays in each home they currently occupied. It is hard to imagine a clearer manifestation of the way shared domestic experiences connected their childhood, youth, and now encroaching old age.

William's purchase of a country house in Fulham in 1783 was the first step toward retirement for the Sharps. Retirement was not one event but a gradual reduction in the size of their households and public endeavors. After James's death his widow Catherine continued to run the business and reside at the Leadenhall Street house, and it continued to be a site of Sharp gatherings. In 1787 Granville joined her there, helping to manage the household and the business. By 1787 William's declining eyesight made him retire from seeing patients, so he, Catherine, and their daughter, 17-year-old Mary, sold the Old Jewry home and moved to Fulham full-time. In 1792 widow Catherine, assisted by Granville, sold the manufactory and "extensive Premises" on Leadenhall Street to the East India Company.[153] They also auctioned off many of the furnishings, including a harpsichord and a chamber organ.[154] Catherine and her daughter moved first to a home on Charlotte Street and then retired to Clare Hall in South Mimms, a country house she shared with her daughter and her recently widowed sister, who was

---

[151] Frances Sharp, travel diary, 1785.

[152] Catherine Sharp (niece), annotations of Granville Sharp's diaries, July 1–August 31, 1785.

[153] Note by Catherine Sharp (daughter of Catherine and James) in her extractions of Granville's diary. Catherine Sharp (niece), annotations of Granville Sharp's diaries, February 14, 1792, book 2, 71, D3549/13/4/2.

[154] Catalogue and Sale of Leadenhall House, February 29–March 2 1792, D3549/12/2/9.

also William's sister-in-law. Granville took rooms at 1 Garden Court, Middle Temple, in addition to his accommodations at Elizabeth's and William's, and Frances moved permanently to Wicken. While visits and musical gatherings continued after 1787, they did so in reconfigured household constellations.

In some ways the Sharps' domestic arrangements could look more like those of early industrial and trade families of the era who made their money from business and, after the death of initial founders of a business, maintained the business as their principal means of income, instead of living on interest from investments.[155] However, the Sharp social connections to land-owning families set them apart from most business families and created a retirement life much more like gentry lifestyles. Retirement from business did not mean, however, retirement from social and musical gatherings. Before he moved there, William had leased a docking space at Fulham for a "pleasure barge."[156] William made many changes and built Egmont Villa, where Granville had his study and later where Mary lived after her marriage.[157] Fulham's size meant that while the large parties of Old Jewry were no longer possible, William's household was hardly diminished or isolated. Before the Sharps took up residence, Fulham House, as it was called, had "stabling for eight horses and rooms over them for servants with two coach houses, a very good wash house, brew house and laundry, two very good gardens, one a pleasure garden, the other a kitchen garden, both planted and stocked with the best fruit, likewise and exceedingly fine shady elm walk nearly a quarter of a mile in length."[158]

Conclusion

Beginning with the Sharps' perspective as unmarried adults reveals the domestic, financial, material, and emotional labor of unmarried family members working

---

[155] Barker, *Family and Business During the Industrial Revolution*, 16–47, 102–103.

[156] William Sharp, lease of piece of ground for docking a sailing ship, 1784, D3549/10/1/7. James also leased barge houses at Lambeth. The Stationers' Company, counterpart lease of a piece of ground and bargehouse at Stonegate, Lambeth, July 7, 1778, TSC/1/G/08/Bargehouses/01, TNA, digital image at Adam Matthew, *Literary Print Culture: The Stationers' Company Archive*, accessed September 8, 2022.

[157] Charles James Fèret, *Fulham Old and New: Being An Exhaustive History of the Ancient Parish of Fulham* (London: Leadenhall Press, 1900), 1:111–112, 3:220–221; Barbara Denny, *Fulham Past* (London: Historical Publications, 1997), 84. Fèret states that William built Egmont Cottage in 1780, but William's tax assessments and Sharp family letters show he remained at Old Jewry until 1787. William Sharp, land tax assessment, 1771, St. Mildred Poultry precinct, London, London Metropolitan Archives, digital image at *London, England, Land Tax Records, 1692–1932*, image 7 of 48, https://www.ancestry.co.uk, accessed January 11, 2021; William Sharp, land tax assessment, 1786, Old Jewry, London, London Metropolitan Archives, digital image at *London, England, Land Tax Records, 1692–1932*, image 35 of 40, https://www.ancestry.co.uk, accessed January 11, 2021; William Sharp, land tax assessment, 1787, Fulham, Middlesex, London Metropolitan Archives, digital image at *London, England, Land Tax Records, 1692–1932*, image 2 of 24, https://www.ancestry.co.uk, accessed January 11, 2021.

[158] Denny, *Fulham Past*, 84.

134 BEING SINGLE IN GEORGIAN ENGLAND

in concert with married kin. Their parents saw the common letters as a symbolic representation of brotherly care for younger sisters. This common gendered expectation was fulfilled in the years immediately following their parents' deaths, as the sisters moved south and joined their brothers' households. However, as the years passed and domestic arrangements no longer reflected female dependency, that aspect of their parents' hopes faded in importance. In its stead was something longer lasting: the practice of and trust in shared domestic and social arrangements among all siblings.

The Sharps built their foundation for domestic governance when most of the siblings were unmarried, thus exposing a layer of household management that is sometimes obscured when married men (or widowed women) are the focus of analysis.[159] Household governance was an important indicator of socially acceptable adult status across the social spectrum. However, the Sharps had completely, pardon the pun, uncoupled the idea of householding from marriage.[160] Many of their households superficially reflected eighteenth-century expectations because they were male headed and the hierarchies of householder and servant or tenant remained unchallenged. But the sibling interactions around household management were shaped more by unity and collaboration than by hierarchy and deference. Marriage was not the origin of Sharp household formation and governance; it was an aspect added later, sometimes over a decade later, to an existing household and socializing patterns based on sibling ties.

While the puns, the boats, and the concerts were particular to the Sharps, the incorporation of single and married family members into shared households, shared finances, and shared social support was present in many families.[161] The Sharps were particularly good at providing domestic stability coupled with social and emotional abundance to both married and unmarried family members. The shared domestic economy was spread between siblings and was established before spouses were added. Things described as husbandly or wifely in household manuals were performed by Sharp siblings.[162] With or without spouses, the siblings provided a broad network of social and financial credit. Siblings as household partners might have also diminished, or at least diffused, the hierarchal tensions sometimes associated with household management.[163] Even as the siblings rotated between

---

[159] Henry French and Mark Rothery, *Man's Estate: Landed Gentry Masculinities, 1660–1900* (Oxford: Oxford University Press, 2012); Karen Harvey, "Men Making Home in Eighteenth-Century Britain," *Gender and History*, 21, no. 3 (2009): 520–540.

[160] Vickery, *Behind Closed Doors*, 3–24.

[161] Naomi Tadmor, *Family and Friends*, 176–182; Amy Froide, "Learning to Invest: Women's Education in Arithmetic and Accounting in Early Modern England," *Early Modern Women: An Interdisciplinary Journal*, 10, no. 1 (Fall 2015): 11–14; Amy Harris, "The Longest Relationship: Analyzing Sibling Co-Residence," in Rosemary O'Day and Susan Cogan, eds., *Sibling Relationships in Early Modern England*, forthcoming.

[162] Harvey, *Little Republic*, 30.

[163] Harvey, *Little Republic*, 34, 115; Amy Harris, "'That Fierce Edge': Sibling Conflict and Politics in Georgian England," *Journal of Family History*, 37, no. 2 (April 2012): 155–174.

homes, they were not guests; they were essential components and participants in each household. Undoubtedly, the Sharps' financial good fortune prevented some conflicts that debt and financial setbacks caused in other households.[164] The Sharps' success, however, was not solely due to financial abundance. Their domestic achievements highlight that harmonious household durability was possible when both single and married members saw themselves as participating in the same collective enterprise, one where the distinctions between independent homeowner and dependent kin nearly disappeared.

From William starting a household in 1750 and throughout the eighteenth century, the Sharps created and sustained shared households that were not delineated along hierarchies of marital status and dependence. Except for John, the Sharps built the foundation for domestic and social abundance while they were unmarried. Marriage may have augmented James and William's social networks in London, but it did not alter their fundamental approach to domestic and social arrangements. Additionally, their abundance continued to require the cooperation of widowed Elizabeth and the other unmarried siblings. And while marriage had provided Elizabeth with a large estate to manage, that management was done without a spouse.

By the late 1760s the Sharps had reached a peak of social and familial success. Though the griefs of 1770–72 diminished the luster of their family gatherings, by the late 1770s they were clearly still enjoying a golden era. They were also increasingly prominent in London social circles—a fact they recognized and which was perfectly captured in the family portrait commission in 1779 (see Plate 1). In a way, their unified sibling households became a self-perpetuating story of domestic success as their public profiles, large parties, philanthropy, and social connections all blossomed. Outside observers often ascribed the Sharps' success to their familial cohesion. From intimate family musical evenings to large "glee evenings" with more than three hundred guests, the siblings built a most enviable family culture.

Their household efforts were not discrete: the siblings, in-laws, and nieces all shared in communal family labors.[165] The sisters-in-law did not seem to have been as musically inclined as the Sharps, but they fully participated in travel and social arrangements.[166] All siblings did domestic favors for each other. Judith, for example, sketched the Hartburn house elevation and improvements as John made

---

[164] Grassby, *Kinship and Capitalism*, 297–300.

[165] Such kin-keeping activities were often shared by elite men and women in the eighteenth century, unlike their Victorian counterparts, for whom such work became feminized. See Dallett Hemphill, *Siblings: Brothers and Sisters in American History* (Oxford: Oxford University Press, 2014).

[166] Others have argued that Catherine Barwick and Catherine Lodge, William's and James's wives, did not enjoy musical gatherings, were "driven to distraction by the brothers' music-making," or had "secret despair" because of the fortnightly Sunday concerts. While it is quite clear the two sisters-in-law did not share in the Sharps' musical talents, I have seen no evidence of a general dislike of Sharp musical performances on their part. See Crosby, "Private Concerts," 38, 62; Edward Lascelles, *Granville Sharp and the Freedom of the Slaves in England* (New York: Negro Universities Press, 1928), 119.

changes to his home (lower image, Plate 5).[167] Similar small acts that linked married and unmarried Sharps in one another's households and family maintenance were repeated in a variety of activities. The Sharps wrote and performed music together, pitched in to purchase lottery tickets, managed each other's accounts, and, as the family portrait immortalized, spent their summers sailing the Thames, enjoying good food, company, and music.[168] They also traveled to care for one another when ill and sat by the bedside of dying siblings.

Households and boats were the physical spaces where the Sharps grounded their domestic and social abundance; religious practice and belief permeated daily routines; books, music, and letters moved between the households, figuratively tying people and places together. The Sharps established their own overflowing, even enviable, festivities. Beyond their family circle, the Sharps were well connected to literary, philanthropic, musical, medical, industrial, and ecclesiastical worlds, but those worlds did not constitute the center of their sociality. The Sharps drew people into their circle by creating their own influential network where they set the rules of engagement and patronage. The importance of those connections was always secondary to the social capital they created for themselves on board the barges or in their homes.

[167] Judith Sharp, house plans sketches for Hartburn, Northumberland, D3549/8/1/6.
[168] Elizabeth Sharp Prowse, memorandum and commonplace book, August 5 and 8, 1770, D3549/14/1/1.

Interlude 3
Portrait

Johan Zoffany's *The Sharp Family* (1779–81) (see Plate 1) depicts the Sharp siblings, sisters-in-law, and nieces as well as the boat master, the cabin boy, Zoffany's dog, a kitten, a variety of musical instruments and a boat book or book of music. The family gathers on board the *Apollo*, depicted anchored between Fulham and Putney on the Thames, with Fulham House and the yacht, *Union*, in the background. At the top of the painting William waves his hat in front of a fluttering flag—a flag bearing "the arms of Mr. & Mrs. Wm Sharp – & of Mr. and Mrs. James Sharp in separate Shields, tyed together with a Blue Riband Held by a Spread Eagle – The Work of Mrs. Judith Sharp, in Patchwork and Embroidery."[1]

The portrait is a beautiful example of an eighteenth-century conversation piece, the popular art form depicting intimate and casual gatherings of families and friends.[2] Zoffany was known for crafting such pieces and the movement and color typical of his work made an excellent choice in capturing Sharp family sociality.[3] Commissioned by William, the portrait, completed in stages between late 1779 and early 1781, memorialized Sharp musical ability and sociability. It also neatly captured the importance of unmarried and childless kin to the family culture.

Below and to the right of William, in a diagonal, sits his wife Catherine with their daughter Mary on her lap. William and Catherine are dressed in the Windsor uniform, underscoring William's connection to the royal family as a sometimes physician to the king. Catherine holds the hand of James' wife (also Catherine) on the left. To the right of William is Judith strumming her angélique (a type of lute with two peg boxes) and Jemima, John's daughter, standing between William and Judith. Along the bottom of the painting (from left to right) sits James (to the right of the cabin boy and boat master), his daughter Catherine, then Granville and Elizabeth facing one another over a pianoforte, Granville holding his double flageolet in the hand reaching behind niece Catherine. The bottom right of the painting is occupied by youngest sister Frances, eldest brother John, and his wife (and first cousin) Mary. James holds his instrument, a serpent, and at

---

[1] Catherine, the niece, provided the information about the flag on a paper attached to the back of the portrait (removed in 1837). According to Catherine, the family paid four hundred guineas for the portrait. See papers about musical activities and the portrait in D3549/12/1/2.

[2] Kate Retford, *The Conversation Piece: Making Modern Art in Eighteenth-Century Britain* (New Haven: Yale University Press, 2017), 307–313.

[3] Mary Webster, *Johan Zoffany, 1733–1810* (New Haven and London: Yale University Press for the Paul Mellon Centre for Studies in British Art, 2011), 388–394; Martin Postle, *Johan Zoffany RA: Society Observed* (New Haven: Yale University Press, 2011), 110–112, 258–260.

Being Single in Georgian England: Families, Households, and the Unmarried. Amy Harris, Oxford University Press.
© Amy Harris 2023. DOI: 10.1093/oso/9780192869494.003.0008

138 BEING SINGLE IN GEORGIAN ENGLAND

his side is John's cello. On the piano rests Granville's clarinet and William's French horns. Frances and niece Catherine, the vocal performers, hold sheet music in their hands as if they are about to sing.

Zoffany, who was roughly the same age as Elizabeth and Judith, had been friends with the Sharps for years. He had attended some of their concerts and been on board the barge. His love of music put him in many of the same circles as the Sharps; his portrait of the prominent father–son cellists, Giacobbe and James Cervetto, who had performed with the Sharps, was also painted in 1780. The two years it took to complete the Sharps' portrait put Zoffany in regular contact with them both at his studio and their various homes. Zoffany and Granville traveled together to Wicken in December 1780 to complete the painting, particularly Elizabeth and Granville at its center, before Zoffany exhibited it at the Royal Academy in 1781.[4]

The portrait was not well received at the exhibition, nor by some later observers. A twentieth-century critic noted that "in colouring and in technique it is one of Zoffany's best works, but as a composition it leaves a great deal to be desired."[5] A contemporary described it as "abominable" because the figures were "piled up in a style of grouping that it is impossible to dwell upon without pain."[6] Walpole admired the individual figures, but remarked that it had "a great want of keeping on the whole."[7] Another contemporary observer found the composition unsuitable: "how has [Zoffany]...jumbled together without the smallest attention to harmony the *flats* and *sharps* of one of the most musical families of Great Britain."[8]

As a celebration of all things Sharp, however, it was a rousing success. The jumble was intentional—a perfect reflection of Sharp family dynamics. The combination of sober looks and inside jokes, the mixture of relationships and generations, the canvas crowded with music and instruments, the boats accompanied by Fulham House in the background highlighting the importance of domestic felicity, even the dark cloud contrasting with the illumination on the figures and their sumptuous clothing seem a perfect depiction of Sharp sociability and tight connections. They were also not bothered by the artistic critiques nor the satirical poems that were sometimes published after one of their extravagant water schemes. They even pasted one such poem into one of their visiting books.[9]

Zoffany's familiarity with the family allowed him license to participate in Sharp puns and jokes. For example, Granville is holding double flageolet behind James's head to form the cuckold symbol. At first blush this is a shocking element, but it was better understood as a sign for Vulcan, the Roman god of the forge, a clear

---

[4] Granville Sharp, diaries, extracted by Catherine Sharp (niece), December 23, 1780, book 1, page 106, D3549/13/4/2.

[5] Victoria Manners and G.G. Williamson, *John Zoffany, R.A. His Life and Works, 1735–1810* (London: John Lane, 1920), 72.

[6] Retford, *The Conversation Piece*, 312.   [7] Webster, *Johan Zoffany*, 393.

[8] Retford, *The Conversation Piece*, 312.   [9] Crosby, "Private Concerts," 52.

INTERLUDE 3: PORTRAIT   139

reference to James's profession. His wife was therefore referred to as Venus, Vulcan's wife, and that might explain Catherine's wistful, almost mournful, glance at her husband.[10]

There were other references to professions and activities. William and his wife in Windsor costume, he in a military pose with flag behind, played on popular portraiture and signaled his connection to royal family. It was also perhaps a nod to their recent hosting of royal visitors. John is wearing his black formal clerical attire and a wig style used by high-ranking church officials.[11] And Judith is wearing a riding habit.

The elegant and elaborate clothing, not to mention the ornate hats and wigs, visually conveyed abundance and affluence shared by the group. Physical proximity also highlighted warmth and closeness. The clasped hands of the two Catherines is the most obvious physical connection between sitters, but Catherine William's wife's other hand appears to touch Frances's hat, while Frances's back is partially supported by her chair and partially supported by John's arm that rests atop the chair. Judith has a blue ribbon tied around her instrument, that goes over her shoulder and behind her in a way that suggests it is connected to Jemima. Granville's hand holding the double flageolet also makes his arm a support behind niece Catherine's back.

One critic found the coloring "repulsive," but color also connects various sitters and elements.[12] Most of the siblings and niece Mary are depicted with deep blue eyes. James's coat reflects the rich brown of the pianoforte, the French horn, and the angélique. Shades of blue and teal link Catherine, William's wife, Jemima, Judith, niece Mary, and Frances. The orange and peach colors of Jemima and Catherine's hats and dresses draw them together. William and John's black coats connect with John's wife Mary, Judith, Catherine William's wife, and James's hats, as well as Catherine, James's wife's shawl. The tawny color of Judith's riding habit matches William's waistcoat. Granville's olive-colored coat and waistcoat are echoed in the green trim of sister-in-law Mary's wrap. In the heart of the painting the pearly fabrics of James's wife, Elizabeth, and niece Mary's dresses and hats form a luminous triangle. And behind it all is the deep red of the *Apollo* and the background of the family flag.

The composition connects all family members by touch, color, or sight line. Just who is married or unmarried, who is spouse to whom, who might live in the same house, or who is parent to whom is not clear. Given the Sharps' domestic

---

[10] I can find no contemporary evidence for this claim. However, the 1972 publication it seemed to have originated with mentions the support of Olive Lloyd-Baker, the owner and organizer of the Sharp family papers in the mid-twentieth century. That suggests that she provided additional family documents or passed on family knowledge to the author. C.S. Smith, "James Sharp: Pioneer of Rolling Carts," *Country Life*, December 7, 1972, 1596–1598.

[11] William Gibson, "'Pious Decorum': Clerical Wigs in the Eighteenth-Century Church of England," *Anglican and Episcopal History*, 65, no. 2 (June 1996): 145–161.

[12] Webster, *Johan Zoffany*, 393.

140   BEING SINGLE IN GEORGIAN ENGLAND

arrangements, that mixing of genders, marital statuses, and generations was undoubtedly purposeful. Prominent men commissioning portraits to depict their affectionate relationships with their children was not uncommon in the 1770s and 1780s, but William's choice—an insistence on all family members mingled together—further indicates the idiosyncratic nature of the figures' positions intentionally reflected Sharp notions about family identity and relationships.[13]

[13] Kate Retford, *The Art of Domestic Life: Family Portraiture in Eighteenth-Century England* (New Haven: Yale University Press, 2006), 141–146.

5

Aunting and Uncling

She "early imbibed the best principles...from...her Equally excellent uncles and aunts."[1]

Mary Sharp Lloyd-Baker obituary

Introduction

In the spring of 1767, Thomas wrote John from London. Being pestered by Judith and James about the Bamburgh paving stones, Thomas quickly dispensed with those details in order to dwell on a topic of greater interest: the southern siblings' bustling efforts to buy clothing for Jemima, to clothe the 4-year-old "from Top to Toe."[2] Thomas's task was to provide for Jemima's shift—an assignment that disappointed him since it was unlikely to excite the child, though it would make his sister-in-law happy. "I w[oul]d have pitched on something th[a]t w[ould]d have pleased [Jemima] better," he dryly remarked. He also noted that the siblings were pleased to hear Jemima's speech had improved. The scene Thomas described— several adult Sharps playfully jockeying for who got to send the items their little niece would enjoy the most and thereby win her favor—is endearing in its light-heartedness and revealing of how important the much-longed-for child was to all the Sharps.

Throughout the second half of the Sharp siblings' lives, being aunts and uncles was an essential element of family interactions. Its importance is thrown into high relief when observing the unmarried siblings, but it was not exclusive to them. Even for those who became parents, being an aunt or uncle was an integral part of Sharp family life beginning with the birth of Ann Jemima in 1762, when the siblings were in their thirties and forties.[3] Their experience reveals that aunting and uncling have their own dynamics distinct from parenting. In many ways the single Sharps enjoyed greater freedom in their relationships with their nieces and nephew as they did not carry the same responsibility for training the

---

[1] Mary Sharp Lloyd-Baker, obituary, copied from *Christian Observer*, April 1813, correspondence to and from Mary Sharp Lloyd-Baker, 1792–1813, D6919/2/2.

[2] Thomas Sharp to John Sharp, April 7, 1767, NRO 452/C/3/2/4/9, NAW.

[3] Elizabeth Sharp Prowse, memorandum and commonplace book, February 27, 1773 and October 10, 1804, D3549/14/1/1.

Being Single in Georgian England: Families, Households, and the Unmarried. Amy Harris, Oxford University Press.
© Amy Harris 2023. DOI: 10.1093/oso/9780192869494.003.0009

142   BEING SINGLE IN GEORGIAN ENGLAND

children.[4] Over their lifetimes the nieces' relations to their aunts and uncles evolved to become more like that of much feted younger sisters. Because no Sharp aunt or uncle had to assume a parental role for an orphaned niece or nephew and because the married Sharps had few children, aunting and uncling were particularly intensive among the Sharps. Those conditions also made aunting and uncling highly visible aspects of family life.

The Sharps had limited parenting experience since some siblings never married and others were late to marry, experienced infertility with staggering frequency, or both. Being aunts and uncles, however, meant that while not all were parents, they were far from being childless. It is useful to think of generation, the early modern term used for biological reproduction, in the context of aunts and uncles.[5] Aunts and uncles participated in socially, materially, and emotionally sustaining the next generation. Because aunts and uncles were generationally removed from their nieces and nephews, their relationships had hierarchal elements, especially when nieces and nephews were young. However, their relationships could evolve to be less axiomatically hierarchical in ways parent–child relationships could not. Additionally, while uncles and aunts were a generation older, they were not necessarily chronologically older. Many people became uncles or aunts when they were very young and might have been raised alongside nieces and nephews, as cousins would be.

Similar to parenting, aunting and uncling were shaped by social class and gender, but they held fewer expectations—for example, aunts and uncles were not blamed if children misbehaved or were not fully prepared for their adult roles.[6] Aunts and uncles were expected to support parents' efforts to launch children into appropriately gendered professional and social networks, but their activities were less prescribed; aunts and uncles had the potential for more innovation and freedom in relations with their nieces and nephews.

Despite their absence in most historical literature, aunting and uncling were familial relations most people participated in, even if they were also parents. Aunts and uncles interacted directly with nieces and nephews and in concert with parents, but they were not merely surrogate parents. True, in cases where nieces and nephews were orphaned, aunts and uncles became *in loco parentis* and were expected to act as such.[7] However, being an aunt or uncle was a qualitatively different relationship than parenthood. By reading the contributions of aunts and uncles only in comparison to parenting, whether as a support for parenting or as a partial substitution, we distort its unique contours. Similarly, when uncles and

---

[4] The Sharps also often acted as godparents, but these relationships were largely ceremonial or even charitable. See Chapter 6.

[5] Lisa Forman Cody, *Birthing the Nation: Sex, Science, and the Conception of Eighteenth-Century Britons* (New York: Oxford University Press, 2005), 21.

[6] Joanne Bailey, "The History of Mum and Dad: Recent Historical Research on Parenting in England from the 16th to 20th Centuries," *History Compass*, 12, no. 6 (July 2014): 489–507.

[7] Patricia Crawford, *Blood, Bodies, and Families in Early Modern England* (New York: Routledge, 2004), 219–222.

AUNTING AND UNCLING   143

aunts are grouped with other relatives who performed parent-like tasks, the specific dynamics of different types of family relations become blurred.[8] Aunting and uncling are not parenting of a lesser sort any more than being a parent is some lesser form of aunthood or unclehood. They were merely different types of relationships, even when their scope of action overlapped.

Aunts have received more attention than uncles, particularly "maiden aunts" and their connection to nieces, often cast as surrogate mothers or orchestrators of nieces' marriage prospects.[9] When uncles are discussed, it is usually about the ways they provided professional and instrumental support for nephews.[10] Families of all social statuses relied on uncles' labor; they provided professional support, funding, and apprenticeships as well as acting as guardians in wills.[11] Uncles' formal support of nephews and nieces is evident in many early modern families, sometimes in conjunction with a parent and sometimes separately. Aunts might also act in this capacity, but given their often limited professional networks, they did so less frequently.[12] Uncles and aunts loaned or bequeathed money to nieces and nephews and also acted as tutors or teachers.[13]

The emotional and material connections between single aunts and their nieces have long been recognized as a central relationship in each of their lives. Nearly universally, these connections are described in terms of providing childless women with children and motherless girls with surrogate mothers.[14] Paralleling those descriptions is the evidence for the importance of uncles in the training of nephews.[15] The Sharps' experiences provide alternative perspectives to both of these depictions.

The Sharp Siblings as Nieces, Nephews, and Cousins

In a time when few adults had living grandparents, aunts, uncles, and older cousins acted as important connections to previous generations. The Sharps had

---

[8] French and Rothery, "Upon Your Entry," 421.

[9] Froide, *Never Married*, 65–69; Lee Chambers-Schiller, "'Woman Is Born to Love': The Maiden Aunt as Maternal Figure in Ante-bellum Literature," *Frontiers: A Journal of Women Studies*, 10, no. 1 (1988): 34–43; Amy Erickson, *Women and Property in Early Modern England* (London: Routledge, 1993).

[10] Ilana Krausman Ben-Amos, *Adolescence and Youth in Early Modern England* (New Haven: Yale University Press, 1994), 54–68, 165–170.

[11] Richard Grassby, *Kinship and Capitalism: Marriage, Family, and Business in the English-Speaking World, 1580-1740* (Cambridge: Cambridge University Press and Woodrow Wilson Center Press, 2001), 179, 184, 234, 236, 279; Naomi Tadmor, *Family and Friends in Eighteenth-Century England* (Cambridge: Cambridge University Press, 2001); Felicity Heal and Clive Holmes, *The Gentry in England and Wales 1500-1700* (Stanford: Stanford University Press, 1994), 24, 43, 66, 225, 255, 265, 329.

[12] Heal and Holmes, *The Gentry in England and Wales*, 260.

[13] Heal and Holmes, *The Gentry in England and Wales*, 160, 251.

[14] Froide, *Never Married*, 65–69.

[15] Grassby, *Kinship and Capitalism*, 282–285; Ben-Amos, *Adolescence and Youth*, 165–170.

144 BEING SINGLE IN GEORGIAN ENGLAND

no lasting relationships with any of their grandparents. Only two were alive when the older Sharp siblings were born and they died before there was time to develop lasting relationships. Their Grandfather Wheler died when John was only a few months old, and their Grandmother Sharp died a few weeks after William's birth, when oldest brother John was only age 6. Similarly, beyond their uncle Haseltine, only one Wheler aunt and one uncle and two Sharp aunts survived beyond the early 1730s. Hence, while the Sharp siblings had relationships with their surviving aunts and uncles, those were more limited than relationships with cousins. Because their parents had been the younger siblings of large cohorts, many cousins from both sides were substantially older than the Sharp siblings. This age disparity partially explains why their cousin, the elder Elizabeth Sharp Prowse, acted more as an aunt to them.

Since the older Elizabeth Sharp Prowse was born in 1712, she was the age of an aunt to the Sharps who were born in the 1720s and 1730s. She had limited kin beyond the Sharp siblings, so it is not surprising she channeled her auntly obligations and desires to her cousins. Her father died when she was 14, and her mother passed away in 1747, when she was 35. Though she married and had children, she had no nieces or nephews and had only one living sister in the 1750s, when she became increasingly important to the Sharp siblings after their parents' deaths. While she was especially close to her namesake cousin, and particularly generous to her, she maintained lifelong support of the other Sharp siblings. When she died in 1780, the younger Elizabeth noted: "[She had] been a real mother to me, and I may say to all my dear bros: and sisrs:…and there was nothing that lay in her power, but what she did, or would have done for any of us." The younger Elizabeth extoled her cousin's virtues: "steady religious Principals and knowledge in History made her company admired by old and young…her example was great to endeavor to follow."[16] The elder Elizabeth left generous bequests to her Sharp and Dering cousins, including continuing Elizabeth's life interest in Wicken (and incidentally requiring her to remain a widow, a standard practice to prevent property from transferring to a new husband's possession under coverture). She delineated how Wicken and other lands in Northamptonshire and Lincolnshire would devolve on her descendants, giving it to her daughters and their heirs in succession; then, if they did not have heirs, to her sister; and then to William, James, and Granville and their heirs if all other lines died out.[17] Each Sharp sibling received £50 "in Testimony of ffriendship & affection." Granville and Elizabeth

---

[16] Elizabeth Sharp Prowse, memorandum and commonplace book, typescript, June 19, 1780, page 62, D3549/14/1/2.

[17] Granville Sharp, diaries, extracted by Catherine Sharp (niece), book 1, page 102, 1780, D3549/13/4/2.

received an additional £500 each, Elizabeth's for being "the best of Wives to my dear Son a most dutiful & affectionate Child to me."[18]

Cousins and the aunts and uncles that survived long enough for the Sharp siblings to know them were part of their financial and social support. Legacies from aunts, uncles, and cousins provided supplemental income of particular use to the younger and never-married siblings: Judith, Granville, and Frances. Gender limited Judith and Frances's professional prospects, and their social status prevented them from pursuing trade and employment. Granville's choice to refuse a parish living or to seek other employment meant legacies and investments granted him, like his sisters, substantial financial and material autonomy he would not have had otherwise. For example, in his 1780 will, their cousin John Mangey left bibles, manuscripts, stocks, and Durham land holdings to Granville.[19] The Dering cousins, with whom the Sharps were particularly close, also used their wills to make bequests that affirmed their close connection. Judith Dering even referred to Jemima as her niece (their technical relationship was cousin once removed).[20] And it was not only the single siblings who benefited: when uncle Granville Wheler died in 1770, he left Westminster land and tenements to William and James, while his remaining nieces and nephews received £50 for mourning.[21]

In return, the Sharp siblings were an important support to their elderly aunts and uncles as they aged. In addition to regular visits to Otterden, Kent, where uncle Granville Wheler lived, the siblings visited and monitored the well-being of "good Old Aunt Mangey." Aunt Mangey was Dorothy Sharp Mangey, who had acrimoniously separated from her husband in the 1740s. When she had a "bad accident which confined her to her Bed," Elizabeth and William immediately traveled to Dunmow, Essex, to spend two days with her.[22] Dorothy was confined to a chair the remainder of her life, and Sharp siblings continued to visit until her death in 1780.

Similarly, the Sharps and their cousins provided each other with social and material support, acted as executors for each other's wills, and inherited from one another. Letters between siblings and personal diaries show that the Sharps

---

[18] Elizabeth Prowse, will, written February 14, 1778, codicil written March 10, 1779, proved July 19, 1780, Prerogative Court of Canterbury, PROB 11/1067s, TNA, digital image at https://www.ancestry.co.uk, accessed November 3, 2019. In the codicil she revoked the £500 to Elizabeth, due to a previous loan of £1000 used to improve the Wicken estate.

[19] John Mangey, will written October 25, 1780, codicils written January 21 and August 10, 1782, proved November 29, 1782, Prerogative Court of Canterbury, PROB 11/1097, TNA, digital image at https://www.ancestry.co.uk, accessed March 18, 2016.

[20] Judith Dering, will written March 21, 1807, proved December 31, 1813, Prerogative Court of Canterbury, PROB 11/1550, TNA, digital image at https://www.ancestry.co.uk, accessed March 18, 2016.

[21] Granville Wheler, will written May 2, 1770, proved May 30, 1770, Prerogative Court of Canterbury, PROB 11/958, TNA, digital image at https://www.ancestry.co.uk, accessed March 18, 2016.

[22] Elizabeth Sharp Prowse, memorandum and commonplace book, February 20, March 3, and March 24, 1769, January 26, 1777, 30, 54, typescript, D3549/14/1/2.

146   BEING SINGLE IN GEORGIAN ENGLAND

regularly corresponded with and dined with their various cousins. Elizabeth was particularly close with her Mordaunt and Rogers cousins/nieces and nephews— the children of her sisters-in-law, who were also her first cousins once removed. As Mordaunts were slated to inherit Wicken after Elizabeth's death, it is understandable that their interactions were more frequent and their social lives more intertwined compared with the other Sharp siblings. However, the Sharps who frequented Wicken also had regular visits with the Mordaunt and Rogers cousins, often relating more as aunts and uncles than as cousins, due to age—much like their cousin Elizabeth had done for them. If the various cousins were visiting Wicken at the same time, they enjoyed "a great deal of Company & visiting; musick, archery, and other amusements every day."[23]

Emotional connections to their cousins, particularly their Dering cousins, were strong even as the siblings aged and their cousin circle expanded. When the Dering cousins became parents, the Sharp siblings maintained close ties with those children. For example, when an otherwise healthy, 39-year-old Ann Dering (daughter of their cousin John) suddenly died in 1789, Granville wrote that had he not been so occupied with his sister's accounts, he would have "certainly set out directly for Norfolk" to be "of some assistance to poor Thurloe, under this 2nd grievous affliction."[24] Thurloe was Ann's brother, whose wife of less than four years had died less than a month before Ann.[25] Perhaps Granville considered Thurloe in particular need of comfort, for Thurloe had been orphaned when he was 11 and Ann had been his only surviving sibling.

Horizontal sibling and cousin relations overlapped with aunt and uncle relationships in a network of reciprocal care and labor. The Sharps benefited from their cousins' wills, and in turn, the siblings helped to settle accounts and execute wills. In 1772, Elizabeth noted she and her siblings inherited substantial amounts from their maternal cousin Grace Middleton.[26] That inheritance required years of continued work on John's part, as his co-executor, another cousin, died before the will was fully executed.[27] Cousin Ann Dering's will was brief, but it highlights the cousins' mutual support.[28] She left the bulk of her possessions to a sister, who was also executrix, and directed her to pay £25 Ann owed James Sharp. Her books were to be divided between two sisters, a diamond ring left to her niece, and a watch left to her sister-in-law. In a codicil, she indicated that if there was enough money, five guineas should be given to Granville for a ring "in remembrance of

[23] Granville Sharp to Jemima Sharp, August 8, 1788, D3549/13/1/S8.
[24] Granville Sharp to John Sharp, December 5, 1789, D3549/13/1/S8.
[25] Church of England, Denver, Norfolk parish registers, burial of Rebecca Dering, November 12, 1789, FHL DGS 4115527, image 832 of 877.
[26] Elizabeth Sharp Prowse, memorandum and commonplace book, March 24, 1772, 41, typescript, D3549/14/1/2.
[27] Accounts of Braems Wheler, executor of Grace Myddleton, 1772–74, CADD 99 and CADD 101, PGL; Account of John Sharp, surviving executor of Grace Myddleton, 1775–78, CADD 100, PGL.
[28] This Ann Dering was aunt to the Ann who died in 1789.

the trouble he had on our [the Dering sisters'] account." The holographic will that survives was clearly a draft, so after her death, Granville and another cousin-once-removed signed an affidavit that the will and codicil were in her handwriting and in her style. Two days later, January 19, 1781, Ann's brother, Heneage Dering (who lived in London presumably), acted as lawyer for one of the surviving sisters (who lived in Ripon) to grant her the rights to execute the will.[29] The will and codicil were a combined fourteen lines, but they succinctly reveal how three unmarried Dering sisters, one unmarried brother, their nephew, and two of their Sharp cousins were connected socially and materially.

Infertility and Gendered Reproduction Concerns

The concentrated nature of Sharp aunting and uncling was partially possible because infertility meant there were few children to compete for attention from the older generation: no sibling parented more than one child. James and Catherine, were parents to two children but only for the six months between the birth of Catherine in June 1770 and the death of Jack in January 1771. Jack's birth nine months after their marriage suggested James and Catherine would have several children, but it was five years until their next child, longer than the typical two-to-three-year interval between children.[30] After their daughter Catherine's birth, James and Catherine had no additional children, and there is no indication Catherine had any additional pregnancies, despite being only 25 when she had her last child, more than a decade younger than most women when they had their last child.

Similarly, after five years of marriage, Elizabeth was widowed when she was 34, but she had no children and left no record of having ever been pregnant. As Elizabeth noted in her diary, John and Mary were married ten years before Jemima's birth in 1762, much longer than the common experience of having a child within a year or two of marriage. Mary was 42 at the time, and that was likely her last pregnancy. Thomas and his wife, Catherine, had a child within a year of their marriage, but the boy was premature, stillborn, and Catherine died within a few hours of delivering him. William's wife, Catherine, was regularly pregnant, but she miscarried or gave birth to stillborn babies eighteen or twenty times in the first fourteen years of their marriage. In July 1773, William and Catherine experienced the birth of a son and Elizabeth noted that Catherine was

---

[29] Ann Dering, will and codicil, written June 22, 1779, proved January 19, 1781, Prerogative Court of Canterbury, PROB 11/1073, TNA, digital image at https://www.ancestry.co.uk, accessed October 8, 2019.

[30] E.A. Wrigley, "Explaining the Rise in Marital Fertility in England in the 'Long' Eighteenth Century," *The Economic History Review*, 51, no. 3 (August 1998): 436.

148 BEING SINGLE IN GEORGIAN ENGLAND

"safe in her Bed, but with her usual Ill luck a fine child, but still boarn."[31] It is no wonder that the birth of Mary in April 1778 was celebrated by her parents and their siblings. Elizabeth was in attendance and noted that her brother and sister-in-law were "blessed with a Little Girl...the only time of her success...that this great Blessing was felt most thankfully by us all."[32]

The married siblings' fertility was unusually low and the number of miscarriages and stillbirths was unusually high, especially in contrast with rising marital fertility rates and declining infant mortality rates during the eighteenth century. Married women typically had four to six children by their late thirties; approximately 4–5 percent of births were stillbirths.[33] Some of the Sharps' fertility concerns could be attributed to endogamy: John and Mary were first cousins, Elizabeth and George were first cousins once removed. But there might also have been fertility problems among the Sharp family overall. Their aunt Ann Sharp Dering had eight children, but their other Sharp uncle and aunt had only four children between them. The three brothers' wives who were not related to the Sharps had an unusual level of infertility and pregnancy difficulties. Perhaps the Sharp brothers had fertility problems that affected fetal development. Elizabeth's lack of children hints that the sisters also may have had fertility problems, but because Judith and Frances did not marry or become mothers, their fertility is impossible to determine.

Though the frequency was higher among the Sharp women, miscarriages and stillbirths were common for eighteenth-century women, no matter their social status.[34] Pregnancies and miscarriages were not always easily distinguished from other uterine conditions; therefore, women who desired to become pregnant faced repeated episodes of uncertainty and anxiety.[35] And in the case of Catherine, William's wife, any apprehension she felt was excruciatingly prolonged and compounded as she apparently gave birth to more than one full-term, but stillborn, baby. Such worries were intensified with the pain, potential threat to life, and grief as she and her Sharp sisters-in-law experienced repeated pregnancy losses. Pregnancy loss and infertility were often understood in a religious context, but

---

[31] Elizabeth Sharp Prowse, memorandum and commonplace book, July 26, 1773, typescript, D3549/14/1/2.

[32] Elizabeth Sharp Prowse, memorandum and commonplace book, April 19, 1778, typescript, D3549/14/1/2. Elizabeth's family lineage chart shows that William and Catherine had at least one additional stillborn child in 1781. Elizabeth Sharp Prowse, lineage chart, D3549/1/2/4.

[33] Chris Galley, "The Stillbirth Rate in Early Modern England," *Local Population Studies*, 81 (2008): 75–83.

[34] Joanna Martin, *Wives and Daughters: Women and Children in the Georgian Country House* (London: Hambledon, 2004), 176–178.

[35] Paige Donaghy, "Miscarriage, False Conceptions, and Other Lumps: Women's Pregnancy Loss in Seventeenth- and Eighteenth-Century England," *Social History of Medicine*, 34, no. 4 (November 2021): 1138–1160; Joanne Begiato, "'Breed' a 'Little Stranger': Managin Uncertainty in Pregnancy in Later Georgian England," in Jennifer Evans and Ciara Meehan, eds., *Perceptions of Pregnancy from the Seventeenth to the Twentieth Century* (London: Palgrave Macmillan, 2017): 13–14.

there is no surviving evidence from the Sharps about whether or how they viewed infertility through a scriptural or religious lens. It is likely, however, they shared their contemporaries' perspective that pregnancy was always dangerous with the possibility of miscarriage or stillbirth always looming.[36]

While miscarriage and stillbirths were female experiences, fathers were also implicated in early modern ideas about conception and infertility. Discussions of fertility and childbirth sometimes blamed miscarriages on men's thoughts or actions and emphasized the importance of marital harmony for conception and successful births.[37] There is no direct evidence in their papers to explain the Sharp brothers' thoughts about infertility, miscarriage, and stillbirths. But in an era when "pregnancy and childbirth were something that couples often saw as a joint venture," it is likely that the brothers and their wives were troubled, frustrated, or grieved by their lack of children.[38] And John and William, who were nearly 40 and nearly 50, respectively, when their first living child was born, might have shared the early modern concerns that linked old age to infertility and lack of sexual desire/desirability.[39]

Because parenthood was an important marker of adulthood and gender identity, infertility or childlessness carried potential stigma. Because the sisters either never married or did not remarry, they did not experience long-term marital infertility as their sisters-in-law did. They did however, experience decades of childlessness. As will be discussed later, their socially recognized role as aunts diminished negative perceptions of their childlessness. The Sharps' communal celebration of children's births may have helped them avoid the stigma of infertility or childlessness.

The married brothers, however, confronted a different concern. For middle-class and genteel men of the late eighteenth century, fatherhood and its attendant connections to fertility were increasingly tied to notions of masculinity.[40] Unlike earlier theories about the necessity of female sexual pleasure for procreation, late eighteenth-century women, particularly from the prosperous and educated classes, were often seen as passive incubators of offspring rather than active contributors to conception.[41] This belief meant that infertility issues could easily be

---

[36] Donaghy, "Miscarriage, False Conceptions, and Other Lumps," 1147–1150.

[37] Jennifer Evans with Sara Read, "'before midnight she had miscarried': Women, Men and Miscarriage in Early Modern England," *Journal of Family History*, 40 (January 2015): 3–23; Leah Astbury, "When a Woman Hates Her Husband: Love, Sex and Fruitful Marriages in Early Modern England," *Gender and History*, 32, no. 3 (October 2020): 523–541.

[38] Evans with Read, '"before midnight she had miscarried,"' 17.

[39] Sarah Toulalan, "'Elderly years cause a total dispaire of conception': Old Age, Sex and Infertility in Early Modern England," *Social History of Medicine*, 29, no. 2 (May 2016): 333–359.

[40] Henry French and Mark Rothery, *Man's Estate: Landed Gentry Masculinities, 1660–1900* (Oxford: Oxford University Press, 2012), 198–222; Helen Berry and Elizabeth Foyster, "Childless Men in Early Modern England," in Berry and Foyster, eds., *The Family in Early Modern England* (Cambridge: Cambridge University Press, 2007), 158–183.

[41] Angus McLaren, *Reproductive Rituals: The Perception of Fertility in England from the Sixteenth Century to the Nineteenth Century* (London: Methuen, 1984), 13–29.

laid at a man's feet and used to undermine his masculinity. While men and women were regarded as more equally responsible for conception in earlier centuries, sex-based differences were consistently explained using a "one-sex" model which described female bodies as a less advanced version of male bodies. Infertility was nearly universally blamed on the woman. Over the course of the eighteenth century, however, as a two-sex model of human sexual difference became more prominent, there was increased consideration of the possibility that infertility could originate with the man. Medical treatises regularly considered both female barrenness and male impotence (with a broader application than today's definition), though personal accounts and family remedy books were careful to disguise discussions of male infertility or sexual dysfunction.[42] Without firsthand accounts, we can only speculate what the married brothers thought about long-term childlessness, but they likely also experienced anxiety and grief, though they were spared the relentless physical burden of multiple pregnancies and miscarriages.[43]

Additionally, gendered concerns about reproduction and infertility connected to ideas of race and nationalism that touched the Sharps who were childless as well as those who became parents.[44] Granville, like many contemporaries, expressed concerns about mixed-race unions, claiming they would weaken the national stock of England. While he expressed dismay that the mixed-race children of British planters would increase the number of black servants, "which is already too numerous," he did not connect his concerns over insufficient numbers of white children to his own childlessness.[45] Despite relatively progressive views about slavery, Granville's rethinking of social distinctions did not go so far as to challenge hierarchically gendered and racial views on marriage and parenting.

On a personal and familial level the Sharps' concerns were framed in more local terms—about perpetuating their family. The hopes for any child were celebrated by all the siblings, no matter their marital status. All the siblings, except John, were aunts or uncles before they were parents, if they became parents. When Jemima was born in November 1762, the unmarried sisters and brothers were 24 to 37 years old—ages when most of their cohort could expect to be married parents. Jack's birth in 1765, only ten months after his parents' marriage was a moment of shared joy as well. For the next five years the aunts and uncles

---

[42] Jennifer Evans, *Aphrodisiacs, Fertility and Medicine in Early Modern England* (Woodbridge: Boydell, 2014), 51–86.

[43] Amanda Vickery, *The Gentleman's Daughter: Women's Lives in Georgian England* (New Haven: Yale University Press, 1998), 94–108.

[44] Katherine Paugh, *Politics of Reproduction: Race, Medicine, and Fertility in the Age of Abolition* (Oxford: Oxford University Press, 2017); Cody, *Birthing the Nation*, 11.

[45] Granville Sharp, *A Representation of the Injustice and Dangerous Tendency of Tolerating Slavery* (London, 1769), 74–75, 109, cited in Daniel Livesay, *Children of Uncertain Fortune: Mixed-Race Jamaicans in Britain and the Atlantic Family, 1733–1833* (Chapel Hill: University of North Carolina Press, 2018), 120.

poured their affection and attention into Jemima and Jack, seamlessly incorporating them into the smooth waters of Sharp socialization.

The Sharp Nieces and Nephew

Jemima

Judith and Frances were in attendance when, in November 1762, after ten years of marriage, Mary and John had their only child: Ann Jemima. Jemima, as she was called, often traveled or resided with her aunts, particularly Judith. Before she was 5, she regularly spent weeks or even months with Judith whenever Judith stayed with the southern siblings.[46] Immediately upon her birth, family friend Catherine Talbot, calling herself a cousin, wrote to Jemima, welcoming her "into this unquiet World." The letter reveals Talbot's understanding of infancy to be like a tabula rasa, when the "gaieties & Follies of Life have no attraction" and when Jemima would remain "perfectly Ignorant of party Distinctions and Look with perfect indifference on all Human Splendors," but suggested that in time she would learn correct gendered behavior from her mother and aunts. Bluestocking Talbot also sarcastically described "so many Charitable Poets," who had claimed women to be jealous and full of "Whim & Flutter and Affectation." She continued sardonically to remark that if women were to "make their Homes delightfull" to men, and if men "provoke" them, then women should make homes "as Miserable uncomfortable."[47] This was perhaps unusual advice for a baby, but it might have been a recognition that the unmarried Sharp aunts would help Jemima avoid such potential pitfalls by providing her with a model of exemplary singleness.

Jemima's aunts and uncles were immediately and consistently informed of her care and development. When she was less than 6 months old her parents dismissed her nurse. This fact is known because Granville wrote to John in the spring of 1763 expressing his hope that while the nurse turned out "so contrary to your expectation," there would be not "any real harm" to Jemima.[48] Similarly, the 1767 letter from Thomas mentioned in the introduction of this chapter, showed how all the southern siblings were kept apprised of Jemima's growth and were eager to shower her with gifts. In Catherine Talbot's letter to the infant Jemima, she predicted that Jemima would be partial to her "very good Aunts, that will contribute all they can toward spoiling you." Talbot did not include Jemima's uncles, but if

---

[46] Elizabeth Sharp Prowse, memorandum and commonplace book, November 15, 1762, January 2, February 18, and May 9, 1768, typescript, D3549/14/1/2.
[47] Catherine Talbot to Jemima Sharp, c.1763, D3549/9/1/14.
[48] Granville Sharp to John Sharp, April 9, 1763, COLL 1891/3/2, YMA.

152 BEING SINGLE IN GEORGIAN ENGLAND

Thomas's letter is representative, both groups made a competitive sport out of spoiling her.

It is possible that Jemima was born with at least some hearing loss, or perhaps lost some hearing because of a disease or an injury in infancy. There is no direct mention of her hearing loss in any letter or diary; instead, letters from her aunts and uncles to her parents discuss her learning and the practicalities of nurses, tutors, and ear trumpets. In the April 1767 letter, Thomas reported to John that all of the southern siblings were "heartily glad to hear that little Jimima improves in speaking."[49] As Jemima was four and a half years old at that point, this report suggests she might have had speech difficulties, perhaps connected to hearing loss. However, she appears to have had some hearing, as she was taught to read, write, and play the harpsichord without any mention of additional accommodations for hearing loss.

More clues about her deafness appear in surviving texts from the 1770s, perhaps reflecting a worsening of her hearing or adaptations needed as she grew and became more independent. Eighteenth-century medical texts as well as home remedy books offered many solutions for deafness that the Sharps might have attempted or at least encountered.[50] It was not always clear if the recipes were meant for temporary, chronic, or permanent deafness, but all agreed on the necessity of curing it. One family recipe recommended combining juices from onions, betony, rosemary, almonds, and eels into a tincture to be poured into the ears.[51]

In any event, Jemima's aunts and uncles, particularly Judith and Granville, were consistently involved in decisions about her needs.[52] In the fall of 1776 Jemima was with Judith for an extended visit to the southern family members. The 14-year-old was "very happy" with the opportunity to see the family, especially her 6-year-old cousin, Kitty (Catherine). In a letter to John about his "Dareling," Judith described her "as healthy & as happy as any thing can be, & she plays, upon the Harpsichord every day at her own desire." But the principal point of Judith's letter focused on finding a proper tutor for Jemima. Judith, making no direct reference to Jemima's deafness, gave the following report:

---

[49] Thomas Sharp to John Sharp, April 7, 1767, NRO 00452/C/3/2/4/9, NAW.

[50] Andreas Elias Buchner, *An easy and very practicable method to enable deaf persons to hear: Together with A brief Account of, and some Reflections and Observations upon, the several Attempts formerly made for the Benefit of such Persons* (London: Hawes, Clarke, and Collins, 1770), *Eighteenth Century Collections Online*, accessed November 3, 2020; *A Collection of Above Three Hundred Receipts in Cookery, Physick, and Surgery, for the Use of All Good Wives, Tender Mothers, and Careful Nurses* (London: Richard Wilkin, 1714), Google Books, accessed November 3, 2020.

[51] Elizabeth Strachey (1670–1722), "A book of receipts of all sorts," 1693, page 5, NLM ID 101202660, National Library of Medicine digital collections, http://resource.nlm.nih.gov/101202660. My thanks to Lindsey Meza for alerting me to this source as well as the *Collection of Above Three Hundred Receipts* cited above.

[52] James Sharp to John Sharp, June 28, 1775, NRO 00452/C/3/1/93/4, NAW.

My Brother has seen Sr. John Pringle who gives a high Character of this Mr. Pellfare & says he is no ways inferior to Mr. Braidwood, but one must make some allowance for the Character one Scotchman gives of an other, however Brother Will, thinks it may be worth the trial if you approve of it. & as he comes to...[see] her, I think we may be a very good judge in one month whether he can be of use to her or no.[53]

Sir John Pringle was a Scottish military physician who, until 1778, worked in London. He had an excellent reputation as a research-based physician.[54] It is not clear who Mr. Pellfare was, but it was high praise to compare him to Thomas Braidwood, a recognized expert in education of the Deaf. Braidwood set up an academy for deaf and mute people, teaching them to speak, read, and write. He had pupils in Edinburgh at the time Judith wrote John, so hiring a comparable tutor who was available in England was an important decision. Perhaps Jemima's hearing had declined, or perhaps she had outgrown her previous tutors' skills or expertise.[55] That same year the family hired a Miss Leadbetter to live with Jemima. This decision was undoubtedly made to help Jemima navigate the hearing world, but it also signaled that the 16-year-old should have some independence from her parents and aunt. It also allowed Judith greater freedom—she departed for an extended visit to the south in May 1779.[56]

The aunts and uncles continued their efforts to improve Jemima's hearing or to help her navigate the hearing world. The following fall, Granville wrote John to report that he had purchased the ear trumpet John requested (at a cost of 17s. 6d.) as well as "a silver...Case for the Ear, such as is used by Lady Rivers, & many other Ladies, & is so small that it may be concealed by the dressing of their Hair." Those most subtle sound enhancers were costly, so Granville "only sent one by way of specimen at 10£ 6d, which will suit either ear) that you may try whether it is of a proper size for my Niece, & whether she would like to wear ear caps of this sort." He also explained that the caps had sharp edges that would need to be covered in silk "to prevent the edge from hurting the back part or stem of the Ear next the head, where it rest. The Open Edge of the Instrument must be placed forwards to receive the sounds; but the shape of it, I think, will be sufficient to direct you to the right mode of applying it."[57]

---

[53] Judith Sharp to John Sharp, October 22, 1776, NRO 00452/C/3/2/6/43, NAW.

[54] J.S.G. Blair, "Pringle, Sir John, first baronet (1707–1782), military physician," *Oxford Dictionary of National Biography*, Oxford Dictionary of National Biography, Oxford University Press, September 23, 2004, accessed August 5, 2021.

[55] Alexander Gordon and Michael Bevan, "Braidwood, Thomas (1715–1806), teacher of deaf people," *Oxford Dictionary of National Biography*, Oxford University Press, September 23, 2004, accessed August 5, 2021.

[56] Elizabeth Sharp Prowse, memorandum and commonplace book, November 30, 1778–May 6, 1779, 60, typescript, D3549/14/1/2.

[57] Granville Sharp to John Sharp, October 18, 1777, D3549/9/1/4.

154 BEING SINGLE IN GEORGIAN ENGLAND

Since the eighteenth century, Deaf history has always been a negotiation between Deaf autonomy and integration into hearing culture.[58] The Sharps pursued integration, as was common for their time. At the same time, they did not impose a category of deafness, disability, or loss onto Jemima, though they sometimes did so with strangers who were far removed from their daily lives, such as the enslaved, the poor, and those who spoke in a different dialect. As the common letters demonstrate, when they were younger, the Sharp siblings occasionally engaged in some of the cruel humor often exhibited by the socially well-positioned, but that behavior decreased over time. Perhaps, as with so many families since the late eighteenth century, interaction with family members from a stigmatized group could reduce the stigma, at least within the family circle.[59] Jemima was born when categories around hearing or speaking disabilities might contain pejorative understandings about sin or evil, but these were not the hardened categories of the nineteenth century or the eugenic categories that followed.[60]

There is no indication Jemima learned to sign—regional predecessors to British Sign Language were in circulation, if not exactly standardized at the time—since doing so would have required that her listener also be able to sign, and there is no mention of signed language among family members. Judith's letters show that Jemima interacted with tutors who encouraged speech and adaptation to the hearing world. Signed language became an important vehicle for group identity and belonging for Deaf people in the nineteenth and twentieth centuries. Even if such avenues had been open to Jemima in the eighteenth century, it is not clear that her family would have encouraged pursuing them. For the Sharps, their belonging and identity revolved around being a Sharp more than any other category or characteristic. Predictably, therefore, family members worked to incorporate Jemima into their already-established family culture. While her hearing loss was something they tried to ameliorate, her deafness did not define her relationship to them. She participated in all family activities and entertainments, including playing the harpsichord with Judith and riding horseback with Elizabeth.[61] Like her younger cousins, Jemima was taught a love of music, books, and travel,

---

[58] Emily Cockayne, "Experiences of the Deaf in Early Modern England," *The Historical Journal*, 46, no. 3 (September 2003): 493–510; Brian H. Greenwald and Joseph J. Murray, eds., *In Our Own Hands: Essays in Deaf History, 1780–1970* (Washington, D.C.: Gallaudet University Press, 2016); Richard Ian Kimball, "'As Good as the Best': Gallaudet Football and the Battle Against Normalization at the Turn of the Twentieth Century," in Christian K. Anderson and Amber C. Falluca, eds., *The History of American College Football* (New York: Routledge, 2021).

[59] Deborah Cohen, *Family Secrets: Shame and Privacy in Modern Britain* (Oxford: Oxford University Press, 2013).

[60] Chris Mounsey, ed., *The Idea of Disability in the Eighteenth Century. Transits: Literature, Thought & Culture, 1650–1850* (New York: Bucknell University Press, 2014); Madeline C. Burghardt, *Broken: Institutions, Families, and the Construction of Intellectual Disability* (Montreal: McGill-Queen's University Press, 2018).

[61] Elizabeth Sharp Prowse, memorandum and commonplace book, September 17, 1776, D3549/14/1/1.

though unlike Catherine, she never participated in public musical performances. The sound of music was an essential element of Sharp sociality and identity, but with little evidence from Jemima herself, we cannot know how she experienced the family's musical culture.

Jack

James and Catherine's son Jack's birth in February 1765 was noted by Elizabeth in her diary, but without any special comment on the birth. Similarly, the surviving letters from that time (principally those from Granville to John) do not make a mention of baby Jack. Presumably, both he and his mother were well, or there would have been a report about recovering health. Since Jack was born within a year of his parents' marriage, his arrival might have appeared expected, a fortunate blessing, but not an extraordinary experience, as Jemima's birth had been. At the time of Jack's birth, William was getting close to marriage, and the unmarried siblings still had the possibility of marrying and having children in the future. The birth of a nephew may have seemed something likely to be repeated many times in the years to come.

No matter the lack of fanfare about his birth, Jack was soon incorporated into his aunts' and uncles' socializing. Three-year-old Jack traveled with Frances to Wicken in the spring of 1768. That fall, he traveled with Elizabeth and Frances, spending nearly two weeks at Wicken before returning with them to his parents at Leadenhall Street. Early in 1769 he traveled with the entire family when they gathered at their uncle Granville Wheler's estate in Otterden, Kent. Three months after that, 4-year-old Jack traveled with Elizabeth and Frances to Wicken, where he stayed for two and a half months. While there he was part of the party who welcomed Elizabeth's newlywed sister-in-law. At the end of 1769, Jack and his parents spent three weeks during Christmastime with Elizabeth at Wicken.[62] In less than two years, little Jack had completed five journeys, all but one without his parents but none without at least one aunt.

The Sharps encouraged a cousin connection between Jack and Jemima, who was two years' Jack's senior. Though no letters between them survive, there is evidence the young cousins were, like many other genteel young people, taught to maintain correspondence with other young people.[63] James wrote John in

---

[62] Elizabeth Sharp Prowse, memorandum and commonplace book, April 15 and October 14, 1768, February 3, May 10, July 8, July 25, and December 5, 1769, D3549/14/1/1.

[63] Amy Harris, "'This I beg that my Aunt may not know': Young Letter Writers in Eighteenth-Century England, Peer Correspondence in a Hierarchical World," *Journal of the History of Childhood and Youth*, 2 no. 3 (Fall 2009): 333–360; Adriana Benzaquen, "'Pray lett none see this impertinent Epistle': Children's Letters and Children in Letters at the Turn of the Eighteenth Century," in Andrew O'Malley, ed., *Literary Cultures and Eighteenth-Century Childhoods* (London: Palgrave Macmillan, 2018): 75–96.

156 BEING SINGLE IN GEORGIAN ENGLAND

February 1769 about several topics, including carriage wheel design, replacement strings for John's double bass, a reminder about a charity owed by the trust John oversaw, and discussion of other financial transactions. In the middle of the letter, James noted that Jack had received a letter from "Cousin Jemmima... which has given high delight and he promises to answer it very soon."[64] Jemima was 6 at the time, and Jack had just turned 4.

The biggest impact of Jack's birth was the fact that there was now a male Sharp heir. Jemima was loved and doted upon by all her aunts and uncles, but Jack's birth signaled something new: a carrier of the surname. And it was not just his parents and aunts and uncles who funneled those often unspoken expectations to Jack. He was the only great grandson of Archbishop Sharp; the Sharps' only paternal uncle had only one son who did not survive to adulthood. Jack was therefore freighted with three generations' expectations of a male heir to perpetuate the surname along with their values and potential professional prominence. Within two years of Jack's birth, James wrote a will that gave John one-third of his estate and stipulated that some of that inheritance would go to Jack's aunts and uncles upon his majority or death, thus linking Jack's fortunes to his aunts' and uncles'. James recommended that, since he had "by great care and application acquired beneficial and extensive trade," even after his death it would be of "great benefit and advantage... to have it carried on" by his wife Catherine and Jack. The will also provided for Jack's education and maintenance until he could be launched into a profession.[65] Jack's first five years were therefore full of family visits and careful planning for his future. All of that collapsed as 1770 drew to a close. He and his uncle Thomas fell ill in early December, perhaps from the same communicable disease. Thomas recovered, but Jack succumbed at the end of January 1771.

Catherine

After Jack's birth, James and Catherine did not have another child for five years; baby Catherine was born in June 1770. Within two months of her birth, Frances took baby Catherine with her when she traveled from London to Wicken. Catherine's parents eventually joined them in Wicken, but in early August, the adult Sharps—and presumably Jack—went on a "water scheme" journey along the Thames, leaving Catherine at Wicken with her nurse.[66] The young Sharps were involved in their aunts' and uncles' social patterns, but when they could not safely participate in those activities, the Sharps arranged for their care like their

[64] James Sharp to John Sharp, February 10, 1769, D3549/9/1/4.

[65] James Sharp, will, written November 21, 1766, proved November 7, 1783, Prerogative Court of Canterbury, PROB 11/1110, TNA.

[66] Elizabeth Sharp Prowse, memorandum and commonplace book, June 5, July 7, and August 4–10, 1770, D3549/14/1/1.

prosperous contemporaries: servants provided labor and childcare that made genteel recreation possible. The Sharps continued to receive news about baby Catherine while they sailed the river. When Elizabeth received news that lightning had struck Wicken, killing a horse, she reported: "When I found my dear little Catherine safe and no harm to any one in my family or the house I felt most thankful."[67]

That same summer, Thomas married Catherine Pawson, and she was pregnant not long after. It appeared the Sharps would have many opportunities to incorporate new nieces and nephews into their family circle. But the deaths of Jack, Catherine, and the baby in early 1771 put an end to such hopes. Jack's death in January was particularly difficult for the siblings, compounded by other deaths in their extended family in March. Elizabeth and Frances were traveling in the North, principally to meet their new sister-in-law, when they learned the news of Jack's death. Then, six weeks later, when their sister-in-law gave birth to a premature stillborn son and then died, they were there to grieve with Thomas, likely joined by John, Mary, Judith, and Jemima.

In early April 1771, James and his wife were preparing to have 10-month-old Catherine inoculated for smallpox. Though smallpox inoculation had been practiced for nearly half a century, it still carried risks. William regularly performed this service for his family members and they recorded each other's recoveries. James and Catherine, however, were especially desirous that Elizabeth and Frances would be with them when the baby was inoculated "in case any thing happened [to] little Catherine as all their spirits were much depressed by their late loss." Elizabeth and Frances left Durham for Leadenhall Street, arriving April 20 and "found dear little Catherine well, and glad all to meet after our late affliction."[68] Once again, the siblings drew together for comfort in shared grief. This grief, however, was not expressed in the same way their father drew on Christian beliefs to comfort their mother when 2-year-old Grace died in 1728. Elizabeth's record of Jack's death and its aftermath emphasizes the emotional impact; there is no reference to spiritual consolation. Given the Sharps' strong religious beliefs, particularly Elizabeth's deep devotion, the absence of religious or spiritual framing of the death and grief is probably not a sign of declining belief. Though the Sharps expressed no desire to allow grief to evolve into joy as their parents' generation did, and as many of their mid-century contemporaries did, their belief in providentialism means they likely saw submission to God's will as expected, even as they grieved.[69]

---

[67] Elizabeth Sharp Prowse, memorandum and commonplace book, August 10, 1770, D3549/14/1/1.

[68] Elizabeth Sharp Prowse, memorandum and commonplace book, April 9 and 20, 1771, D3549/14/1/1.

[69] Katie Barclay, "Grief, Faith and Eighteenth-Century Childhood: The Doddridges of Northampton," in Katie Barclay and Kimberley Reynolds with Ciara Rawnsley, eds., *Death, Emotion and Childhood in Premodern Europe* (London: Palgrave Macmillan, 2016), 178–179.

158 BEING SINGLE IN GEORGIAN ENGLAND

Despite Catherine's birth in 1770 and Jack's death in 1771, James never updated his will. The care with which he planned Jack's financial and professional future was unnecessary for a daughter who would be well educated and well supported financially but who would not be prepared for a career. These gendered attitudes toward children were unremarked upon and went unchallenged by the Sharps. Perhaps more conflict or concerns would have developed if there had been more nieces and nephews, but without them, Catherine was her parents' heir at law, and no will would be required for her to inherit from them. In all other ways, Catherine was universally cherished and raising her drew consistent focus from her aunts and uncles, particularly the unmarried ones. She was taught to sing and dance and began performing at musical gatherings before she was 5 years old; Elizabeth gave Catherine a music book when she was 6.[70] Throughout her childhood, she was often with Elizabeth and Frances, Elizabeth consistently referring to her as "dear little Catherine."

Mary

Mary's birth in April 1778, eight years after Catherine's birth, was universally celebrated by the siblings. William and Catherine had been married for more than twelve years when Mary was born. Three days after the birth, Granville was happy to inform John that Catherine was recovering well and that "the little Babe is also very well."[71] In the previous twelve years, Catherine had suffered numerous miscarriages or stillbirths. She might have had at least one additional failed pregnancy in 1779, so over time Mary's birth and survival were regarded as even more fortuitous.[72] It is hardly surprising that Elizabeth, who attended the birth, described Mary's birth as a "great Blessing...felt most thankfully by us all."[73] Within six weeks of her birth, Mary's parents took her to Wicken to visit for a few days. Of this visit, Elizabeth wrote: "This little exertion thought good for my sisr. but very soon after, the child was left with me with her nurse for the Summer."[74] A later observer noted that Mary "early imbibed the best principles of Christianity from the Lessons & example of her Excellent Parents, & of her Equally excellent uncles & aunts" and noted her special closeness to Elizabeth and Frances, "with

---

[70] Crosby, "Private Concerts," 38.

[71] Granville Sharp to John Sharp, April 21, 1778, D3549/13/1/S8.

[72] In March 1779 Granville reported to John that "My Sister Will has been down stairs since her indisposition, & seems pretty well again." This was only eleven months after Mary's birth, but since Mary was apparently given to a wet nurse, it would not have been unusual for Catherine to have become pregnant again, especially considering in the first twelve years of her marriage she had been pregnant at least eighteen times. Granville Sharp to John Sharp, March 1779, D3549/13/1/S8.

[73] Elizabeth Sharp Prowse, memorandum and commonplace book, April 19, 1778, D3549/14/1/1.

[74] Elizabeth Sharp Prowse, memorandum and commonplace book, April 28, 1778, D3549/14/1/1.

AUNTING AND UNCLING   159

whom much of her Infancy & youth were spent."[75] Around the same time, James and Catherine visited Wicken and left niece Catherine with her aunts and infant cousin. As with Jemima, Jack, and Catherine before her, Mary was immediately embedded in Sharp socializing and visiting patterns and was encouraged to develop relationships with her aunts, uncles, and cousins.

While the Sharp aunts were crucial teachers for Mary, Granville was also heavily involved, and even John was kept apprised of his nieces' activities and development. When Mary was 11 months old, Granville wrote John: "Niece Catherine is purely recovered, & sits up...Little Mary is weaned, & seems to thrive and grow fatter and firmer than she was when she sucked."[76] In this same letter Granville discussed mislaying a letter about lace, going to find deeds for Bamburgh, a parliamentary committee on River Lea navigation (along with James), and politics and the slave trade. Imparting information about the nieces and reporting on their care was just another part of the interests and responsibilities Granville shared with his brother. Early modern fathers often monitored the care of their children, including the timing of weaning, walking, and speech, but this letter between two uncles, one unmarried and childless and the other a married father, suggests that care of infants and children was not confined to paternal roles.

Like Catherine, Mary was often at Wicken or traveling with Elizabeth and Frances. At her home and while with her aunts, she learned to sketch, paint, write poetry, and play the harp. She also might have received artistic advice from the painter Zoffany during a 1798 visit she and her father made to his house.[77] She, her mother, aunts, and cousins regularly visited, dined, shopped, and read together. She traveled with her parents, to visit aunts and uncles at Wicken Park, Clare Hall, or Granville's rooms. On one occasion, she and Granville rode horses, accompanying her parents in a chariot.[78]

Little of Frances's writing survives, but Elizabeth consistently remarked on Frances's deep affection for her nieces and that she expressed enjoyment in their company. Simultaneously, Elizabeth did the same with the children of her sisters-in-law, the Mordaunt and Rogers children. The push and pull of aunting duties to two sets of children was not always easy to navigate. In September 1778 Elizabeth and Frances had 5-month-old Mary with them at Wicken. Elizabeth's sister-in-law wrote from Walton Hall in Warwickshire asking Elizabeth to receive her three youngest children at Wicken because several Walton servants had an infectious fever. Elizabeth had to decline, however, because baby Mary was scheduled to be inoculated against smallpox the following week, and Elizabeth did not want to risk her catching an illness before the inoculation. The Mordaunt children were

---

[75] Mary Sharp Lloyd-Baker, obituary, April 1813, copies from *Christian Observer*, D6919/2/2.
[76] Granville Sharp to John Sharp, March 1779, D3549/13/1/S8.
[77] Mary Sharp Lloyd-Baker, diary, June 13, 1798, D3549/24/1/2.
[78] Mary Sharp Lloyd-Baker, diary, July 12, 1798, D3549/24/1/2.

160   BEING SINGLE IN GEORGIAN ENGLAND

safely ensconced elsewhere and after the servants at Walton recovered, they returned home without coming to Wicken. Being unable to help all of her nieces and nephews weighed heavy on Elizabeth's mind: "I don't know that I ever felt more hurt at any thing then not being able to receive them, when offered at so distressing a time."[79]

Wicken Park was attractive to all of Elizabeth's nieces and nephews. For the Sharp nieces it was an ideal place to spend childhood. While Catherine and Mary lived near each other in London, and while the siblings often gathered in London, Wicken allowed the nieces extended contact with their aunts, Granville, and occasionally Jemima, often in the absence of the girls' parents. This contact meant the parents were willing to let their daughters form family connections not mediated or observed by either parent. When she was 14, Mary wrote a poem rhapsodizing about her fond memories of playing among Wicken's lush trees and flowers: "Oft in your verdant meadows have I seen / The Suns last parting rays just gild the green."[80] Catherine and Mary were always appreciative of their time there and were clearly shaped by the time they spent with aunts and uncles during those visits. Over family meals, during household prayers, and while socializing in rooms crowded with "books of music heaped / And instruments like trophies hung around...And with them mixed the quiver, bow, and belt / That spoke of pastimes," the Sharp nieces experienced a childhood perhaps even richer than the stellar childhoods their aunts and uncles experienced. At Wicken, their childish drawings and paintings were lovingly displayed on the walls. And in music, reading, and "friendly converse," the nieces spent evenings "when loud the winter wind / Without was heard to roar while the brick flame / Within, its cheering warmth spread round the room / Our group of friends, with various piecing work / Of use or fancy, urged the fleeting hours."[81]

The patterns of long visits with aunts and uncles began immediately after birth, and as they grew, Jemima, Catherine, and Mary were often with aunts and uncles without parents. In the summer and fall of 1772, for example, Catherine spent five months at Wicken, her parents and other aunts and uncles visiting occasionally.[82] It is possible to see these visits as single sisters providing free childcare, but surviving documents give a different impression. Uncles, particularly single Thomas and Granville, were important in their nieces' lives. Parents reimbursed aunts and uncles and negotiated with them about proper tutors and activities for the children. Letters between the siblings show genuine and individualized connections to the nieces, not just duty to their siblings. While they sometimes shared parental duties—things like buying shifts and ear trumpets and planning

[79] Elizabeth Sharp Prowse, memorandum and commonplace book, September 17, 1778, D3549/14/1/1.
[80] Mary Sharp Lloyd-Baker, "On Returning to Wicken," May 1792, D6919/2/2.
[81] Mary Sharp Lloyd-Baker, "Wicken," 7, D6919/2/4.
[82] Elizabeth Sharp Prowse, memorandum and commonplace book, October 12, 1772, D3549/14/1/1.

AUNTING AND UNCLING   161

for Jack's future were things parents also did—in the process of buying shifts and negotiating financial support, the Sharp aunts and uncles developed their own meaningful relationships with their nieces and nephew that were not managed by parents.

Being Aunts and Uncles Over the Life Course

The instrumental obligations to kin that helped shape aunt/uncle and niece/nephew relationships are well understood.[83] Similarly, a variety of scholars have noted examples of aunt/uncle and niece/nephew relationships that were warm and meaningful.[84] The ways that relationships and emotional ties developed over the life course are not as well understood. Like parenting, aunting and uncling did not end with childhood but continued to influence adult nieces and nephews.[85] Not all the siblings had the same relationship with each of their nieces; they were shaped by marital status and, to a lesser extent, by gender.

The elder Elizabeth Sharp Prowse acted as a motherly figure to her orphaned cousins the Sharps; however, her example is not a precise match for what the Sharps did for their nieces and nephew. Because their nieces' parents survived, the Sharp aunts and uncles did not have to assume a parenting role, as their cousin Elizabeth had for them, and as other well-studied aunts did for orphaned children in the eighteenth century. Elizabeth's role as surrogate parent was buttressed by her also being the younger Elizabeth's mother-in-law. The Sharp siblings had no such tripling of cousin/aunt/mother relations. Additionally, because their parents were still alive, the Sharp nieces had room for relationships with their aunts and uncles not based on surrogate parent–child dynamics, allowing their connections to develop on their own terms. The results were less hierarchical than if the aunts and uncles had assumed surrogate parenting responsibilities. The first of the nieces to be orphaned was Jemima, but she was in her late thirties at the time. Catherine's father died when she was 13, but her relationship with her aunts and uncles, built by long visits, was already well established. Catherine's mother survived until Catherine was in her mid-sixties. Mary was 30 when her father died, and her mother outlived her. So, there was no space for Sharp aunts and uncles to completely act *in loco parentis*. Their experiences, therefore, offer an unobstructed view of aunting and uncling.

Literacy and musical training were the first lessons taught to the young nieces. The timing of Granville's *A Short Introduction to Vocal Music* (1767), written to

---

[83] Berry and Foyster, "Childless Men," 181.

[84] Froide, *Never Married*, 64–71; Fletcher, *Growing Up in England: The Experience of Childhood, 1600–1914* (New Haven: Yale University Press, 2008), 260–261, 304.

[85] Joanne Bailey, "The 'Afterlife' of Parenting: Memory, Parentage, and Personal Identity in Britain c.1760–1830," *Journal of Family History*, 35, no. 3 (July 2010): 249–270.

162 BEING SINGLE IN GEORGIAN ENGLAND

instruct children, is unlikely to have been mere coincidence, coming as it did when Jemima was 4 and Jack 2. Though meant for children, the short treatise covered a large range of musical content, including music theory, notation, rhythm, and sight singing. He did recognize that learning how to properly express and pronounce while singing was something that could not be conveyed in writing and would require lessons with a music master. The booklet was not meant to be an exhaustive introduction, "a farther and complete understanding of vocal music can only be acquired by being long conversant in the science," Granville acknowledged.[86] His vision for children encountering such a complex text included the careful "assistance of some understanding person" to read with the child and help them apply the lessons. He clearly intended it mostly for boys—not those who were "bred musicians by profession" but those who had other school studies limiting the time they could devote to formal musical training and who "yet may be enabled...to bear a Chorus Part in the service of God."[87] It is probable, however, when confronted with his nieces' need for musical training that Granville became such an "understanding person."

Judith also had increased interest in musical education after her nieces were born. The collection of folk songs recorded by the siblings' mother was expanded by Judith in the 1770s. Though Judith's signature in the book is dated 1756, it does not contain many songs produced between the 1740s and the 1760s; it appears Judith resumed her mother's efforts only once the nieces were old enough to participate in Sharp musical activities.[88] Her 1768 request for her London brothers to send sheet music to Northumberland might have been the beginning of her work on the songbook, since Granville included several ballads in the package.[89] Despite Granville's focus on boys who could participate in church choirs, his description of an "understanding person" to teach them anticipated Anna Letitia Barbauld's 1778 book advocating for children to learn about the world via conversation with an "affectionate, rational Mamma" during "prosaic domestic activities."[90] Judith's songbook suggests that Barbauld's understanding person could easily be an affectionate aunt as a mamma who taught children music, reading, and curiosity through everyday observations and activities. And one can imagine Judith or Granville reading stories to the nieces as they played, worked, or nodded to sleep.[91]

Over time, particularly close relationships developed between different groupings. Judith and Jemima usually traveled and resided together. Jack, Catherine,

---

[86] Granville Sharp, *A Short Introduction to Vocal Music* (London: first printed in 1767, reprinted in 1777), 2nd edn., 30, MT 870 S5 1777, WACML.

[87] Sharp, *A Short Introduction*, iv.   [88] Judith Sharp, songbook, D3549/8/1/3.

[89] Granville Sharp to John Sharp, January 24, 1768, COLL 1891/3/19, YMA.

[90] Jessica Wen Hui Lim, "Barbauld's Lessons: The Conversational Primer in Late Eighteenth-Century British Children's Literature," *Journal for Eighteenth-Century Studies*, 43, no. 1 (2020): 103.

[91] Abigail Williams, *The Social Life of Books: Reading Together in the Eighteenth-Century Home* (New Haven: Yale University Press, 2017), 36–63.

AUNTING AND UNCLING   163

and Mary spent much of their childhood at Wicken with Elizabeth and Frances. Granville was close to all his nieces, as he too spent long visits at Wicken and carried on a regular correspondence with Jemima. Long visits, shared domestic space, and temperament combined to create long-lasting ties between the nieces and their aunts and uncles. The family portrait highlights these ties, by placing Jemima between an aunt and uncle and placing Catherine halfway between her parents but with her uncle's arm around her back. It looks like Jemima might have sat with Judith instead of her parents for the portrait. Mary, a small child, was understandably painted on her mother's lap.

There were gendered differences in the Sharps' experience as aunts and uncles. The nieces spent much time with their single aunts, sometimes for months at a time.[92] While the nieces' relationships with their aunts were deep and lasting, it echoed the experience of many eighteenth-century women, particularly wealthy unmarried women. The most striking insight from the Sharps' experience is what the brothers' experience of uncling reveals. Focusing on uncling provides a different perspective on connections between masculinity, reproduction, and generational connections. Fatherhood's social importance to ideas of patriarchal national, social, and familial order meant it was more than a matter of biological reproduction; fatherhood and paternity were not synonymous.[93] Fathers consistently monitored their pregnant wives' and their children's health, wrote letters seeking advice from other fathers, sought remedies for children's illness, and worried about their children's social, gendered, and financial future.[94] They were affectionate, protective, and knew their children well.[95] Fathers were also meant to inculcate manly virtues in their sons, thereby solidifying their own manliness.[96] Uncling complicates this picture. Fatherhood was important, but the Sharps' uncling demonstrated masculine domestic and familial roles that were not dependent on fatherhood or paternity.

The Sharp uncles, particularly Granville and Thomas, were involved uncles from their nieces' and nephew's infancy. Granville maintained this pattern with Elizabeth's Mordaunt nieces and nephews (technically his cousins twice removed).

[92] Elizabeth Sharp Prowse, memorandum and commonplace book, September 20–November 14, 1780, D3549/14/1/1.

[93] Alexandra Shepard, "Brokering Fatherhood: Illegitimacy and Paternal Rights and Responsibilities in Early Modern England," in Steve Hindle, Alexandra Shepard, and John Walter, eds., *Remaking English Society: Social Relations and Social Change in Early Modern England* (Woodbridge: Boydell & Brewer, 2013), 44. Fatherhood was important throughout the early modern European and Atlantic world; see Benjamin Roberts, "Fatherhood in Eighteenth-Century Holland: The Van der Muelen Brothers," *Journal of Family History*, 21, no. 2 (April 1996): 218–228; Lori Glover, *All Our Relations: Blood Ties and Emotional Bonds among the Early South Carolina Gentry* (Baltimore: Johns Hopkins University Press, 2000).

[94] Lisa Smith, "The Relative Duties of a Man: Domestic Medicine in England and France, ca. 1685–1740," *Journal of Family History*, 31, no. 3 (July 2006): 237–256.

[95] Joanne Bailey, "'A Very Sensible Man': Imagining Fatherhood in England, c.1750–1830," *History*, 95, no. 3 (July 2010): 267–292.

[96] Anthony Fletcher, *Growing Up in England*, 149.

164   BEING SINGLE IN GEORGIAN ENGLAND

When he socialized with the Mordaunts and Rogerses and their children, he joined in the activities with them, whether that was archery at Wicken or visiting museums in London.[97] Additionally, having only nieces highlights how important uncling could be to single, childless men. Granville was not going to launch his nieces into his professional network. Instead, the relationship involved an emotional connection. Stripped of the father–daughter hierarchy and the instrumental expectation of uncle–nephew relations, and without competition for having his own children, Granville's relations with his nieces had a measure of freedom and enjoyment that was perhaps not possible for many fathers.

From surviving documents, Granville's and Thomas's connections to their nieces is more evident than the married brothers'. (While Thomas married, it was only after Jemima, Jack, and Catherine were born, and he died less than three years after his marriage.) However, even for the married brothers, relationships with their nieces were an important element of their family life. The only ones to become grandparents, William and Catherine, did not do so until he was 72 and she was 59. They were grandparents for only nine and thirteen years, respectively. But William had been an uncle for nearly three years when he married, and he and Catherine were uncle and aunt for more than four decades. By the time William and Catherine became grandparents, only three Sharp siblings and one sister-in-law were alive. Therefore, while grandparenting was important to William and Catherine, it never became a central aspect of Sharp family culture. For eighteenth-century women and men without grandchildren, nieces and nephews and grandnieces and grandnephews were important relationships and important heirs.[98] John, for example, continued his connection to the Dering cousins' children, who were also his grandnieces and grandnephews by marriage, throughout his life. Residing in the North meant he often requested that Granville act in his stead at Dering christenings, marriages, and funerals.[99] And it was a combination of married fathers and uncles who purchased and named three boats in the 1770s: the *Jemima*, the *Catherine*, and a canoe named the *Mary*.

If Judith became or was expected to become a caregiver for Jemima because of her deafness and Judith's singleness, it was never mentioned. It was either an unspoken expectation based on gender and marital status, or it developed organically because of Judith's interest in doing so; there is no trace of any discussion or negotiation around Judith's closeness to Jemima. There is a 1776 account notation by Granville that Judith received £5 5s. from John and Mary "on acco[oun]t of Niece Jemima."[100] Whether this was payment for Judith's time caring for Jemima

---

[97] Granville Sharp, diaries, extracted by Catherine Sharp (niece), book 2, 113–114, June 24–July 16, 1795, D3549/13/4/2.

[98] Susannah R. Ottaway, *The Decline of Life: Old Age in Eighteenth-Century England* (Cambridge: Cambridge University Press, 2004), 169; Tadmor, *Family and Friends* 148–149.

[99] Granville Sharp to John Sharp, January 26, 1782, D3549/13/1/S8.

[100] Granville Sharp to John Sharp, January 3, 1777, D3549/13/1/S8.

AUNTING AND UNCLING   165

or as a reimbursement for money she spent on Jemima's care is unclear. If it was the former, that practice ended in 1778 when John and Mary hired a live-in companion for Jemima, indicating Judith's company for Jemima was neither compulsory nor employment based. Similarly, Granville's relationship with Jemima was colored by warm affection as much as any sense of duty. The year 1778 might have also signaled a change in Jemima's relation to Judith and Granville. In 1777, Granville referred to Jemima as a "good girl," but after that date, he no longer called her a girl, instead simply calling her "niece." In a surviving 1778 letter, amid reports of family activities at Wicken, Granville requested that Jemima report financial and legal details to her father and discussed the Sierra Leone colony.[101] The content and the requests are hardly things one would share with a child, and his tone was the same he used with his sisters. Jemima turned 16 in November of 1778, and it appears, as with most eighteenth-century youth in their mid-teens, her aunt and uncle began expecting her to leave girlhood behind and assume more young adult responsibilities.

Her uncle William took a bit longer to fully recognize her adult status. In a February 1799 letter, William remarked to Judith that he was pleased to learn Jemima "is become a woman of business, & manages her own affairs with so much prudence and ability."[102] Jemima was 36 at the time and had long been managing her own affairs. Judith and Granville, because of more consistent interactions with her, had long recognized her as capable and independent. Jemima's independence flowered in the 1790s, when she acquired a home in Durham with Judith. Judith's involvement is understandable, but Granville also played a key role. He drew plans for home renovations and acted as a go-between for the women and their legal advisors in London.[103] Much as he had done for his siblings beginning in the 1760s, Granville continued to manage accounts for Jemima and other nieces well into the nineteenth century. He and Jemima continued to correspond about various anti-slavery initiatives, and while their relationship developed a peer-like quality, Jemima continued to recognize their generational difference by signing letters as "your ever dutiful niece." Judith, Granville, and William also continued to support Jemima's property rights in Durham and Doncaster, Yorkshire, which rectory lease she inherited from her father, and her family offered fierce loyalty during an ongoing dispute about Doncaster tithes. In turn, Jemima made William, and by descent, cousin Mary, her heirs.[104]

---

[101] Granville Sharp to Jemima Sharp, August 8, 1788, D3549/13/1/S8. The letter has been miscategorized with her father's correspondence with Granville.

[102] William Sharp to Judith Sharp, February 18, 1799, D3549/16/1/1.

[103] Granville Sharp to Joseph Hill, January 3, 1799, Add.MS.1030, PGL.

[104] Papers concerning Doncaster rectory, 1684–1822, D3549/23/2; *Ann Jemima Sharp vs. Sir George Cooke*, 1815, C13/1413/32, TNA; John Edward Jackson, *The History and Description of St. George's Church at Doncaster* (London: J.B. Nichols and Sons, 1855), lv–lix.

166 BEING SINGLE IN GEORGIAN ENGLAND

In some ways the nieces evolved into younger sisters. Letters the nieces exchanged with their aunts and uncles at the turn of the century were not letters between an adult and a child but between two adults, with their own household and travel schedules and with their own financial independence. As Mary later remarked, letters acted as "a golden link" to home and family for young people entering the world.[105] The transition into sisterly roles for the nieces is particularly visible in Catherine's interaction with Elizabeth and Frances and Jemima's with Judith and Granville. Mary married in her early twenties, and though she maintained close ties with the Sharps, the continued single status of the remaining nieces highlights the ways they evolved into younger sisters. Catherine and Jemima's continued singleness undoubtedly played a role but so did birth order: Elizabeth, Judith, Granville, and Frances were the four youngest Sharp siblings. Catherine was only 13 when her father died in 1783, so her aunts and uncles assumed an increased role in her and her mother's domestic and business arrangements in the 1780s and 1790s. By the end of the century, she had begun working with Elizabeth to record and preserve family papers, and Jemima regularly worked with Judith and Granville as she managed her property and household. In both cases the aunts and uncle followed patterns they learned through interacting with siblings, increasingly treating their nieces as peers.

Without siblings, the three cousins invested considerable time and energy in their relationships even as their domestic arrangements altered. May 1800 marked a turning point for them, when 22-year-old Mary married Thomas John Lloyd-Baker, a young man from a Gloucestershire gentry family she and her parents had associated with beginning in the late 1790s. Granville reported the details to Judith and Jemima: The couple were married by the bishop of London at nine in the morning on May 20 in Fulham church, after which guests, clergy, and family members gathered at Fulham House for a wedding breakfast.[106] Then the family departed for Clare Hall to spend the rest of the day and May 21 with just their "own party," as Elizabeth put it.[107] The newlyweds initially lived in the cottage at Fulham House (three of their first four children were baptized there), but they eventually moved to Hardwicke Court in Gloucestershire.

Thirty-year-old Catherine and 38-year-old Jemima remained unmarried. In April 1788, despite there being "much talk" of Jemima potentially marrying a Mr. Parker, nothing came of it. Despite John's willingness to give a generous marriage settlement, Elizabeth remarked that she did not think Jemima ever inclined to the marriage.[108] Sharing a household with Judith and surrounded by

---

[105] Mary Sharp Lloyd-Baker, "Wicken," 3, D6919/2/4.
[106] Granville Sharp to Jemima Sharp, May 19, 1800, D6919/2/2.
[107] Elizabeth Sharp Prowse, memorandum and commonplace book, May 20, 1800, D3549/14/1/1.
[108] Elizabeth Sharp Prowse, memorandum and commonplace book, April 23, 1788, D3549/14/1/1. There is no indication that being deaf disadvantaged Jemima's marriage prospects. This reflects findings about eighteenth-century Belgium, where deafness could impact marriage opportunities, but was

additional aunts and an uncle also disinclined her (unless almost unattainable standards were met). This was a common pattern; women often "learned" singleness from their aunts and single woman ran in families.[109] It is easy to see why marriage was not a priority for Jemima and, perhaps by extension, for Catherine.[110]

With six pregnancies and two children who died as infants in the first nine years of her marriage, Mary's daily life differed greatly from Catherine's at Clare Hall north of London and from Jemima's in Durham. But letters, gifts, and, when possible, visits maintained strong cousin ties. In 1788, 10-year-old Mary gave Catherine a lapis lazuli heart. When it was later broken, Mary replaced it and composed a poem about its symbolism:

> May this a faithful Emblem prove
> Nor Ever from your Bosom rove
> But rest there firm & true;
> Its small dimensions justly may
> My Merit, not my Love, portray,
> My Constancy its true.

Catherine continued to treasure the gift until she passed it to Mary's granddaughter in 1837.[111]

Conclusion

In a family like the Sharps, where low marriage rates and low fertility rates reduced the experience of parenting, aunting and uncling assumed a larger place in the family culture. Aunt and uncle relationships are often understood as a type of surrogate parenthood, but the Sharps' experience shows that aunting and uncling were their own relationships with their own boundaries and possibilities; while their roles overlapped in some ways with parenting, they also contained aspects parent–child relations did not have.[112] Just as mothering was not only

---

not a universal determinant for whether a person married or not. Sofie de Veirman, Helena Haage, and Lotta Vikstrom, "Deaf and Unwanted? Marriage Characteristics of Deaf People in Eighteenth-Century Belgium: A Comparative and Cross-Regional Approach," *Continuity and Change*, 31, no. 2 (August 2016): 241–273.

[109] Froide, *Never Married*, 54.

[110] Amy Harris, "'She Never Inclined to It': Childhood, Family Relationships, and Marital Choice in Eighteenth-Century England," *Journal of the History of Childhood and Youth*, 12, no. 2 (Spring 2019): 179–198.

[111] Note on lapis lazuli heart, January 1837, in loose papers of Mary Sharp Baker, D6919/2/2.

[112] Joanne Bailey, *Parenting in England, 1760–1830: Emotion, Identity, and Generation* (Oxford: Oxford University Press, 2012), 210–214.

168   BEING SINGLE IN GEORGIAN ENGLAND

nurturing and fathering not only providing, so too aunting was not solely about emotional and marital support for nieces and uncling about professional support for nephews.

For unmarried or childless men, sibling relationships, particularly with their sisters and sisters-in-law, could offer avenues to a type of surrogate husbandhood and fatherhood. But when uncles, even uncles who were also fathers, invested in relationships directly with nieces and nephews, the relationship evolved beyond surrogate parenting into something fulfilling and defined on its own terms. Hierarchies based on generational differences leveled out over time for the Sharps, particularly the single Sharps and their nieces.

Aunting and uncling is not a matter of biological reproduction, but it is a matter of social reproduction. Through long visits, letters detailing the health and development of the children, investment in their education, and gifts, the Sharp aunts and uncles were essential to the raising of the next generation. Their importance was particularly true for the unmarried and childless Sharps whose relationships with their nieces and nephew were untrammeled by competing obligations to spouse and children. In the long term this also reduced two nieces' inclination to marry.

6

For All the World

"[E]very of us must exercise private benevolence according to his substance; we must set apart ^a decent portion^ of our worldly goods for this purpose, & strive to lay it out in the most beneficial manner, to do as much good with it as we can."[1]

John, sermon draft

"The Queen O Wicken, parent, patroness

Defender of the poor"[2]

Niece Mary's description of Elizabeth

Introduction

In September 1767 Catherine, William's wife, wrote a letter to Elizabeth and Judith at Wicken. She wrote that the London brothers were consulting legal experts about ways they could help a formerly enslaved man, Jonathan Strong, whose former master was trying to reclaim him. The case was likely to make "fine work for the Lawyers," but the brothers thought it "a pubblick consern and will go thro with it," she reported. She then indicated Strong was staying with her and William in Mincing Lane.[3] In the letter Catherine referred to Jonathan Strong as "a black boy Bro G took some care about 2 years ago." Typically, the story of Sharp philanthropic and reforming activities starts there—with Granville and the anti-slavery movement. But it is impossible to imagine Granville's work without the involvement of his siblings and nieces. Every treatment of Granville's life, from nineteenth-century hagiography to current historical scholarship, discusses his siblings and their support. The force of their personalities and the importance of Granville to them and they to him is so obvious, that they cannot be left out of his story. Similarly, because Granville was single, his connection to his siblings and nieces is highlighted as comprising his most important personal relationships and his most important allies.

---

[1] John Sharp, sermon draft, *c.*1750, Archdeacon Sharp sermons, GB-0036-SHS, Box 1, Sermon 27, Durham Cathedral Library (DCL).

[2] Mary Sharp Lloyd-Baker, "Wicken," 1, *c.*1810, D6919/2/4.

[3] Transcript of letter from Catherine Barwick Sharp to Judith Sharp, Elizabeth Sharp Prowse, diary and commonplace book, September 26, 1767, 55, D3549/14/1/1.

Being Single in Georgian England: Families, Households, and the Unmarried. Amy Harris, Oxford University Press.
© Amy Harris 2023. DOI: 10.1093/oso/9780192869494.003.0010

170 BEING SINGLE IN GEORGIAN ENGLAND

However, Granville's work was just one part of a family mosaic, not an isolated set of actions attributable solely to his unique drive or intelligence. Similarly, the charitable and reform work of John, Elizabeth, James, and William has been studied in isolation.[4] The full impact of the Sharps' work is only evident when all their stories are brought together. Doing so also allows speculation about the Catherines', Frances's, and Judith's roles, since little documentary evidence survives for their charitable activities. Bringing the siblings' stories together reveals the depth of their sincere, though paternalistic, desires to help their social inferiors. No matter how communal, even egalitarian, their internal relationships were, all their charitable endeavors reflected eighteenth-century hierarchies embodied in paternalism, or perhaps more accurately for the sisters, maternalism. The practice of charitable paternalism/maternalism might also have had a particular attraction to the Sharps, since most were childless the majority of their lives.

The Sharps' progenitors were credited with a tradition of generosity to the vulnerable.[5] As with so much of their family culture, the Sharp siblings built on previous generations' practices of social and religious reform and charitable endeavors. Charitable support of the poor, ill, enslaved, and dispossessed became central to the Sharps' sense of self and family identity. Their father once praised John for cultivating "benevolence...by the habitual and successful exercise of this good work" in helping the poor, widowed, and orphaned.[6] The scope of the siblings' activities, however, far outstripped that of their grandparents and parents. John's extensive charitable work at Bamburgh and William's weekly offer of free medical treatment for the poor were the siblings' first formal charitable actions. Between the 1760s and 1780s the siblings' philanthropic efforts ranged from formal institutions they joined and organizations they established to more informal, local actions. Granville's effort included numerous publications and had the furthest geographic reach. The others' work tended to be local or regional and they published far less. In addition, they participated in informal forms of private charity and unremunerated service. They continued such work throughout their lives, though after 1790 retirement from business, age, declining health, and death narrowed the scope of their philanthropic and reform activities.

---

[4] J.A. Woods, "James Sharp: Common Councillor of London in the Time of Wilkes," in Anne Whiteman, J.S. Bromley, and P.G.M. Dickson, eds., *Statesmen, Scholars and Merchants* (Oxford: Clarendon Press, 1973), 276–288; McDonagh, "'All towards the improvements of the estate': Mrs. Elizabeth Prowse at Wicken, 1764–1810"; Alun Withey, "Medicine and Charity in Eighteenth-Century Northumberland: The Early Years of Bamburgh Castle Dispensary and Surgery, c.1772–1802," *Social History of Medicine* (2016): 1–23; Sean P. Hughes and G. Anne Davies, "Why is William Sharp's Name Forgotten When His Novel Method for Treating Factures of the Ankle is Still Used Today?," *Journal of Medical Biography* (March 2022).

[5] Hoare, *Memoirs of Granville Sharp*, 455–456.

[6] John Sharp, sermon draft, c.1750, Archdeacon Sharp sermons, GB-0036-SHS, Box 1, Sermon 27, Durham Cathedral Library.

FOR ALL THE WORLD   171

Given the Sharps' strong collective identity, it is not surprising to discover how intertwined their charitable activities were. Catherine's 1767 letter reveals her otherwise invisible role in supporting Jonathan Strong's suit and highlights the importance of Elizabeth, Frances, and Judith's involvement, while also pointing out that James and Granville worked together on the case. From 1765, when Granville began his efforts, James and William supported anti-slavery activities by providing care for Strong. When Strong's previous enslaver tried to reclaim him, he sued James and Granville for theft. Additionally, all the brothers (and presumably the sisters, though letters detailing such work does not survive), edited and gave feedback about Granville's anti-slavery writing, exchanged his pamphlets, and carefully monitored how his works were received by other authors; they also preserved records of this shared work. Beyond Granville's actions, the siblings participated in formal (institutional) philanthropy and informal (personal) charity as well as social and political reforms.

Foundations of the Sharp Siblings' Philanthropic and Reform Efforts

Earlier Generations' Charitable and Philanthropic Activities

The Sharps built on earlier traditions of Anglican volunteerism and increasing attention to pastoral care.[7] Caring for the poor was a principal area of charitable action and clerical preaching.[8] Whether the action was private charitable acts or membership in a public philanthropic society, it was cast in paternal terms.[9] Sir George Wheler, in addition to bequests to the poor and funding apprenticeships for poor children, funded a charity school for girls at Houghton le Spring, Durham. The bequest provided a generous annual salary for a schoolmistress, employment of the free school's usher, clothes for girls attending the school, repairs of the school's gatehouse, and "books, pens, ink and paper, and materials for sewing, knitting, etc." for the students.[10] He was also involved with the Society

---

[7] Brent Sirota, *The Christian Monitors: The Church of England and the Age of Benevolence, 1680–1730* (New Haven: Yale University Press, 2014), 149.

[8] Sarah Irving-Stonebraker, "The Surprising Lineage of Useful Knowledge," in Justin Champion, John Coffey, et al., eds., *Politics, Religion, and Ideas in 17th and 18th Century Britain: Essays in Honour of Mark Goldie* (Melton: Boydell and Brewer, 2019), 277–291.

[9] Lancelot Addison, *A Modest Plea for the Clergy; Wherein is Briefly Considered, the Original, Antiquity, and Necessary Use of the Clergy, and the Pretended and Real Occasions of Their Present Contempt* (London: W. Taylor, 1709), 83.

[10] Frank H. Rushford, *Houghton Le Spring: A History* (Durham: Durham County Press, 1950), 24, 69, Du/L6, Society of Genealogists (SoG). This Girls' Blue Coat School (a common term for charity schools) opened in 1719 and served twenty-eight students at a time. It merged with another local school in 1855.

172   BEING SINGLE IN GEORGIAN ENGLAND

for the Propagation of the Gospel in Foreign Parts and the Society for Promoting Christian Knowledge.

Archbishop Sharp's dislike for the reformation of manners societies was partially due to dislike of dissenting sects and partially a distaste for what he saw as "witch-hunting" tendencies within the societies.[11] Instead he was consistently motivated by pastoral concerns for the clergy in his province. In the eighteenth century most northern clergymen struggled financially and many lived in poverty.[12] The archbishop worked to alleviate the situation via his advocacy for what became called Queen Anne's Bounty—a reform effort to augment poor clergymen's income by reapportioning tithes.

The Sharp siblings' father, Thomas Sr., worked consistently to support poor clergy, even beyond the scope of Queen Anne's Bounty.[13] He and his wife Judith provided support for the poor of Rothbury and many of his sermons focused on charity and supporting the widows and children of poor clergymen.[14] The Sharps' extended kin also continued the tradition by using their wills to provide for poor clergy, often obligating the siblings to continue the work when they acted as executors.[15] Thomas Sr. became a trustee of Lord Crewe's charity in 1736. As trustee he facilitated the charity's mission to support poor clergy and build schools, and undertook other charitable efforts in the City of Durham and Lincoln College, Oxford. He also began repairs on Bamburgh Castle on the Northumberland coast, one of the charity's properties. He regularly toured trust properties to inspect efforts to build schools, repair parsonages, and "mak[e] grants to individuals which ranged over very kind of need."[16]

Sharp Siblings' Philanthropic and Charitable Activities before the 1760s

Thomas Sr.'s concern with poor clergy and their dependents was perpetuated by John. As John once wrote the bishop of Durham, "I am very desirous to do all the

[11] Barry Till, "Sharp, John (1645?–1714), archbishop of York," *Oxford Dictionary of National Biography*.

[12] M.F. Snap, "Poverty and the Northern Clergy in the Eighteenth Century: The Parish of Whalley, 1689–1789," *Northern History*, 36, no. 1 (March 2000): 83–97.

[13] Thomas Sharp, "An Apology for the Annual Collections Made toward the Support of Clergymens Widows and Orphans, within the Counties of Durham and Northumberland, being a Sermon Preached at the Yearly Meeting of the Sons of the Clergy," Newcastle upon Tyne, October 23, 1746 (Newcastle upon Tyne: John White, 1746), Y 1746.Sharp, NYHS.

[14] Thomas Sr. published at least eighteen sermons and religious texts during his lifetime and his sons posthumously published a collection of his works in 1763.

[15] John Mangey, will, written October 25, 1780, codicils written January 21 and August 10, 1782, proved November 29, 1782, Prerogative Court of Canterbury, PROB 11/1097, TNA, digital image at https://www.ancestry.co.uk, accessed March 18, 2016.

[16] C.J. Stranks, "The Charities of Nathaniel, Lord Crewe and Dr. John Sharp, 1721–1976," Durham Cathedral Lecture, 1976, 10, http://www.lordcrewescharity.org.uk/phpmedia/docs/7feb-d25997011e9960b528a989936fb3.pdf.

Good I can…& I don't know how I can employ myself more usefully to that end, than by endeavouring to get all the poor Cures in this Archdeaconry Augmented, that are capable of being so." He planned to augment the income for one or two a year and, in typical John style, promised that should the bishop approve the plan, he would be "indefatigable in the prosecution of it."[17]

The Sharps were embedded in the eighteenth-century rise in voluntarism within the Church and increased philanthropic activities beyond clerical concerns. As John sermonized, public and private charity were essential aspects of Anglican worship. "[E]very of us must exercise private benevolence according to his substance; we must set apart ^a decent portion^ of our worldly goods for this purpose, & strive to lay it out in the most beneficial manner, to do as much good with it as we can," he wrote in the early 1750s.[18] He also reminded listeners to ensure their charitable efforts did not interfere with their responsibilities to their household. "I need not be understood to insinuate," he wrote, "by this that a man shd carry his Love to his neighbour so far as to do hurt to himself. We are only commanded to do actions of Love & charity in proportion to every mans estate; but were we to carry them to that length as to do…any real disservice to ourselves & our families."[19]

John was in his late twenties, single, and newly appointed vicar of Hartburn when he wrote the sermon about benevolent obligations. He took his own counsel seriously and when he became trustee of Lord Crewe's Charity in his father's stead in 1758, he applied his indefatigable energy (and the trust's surplus funds) to improving the conditions at Bamburgh. That summer the trustees agreed to give him the £15 that had been set aside to repairing the castle. They severely underestimated not only the cost of repairing and running the castle, but also the drive and imagination of their newest trustee. John's first task was to refurbish parts of the castle in order for the manorial courts to resume regular meeting (something they had not done since 1748) and to establish schools for boys and girls, to be held within refurbished spaces inside the castle. He and Mary subsequently made Bamburgh their second home, living in repaired living quarters within the keep. The living quarters were "fitted up at the join expense of Lord Crewe's Trustees" and Thomas, when he was appointed curate for Bamburgh, which had no house attached to it.[20] John and Mary lived there half of the year and Thomas joined in their charitable endeavors. From the beginning of his trusteeship, John used his own funds to augment the trust's expenditures on Bamburgh improvements. The trust would often reimburse him, but it appears his early strategy was to ask for limited funds for whatever project or wages he was

[17] John Sharp to the Bishop of Durham, March 8, 1764, NRO 384/1, NAW.
[18] John Sharp, sermon draft, c.1750, Archdeacon Sharp sermons, GB-0036-SHS, Box 1, Sermon 27, DCL.
[19] John Sharp, sermon draft, undated, GB-0036-SHS, Box 1, DCL.
[20] John Sharp, visitation answers, 1782, NRO 452/C/3/2/12, NAW.

174   BEING SINGLE IN GEORGIAN ENGLAND

requesting, pay the overage himself, and then, once he could show them results, seek reimbursement for the full sum. He must have been particularly skilled and persuasive. His first request, for £5 a year for repairing rooms for the manorial courts, was easily granted, and when he reported that he had had to supplement with over £300 of his own money, the trust reimbursed him.

Like John, William began incorporating charitable service into his routine as soon as he became a householder. When he completed his apprenticeship in 1750, he had the good fortune to inherit his retiring master's house and surgery. He began seeing poor patients free of charge. In 1755 he was elected an assistant surgeon to St. Bartholomew's Hospital and his reputation continued to grow, as did the line of patients without financial means outside his Mincing Lane door.

Formal Philanthropic, Political, and Reform Activities, 1760s–1780s

After 1760, John and William's work greatly expanded, and the other siblings followed suit as they matured and acquired businesses and homes. The Sharps were not confined to serving within existing philanthropic or reform organizations; much of their charitable work was done outside the major charitable organizations of their time. As with their social network, their charitable networks were often created or greatly augmented by their own activities.

Activities at Bamburgh, Northumberland

In the thirty-four years he managed Bamburgh Castle and its associated charities, John constantly improved and expanded the scope of Crewe's charity. Though little is known of Mary's contribution, surviving evidence about the closeness of their relationship and their shared responsibility for household finances suggests she was instrumental. In fact, it is possible that John learned his shrewd financial skills from her since she was the one who imposed an annual budget on his Bamburgh expenditures because his free spending in their "rather strait" circumstances had her begrudging the money spent on the Castle.[21] It is easy to imagine her influence, for example, behind John's turning a fishery owned by the trust from something that produced about £150 per year when he became a trustee to one worth £535 annually less than a decade later.[22] The scale of what John and Mary established at Bamburgh is staggering. Early efforts might have been modest; refurbishing rooms for manorial courts and for schools was useful, but not

---

[21] Mary Sharp to Judith Sharp, May 14, 1770, D3549/16/1/1.
[22] Stranks, "The Charities of Nathaniel, Lord Crewe," 14.

exactly transformative. In the following decades, however, John used his position to make the coast safer for sailors and to enact a variety of poverty-relieving and health-promoting initiatives that served numerous groups.

John seemed particularly concerned with local conditions at Bamburgh. The coast could be dangerous in storms, so he began a series of initiatives to rescue survivors from shipwrecks as well as to salvage the wrecks for castle building materials, to provide for their medical care, and to establish a fund to support widows and children of sailors who did not survive. One of his first efforts to relieve poverty was a "corn charity" in 1766. With an initial outlay of £30 from the trustees, he began purchasing wheat "for the relief of the Poor in Bambroughshire, when the price of wheat shall happen to be above 5s [per] Bushell."[23] Eventually the corn charity grew to include four granaries and a windmill built to supply grain, beans, and peas to the area's poor, free of charge or at a subsidized cost. Anyone within forty miles of Bamburgh was welcome to avail themselves of the grain (dispensed twice a week) and the "cheap shop" at the castle where they could buy "candles, butter, pepper, blue, pins, alum, and rice specially imported from Carolina" at a reduced cost.[24] The number of people who must have bene-fited from these commodities was enormous. For example, the trustees spent at least £100 for grain dispensed just between 1767 and 1769—a sum that on the open market could have purchased sixty-one quarters (over 1700 pounds) of wheat.[25]

John's next innovation was a dispensary at the castle. The castle already had upwards of thirty beds, largely for ill and injured seaman who had been rescued from shipwrecks. John noted that Bamburgh's isolated location—fifty miles from the Newcastle Infirmary and over seventy miles from Edinburgh Infirmary—meant the poor, who were "so very necessitous," could "neither pay a surgeon for attendance or advice, or be at the necessary expence of Drugs when sick."[26] In the middle of the eighteenth century, dispensaries, with their smaller size and empha-sis on outpatient care, were increasingly popular alternatives to in-patient care at large hospitals and infirmaries. John's implementation of such a plan was not, therefore, unprecedented.[27]

The trust's funding and John's astute leadership, however, made Bamburgh unique in England's medical care landscape. Without a board of governors or

---

[23] Lord Crewe's Trustees order book, October 9, 1766, page 99, NRO/452/B/1/1, NAW, digital image at http://www.familysearch.org, Image Group Number 100725245, image 102 of 375.

[24] Stranks, "The Charities of Nathaniel, Lord Crewe," 12.

[25] Lord Crewe's Trustees order book, September 14, 1767, November 26, 1768, November 27, 1769, pages 99–100, 113, 123–124, NRO/452/B/1/1, NAW, digital image at http://www.familysearch.org, Image Group Number 100725245, images 107–108, 121, 131–132 of 375.

[26] Lord Crew Charity, castle notebook, August 20, 1772, page 141, quoted in Alun Withey, "Medicine and Charity in Eighteenth-Century Northumberland: The Early Years of Bamburgh Castle Dispensary and Surgery, c.1772–1802," Social History of Medicine, 29, no. 3 (August 2016): 471.

[27] Withey, "Medicine and Charity," 472.

subscribers setting the rules and budget, John enjoyed the confidence of his fellow trustees and was left largely unhindered to do what he thought best. He consulted with experts from every possible field, including his brother William, who helped him find surgeons for Bamburgh and who donated a sedan chair for transporting patients.[28] In addition to treating injuries and illness, the dispensary offered smallpox inoculation, something not widespread in the North before this date, but something John was familiar with due to William's implementation of the practice among his family and patients. Along with the dispensary, there was an on-site apothecary, a surgery, the beds for injured seaman, a hot bath for recuperating patients, not to mention kitchens and dining facilities, tools, equipment, and furniture—and of course a retinue of servants, temporary laborers, surgeons, nurses, and midwives to manage day-to-day operations. The scale of the dispensary's work was remarkable. At its highest, the dispensary served 2000 patients a year, of every age and gender.[29]

John and Mary's residence at the castle for a portion of every year meant that unlike a hospital's or charity's board of governors, John was aware of the details of how poor people lived and struggled. He clearly saw how poor education, inadequate wages, unexpected illness, disability, or death perpetuated poverty. He heard or read the individual accounts from people petitioning the charity for support. His awareness of the realities of poverty made him, unlike many of his contemporaries, unconcerned with moralizing about poor people's behaviors and made him entirely uninterested in denominational differences. His sermons show a consistent concern for loving one's neighbors, but it is telling that he did not publish them as his father and grandfather had done. Instead, he dedicated his time and intellectual labor to addressing human suffering as effectively as possible. A 1779 visitor described all of John's "schemes" as having a "humane and useful tendency" and a twentieth-century archdeacon described John's approach: "No theory was involved. It had been a practical response to obvious need."[30] While patients had to have a certificate from their parish priest or dissenting minister indicating they needed the services of the dispensary, being treated there was "remarkably devoid of caveat."[31] John's prioritizing practical care over assessments of worthiness seems to have influenced the local clergy, established and nonconformist, because they freely granted certificates. Over time John developed and then expanded every philanthropic initiative at Bamburgh. It was, as a scholar has

---

[28] Alun Withey, "The Hidden Hospital: Bamburgh Castle Infirmary and Dispensary," *History Today*, August 11, 2015, https://www.historytoday.com/hidden-hospital-bamburgh-castle-infirmary-and-dispensary.

[29] Withey, "Medicine and Charity," 478, 486.

[30] William Hutchinson, *A View of Northumberland: With an Excursion to the Abbey of Mailross in Scotland* (Newcastle: W. Charnley and Messrs Vesey & Whitfield, 1778), 175; Stranks, "The Charities of Nathaniel, Lord Crewe," 16.

[31] Withey, "Medicine and Charity," 482.

recently put it, "a self-contained welfare state in miniature."[32] It is no surprise John considered the castle "a child of my own."[33] John's characterizing Bamburgh's charitable undertakings in paternalistic terms was a standard eighteenth-century trope. Such an association may have also provided John (and perhaps Mary) with a large fictive posterity alongside their daughter Jemima.[34]

Details about Thomas and Mary's role in Bamburgh's practical philanthropy are not recorded, but from a few scattered references in the Sharps' correspondence it is clear they both acted as a sort of assistant managers, supervising workmen, handling disputes between servants, and offering advice to John. In a letter reporting about repairs at the castle, Thomas once recounted how he managed the care of guests at Bamburgh. Thomas scolded his servant, Rutherford, for how he handled castle visitors. When visitors came, Rutherford let the housekeeper show them the gallery and the kitchen and then he would take them to show the remainder of the castle so that he would get the monetary benefits that might come from doing this instead of her. Drawing away guests, as Thomas wrote, "by his Officiousness." Thomas seemed more troubled by the inhospitality—to guests and the housekeeper—than by the petty fraud.[35] It is also probable, given how synchronous their thoughts were about household management and family relationships, that Mary and Thomas shared John's practical approach to alleviating suffering and poverty. Being the younger, unmarried brother made perpetuating patterns established when they were younger all that much easier. Thomas had followed in John's footsteps throughout his life; he was happy to follow John's leadership and work alongside him.

Though it is lengthy, it is worth quoting John's own response when asked about the scale and scope of Bamburgh charities:

Schools for 130 Children – apartments for the 3 Masters & Mistress; Large Granaries forlorn, so as to supply all the Poor that come for it at a certain moderate Price even in the scarcest Years – Publick Library; Rooms for the reception of Shipwrecked Seamen – General Dispensary for Sick & Wounded Poor – an Infirmary for particular Objects:

Baths of different kinds – Barrack for a Detachment of Men in time of War – Armoury – Powder Room – Powder Magazine – A Ten Gun Battery of heavy Metal from 32 Pounder…which commands a pass between the castle & the Islands through which ships of the greatest Burden may sail; & if chased have a chance to be secured from Privateers – An upper Battery of Swivels on the top of

[32] Withey, "Medicine and Charity," 474.
[33] John Sharp to Judith Sharp, May 14, 1770, D3549/16/1/1.
[34] Lawrence Stone and Jeanne C. Fawtier Stone, *An Open Elite? England 1540–1880* (Oxford: Clarendon Press, 1984), 412–419.
[35] Thomas Sharp, Bamburgh, to John Sharp, Hartburn, Northumberland, December 6, 1760, D3549/9/1/4.

178   BEING SINGLE IN GEORGIAN ENGLAND

the Green Tower of Keep, to cover the under one, in case an Enemy Should make good their Landing, Repositaries for shipwrecked Stores and also for Implements for the assistance for vessels in distress.[36]

John recognized that Bamburgh's situation was unique. "It was owing to the *peculiar situation* of this castle, and accidental circumstances, more than to any other cause, that so many charities have been thought of, and instituted here," he wrote. If there was a need, John designed a solution and convinced the other trustees it would be money well spent. Everything was done to make the castle "habitable, commodious, and more extensively useful," while funding came from his personal income and from "some assistance from...relations and friends."[37] Though John did not mention it, the most peculiar part of the endeavor was the Sharps themselves. Mary's budgetary lessons, John's indefatigable energy, and Thomas's unstinting support came together to create an extraordinary response to every local need. In the end their efforts provided medical, educational, and financial assistance to thousands.

Activities in London

William's free medical services may have been the first charitable endeavor for the London-based siblings, but over the 1760s and 1770s James and Granville established their own reforming and philanthropic efforts and the family's combined efforts expanded. Beginning in the late 1760s the London-based brothers began joining various philanthropic and voluntary societies and organizations. James and Granville worked on proposals to improve the banks and docks of the Thames. All three joined St. Bartholomew's board of governors and William and Granville joined the Society for the Propagation of the Gospel in Foreign Parts. Throughout this period the brothers became increasingly intertwined with each other's efforts. James's helping John acquire paving stones for improvements at Bamburgh and William's advising John about surgeons and medical care there have already been noted. On another occasion, William, James, and Granville sent a petitioner to John. James's former apprentice, George Higginson, had lost all of his considerable fortune when his business of exporting toys and jewelry to India collapsed during the credit crisis of 1772–73 and he declared bankruptcy. Granville, William, and James offered some assistance as Higginson attempted to reestablish himself. They then

---

[36] John Sharp to Edward King, Esq., March 5, 1786, Add MS 1014, PGL.
[37] "Copy of a Letter from Dr. Sharp to John Ramsay, Esq. of Oche, by Stirling, North Britain," *Gentleman's Magazine*, 63, part 1 (May 1793): 387–389.

asked John if Crewe's charity could also help the man. The trustees approved the request and granted Higginson twenty guineas.[38]

Like John, William too received praise from outside observers. A poem written in his honor proclaimed "Sharpe's all gen'rous soul, / In charitable deed, knows no control / That still attentive to affliction's call, / With sympathizing heart he feels for all."[39] And he followed John's pattern of being more concerned with addressing needs in his neighborhood than in publishing his ideas or engaging in professional debates. William, like many mid-century surgeons and physicians, was an enthusiastic proponent of smallpox inoculation, but he did not participate in the defense and advocacy of the practice in print.[40] His only publication, a letter he sent to another St. Bartholomew surgeon, detailing a new method for treating broken ankles, was published in 1767.[41] Though the method is still used today, William apparently did nothing to promote his invention, nor advertise his surgery.[42] William had been in business for fifteen years and a surgeon at St. Bartholomew's for a decade when he married Catherine Barwick. However, it is probable that the marriage and the £3500 in stock she brought with her augmented William's ability to provide services for the poor without needing to advertise his services or supplement his income and reputation by writing textbooks or medical treatises.

James was unique among the siblings because he held political office and used it to push for political reforms and social improvements. He was a member of the London Common Council from 1765 until his death in 1783. He consistently voted for reform and even radical positions.[43] His wife Catherine's thoughts on James's politics are unknown, but as her brothers voted for many of the same candidates James voted for in 1768, it is probable she shared at least some of his beliefs.[44] As happened so often for the Sharps, the timing of his election to the Common Council was fortunate for James's interests. By the mid-1760s the Common Council had become more engaged in public works than previously.

[38] Granville Sharp to John Sharp, July 24, 1773, NRO 452/C/2/2/5/20, NAW.

[39] George Brown, undated poem honoring William Sharp, D3549/10/1/10.

[40] Deborah Christian Brunton, "Pox Britannica: Smallpox Inoculation in Britain, 1721–1820" (PhD thesis, University of Pennsylvania, 1990), 66–97; Barbara Denny, *Fulham Past* (London: Historical Publications, 1997), 100.

[41] William Sharp, *An Account of a New Method of Treating Fractured Legs. Read Before the Royal Society of London, on February 12, 1767. To Which Is Prefixed a Letter on that Subject to James Parsons, M. D. A Member of that Respectable Society, Dated November 6, 1766* (London, 1767).

[42] William's innovative splint was advertised in 1768, but by someone selling them in the Minories, not by William. "For Fractured Limbs," *Gazetteer and New Daily Advertiser*, September 20, 1768.

[43] J.A. Woods, "James Sharp: Common Councillor of London in the Time of Wilkes," in Anne Whiteman, J.S. Bromley, and P.G.M. Dickson, eds., *Statesmen, Scholars and Merchants: Essays in Eighteenth-Century History Presented to Dame Lucy Sutherland* (Oxford: Clarendon Press, 1973), 276–288.

[44] James and John Lodge, Little St. Helen's, Clothworkers' Company, *The Poll of the Livery of London for Four Citizens to Represent the Said City in Parliament* (London: John Rivington, 1768), 63, London Metropolitan Archives, digital image at *UK, Poll Books and Electoral Registers, 1538–1893*, https://www.ancestry.co.uk, accessed May 2, 2022.

180   BEING SINGLE IN GEORGIAN ENGLAND

It was also enjoying a more powerful voice in local and national politics (a power that gradually declined after the 1770s).[45] Both factors were parallels to James's interests in political reform and in improving transportation networks—both of which he "calculated for the benefit of mankind in general."[46]

Though he had not voted for John Wilkes in 1768, James opposed Parliament's refusal to seat Wilkes in 1769. He supported, and often wrote, various remonstrances the Council adopted. In particular, he wrote and presented a remonstrance calling for the king to dismiss Parliament in May 1770.[47] After the Sharps entertained the royal family in August 1770, James had two conversations with the king. While they mostly discussed music, James was clear that his loyalty to the crown did not mean he would cease opposing government actions he disagreed with. "I am very sure," he told the king, "the City of London will rejoice to do every thing in their power, that may any way contribute to your Majestys pleasure or convenience provided it does not interfere with the publick good."[48] The king apparently did not hold this against James, whom he described as "very sensible and clever" even if his principles led him to be a "bill of Rights man."[49]

That November the Common Council sent another remonstrance, this one conveyed by a procession that included James in his coach. Thomas reported to Elizabeth, Judith, and Frances that he hoped "they may be better received than usual, for I am told their Remonstrance is a very Mild & proper one." Thomas indicated that Wilkes did not go with the procession, "lest it sh[oul]d in flame the Populace & occasion the soldiers to fire upon them."[50] Thomas was referring to the 1768 St. George's Fields Massacre, when Wilkes was imprisoned and his gathered, protesting supporters were fired on. In 1771 James was part of the Common Council majority who voted for Wilkes because he supported "the privileges and franchises of the city, and defended our excellent constitution."[51]

While James was active in the various council committees and advocated for governance on more democratic grounds, his main passion was to improve transportation networks, principally the canal system. The rolling carts might have been a purely practical solution to improve the condition of English roads, but his passion for improving English waterways was driven by a belief that improved communication and transportation were essential to London retaining its

---

[45] Ian Doolittle, "The City of London in the Eighteenth Century: Corporate Pressures and Their Consequences," in Elaine Chalus and Perry Gauci, eds., *Revisiting The Polite and Commercial People: Essays in Georgian Politics, Society, and Culture in Honour of Professor Paul Langford* (Oxford: Oxford University Press, 2019), 101–118.

[46] James Sharp, obituary, 1783, clipping in family scrapbook, D3549/12/14.

[47] Woods, "James Sharp," 285.   [48] Quoted in Woods, "James Sharp," 285–286.

[49] Quoted in Woods, "James Sharp," 286.

[50] Thomas Sharp to [Elizabeth Sharp Prowse, Wicken], November 21, 1770, portion inserted after the entry for May 26, 1759, Elizabeth Sharp Prowse, memorandum and commonplace book, D3549/14/1/1.

[51] "News," *London Evening Post*, March 21, 1771, 4.

FOR ALL THE WORLD   181

"Superiority in Foreign as well as Country Trade."[52] In an impassioned address to the Common Council advocating for a canal between Waltham Abbey some forty miles north of London and Moorfields on the city's northern boundary, he delineated the benefits, costs, and necessity of such a canal for expanding domestic trade and improving London's port. His closing remarks echoed paternalistic ideas about the council's obligations and demonstrated that his council work and engineering improvements were central to his understanding of civic responsibility and charitable endeavor. "Shall we delay setting heartily about this desirable Work?...I trust we shall not. It is our Duty; it is Justice; it is the greatest of all Charity, to impart to Man the Means of earning his Bread; it is Charity to our Country; it is Charity to Mankind." In typical Sharp fashion he did not see conflict between his own comfortable, even abundant circumstances, and the lack he wanted to address: "we may derive Wealth to ourselves by supplying the respective Wants of others," he concluded.[53] A family friend later wrote of James that "his unshaken integrity gave him great influence in the city."[54] This exaggerated James's power, as he was not successful in convincing others to build the Waltham Abbey–Moorfields canal, but he channeled his energies, as well as some of Granville's, into improving the Thames instead. He also continued work on other Common Council committees and invested in other canal projects in the counties.

James may have seen his work to improve roads and canals as a service to his fellow countrymen, but his passion and innovations were not universally appreciated. On the nights of June 5 and 9, Edward Mayor, carman, and John Darlow, wheelwright, had threatening letters thrown into their yards. The letters' author threatened to burn down their houses if they kept making or using carts after James's design. While both letters mention James by name, the second was particularly pointed: "that Damd Son of a Bich Sharp shall Feal our Resentment furst as he has got one at work the furst Day the new one Comes Out." James wanted the culprit caught but he did not seem unduly troubled by the events. What motivated the antagonism is not exactly clear, but it likely came from those threatened by what the mechanical inventions would mean for existing labor practices, perhaps akin to a sort of proto-Luddism. Undeterred, James offered £50 on the conviction of the perpetrator(s) in addition to the king's offer of immunity to any participant who identified the letters' author. Aware of the groups likely to be disgruntled with his invention, James sardonically added to the news account of the incident:

---

[52] Robert Whitowrth, *A Report and Survey of the Canal, Proposed to Be Made on One Level, from Waltham-Abbey to Moorfields...To Which is Subjoin'd an Address to the Right Honrouable the Lord-Mayor, and the Worshipful the Aldermen and Common-Council, of the City of London...by James Sharp* (London, 1773), cover.

[53] Robert Whitowrth, *A Report and Survey of the Canal*, 16.

[54] Hoare, *Memoirs of Granville Sharp*, 22.

182   BEING SINGLE IN GEORGIAN ENGLAND

> Mr. Sharp thinks it proper to declare, that he has undertaken the making carts of this construction for the public, with no other view than the preservation of roads and pavements; and will with pleasure give any assistance in his power to such wheelers, coach-makers, &c. as chuse to build rolling carriages of this sort.[55]

Later in 1768 James wrote John that he was working on a smaller-scale rolling cart and in January 1769 he reported he had built sixteen and was "building more as fast I can"—a rather clear rebuttal to the threats that had been as much focused on his efficiency as on the carts themselves.[56]

Unlike William and James, Granville's philanthropic work is well-known even today. In fact, it is the main reason scholars have written about the Sharps. At the heart of his efforts was the struggle to end the transatlantic slave trade, an effort that has been lionized and analyzed for two centuries. His brothers' contributions and support have also generally been recognized. And with good reason. In July 1775, after seeing the requests for additional ordnance in response to the Battle of Bunker Hill, Granville took a leave of absence from the Ordnance Office, not wanting to be "any way concerned in that unnatural business."[57] He repeatedly prolonged his furlough: "I cannot return to my ordnance duty whilst a bloody war is carried on, unjustly as I conceive, against my fellow subjects," he wrote that September. He hesitated to quit outright, however, since after nearly two decades at the office it was, he wrote, "now become my only profession and livelihood."[58] Several extensions of his furlough eventually led to his resignation in July 1777. During those two years James and William reassured Granville that they would support him financially if he chose to devote himself to public service outside paid positions. "If…you should think it proper to give up your employment," James wrote him in October 1775, "I will now speak for my brother William as well as for myself – we are both ready and willing, and, God be thanked, at present *able*, to take care that the loss shall be none to you." James, anticipating Granville's potential response, assured him "all that we have to ask in return is, that you would continue to live amongst us as you have hitherto done, without imagining that you will, in such a situation, be burthensome to us." James continued, playing on the same themes he discussed when considering marriage some thirteen years before, "if we have the needful amongst us, it matters not to whom it belongs—the happiness of being together is worth the expense, if it answered no farther purpose." James was primarily motivated by Sharp emotional and social bonds. "I have no doubt," he stated, "but the mutual assistance we are of to each other, and the consequence we acquire by it, is more than adequate to any

---

[55] "News," *Gazetteer and New Daily Advertiser*, June 13, 1768.

[56] James Sharp to John Sharp, November 30, 1768 and January 12, 1769, D3549/9/1/4.

[57] Hoare, *Memoirs of Granville Sharp*, 123.

[58] Charles Stuart, *A Memoir of Granville Sharp* (New York: American Anti-Slavery Society, 1836), 22.

third employment we might reasonably hope could be obtained." At the end of the letter William added his comments, at pains to convince Granville he was in agreement with James and that if anyone owed anyone anything, it was William who owed Granville; he concluded the letter with "I most heartily approve of what my brother has written above; and I hope you will think of the matter as we do. Much love, as due, from your affectionate Brother."[59] Granville was 41 and he never acquired other employment, instead spending the rest of his life engaged in anti-slavery and other reform efforts, always with the approval and support of his siblings.

Granville's decision to the leave the Ordnance Office and his brothers' unstinting support of his activism really began in 1764. That year he encountered Jonathan Strong among the queue outside William's surgery. Jonathan had been beaten by his enslaver so severely he had been left for dead. How he made his way to the surgery is unknown, but when Granville saw Strong's injuries, he rushed into William's house to have Strong treated immediately. William acquired a bed at St. Bartholomew's for Jonathan and when he recovered sufficiently (his sight was never fully restored) the Sharp brothers found him a position as an apothecary's servant. Two years later Strong's former owner encountered him as he was running an errand for the apothecary. Seeing Strong was capable of working, and ironically incensed he had lost the benefits of Strong's labor, he sold him to another Jamaican planter who kidnapped Strong and had him held in jail. Strong sent word to Granville, who with a combination of fiery anger, social connections, and quick thinking, was able to secure Strong's release. As the opening of this chapter explained, in the immediate aftermath, Strong found a safe haven at William and Catherine's house. Strong's original enslaver challenged Granville to a duel, but unimpressed by that lingering element of an early modern male code of honor, Granville declined, stating the law would settle the matter. There ensued a seven-year legal battle as Strong's new owner sued James and Granville for theft of property. Due to various delays the case was never fully argued and Strong remained at liberty until his death in 1773.

The case galvanized Granville, whose novice attempt at legal argumentation in the case exposed a gap in his understanding and convinced him slavery itself, not just Strong's particular case, needed addressing.[60] As there was ambiguity in what the legal precedent was for slavery in Britain, Granville spent years studying the law and history of slavery. The product of that study led to his first anti-slavery publication in 1769. *A Representation on the Injustice of Tolerating Slavery* was one of the first English treatises arguing that slavery was antithetical to the English

---

[59] Hoare, *Memoirs of Granville Sharp*, 126–127.

[60] Hoare, *Memoirs of Granville Sharp*, 498. That Granville thought he could teach himself the law the way he taught himself Greek and Hebrew is not surprising when considering legal training still had ad hoc aspects combining expertise and practice. See W.M. Jacob, *The Clerical Profession*, 3–4.

184 BEING SINGLE IN GEORGIAN ENGLAND

constitution (and Christian principles). While it would take until 1807 for the British to end the slave trade and until 1833 for slavery to be abolished in the British Empire, Granville's arguments led directly to the Somerset case in 1772. In a case paralleling Strong's, James Somerset, an enslaved African brought to Britain, escaped his owner, who recaptured him, and imprisoned him on a ship with orders to sell him upon arrival in Jamaica. Supporters were able to secure a writ of *habeas corpus* and the case went to trial. Though it was meant to decide whether Somerset had been illegally detained, the case came to be a referendum on whether property rights extended to slavery, something not guaranteed in the English constitution. In the end, Lord Mansfield, Lord Chief Justice of the King's Bench ruled that enslaved people brought to Britain could not be compelled to return to slave-holding colonies.[61] Many, however, interpreted it to mean arriving in Britain functionally freed a person from slavery. Debate over the implications of the Somerset decision raged on both sides of the Atlantic for decades and Granville continued to publish and correspond about abolishing slavery for the remainder of his life.[62]

As the movement for abolition gathered steam at the end of the century, Granville's stature only increased in reform-minded circles. By the 1780s he regularly corresponded with prominent reformers across the French and British Atlantic worlds. He was proud of his ability to interact with those he did not agree with, remarking that his apprenticeship with men from a variety of religious backgrounds had taught him to distinguish between "the *opinions* of men and their *persons*."[63] Olaudah Equiano, the Archbishop of Canterbury, Phyllis Wheatley, James Oglethorpe, Benjamin Franklin, Marquis de Lafayette, Benjamin Rush, and Methodist and Quaker abolitionists were among his associates or correspondents.[64] Granville also continued to advocate for individuals, including enslaved people, who approached him for help or whose plight he read about in the press. For example, in 1768 and 1769 when he found newspaper notices about selling a Black boy and girl, he wrote an alderman and the Lord High Chancellor, respectively, petitioning them to prevent the sales as being illegal. He pleaded with the alderman to "consider the subject more seriously than you have hitherto done."[65]

Granville had consistent opportunities to advocate for individuals, particularly after he was appointed to Bridewell's prison committee in 1792, attending meetings

---

[61] James Oldham, *English Common Law in the Age of Mansfield* (Chapel Hill: University of North Carolina Press, 2004), 305–323.

[62] Matthew Mason, "North American Calm, West Indian Storm: The Politics of the Somerset Decision in the British Atlantic," *Slavery and Abolition*, 41, no. 4 (2020): 723–747.

[63] Lascelles, *Granville Sharp*, 4.

[64] Jemima Sharp, Durham, to Granville Sharp, Garden Court, Temple, London, February 20, 1811, D3549/13/1/S6; John A. Woods, "The Correspondence of Benjamin Rush and Granville Sharp 1773–1809," *Journal of American Studies*, 1, no. 1 (April 1967): 1–38.

[65] Hoare, *Memoirs of Granville Sharp*, 48–49.

and hearing petitions on a weekly basis. There is no direct evidence, but it is possible that work with prison committees affected how he reacted when he was the victim of a petty crime. In July 1793, while walking down Chancery Lane, he had a monographed silk handkerchief pick-pocketed. The thieves, a 14-year-old boy and an 18-year-old young man, might have been in desperate circumstances, as they had stolen similarly small items earlier that year.[66] At the trial Granville was at pains to testify only that he had lost his handkerchief; he had not witnessed or even noticed the crime until his handkerchief was returned to him by a witness. The boys were convicted and sentenced to be transported. Granville advocated for a lighter sentence, suggesting they join the "king's service," and offering to provide them with clothing. He was able to extract a promise that their sentence would be delayed until the next sessions to "allow time for their entering [the military] or getting imployment."[67]

There have been dozens of accounts about Granville's work and William and James's role in his work, though usually as supporting cast in his heroic drama. Those accounts, however, barely skim the depths of Sharp sibling support for Granville. In addition to Catherine's care of Jonathan Strong, Granville sought support from all his siblings, and once they were older, his nieces. He had frequent correspondence with John, asking for John's advice on writing content and style. Being largely self-taught, Granville sought John's more formally educated counsel. Other family members tracked Granville's publications, the responses to them, and noted when he was honored. Granville's diffused residences among the London and Northamptonshire homes and his constant travels between them, as well as to the North, facilitated face-to-face support. He knew his work was not possible without his family's support. He once wrote John that he knew "every thing that nearly concerns me is equally interesting to all my Dear brothers and Sisters."[68] It is not surprising that the youngest brother whose every action had been supported and praised by his older brothers and sisters, should emerge as unshakably confident that his work would be counted as worth recording by his family.

Granville and James were particularly connected, as they worked together on the Strong case and on a host of other reforms: improving the Thames's banks, parliamentary reforms, ending press gangs, supporting a narrow measure of Catholic emancipation, and supporting the American colonists' claims. In 1771, a press gang broke into James's manufactory and made away with four men before

---

[66] Old Bailey Proceedings, *London Lives, 1690–1800*, t17930911-14 (http://www.londonlives.org, version 1.1., June 17, 2012), September 11, 1793, trial of George Whiteman and George Mackay; Criminal Registers for Middlesex, January 9, 1793, prisoner George Mackay, HO 26, piece 2, page 43; June 20, 1793, prisoner George Whiteman, HO 26, piece 2, page 88, TNA, digital image at *England and Wales, Criminal Registers, 1791–1892*, https://www.ancestry.co.uk, accessed January 2, 2022.

[67] Granville Sharp, diaries, extracted by Catherine Sharp (niece), book 2, 92–94, July 11, July 16, September 11, 1793, D3549/13/4/2.

[68] Granville Sharp to John Sharp, October 31, 1787, D3549/13/1/S8.

186   BEING SINGLE IN GEORGIAN ENGLAND

they could be stopped, but Granville did not begin working with James Oglethorpe to end the practice until the war with America. In 1776, Granville and his brothers drafted an agreement to protect John Tilley, their waterman, from being pressed into service.[69] Granville also helped found the Society for Effecting the Abolition of the Slave Trade (though he wanted to abolish slavery completely, not just the slave trade). He engaged in other reform movements with varying elements of philanthropy. He wrote against child labor, enthusiastically supported the early stages of the French Revolution, advocated for an American episcopate, sat on prison and hospital boards, and joined or helped to found the Protestant Union, the British and Foreign Bible Society, and the Society for the Conversion of the Jews.[70] His participation in the latter three organizations reflect an eighteenth-century British sense of Christian paternalistic duty to other races and religions.

As that list of his activities and memberships suggests, Granville was no radical, even if he has often been described that way. "He was fully confident that [his reform efforts] rested securely on the twin pillars of his faith, the guarantee of freedom in Britain's unwritten constitution and a righteous Anglican God," most clearly demonstrated by his participation in Christian proselytizing organizations.[71] His stance was typical of many in the anti-slavery movement; they were patriotic, mainstream Anglicans who were conservative politically, socially, and religiously—motivated by ideas of divine providence and reform-minded, but not radical.[72] Granville looked askance at Welsh Methodists that "far exceed common Enthusiasm & seem to discover apparent marks of demonical delusion."[73] He was scandalized by the popularity of women playing men's roles and vice versa in *The Beggar's Opera*. He called Hume an "arrogant infidel," and had no patience for Irish independence or full Catholic emancipation. He was alarmed by the Gordon

---

[69] Elizabeth Sharp Prowse, memorandum and commonplace book, January 4, 1771, D3549/14/1/1; Memorandum of agreement for John Tilley, protection against impressment, November 1776, D3549/12/1/7; Hoare, *Memoirs of Granville Sharp*, 192–193, 383–387; Granville Sharp, diaries, extracted by Catherine Sharp (niece), book 1, page 100, April 10, 11, 13, 1780, D3549/13/4/2; John Sainsbury, *Disaffected Patriots: London Supporters of Revolutionary America 1769–1782* (Montreal: McGill-Queens University Press, 1987), 75–83, 93, 128, 148.

[70] His advocacy for an American episcopate so endeared him to American Anglicans that several granted him honorary degrees: the College of Rhode Island (1786), Harvard University (1788), and William and Mary (1791). Terry L. Meyers, "Thinking about Slavery at the College of William and Mary," *William & Mary Bill of Rights Journal*, 21, no. 4 (May 2013): 1215–1257; Frederick V. Mills Sr., "Granville Sharp and the Creation of an American Episcopate: *Ordo Espicoporum Est Robur Ecclesiae*," *Anglican and Episcopal History*, 79, no. 1 (March 2010): 34–58; Granville Sharp, Old Jewry, to John Sharp, July 18, 1786, D3549/13/1/S8; Hoare, *Memoirs of Granville Sharp*, 436, 443–444; Granville Sharp to John Sharp, July 6, 1789; Nicholas Rogers, *The Press Gang: Naval Impressment and Its Opponents in Georgian England* (London: Continuum, 2007), 21–22.

[71] Hochschild, *Bury the Chains*, 46.

[72] Nicholas Hudson, "'Britons Never Will be Slaves': National Myth, Conservatism, and the Beginnings of British Antislavery," *Eighteenth-Century Studies*, 34, no. 4 (Summer 2001): 559–576; John Coffey, "'Tremble, Britannia!': Fear, Providence and the Abolition of the Slave Trade, 1758–1807," *The English Historical Review*, 127, no. 527 (August 2012): 844–881.

[73] Granville Sharp to John Sharp, December 14, 1784, D3549/13/1/S8.

Riots and volunteered to be head of pikemen as a defense if needed.[74] His insistence that American bishops only be consecrated by Church of England authorities led to conflict with others who advocated for the legitimacy of Scottish or American consecration. Being "zealous for the Church of England" consecration led him to be "very whimsical & impudent," one of his opponents wrote.[75] Even with these limits to Granville's reform interests, his approach to social reform and philanthropy took two avenues: a philosophical one represented by publications, committees, and society memberships, and a personal one based in an individual's needs. His writing produced "some of the age's most compelling abolitionist arguments," and once he knew of a person's problem, he worked tirelessly to help her or him.[76]

While publishing his work was a central activity for Granville, John, William, James, and Elizabeth published much less and participated in fewer societies. Their awareness of suffering in their immediate neighborhoods inspired their actions. Beyond personality differences, the siblings' dissimilar approaches might reflect their householding status. Though they practiced a much more horizontal approach to household governance among themselves, this did not mean their houses did not have dependents: servants, apprentices, and the neighborhood poor. Granville, however, had no household and its attendant dependents to manage. Instead, he had various places of retreat for quiet study, and he frequently circulated through his siblings' various neighborhoods. That combination meant his two preferred methods of charitable endeavor, philosophical and personal, were a perfect match for his domestic situation.

Granville's most ambitious scheme was a project to resettle poor, formerly enslaved Africans (and some whites) in Sierra Leone in 1787–88 and, when that utterly failed, to establish the Sierra Leone Company.[77] Though the initial project was a failure and the company's charter focused on trade and not Granville's self-governing plans, those disappointments did not dampen Granville's belief that local self-governance was the best path to liberty and peace. In fact, when he first heard of the poor conditions in Granville Town (Sierra Leone), he attributed it to "nothing but the intemperance of the people, & their enervated indolence in consequence of it" and not any miscalculation of the difficulties the settlers would encounter by encroaching on existing African political and social structures,

---

[74] Granville Sharp, commonplace books, vol. 1, page 1, D3549/13/4/1; Hoare, *Memoirs of Granville Sharp*, 206, 456.

[75] Charles Inglis, October 21, 1785, *Journal of Occurrences*, Inglis Family Papers, MS C-3, University of New Brunswick, quoted in Brent Sirota, "'The Manifest Distinction Established by Our Religion': Church, State and the Consecration of Samuel Seabury," *Religion and American Culture: A Journal of Interpretation*, 32, no. 1 (2022): 68–107.

[76] Manisha Sinha, *The Slave's Cause: A History of Abolition* (New Haven: Yale University Press, 2016), 22.

[77] Padraic X. Scanlan, *Freedoms Debtors: British Antislavery in Sierra Leone in the Age of Revolution* (New Haven: Yale University Press, 2017).

188   BEING SINGLE IN GEORGIAN ENGLAND

let alone disease and death.[78] Though many contemporaries did not share his optimism about the Sierra Leone schemes, he assumed his drive and sense of righteous imperative would carry the day.[79] Additionally, he wrote John that "Numbers of people both white & Black are daily applying to me to go there," an experience that reinforced his confidence in the project's potential usefulness.[80] Dedication to the Sierra Leone project also reflected his convictions that local governance was the surest way to ensure liberty and social stability. He thought the system of frankpledge, a form of local governance he knew from his studies, was the ideal form of government.[81]

These ideas can seem idealistic, if not naïve. Sometimes Granville's optimism, zeal, and even stubbornness could outpace his practical abilities. Some of his confidence can be attributed to his previous successes and to the fact that his brothers' support had allowed his philanthropic work to develop mostly outside the bureaucratic constraints of large institutions. His older brothers' experiences had made them more practical in their ambitions. James could see the limitations of his grand canal schemes and be content with partial success. John recognized that his success in Bamburgh was partially a happy accident. Granville generously offered help when he learned of individual circumstances, as with the pickpockets or the bankrupt Higginson, but in many ways the abstraction of legal cases, correspondence, and publications prevented him from fully apprehending the practical difficulties in something like the Sierra Leone colony. Granville was not alone in this, however, as his thoughts about Sierra Leone perfectly capture late eighteenth-century Christian beliefs in English constitutionalism and a trust that British paternalism could improve the condition of humanity.

The language of paternalism informed Granville's attempts with Sierra Leone and his other endeavors. To be clear, this was a "Christian paternalism [that] inspired antislavery attitudes and was not yet yoked to proslavery dogma."[82] Granville and other contemporary white abolitionists saw the enslaved as oppressed children requiring their assistance, not, as later proslavery Christians claimed, childlike creatures incapable of self-governance. Similar to Catherine denoting Strong, an adult man, as "boy," Granville described the struggling colony as his "poor little ill thriven swarthy Daughter."[83] In his first anti-slavery

---

[78] Granville Sharp to John Sharp, January 19, 1788, D3549/13/1/S8.

[79] Anne Stott, *Wilberforce: Family and Friends* (Oxford: Oxford University Press, 2012), 54–55; Cassandra Pybus, "'A Less Favourable Specimen': The Abolitionist Response to Self-Emancipated Slaves in Sierra Leone, 1793–1808," *Parliamentary History*, 26 (2007): 97–112.

[80] Granville Sharp to John Sharp, January 19, 1788.

[81] He might have also been influenced by John's work with the manorial court at Bamburgh. Manor of Bamburgh, court leet, view of frankpledge, and court baron records, 1779–1797, NRO 452/D/2/2, NAW.

[82] Sinha, *The Slave's Cause*, 16.

[83] Granville Sharp to John Sharp, October 31, 1787; Granville Sharp to John Sharp, September 23, 1791, D3549/13/1/S8.

publication, Granville wished that when Europeans had first encountered Africans, they had been inspired by Christian principle to "communicate to the ignorant Africans that superior knowledge which providence had favoured them with."[84] Similarly, Lafayette remarked in a letter to Granville, "Circumstances" might have made them "in Many Respects Superior to our Black Brethren, That We May Cease to Place ourselves Beneath Them in The Pursuit of This Disgraceful Trade."[85] While Granville (and his siblings) were appalled by the violence and cruelty of slavery, they did not challenge the racial hierarchy at its heart.[86]

Charitable Activities Outside Formal Institutions in the 1760s–1780s

The Sharps engaged in a variety of charitable actions outside institutional or political structures. They lent their names and patronage to godchildren and dispensed money to the poor. For example, Granville, in addition to his godchildren, had various acquaintances whose wills asked him to act as their children's guardians, requests he usually complied with.[87] In essence, Granville's philanthropic work granted him a type of fictive or surrogate fatherhood. For the sisters, most of their charitable or reform activities concentrated in informal actions based in their neighborhoods and households. Why the sisters did not join philanthropic societies like many women of their standing did, is not known.

The Sharps' philanthropic and charitable work was not discrete; together they engaged in a variety of more informal and even ad hoc activities in support of the poor or those they deemed unjustly treated. James donated his specially designed stoves for the Foundling Hospital, and he and Elizabeth donated money to support hurricane victims in Barbados and Jamaica in 1781.[88] Elizabeth found positions for abandoned children at Wicken. John helped Granville ensure a woman would not lose the legacy that was hers by law.[89] Many actions reflected a paternalistic or maternalistic *noblesse oblige* understanding of social relations and responsibility to alleviate suffering. For example, in 1776, Elizabeth and her

---

[84] Granville Sharp, *Extract from a Representation of the Injustice and Dangerous Tendency of Tolerating Slavery, or Admitting the Least Claim of Private Property in the Persons of Men in England* (London, 1769, reprint Philadelphia: Joseph Crukshank, 1771), 2–3.

[85] Melvin D. Kennedy, *Lafayette and Slavery, From His Letters to Thomas Clarkson and Granville Sharp* (Easton: The American Friends of Lafayette, 1950), HT867.L3, NYHS.

[86] Daniel Livesay, *Children of Uncertain Fortune: Mixed-Race Jamaicans in Britain and the Atlantic Family, 1733–1833* (Chapel Hill: University of North Carolina Press, 2018); Brooke N. Newman, *A Dark Inheritance: Blood, Race, and Sex in Colonial Jamaica* (New Haven: Yale University Press, 2018).

[87] Hoare, *Memoirs of Granville Sharp*, 460.

[88] "West India Sufferers," *London Courant*, January 29, 1781; "Sufferers in Jamaica and Barbadoes," *Aurora and Universal Advertiser*, February 19, 1781; Sharp, *An Account of the Principle*, 18; Elizabeth Sharp Prowse, Wicken estate and personal ledger, May 1, 1781, page 67, 364P/069, NRO.

[89] Granville Sharp to John Sharp, July 6, 1789, D3549/13/1/S8.

190   BEING SINGLE IN GEORGIAN ENGLAND

mother-in-law walked the bulk of the estate, coming in and out of the company of servants and laborers finishing their day's work: "now & then," she wrote, "a shilling from my Mother made it agreable to all partys."[90]

In addition to one-time donations to the poor, the Sharps assumed the combined charitable and patronage duty of godparenting. John, Catherine (James's widow), Elizabeth, Judith, Granville, and niece Catherine each had godchildren, many of them acting in that capacity for niece Mary's children. It is probable that the remaining siblings were also named as godparents. Godparenting non-relatives, or very distant relations, came with few obligations in the eighteenth century.[91] This is reflected in the Sharps' wills; John gave each of his four godchildren £5—a token amount when compared to the £40 he bequeathed a servant.[92] Catherine (James's widow) named only one goddaughter in her will, to whom she left £20.[93] Judith left £50 to a goddaughter, but stated "I believe she is still with her father...in Hexham, Northumberland," suggesting they were not particularly close.[94]

Granville had numerous godchildren and children named for him, likely many of those without his knowledge; his obligations to them were minimal, if they existed at all. He was godfather to Henry Granville, the first African to be baptized in Clapham.[95] Other children were named for him with a combination of "Granville Sharp" plus their surname, particularly among reformers and nonconformists. Granville did not have close relationships with all these children, but some saw the connection as a chance to call on him as a surrogate father. William Granville Sharp, who was not related, wrote Granville in 1802 thanking him for his "fatherly advice," for example. Granville corresponded with William for at least a decade, offering professional advice and support.[96]

Unlike many women of their social class, the three Sharp sisters and three sisters-in-law did not join any philanthropic or voluntary societies. However, like most women of their social class, they engaged in a variety of charitable and philanthropic endeavors among their social connections and in their neighborhoods.[97] They were also intimately connected to their brothers'/husbands' political and

---

[90] Elizabeth Sharp Prowse, memorandum and commonplace book, May 11 and 18, 1776, 51–52, typescript, D3549/14/1/2.

[91] Patricia Crawford, *Blood, Bodies and Families in Early Modern England* (New York: Routledge, 2004), 120; Will Coster, "'From Fire and Water': The Responsibilities of Godparents in Early Modern England," *Studies in Church History*, 31 (1994): 301–311.

[92] John Sharp, will, written April 17, 1792, codicil written April 21, 1792, proved May 2, 1793, Prerogative Court of Canterbury, PROB 11/1232, TNA.

[93] Catherine Lodge Sharp, will, written May 2, 1829, codicil written May 2, 1829, proved March 3, 1835, Prerogative Court of Canterbury, PROB 11/1844, TNA.

[94] Judith Sharp, will, written December 6, 1807, proved May 6, 1809, Prerogative Court of Canterbury, PROB 11/1498, TNA.

[95] Anne Stott, *Wilberforce: Family and Friends* (Oxford: Oxford University Press, 2012), 56.

[96] William Granville Sharp to Granville Sharp, April 26, 1802, D3549/17/1/2.

[97] Donna T. Andrew, "*Noblesse Oblige*: Female Charity in an Age of Sentiment," in John Brewer and Susan Staves, eds., *Early Modern Conceptions of Property* (New York: Routledge, 1996), 293; Eve

philanthropic work. Elizabeth, the patroness of Wicken as niece Mary called her, fully embraced that role. Beyond small gestures of benevolence, Elizabeth made substantial and meaningful improvements for her tenants. Her father-in-law had succeeded in enclosing most of the village, augmenting Wicken Park's original four hundred acres fivefold. Enclosure was often a contentious process as it pitted established common rights against powerful families' desires to consolidate property and wealth. Elizabeth's efforts to improve Wicken tenant farms and cottages, however, seems to have ameliorated the worst abuses of enclosure while also improving living conditions on the estate.[98] She conscientiously considered not just the profit to the estate, but the daily living circumstances of those dwelling and employed there. A sermon given at her funeral stated she consistently employed those rejected by others and those with disabilities or infirmities that "almost every one but herself would have been, not only unwilling to employ, but ashamed to acknowledge."[99] She regularly purchased necessities when she discovered needs on the estate or in the village, as when she spent "nearly £12 on sheets and blankets" upon learning the poor in Wicken did not have adequate bedding during the winter of 1774.[100]

In many ways Elizabeth was like John; when she encountered a need within her scope to address, she set out to meet that need. Elizabeth's meticulously kept ledgers for Wicken highlight how intertwined the Sharps' charitable activities (not to mention household accounts) were. In the same month she noted her donation to hurricane survivors in the West Indies she paid £1 1s. to a lying in charity (from James's account), paid for a piano cover (from his wife's account), bought buckles for niece Catherine, gave a blind man 1s. and gave the children (presumably the village children) 2s. for May Day garlands, among other expenditures.[101] She regularly gave a shilling or two to any poor person she encountered and paid for servants' entertainments, in addition to more systematic support for the local schools and apprenticeships for servants' orphaned children. Mary's elegy to Wicken contains numerous references to Elizabeth's concerted effort to improve education and living standards for every poor or laboring family in Wicken. Even accounting for Mary's rose-colored nostalgia for her aunt, it is clear that Elizabeth devoted considerable time and resources on local charitable actions. Her only limitation seems to have been a distaste for evangelicalism; she once dismissed her dairymaid "for attending the Methodest meetings & inviting

---

Tavor Bannet, "The Bluestocking Sisters: Women's Patronage, Millennium Hall, and 'The Visible Providence of a Country,'" *Eighteenth-Century Life*, 30, no. 1 (Winter 2006): 25–55.

[98] McDonagh, "'All towards the improvements,'" 268–280.

[99] John Owen, *A Discourse occasioned by the Death of Elizabeth Prowse, late of Wicken Park, Northamptonshire; Delivered in Substance at Fulham Church, on Sunday, March 4, 1810* (London: Printed for J. Hatchard by J. Tilling, 1810), 12, D3549/13/5/33.

[100] McDonagh, "'All towards the improvements,'" 280.

[101] Elizabeth Sharp Prowse, Wicken estate and personal ledger, May 1781, page 67.

192   BEING SINGLE IN GEORGIAN ENGLAND

the young of the village to go with her & had some of the preachers to call upon her [at Wicken]."[102]

There are clues among surviving records that Judith, Frances, and the two Catherines participated in the same types of ad hoc charity Elizabeth did, and as was expected of women of their class. Catherine's account books at Fulham show similar gifts of a few shillings to individual poor people or donated at a charity sermon.[103] Judith's actions are hardest to trace in the surviving record, but her possession of a printed copy of John's sermon supporting the Newcastle Infirmary suggests she engaged in conversations about familial philanthropic efforts and made donations accordingly.[104] Additionally, her funeral sermon emphasized her charity and that her death was a loss to "the Neighbourhood & poor in general."[105] Frances engaged in activities similar to Elizabeth because Elizabeth's ledgers show amounts spent on a local girl's schooling, which Frances reimbursed.[106]

The Sharp women also used their wills to provide for servants, poor relations, particularly female kin. Elizabeth left stock in the Grand Junction Canal to pay for a village schoolmaster, her clothing to her maid, various sums to long-time servants, and £100 to the village poor—money left in trust to her by her aunt. Judith left bequests to Jemima's servants, as well as £50 to her goddaughter. Catherine, James's widow, left money to various servants and £20 to the poor of South Mimms. William's widow left £10 to each servant and £50 to Fulham's poor. Frances did not leave a will, so her estate, worth over £1200 was equally divided among her siblings.[107]

All of the Sharps drew limits on their philanthropic or reform ambitions. The most striking is their seeming lack of interest in improving the status of women.[108] Perhaps because the sisters enjoyed domestic, financial, and physical freedom infrequently granted women in eighteenth-century England, and perhaps because the sisters-in-law seemed to have the eighteenth-century ideal partnerships in their marriages, there was little impetus to advocate for structural changes that

---

[102] Elizabeth Sharp Prowse, memorandum and commonplace book, July 29, 1801, D3549/14/1/1.

[103] Catherine Barwick Sharp, account books, 1793–6, pocket expenses 1794, pages 61–2, D3549/23/1/7, pt. 1.

[104] John Sharp, *A Sermon Preached at St. Nicholas's Church in Newcastle, Before the Governors of the Infirmary, for the Counties of Durham, Newcastle, and Northumberland, on Wednesday June 24, 1752* (Newcastle upon Tyne: I. Thompson and Company, 1752), with book plate of "Jud: Sharp," Bamburgh 5 G 10/1, PGL.

[105] Elizabeth Sharp Prowse, memorandum and commonplace book, April 1, 1809, D3549/14/1/1.

[106] Elizabeth Sharp Prowse, Wicken estate and personal ledger, 1776–78, page 169, 364P/068, NRO.

[107] Judith Sharp, will, written December 6, 1807, proved May 6, 1809, Prerogative Court of Canterbury, PROB 11/1498, TNA; Elizabeth Prowse, will, written January 17, 1798, proved March 2, 1810, Prerogative Court of Canterbury, PROB 11/1509; Catherine Sharp, will, written May 2, 1829, proved March 3, 1835, Prerogative Court of Canterbury, PROB 11/1844; Catherine Sharp, will, written May 27, 1813, proved February 26, 1814, Prerogative Court of Canterbury, PROB 11/1552, digital images at https://www.ancestry.co.uk, accessed 2018; Granville Sharp, notes on Frances Sharp's estate, D3549/23/1/33.

[108] Susan Brown, "Rational Creatures and Free Citizens: The Language of Politics in the Eighteenth-Century Debate on Women," *Historical Papers Communications Historiques*, 23, no. 1 (1988): 35–47.

would have made such things possible for others. Additionally, despite their abhorrence of slavery, the Sharps could not help but be caught in its economic wake. Beyond food and household goods produced directly or indirectly by enslaved labor, James's principal place of trade was the Caribbean and the American colonies. His advertising pamphlets, distributed across the British Atlantic, included a description of wagons and carts designed for "West-India Planters Use, are made as well as Trucks particularly constructed for Sugar-Hogsheads."[109] Similarly, John and the other trustees at Bamburgh ordered rice specifically from the Carolinas, demonstrating it was nearly impossible to sever all ties with the slave trade in eighteenth-century England. James and Granville may have tried to convince William Beckford, sometimes alderman and Lord Mayor, that slavery was wicked, but James continued to vote for him, despite Beckford and his family being among the wealthiest Jamaican planters. No matter how anti-slavery the Sharps were, they remained embedded in the slave economy.[110]

Diminution in the 1790s

As the Sharps aged and retired from business, their households and charitable work also slowed, though their philanthropy persisted and their sociability remained vibrant. Granville's notebooks show that though his domestic arrangements did not replicate his brothers' householding status, where he lived and in what style was a matter of serious consideration and enjoyment. As he indicated in his 1787 room rental, quiet space for study was important to him, and his 1792 move was carefully noted in his diary. On January 31 he "Took Chambers in the Temple" and on February 14, "Lay for the first time at my Chambers No 1 Garden Court in the Temple."[111] The move to rooms in the Temple was more than just a place for quiet study—it put him at the heart of the legal community. He also benefited from the 343-acre Fairsted Manor (Essex) he inherited from Elizabeth Oglethorpe (James's widow) in 1787.[112] She recommended it be used for "charitable uses," and Granville sought John's advice about how to best "advantageously dispose of this little Esate for public Charity after my death." In the interim the £150–200 in rent he received annually were a welcome supplement to his income.[113]

---

[109] James Sharp, *An Account of the Principle and Effects of the Air Stove-Grates*, 10th edition (1781), 17, TS 425.S451, NYHS.

[110] Sean D. Moore, *Slavery and the Making of Early American Libraries: British Literature, Political Thought, and the Transatlantic Book Trade, 1731–1814* (Oxford: Oxford University Press, 2019).

[111] Granville Sharp, diaries, extracted by Catherine Sharp (niece), book 2, page 71, January 31 and February 14, 1792, D3549/13/4/2.

[112] Elizabeth Sharp Prowse, memorandum and commonplace book, May 29, 1787, page 73, typescript, D3549/14/1/2.

[113] Granville Sharp to John Sharp, October 31, 1787, D3549/13/1/S8.

194   BEING SINGLE IN GEORGIAN ENGLAND

Even in the Sharps' reconfigured household constellations, visits and musical gatherings continued. Besides spelling an end to his political reform efforts, James's death in 1783 narrowed the scope of the siblings' water adventures. In November 1786 they sold the yacht and "ordered [it] be broke up." They had other boats and continued to sail the river while dining or playing music, though on a much smaller scale than previously. In addition to their trip to Scotland in 1785, they held a glee and musical evenings in 1783 and a small concert in 1786; took a short river trip in June 1787; had a house party in 1788; and continued musical evenings and long visits at Fulham and Wicken well into the nineteenth century.[114] William, Catherine, and Granville made regular visits north, including a winter visit to Durham in 1795–96. When Elizabeth noted that journey, she remarked that she remained at Wicken that winter, the first time she had spent the entire winter there. Her notations underscored Wicken's importance for the Sharps as age dictated a slower pace of life; in 1796 all the siblings except Frances were over age 60. The scale of Sharp sociability became increasingly concentrated on just "our own party," but the enjoyment of family gatherings continued unabated.[115] Elizabeth wrote of the family's long visit at Wicken in 1793 that they were "together most comfortably."[116]

Their charitable work also persisted. Granville continued to be a prodigious author and activist, working with the Clapham Sect to abolish the slave trade and sitting on various boards and committees. William too continued to sit on the hospital board and continued an inoculation program at Fulham. Judith, Mary, both Catherines, and Frances continued with their normal patterns of charitable donations and Elizabeth continued her work at Wicken.

The biggest shift in Sharp philanthropic work concerned the Bamburgh charities. In April 1792, Granville made a hasty trip to Durham "on account of the dangerous illness of my dear Brother...John."[117] Arriving in Durham on the 25th, he met with his brother's curate and chaplain that afternoon and the following day, learning no one was hopeful of John's recovery. Much like with James nearly a decade before, Granville spent the following two days close to John's bedside, likely joined by Mary. Granville was probably there when 69-year-old John passed between ten and eleven on the morning of April 28. The following week Granville acted as chief mourner when John was buried in Durham Cathedral, beside the graves of his parents and grandfather Wheler, and with a spot reserved for his wife.

Immediately following John's death, Mary, Judith, Jemima, and Granville had to negotiate with the Crewe trustees about the disposition of Bamburgh's living

---

[114] Crosby, "Private Concerts," 43–44; Granville Sharp to Jemima Sharp, August 8, 1788.

[115] Elizabeth Sharp Prowse, memorandum and commonplace book, May 20, 1800, D3549/14/1/1.

[116] Elizabeth Sharp Prowse, memorandum and commonplace book, August 26–December 1793, D3549/14/1/1.

[117] Granville Sharp, diaries, extracted by Catherine Sharp (niece), book 2, pages 73–74, April 23, 1792, D3549/13/4/2.

quarters and charities, not to mention arrangements with church officials about John's various livings. Andrew Bowlt, who had been an assistant curate to John and who "live[d] constantly" with John's family was granted permission in July to remain in the castle.[118] Other than the time it took to pack up belongings at Bamburgh, Mary apparently had no desire to spend any longer there than she absolutely had to.[119] Granville "took great Pains in sorting" Bamburgh's records while Mary and Judith "were not Idle" in preparing to depart Bamburgh for Hartburn, but first going to Rothbury to visit a blind friend, a visit Mary characterized as "an act of Charity."[120]

John's death in 1792 meant the loss of Bamburgh and Hartburn as sites of charity and sociability, but with Jemima's acquisition of "a most pleasant" house, Durham remained in the Sharp circuit.[121] Furthermore, John's bequest of over £1200 for the upkeep of the castle tower and donations of books, furniture, and equipment to Crewe's charity, meant Mary, Jemima, and later Granville, spent years perpetuating Bamburgh's charitable work.[122] A Durham clergyman did not think Mary would long survive John's death, but she lived another six years, rather comfortably ensconced with Judith and Jemima in Jemima's house in Durham, less than a quarter mile from where she and John lived when staying at the college. Her death at age 77 in 1798 was not a surprise to the family, but they mourned the loss deeply. Mary and the Sharps grew up together, they were first cousins, and had been siblings-in-law for nearly fifty years. Elizabeth described her as an "affect[ionate] Sisr to all her Dear Husbands Family," who was "truly Friendly & affable to all that knew her."[123] At Mary's death, Granville immediately traveled to Durham and spent two months with Judith and Jemima.[124]

The loss of Mary was compounded the following year when Frances, while visiting their Rogers cousins in Berkeley, Gloucestershire, suddenly became ill and died after a ten-day illness. Elizabeth was devasted, especially as it happened while Frances was away from home and without any siblings in attendance. Elizabeth and Frances had lived together for the majority of Frances's life, their day-to-day interactions had been intertwined for sixty years; it is no wonder

---

[118] John Sharp, visitation answers, 1782, NRO 452/C/3/2/12, NAW.

[119] Thomas Dampier to George Wood, Durham, May 25, 1792, NRO 452/C/3/12/22, NAW; George Wood to Mr. [Thomas] Dampier, June 20, 1792, NRO 452/C/3/12/24 20, NAW; Orders of Lord Crewe's Trustees, 1721–1815, page 271, NRO 00452/B/1/6, NAW.

[120] Mary Sharp to George Wood, Durham, June 9, 1792, NRO 452/C/3/12/23, NAW; Mary Sharp to George Wood, June 16, 1792, NRO 452/C/3/12/24, NAW.

[121] Elizabeth Sharp Prowse, memorandum and commonplace book, April 28, 1792, typescript, D3549/14/1/2; plan of house and garden belonging to Miss Sharp, D3549/17/3/2.

[122] John Sharp, will, written April 17, 1792, codicil written April 21, 1792, proved May 2, 1793; leases and deeds related to Lord Crewe's trust for Bamburgh, 1756–1830, NRO 00452/D/1/1/33/1-5, NAW; Granville Sharp to Joseph Hill, January 3, 1799, Add.MS.1030, PGL.

[123] Elizabeth Sharp Prowse, memorandum and commonplace book, January 26, 1798, D3549/14/1/1.

[124] Granville Sharp, diaries, extracted by Catherine Sharp (niece), book 2, February 2–March 28, 1798, pages 151–154, D3549/13/4/2.

196   BEING SINGLE IN GEORGIAN ENGLAND

Elizabeth described Frances's death as "a great greef." Elizabeth departed for Berkeley in order to attend the funeral and when she returned to Wicken she found Catherine (James's widow) and niece Catherine there to greet and comfort her.[125] The remainder of the family was in the North and did not learn of Frances's passing until three days after her death.[126] The family deaths in the 1790s reduced the Sharps' collective charitable undertakings to Elizabeth's ongoing work to improve the neighborhood around Wicken Park; Judith, Jemima, niece Catherine and both sisters-in-law's donations to local poor individuals; Granville's continued activism, particularly around the growing movement to legislate the end of the slave trade; and William's advocacy for smallpox inoculations in Fulham. Overall, it was a smaller scope for their actions than that they enjoyed in previous decades, but hardly a retreat from philanthropy and social reform.

Conclusion

Granville benefited from being the youngest brother, and next-to-youngest child, long accustomed to his work being enthusiastically supported by his older siblings. John's place as eldest son who assumed their father's ecclesiastical and charitable appointments, coupled with not becoming a father until he was almost 40, channeled some of his parental energy to the care of Bamburgh Castle and the poor. Other siblings enthusiastically joined in these endeavors: Thomas supported all of John's and Mary's efforts in Bamburgh; William provided medical care for the poor; in addition to his support of Granville's antislavery work, James too supported Granville and was a common councilor in London, supporting measures to uphold constitutional rights and improve transportation and communication networks; widowed Elizabeth's management of Wicken Park included care for long-employed servants and the local poor. Judith's, Frances's, and the Catherines' activities are less well-documented, but they too spent money and time on charitable causes and materially and emotionally supported the work of the other Sharps.

While his family's support is always acknowledged, most accounts of the Sharps' philanthropy has focused on Granville, who matched certain ideals of an elite (male) individual heroically working against the slave trade.[127] Such focus has given a distorted picture of Sharp philanthropy and sense of social responsibility. Prince Hoare, a family friend and his first biographer, described Granville

---

[125] Elizabeth Sharp Prowse, memorandum and commonplace book, August 23, September 2, September 11, 1799, D3549/14/1/1.
[126] Granville Sharp, diaries, extracted by Catherine Sharp (niece), book 3, September 5, 1799, page 13, D3549/13/4/2.
[127] Eleanor Morecroft, "Antislavery, Elite Men, and the 'Voice of the British Nation,'" *History Compass*, 15, no. 5 (2017).

as a hero whom the family could not help but "exult in possessing, among the members of their family, such a relative."[128] Twenty-first-century interest in the history of slavery and abolition can make it seem like Granville was the central character and his siblings merely bit players in his drama. In their eighteenth-century context, however, he was part of a network of altruism, philanthropy, and social responsibility. Charity, and participation in philanthropic and voluntary societies, was "an emblem of the donor's power and a mark of his responsibilities."[129] Granville's long-term impact on outlawing slavery was enduring, but his work was one part of a larger family pattern. William, John, and Elizabeth are rarely remembered today, but during their lifetimes they did much to alleviate human suffering.

Injustice, great and small, exercised the Sharps. From anti-slavery and poor relief on one end of the scale and the good treatment of servants and villagers on the other, they were aware of any ill-treatment and their obligation to address it. Their work did not lead them to advocate dismantling social hierarchies, however. John's concern for clerical widows emphasized the "worthy" poor widows; Elizabeth dismissed an enthusiastic Methodist from service; Granville's concern for poor Blacks and the enslaved did not mean he wanted them to marry or have children with white English men and women. And no siblings, not even the sisters, considered advocating for women's rights. Their material and relational abundance may have encouraged care for the poor and oppressed while simultaneously blunting their ability to perceive sexism's stark place in Georgian culture. While their charitable and reform work was grounded in ideas of social hierarchy and paternalism, those attitudes cannot mask their sincerity, nor their successes.

Their father once wrote that perhaps John had a greater measure of a "spirit of benevolence" than was "commonly imagined."[130] It was early in John's career, so Thomas Sr. could not have imagined how true his assessment would be. And not only of John. Inspired by eighteenth-century volunteerism, deeply held religious beliefs, and paternalistic/maternalistic social obligations, the Sharps engaged in common practices of neighborhood benevolence. They also expanded their efforts to improve the suffering of the poor throughout northern Northumberland, the cottagers and poor of southern Northamptonshire, the ill and poor of London, the wrongfully imprisoned, the pressed, the American colonists, and the enslaved throughout the empire.

---

[128] Hoare, *Memoirs of Granville Sharp*, xx.   [129] Andrew, *"Noblesse Oblige,"* 277.
[130] Thomas Sharp to John Sharp, August 21, [1751], among John Sharp's sermons 452/C3/33, GB-0036-SHS, Box 1, sermon 27, DCL.

7

Leaving a Legacy

"A Family Anecdote worthy of remembrance."[1]

Granville Sharp in a letter to John Sharp

Introduction

With established household and social routines, the Sharps entered their golden age between the 1760s and 1780s. As that golden age waned and as they entered the middle and later years, they began to contemplate what the future would hold for their family. Singleness and childlessness encouraged alternative ways of preserving and perpetuating a family legacy. The deaths of John, Mary, and Frances in the 1790s accelerated their legacy-preserving activities. Those changes required grappling with the household items, music, instruments, and books they had collected over the previous decades. That work overlapped with an increased interest in genealogy. In essence, the siblings' experience demonstrates how singleness, late marriage, and childlessness shaped individuals' perspectives about lineage, posterity, and legacy, especially in middle and old age.[2] The enviable Sharp sociability and support had already created a sense and place of belonging matched by few families; efforts to preserve a legacy were an attempt to perpetuate that sense of belonging back in time and forward to the future.[3]

The Sharps' family portrait was just one manifestation of Sharp family efforts to preserve and record their family's history and pass it on to future generations. Elizabeth's description of sitting for the portrait—something the family did as individuals or small groups, never as a whole—reflected the Sharps' efforts to preserve and perpetuate a family legacy. Much like how they occupied a central position in the portrait, unmarried Granville and widowed Elizabeth were at the center of their family's genealogical and preservation activities. And paralleling Granville's arm around their niece Catherine, the siblings drew her into their

---

[1] Granville Sharp to John Sharp, September 23, 1791, D3549/13/1/S6.

[2] Queer theorists have pushed against the conflation of identity, futurity, and children. In some ways, the Sharps queered genealogical practices by uncoupling them from reproduction but retaining ideas of identity and futurity. Lee Edelman, *No Future: Queer Theory and the Death Drive* (Durham: Duke University Press, 2004).

[3] Reinhart Koselleck, *Futures Past: On the Semantics of Historical Time*, trans. Keith Tribe (New York: Columbia University Press, 2004).

Being Single in Georgian England: Families, Households, and the Unmarried. Amy Harris, Oxford University Press.
© Amy Harris 2023. DOI: 10.1093/oso/9780192869494.003.0011

family historical efforts. Similar to how the painting was collaged from various individual sittings, the family legacy was a joint project for all the Sharps, no matter their marital status. Its contours, however, were outlined and molded by the unmarried and childless family members.

Without a tangible legacy in the form of spouses and children, the unmarried and childless Sharps became more creative and took a more expansive view of posterity and legacy. Their ingenuity influenced the married family members, especially as they aged and realized they would not produce any male heirs and that their daughters and nieces might not marry or have children. In essence, when middle or old age, singleness, and childlessness came together, the combination channeled some of the Sharps' prodigious energy to crafting a legacy.[4] In the end, the unmarried and childless Sharps created something that transcended boundaries of nuclear families and lineal descent. Granville and his brothers concentrated on preserving their religious and intellectual patrimony. Elizabeth, Judith, and niece Catherine recorded information about family events and gatherings and created a lineage chart that encompassed all family members, not just the males, the well-married, or the parents.

This gendered division is not particularly surprising, as women's care for family members was central to femininity and had been reinforced by education and even toys and books.[5] Over time, however, singleness came to blur some of the gendered distinctions of kin-keeping as the Sharps worked to shape and preserve their material legacy and values.[6] Ultimately, while the Sharp siblings preserved some hierarchal elements of eighteenth-century genealogical practices, they emphasized shared values and group identity more. The perspective of unmarried or childless family members suggests that eighteenth-century genealogical practices were not always based on status and property, as has sometimes been argued.[7]

Elizabeth and the Sharp Lineage Chart

In addition to making a family chronicle, Elizabeth incorporated dozens of family arms into her family lineage chart, as most gentry and aristocratic families had

---

[4] Lynn Botelho and Susannah R. Ottaway, "General Introduction," in Lynn Botelho, ed., *The History of Old Age in England*, vol. 1 (London: Pickering and Chatto, 2008).

[5] O'Malley, *The Making of Modern Childhood*, 113–114.

[6] Twentieth-century gerontologists identified three types of legacy-making: biological, material, and values. While the Sharp nieces were a biological embodiment of Sharp values, their low numbers and low marital rate increased the importance of the latter two types of legacy. See Elizabeth G. Hunter and Graham D. Rowles, "Leaving a Legacy: Toward a Typology," *Journal of Aging Studies*, 19 (2005): 327–347.

[7] François Weil, *Family Trees: A History of Genealogy in America* (Cambridge: Harvard University Press, 2013); Michael Sharpe, *Family Matters: A History of Genealogy* (Barnsley: Pen and Sword Family History, 2011).

200 BEING SINGLE IN GEORGIAN ENGLAND

done for centuries (see Plate 2). Measuring more than six feet across and three feet high, each crest was hand-drawn and painted in bold colors, mostly by Judith, on a heavy, backed white cloth. Beyond family crests, each individual name was written over a painted colored circle—the same color used for each sibling cohort. The backed fabric was sewn in such a way to allow the chart to be folded like a map, meaning it could be stored in a box not much bigger than a large book. This meant it could be easily worked on and transported. It is not clear if Elizabeth meant for it eventually to be framed and hung, or to remain as a working document.

Heraldry, the careful rules about the construction and display of royal and noble arms, was a late medieval invention that shaped most English genealogical accounts for five centuries. With the diminishment of feudalism in the fifteenth century, and the attendant blurring of lines between powerful landowners and those from less prosperous groups, heraldry became increasingly important to those without titles, particularly land-owning gentry.[8] One strand of this practice was about proving or anchoring family status, but as with the Sharps, there was also the impetus to record family lines when they were on the verge of going extinct.[9] Elizabeth incorporated the family arms for each line depicted on large family lineage chart she began in the 1790s, meaning she probably used reference material beyond family records to ensure she followed correct procedure for combining two sets of arms. Her brothers had a similar interest in the family arms, discussing when their grandfather and his brother had changed it from a peacock's head to an eagle's head on the top. That discussion took place in the exchange Granville and John had about potential family mottos. Charles's youthful preference for "fortune favors the brave" was juxtaposed against Granville's middle-aged preference for "let justice be done though the heavens fall"—a motto more fitting with the outlook and experience of their older years.[10] The timing of this discussion, 1786, suggests these questions might have been connected with Elizabeth's efforts to construct the family lineage chart.[11] Such actions also made Elizabeth similar to her male contemporaries, including heralds in the College of Arms, antiquarians, and individuals in the nascent professional genealogical field.

In other respects, Elizabeth's pedigree was strikingly different from those of her contemporaries. Her widowed and childless state generated a very different perspective on progenitors and posterity. That different perspective reached its full flower in the lineage chart Elizabeth constructed. The other contributors to the

---

[8] Sharpe, *Family Matters*, 54. For a transatlantic example of the connections between social or political power and genealogy, see Karin Wulf, "Bible, King and Common Law: Genealogical Literacies and Family History Practices in British America," *Early American Studies*, 10, no. 3 (Fall 2012): 467–502.

[9] Sharpe, *Family Matters*, 55. Family efforts to prevent future forgetting had been widespread since at least the sixteenth century; see Keith Thomas, *The Ends of Life: Roads to Fulfilment in Early Modern England* (Oxford: Oxford University Press, 2009), 253.

[10] Granville Sharp, to John Sharp, July 7, 1786, D3549/13/1/S8.

[11] Granville Sharp to John Sharp, July 1, 1786, D3549/13/1/S8.

lineage chart were also unmarried and childless: Judith drew and painted the circles representing each person; Granville wrote the narrative explaining how the name Granville came into the family; and niece Catherine worked with Elizabeth to fill in genealogical details. Though the lineage chart was never finished (Catherine continued to fill in details until 1842 but never completed the earlier generations), it represents a unique perspective of family inheritance and legacy—one particularly shaped by Elizabeth's marital status and gender.

The lineage chart is a beautiful piece of handiwork, but that is not what sets it apart; other families, particularly the female members, rendered their genealogy and children in beautiful samplers and tapestries.[12] Instead, its value resides in how it represents Elizabeth's vision of her family and her place among past and future generations. Despite the importance of the Sharp surname to Elizabeth and her family, the chart is not an account of their descent from illustrious Sharps. Instead, the four surnames and arms displayed at the top, depicting early sixteenth-century ancestors, represent four female lines of descent: Palmer and Halton (the Sharps' grandmother's ancestors), Wheler (the Sharps' mother), and Granville (their mother's maternal line).[13] Granted, some of the reasons for depicting these four female lines may be the prominence of those families and lack of records for the Sharps before the early seventeenth century. Nevertheless, Elizabeth could have chosen the Sharps as the starting point, with other lines appearing only when they intersected with Sharps. Or she could have chosen to trace some of those illustrious names back to the Tudors, the Conquest, or Alfred the Great, as other families did. Instead, Elizabeth situated the Sharps in the center—not as lone progenitors but as the centerpiece of a vast kinship network. The ribbon of blue circles in the middle of the chart highlights their centrality—the blue circles are Elizabeth and her siblings, with two earlier generations of Sharp siblings and one later generation of Sharps surrounding them (see upper image, Plate 3).

Elizabeth's style of genealogy and family chronicle was very different from the style of eighteenth-century published genealogies covering the peerage or heraldry. Eighteenth-century genealogies typically focused on patriarchal lineage or the royal and noble houses. Or, in the case of *Genealogical Essay on the Family of the*

---

[12] Preserving family legacies in this way was widespread in early America. The Huntington Library has a collection of eighteenth-century American family trees stitched and sewn, often by young women. For example, see Rebecca Ives Gilman (1746–1823), *Ives Family Coat of Arms*, 1763, Huntington Library. See also genealogical manuscript containing the history of several surnames, including Bustamante, Cordero, Joanes, Manaldo, Odoardo, Ponce, Trevino, and de la Riba, 1755, Documents Collection, 1519–1979, DRT 9, Daughters of the Republic of Texas Library, San Antonio, Texas.

[13] Elizabeth's emphasis on female lines is echoed in other early modern women's genealogy. See Natasha Korda, "Marriage, Identity, and the Pursuit of Property in Seventeenth-Century England: The Cases of Anne Clifford and Elizabeth Wiseman," in *Women, Property and the Letters of the Law in Early Modern England*, 179.

202   BEING SINGLE IN GEORGIAN ENGLAND

Hams, satirized such efforts.[14] From the Tudors to the late seventeenth century, genealogies focused on claiming legitimacy for the nation via the legitimacy of the royal houses, as indicated by the published royal lineages sold in bookshops in the seventeenth and eighteenth centuries. Early modern visitation records did similar work for titled or armorial families beyond royalty. Volumes tracing gentry and peer genealogies, even if those families had no titles or arms, began to be published in the sixteenth and seventeenth centuries and continued to perform similar work in the eighteenth century—establishing the legitimacy of genteel culture and influence.[15] These impulses tended to make genealogical practices incredibly linear, dynastic, and patriarchal.[16]

A comparison with a hand-made pedigree of a contemporary, Fielding-Best Fynney, a married man with children, emphasizes Elizabeth's unique perspective. Fielding-Best created a narrow scroll several feet long that included only dynastic relationships (father to son) until he reached people he personally knew (his siblings and children). At that point he began to provide more information about more family members. Elizabeth, however, provided full information for everyone in the family, even the unmarried, the childless, and those who died as children. She and her siblings rest in the center—in a web of relationships going back seven generations, forward three generations, and outward to third and fourth cousins. She emphasized the strength of lateral kinship instead of lineal descent. Whereas Fielding-Best inherited a line, Elizabeth inhabited a geography of family relationships. Elizabeth, remarkably, considered lateral connections even for those she did not know (including stillborn children), indicating how childlessness and singleness made her aware of other childless or unmarried kin and therefore more cognizant of the need to remember them and incorporate them. Her childlessness and the importance of sibling ties (as opposed to marital ties) are highlighted in how she depicted her siblings, nieces, and nephews. She used blue to depict her siblings and continued to use blue for the next generation, even when the surname changed to Lloyd-Baker. Additionally, her unique marital status as a widow of her second cousin allowed her to depict both natal and marital relationships simultaneously.[17] She and her husband, George Prowse, appear twice on the lineage chart, once as a child/sibling and once as a spouse. Elizabeth's

---

[14] *A Genealogical Essay on the Family of the Hams: Wherein Is Shewn, Their Pretensions to Certain Colleges, as Founders Kinsmen. Together with a Preface, Setting Forth the True Original of the Family of the Belchers. Inscrib'd, with All Due Submissions, to the Learned Society of Antiquarians* (London: Printed for Ned Lackham, 1730), WACML PR 3291.G326. For an elaborate description of armorial rights, see Sylvanus Morgan, *The Sphere of Gentry: Deduced from the Principles of Nature, an Historical and Genealogical Work, Arms and Blazon* (London: William Leybourn, 1661), WACML fCR19 M84s.

[15] Sharpe, *Family Matters*, 58–60, 63–64.

[16] Charles Lyttleton, "Grenville Pedigree, 1750–59," Stow Grenville Collection, Huntington Library, STG Personal Box 38, folder 11.

[17] Elizabeth and Catherine unwittingly echoed a very old pattern of genealogical practice. Medieval genealogies of Christ, centered on the importance of immaculate conception instead of patrilineage, emphasized St. Anne and her daughters over Christ's descent from David. See Pamela Sheingorn,

work was also strikingly different from nineteenth-century authors' descriptions of the family. In an 1889 published pedigree of the Sharps, for example, Elizabeth is completely erased from the family and replaced with her husband, George Prowse. She was not the only one erased; all of the Sharp sisters, William, and all the siblings they lost in childhood are not named but are merely labeled as "and nine others."[18]

Granville penning the note at the top of the lineage chart about how the surname Granville entered their family line might reflect a similar recognition on his part. Granville may have helped Elizabeth compile information about their ancestors when he helped their grandfathers' biographers gather records.[19] Once that biographical information was combined with Elizabeth's efforts, it depicted a broader concept of lineage. As the only unmarried and childless brother, Granville benefited from the space made by Elizabeth to connect to past and future generations.

Niece Catherine did not marry until 1817, and while she did not marry a cousin, she did try to replicate her aunt's technique of tying marital connections into natal relationships by having her husband change his surname to Sharp and thus inserting him into her lineage (a maneuver underscored by his circle on the family lineage chart also being colored blue). That he was a successor to her father and uncle's position of rector at Bamburgh only deepened his inclusion into the Sharp lineage.

Pedigree charts and family chronicles compiled by men tended to focus on the work of married men with children—those who perpetuated surnames. But Elizabeth recorded women and men of all familial statuses. Particularly striking is Elizabeth's inclusion of her siblings who died as infants or as young children, even those who died before her birth. She did not group them as nameless children who died young, as was often the practice in published genealogies, but she recorded their names and birth and death dates and gave them individual circles in the chart. Some of this knowledge clearly predated Elizabeth's memories, underscoring that remembering family events and ancestors was a well-established practice for the Sharps. Undoubtedly, her parents had preserved this information, though only hints of that preservation survive.[20] She did not provide a linear

---

"The Holy Kinship: The Ascendancy of Matriliny in Sacred Genealogy of the Fifteenth Century," *Thought*, 64, no. 254 (1989): 268–286.

[18] William Cudworth, *The Life and Correspondence of Abraham Sharp* (London: Sampson, Low, Marston, Searle, and Rivington, 1889), YMA COLL 1891/13.

[19] In his account of the Sharp family, published in 1889, William Cudworth states that he used notes compiled by Granville in 1798. Cudworth, *The Life and Correspondence of Abraham Sharp*, 261–262; Granville worked with their uncle Granville Wheler to provide materials for a biography of George Wheler: "Ledston Hall Archives: Additional Papers of the Wheler Family 17–20th Centuries," West Yorkshire Archive Service, Leeds, digital copy Newberry Library, MS Folio E 68.552, https://www.catalogue.wyjs.org.uk/CalmView/GetDocument.ashx?db=Catalog&fname=WYL170_pt2.pdf.

[20] Thomas Sharp to Judith Wheler Sharp, March 25, 1728, D3549/8/1/1.

204 BEING SINGLE IN GEORGIAN ENGLAND

progression but instead provided a lattice work of all the ancestors who, collectively, produced the Sharp siblings and their nieces. Her marital status and gender inspired a different, more expansive understanding of family, lineage, and kinship.[21]

Age and a Developing Interest in Family History

Like many early modern and Georgian families, the Sharps' ancestors had engaged in genealogical activities.[22] Their uncle Heneage Dering wrote a combined autobiography and family chronicle when he was 70, hoping his descendants might glean something useful from it; their grandfather Sharp maintained knowledge of his extended kin; their grandfather Wheler wrote an autobiography intended to memorialize their ancestors and inspire his descendants; and in addition to writing a biography of his own father, Thomas Sr. explored possible kinship connections to other northern families.[23] There is no surviving direct evidence of their female ancestors' efforts, but their mother must have engaged in some preservation efforts and genealogy, since her children had knowledge of their Wheler ancestors' lives and read their grandfather Wheler's writings. In each firsthand account, the Whelers and Sharps prefaced their life stories with a genealogical history, a pattern the Sharp siblings and nieces followed. Like most contemporary family chroniclers and genealogists, the Sharp ancestors indicated they were recording the "important details." The Sharp siblings, particularly Elizabeth, had a broader definition of what constituted important. She included family gatherings, not just individual actions and her inclusion of stillborn children was her own invention. For her, if it involved her kinship network, it was important by definition.

The Sharps did not set out in their youth to learn of their ancestors and preserve that legacy for their posterity. They grew up knowing they were the only remnants of Archbishop Sharp's surname line, but beyond that they did not seem unusually knowledgeable or interested in their progenitors. Others might have known the Sharps had "roots deep down in the history and soil of Yorkshire," going back to at least the fourteenth century, but this heritage did not seem to

---

[21] Tadmor, *Family and Friends*. See also Ellen Gruber Garvey, *Writing with Scissors: American Scrapbooks from the Civil War to the Harlem Renaissance* (New York: Oxford University Press, 2012).

[22] Joanne Bailey, "The 'Afterlife' of Parenting: Memory, Parentage, and Personal Identity in Britain c.1760–1830," *Journal of Family History*, 35, no. 3 (July 2010): 249–270; Davidoff, *Family Story* Rotschild Inner life chapter 7.

[23] Heneage Dering, "Autobiographical Memoranda," in *Yorkshire Diaries and Autobiographies in the Seventeenth and Eighteenth Centuries, Publications of the Surtees Society*, vol. 65 (London, 1877); Sir George Wheler, autobiography, 1700, MS 3286, LPA; Thomas Sharp, "Catalog of clergy of Cathedral of Durham," annotated by Granville Sharp, c.1790s, COLL 1891/9/1, YMA; Thomas Sharp, *The Life of Dr. John Sharp: Archbishop of York*, handwritten copy, COLL 1891/9/2, YMA; *The Gentleman's Magazine*, 62, part 2 (1792): 618.

concern the siblings in their younger years.[24] The only evidence of any youthful interest in their family heritage comes from a later recollection of Granville's. In a 1786 letter, he recounted to John how their brother Charles, who died in 1744, once drew the family arms and attached the motto *fortes fortuna juvat*.[25] Beyond that moment, the young Sharps did not concern themselves with family heritage, but their father had written a biography of his father in the hopes it would become an heirloom for his children. At the time, *heirloom* could mean either a physical object or a more abstract sense of family knowledge and values, and it was probably the latter Thomas Sr. had in mind. His desire, however, does not seem to have had an enormous impact when the siblings were young, if Granville's 1763 account of not knowing much about the archbishop was indicative of his siblings' knowledge.[26]

Similarly, between the 1740s and 1760s, the siblings were not considering their legacy beyond their personal concerns about marriage and childbearing. And for the siblings who married, their initial concerns about posterity were predominantly reproductive and patrilineal. For example, James made a will the year after the birth of his son, Jack, that provided for Jack's future. He never updated the will, despite the birth of his daughter in 1770 and Jack's death in 1771.[27] The Sharps' ancestral legacy became more important only as they approached old age and it became clear that there would not be a large posterity. The Sharps' collective fertility problems changed the family landscape as they aged. William's wife with her "usual ill luck" of suffering miscarriage and stillbirths, and the devastating losses of Jack, Thomas's wife and son, and then Thomas himself in 1770–72 meant that as the siblings entered their forties and fifties, it was obvious they would not be able to count on a bevy of daughters and sons to carry on family traditions and the family name. No wonder that their niece Mary's birth in 1778 was a "great Blessing...felt most thankfully by us all."[28]

As the siblings gradually realized they would not have the traditional carrier of a family legacy—a boy bearing their surname—they began, incrementally, to create alternative ways to preserve their family culture, memorialize their ancestors, and provide for a future legacy. Their first efforts to chronicle interactions and connect themselves with earlier generations included the common letters they exchanged, copied, and preserved in the 1750s and Elizabeth's combined diary, commonplace book, and family chronicle. These efforts coincided with the

---

[24] A. Tindal Hart, *Life and Times of John Sharp, Archbishop of York* (London: SPCK, 1949), 13, 38, BX 5199 S5 H3, WACML.

[25] Granville Sharp to John Sharp, July 7, 1786, D3549/13/1/S8.

[26] Thomas Sharp, *The Life of John Sharp, DD, Lord Archbishop of York*, ed. Thomas Newcome, vol. 1 (London: C. and J. Rivington, 1825), iv, v; Granville Sharp to [John] Sharp, April 9, 1763, COLL 1891/3/2, YMA.

[27] James Sharp, will written November 21, 1766, proved November 7, 1783, Prerogative Court of Canterbury, The National Archives, PROB 11/1110, TNA, digital image at https://www.ancestry.co.uk.

[28] Elizabeth Sharp Prowse, memorandum and commonplace book, April 1778, D3549/14/1/1.

206 BEING SINGLE IN GEORGIAN ENGLAND

siblings beginning to establish their own households. Also in the 1750s, details about the frequent musical concerts at William's house or onboard one of the yachts were carefully recorded and preserved in the concert programs and the "visiting books" of those in attendance. Beyond this record of their social lives, the first evidence of the brothers' concerns about family legacy appears in letters they exchanged between 1761 and 1766 concerning the preservation of their grandfather's and father's writings and biographies. Granville and John wrote extensively about the effort, including concerns about how popular they thought a publication might be, but Thomas, William, James, and their cousin Heneage all participated in the discussion and editorial efforts to make the subject matter appealing to potential readers.[29] In recording and preserving the chronicle, the genealogy, the publications, and information about the river concerts, the Sharp siblings came to collectively shape a family legacy beyond children. As the Sharps were accustomed to thinking of themselves as a unit, it is not surprising that once they became concerned about passing on a legacy, they saw it as a group effort. They approached recording and preserving their family's history and culture with the same zeal and cooperative spirit.

When they were young, Granville and William accompanied their father while he visited relatives. They met a man who let them, their horses, and their servants stay at his home even though he did not know them. When the Sharps arrived at the house, the man recognized them as descendants of the Sharp who had given him that living. He hugged them and wept for gratitude for what their grandfather had done for him. But it was not until 1791 that Granville retold this story. He mentioned it to John in case John had never heard it because "it is a family Anecdote worthy of remembrance."[30] Young Granville took for granted a family story that middle-aged Granville valued and preserved. By recounting such family stories, the siblings not only preserved records but also highlighted the content that supported their sense of family identity.[31]

Single family members performed the majority of this work. When John died in 1792 the only married Sharps were William and Catherine. In addition to the single Sharps, Mary, Elizabeth and their two sisters-in-law, and the other Catherine, were widows. Therefore, for the last decades of their lives, most of the siblings experienced old age as unmarried people. Many accounts of the late eighteenth- and early nineteenth-century Sharp family life skim over their activities to concentrate on their deaths and memorials. However, this misses nearly two decades of Sharp sociability and their most concentrated family historical

[29] Thomas Sharp to John Sharp, December 4–5, 1761, NRO 0452/C/3/2/2/6, NAW; Granville Sharp to John Sharp, February 12, 1766, COLL 1891/3/7, YMA.
[30] Granville Sharp to John Sharp, September 23, 1791, D3549/13/1/S6.
[31] Janet Finch and Jennifer Mason, *Passing On: Kinship and Inheritance in England* (London: Routledge, 2001).

activities.[32] It was not just Granville whose appreciation of family legacy was influenced by age. Though they continued to enjoy vibrant family social gatherings into the nineteenth century—the entire family gathered for "a most happy" house party at Wicken in 1806—the siblings also prepared their legacy by distributing material objects and writing wills to ensure their nieces properly preserved objects of family importance.[33]

Sometime in the 1770s or 1780s, Elizabeth returned to her diary and commonplace books (which she began keeping perhaps as early as 1743) and began to compile a family chronology. By the 1790s, her niece Catherine had joined her in this effort. Though the bulk of the writing was about her siblings, sisters-in-law, and nieces and nephews, Elizabeth also included genealogical details about her grandparents, aunts, uncles, and cousins. Some of this work undoubtedly informed the official family pedigree submitted to the College of Arms in 1799, but Elizabeth's work went far beyond the demands of heraldry.[34] In the end, she drafted a collage of Sharp family history, derived in part from her own writings, supplemented with clippings from letters or day books of other family members, and eventually edited by Catherine.

Elizabeth began the book by describing the Sharp family crest, reporting the change in spelling (from Sharpe to Sharp) among their direct ancestors, and explaining the Sharp surname.[35] She and Catherine clearly saw the history as a work in progress, one in which she and other family members invested much time and effort. Its unfinished nature is obvious because there are two versions of her work: an extracted draft version and a bound volume of combined information (though often with fewer details than the draft copy contained) from several sources, including Elizabeth's diary and snippets of information found in letters, newspapers, monumental inscriptions, and their cousin Heneage Dering's notes on their family (see Plate 6). In addition, a descendant of her niece Mary produced a typescript copy of Elizabeth's memoirs in the twentieth century. All of these versions and various efforts of family members demonstrate the painstaking and time-consuming effort Elizabeth, and then Catherine, put into compiling a family chronology and history.[36] What originally began as a diary kept by a young Elizabeth became the foundation for a sprawling account

---

[32] For a similar account, see Patricia Crawford, "Katherine and Philip Henry and Their Children: A Case Study in Family Ideology," *Transactions of the Historic Society of Lancashire and Cheshire*, 134 (1984): 39–73.

[33] Elizabeth Sharp Prowse, memorandum and commonplace book, May 1806, D3549/14/1/1.

[34] Sharp family pedigree and arms, 1800, D3549/1/2/2.

[35] Elizabeth Sharp Prowse, memorandum and commonplace book, page 1, D3549/14/1/1.

[36] Their effort was not without precedent; seventeenth-century English women also engaged in such efforts. Katharine Hodgkin, "Women, Memory and Family History in Seventeenth-Century England," in Erika Kuijpers, Judith Pollmann, Johannes Müller, and Jasper Van Der Steen, eds., *Memory before Modernity: Practices of Memory in Early Modern Europe* (Leiden: Brill, 2013), 297–314.

208 BEING SINGLE IN GEORGIAN ENGLAND

reaching back to her grandparents, outwards to cousins, and forward to the nieces she would leave behind.[37]

By the turn of the nineteenth century, Catherine had assumed much of the work on this project. Though Elizabeth was still writing what would become the draft copy, it was clear that Catherine had an editorial vision of what the final version should be. In an aside to her transcription of a June 1798 entry, Elizabeth mentioned a picture her nephew (on her husband's side) drew of her residence, Wicken Park, "which I had placed here, but Catharine sayd I must place it on the Back of the Picture so shall only coppy it here."[38] Mild bickering between Elizabeth, who was 65 at the time, and Catherine, thirty-seven years her junior, is not all that surprising. What is remarkable, however, is that Elizabeth's passion for preserving her family's legacy had clearly affected 28-year-old Catherine, who might have been considering the prospect that she and her cousins might not have children to whom to pass that legacy. Catherine herself attempted a similar chronicling effort after her aunt's death, but without the sibling and cousin network her aunt enjoyed, there was relatively little left to record, and she seems to have ceased her efforts in 1812.[39] Concurrently with her work on Sharp family history, Elizabeth also recorded a chronicle of Wicken village. Part local history, part history of Wicken Park landowners, part family history, her Wicken chronicle performed the same service as her Sharp family chronicle by organizing information to be used in the lineage chart and by preserving a history for the future.[40]

Some of Elizabeth's efforts were similar to those of other families. They, like the Sharps, chronicled special events, like the Sharps did when they recorded the monarchs' visits to the family yacht on the Thames, but the Sharps and others also recorded the more mundane events of family life.[41] From account books to recipe books, late seventeenth-century and eighteenth-century families found the space to include personal and familial events, record their ancestors' names and dates of birth and death, and preserve family memories and traditions.[42] They also made explicit efforts to write family chronologies that were passed to descendants and maintained by them, as the Tuthill family did when they preserved their ancestor's

---

[37] Elizabeth Sharp Prowse's experience was similar to that of Elizabeth Isham, who wrote seventeenth-century "Books of Remembrance." Like Elizabeth Sharp Prowse, Isham made multiple copies of her writing in an explicit effort to preserve her life and perpetuate its meaning. And like her, Isham also never married. Margaret J.M. Ezell, "Elizabeth Isham's Books of Remembrance and Forgetting," Modern Philology, 109, no. 1 (August 2011): 71–84.

[38] Elizabeth Sharp Prowse, memorandum and commonplace book, June 1798, D3549/14/1/1.

[39] Catherine Sharp (Bowlt), diary, 1810–12, D3549/17/5/4.

[40] Elizabeth Sharp Prowse, account of Wicken, c. late eighteenth century or early nineteenth century, 364P/501, NRO. The catalogue misattributes this work to Elizabeth's sister-in-law Elizabeth Prowse. The familial references within the document and the hand indicate it was Elizabeth Sharp Prowse who wrote it.

[41] The Frogatt family of Derbyshire engaged in similar work when they carefully chronicled the deaths and burials of family members. Frogatt family of Stavely or Stanly, Derbyshire, Stow Grenville Collection, STG Person Box 38, folder 12, Huntington Library.

[42] Ann Yerbury, family notebook, 1703–47, MS 1994.002, folder 2, item 1, WACML.

1681 notebook and continued to record family events in it until 1853.[43] Even in the midst of estate accounts, men and women inserted personal accounts, or "memorandum relating to myself" as one writer put it, and many took time to make an "Acc[oun]t of My Predecessors."[44]

Families also perpetuated genealogical connection through naming patterns. While the English never repeated the strict naming practices of the Scots, they consistently named children for previous generations. By the eighteenth century, the practice of naming children after godparents had waned as the popularity of naming children after parents grew.[45] Names were important markers of possession and identity, even when first names were often reused within the same sibling cohort.[46] The naming pattern among the Sharp siblings demonstrates the family legacy already embodied in their names. The table below provides the Sharp siblings' names and the relative(s) they were named for.

Sharp Sibling	Namesake
John	Paternal grandfather and uncle
Wheler	Mother's maiden name
Thomas	Father, great-grandfather
Grace	Maternal grandmother and aunt
George	Maternal grandfather
Charles	Maternal uncle
William	Maternal and paternal uncles
James	Paternal uncle
Elizabeth	Paternal grandmother and aunt
Judith	Mother
Granville	Maternal uncle and a previous generation's surname
Ann	Paternal aunt
Frances	Maternal aunt

Due to the frequency with which early modern children were named Elizabeth, Mary, John, Thomas, and William, some of these names could be attributed to those larger patterns, but the fact that no Sharp sibling had a name without family connections underscores that carrying the family legacy was a part of their lives from childhood.[47] The pattern they followed was typical of landed and titled

[43] Christopher Tuthill et al., family notebook, 1681–1853, MS 1977.003, WACML.

[44] Renaud Accounts, MS 1977.009, WACML.

[45] Scott Smith-Bannister, *Names and Naming Patterns in England 1538–1700* (Oxford: Oxford University Press, 1997).

[46] Eleanor Shevlin, "The Titular Claims of Female Surnames in Eighteenth-Century Fiction," in Nancy Wright, Margaret W. Ferguson, and A.R. Buck, eds., *Women, Property, and the Letters of the Law* (Toronto: Toronto University Press, 2004), 256–257; Peter Razzell, "Growth of Population in Eighteenth-Century England: A Critical Reappraisal," *The Journal of Economic History*, 53, no. 4 (1993): 753.

[47] Douglas A. Galbi, "Long-Term Trends in Personal Given Name Frequencies in the UK (20 July 2002)," Federal Communications Commission, SSRN, http://ssrn.com/abstract=366240, accessed March 17, 2016.

210   BEING SINGLE IN GEORGIAN ENGLAND

families, though perhaps more unique to the Sharps was their practice of naming the family yachts after their nieces.

Material Objects and Family Identity

Beyond its content, Elizabeth's lineage chart, much like the family portrait, was also a material representation of Sharp family culture and values. Other family members knew of it, handled it, and contributed content. Judith's, Catherine's, and Granville's contributions are obvious, but others were clearly consulted, and the lineage chart was preserved by niece Mary's descendants, thus connecting them not only to Elizabeth, Granville, and Catherine but also to all their mother's ancestors. The lineage chart joined other physical objects the Sharps gathered or created to link a familial past and future. Material objects, particularly gifts and heirlooms, were important for familial memory and belonging in the eighteenth century.[48] The Sharps' long-term shared households deepened their connections and facilitated the sharing and preserving of material objects. In some ways, the Sharps, no matter their marital status, were much like other comfortable Georgians regarding family heirlooms; they were intrigued by family mottos and arms and emphasized their surname over other lines.[49] While all family members engaged in gift exchanges and worked to preserve heirlooms, those activities seemed to be a particular concern of the unmarried family members. William's and John's wills, written by two married fathers, recorded the passing of family heirlooms and the material objects of mourning, but their letters do not show the preoccupation with preserving and passing on material objects significant to their generation that the letters of other siblings and their unmarried nieces did. The Sharps' experience highlights how the unmarried could be just as dedicated as parents in perpetuating family ideals and legacy.[50]

The interiors of wealthy homes like the Sharps' were places of consumption meant to signal social status which also offered a sense of belonging and identity for the family members.[51] The Sharps were keenly aware of the material

---

[48] Ezell, "Elizabeth Isham's Books of Remembrance and Forgetting," 82–84; Susan M. Stabile, *Memory's Daughters: The Material Culture of Remembrance in Eighteenth-Century America* (Ithaca: Cornell University Press, 2004). On the importance of gift exchange, see Margot C. Finn, "Colonial Gifts: Family Politics and the Exchange of Goods in British India, c.1780–1820," *Modern Asian Studies*, 40 (February 2006): 203–231; Ilana Kraus Ben-Amos, *The Culture of Giving: Informal Support and Gift Exchange in Early Modern England* (Cambridge: Cambridge University Press, 2007); Rafaella Sarti, *Europe at Home: Family and Material Culture, 1500–1800* (New Haven: Yale University Press, 2004), 215–216.

[49] Granville Sharp to John Sharp, July 1, 1786, D3549/13/1/S8.

[50] Joanne Bailey, *Parenting in England, 1760–1820: Emotion, Identity, and Generation* (Oxford: Oxford University Press, 2012), 174–198.

[51] Kate Smith, "Warfield Park, Berkshire: Longing, Belonging and the Country House," in Kate Smith and Margot Finn, eds., *The East India Company at Home, 1757–1857* (London: University College London Press, 2018): 175–190.

manifestations of kinship and the legacy they embodied. Their family portrait exemplified this awareness; they commissioned a famous portrait artist, they traveled long distances to sit for him, and they did it after Thomas Jr.'s death, just as their own middle age might have convinced them to preserve their family before it diminished further. They knew the portrait would be passed down, preserved, and hopefully treasured. They also had a tradition of exchanging family portraits and sketches to hang in one another's homes (see Plate 7). As Thomas once told John, "we will make Room for a Picture of y[ou]rself wh[en]ever it shall be drawn, for I am determin'd... to have a good Picture of you."[52] Similarly, Judith had family portraits in her home as well as bracelets with miniatures of her siblings in them.[53] The siblings also exchanged family jewelry and memorial cups, left money for the purchase of mourning rings, and of course bequeathed books and music.[54]

These objects were particularly important for the Sharps as a genteel family with no family home. With the death of their father, the homes associated with their childhood and youth passed to his ecclesiastical successor. The siblings were interested in their ancestral homes, but without one home where all these objects could reside and be venerated in perpetuity, they had to labor to ensure objects, and their meanings, were carefully maintained.[55] John, refurbished the keep of Bamburgh Castle, where Sharp family portraits continue to hang, and designed a doorway for the house at Hartburn that had a bust of their grandfather Sharp above it.[56] The Sharps' wills reference a host of objects intended to perpetuate family identity and culture. In addition to coats of arms and paintings, they had large collections of books, instruments, and music. They also redistributed the possessions they inherited from ancestors or from their own number who died before them. Elizabeth, for example, received a gold plate from a Wheler uncle and passed it on to Catherine, William's widow.[57]

The Sharps' wills show a common pattern: women, particularly unmarried women, were more likely to name a variety of kin in their wills, and they were more likely to make women their primary heirs. They were also more likely to list

[52] Thomas Sharp to John Sharp, Hartburn, April 7, 1767, NRO 452/C/3/2/4/9, NAW.
[53] Judith Sharp, will written December 6, 1807, proved May 6, 1809, Prerogative Court of Canterbury, PROB 11/1498, TNA.
[54] Note about lapis lazuli heart given by Mary Sharp to her cousin Catherine Sharp, 1837, Mary Sharp Lloyd-Baker correspondence, D6919/2/2; Elizabeth Sharp Prowse, memorandum and commonplace book, April 25, 1768, D3549/14/1/1.
[55] On a 1785 journey to Scotland, the family were interested in visiting the ancestral Sharp home in Little Horton, Yorkshire, and were disappointed when their request was denied. Later, Granville took a claimant to the Little Horton estate, to the house where Archbishop Sharp was raised, indicating the Sharp siblings and nieces were familiar with it. Frances Sharp, diary, July 14, 1785, D3549/15/1/1; Granville Sharp to Ann Jemima Sharp, March 29, 1798, D3549/13/1/S6.
[56] Judith Sharp, drawing of Hartburn, Northumberland house, undated, D3549/8/1/6.
[57] Elizabeth Sharp Prowse, will written January 17, 1798, codicil written February 21, 1804, proved March 2, 1810, Prerogative Court of Canterbury, PROB 11/1509, TNA, digital image at https://www.ancestry.co.uk.

212   BEING SINGLE IN GEORGIAN ENGLAND

specific personal items designated for specific individuals, while the married brothers' wills focused on property and money for their widows and daughters.[58] Granville's notes about Frances's estate demonstrate that pattern. Frances died without a will, so her nearest relatives would be her heirs at law. Typically that would have meant equal division among her siblings. Granville made an account showing precisely that and granting each sibling or, in the case of John and James, their surviving heirs, an inheritance of just over £200 each. He then noted, however, that Frances had long made her wishes known, and so all the heirs agreed the estate should be divided according to those wishes: small amounts went to her sisters Elizabeth and Judith and the remaining money went to nieces Catherine and Mary. Mary, who was engaged at the time, received far less than unmarried Catherine. Frances's four surviving siblings and siblings-in-law and niece Jemima were already well provided for (Jemima had inherited property and money from her parents' wills), so it is no surprise Frances's siblings agreed to surrender their £200 to benefit Catherine and Mary.[59]

The heart of the Sharp efforts to preserve the material past and perpetuate it to the next generation was best represented in their bestowal of music and books—in other words, those things that they identified as central to Sharp family identity. Their father had composed and performed music throughout his life and their mother had taught them folksongs. The Sharp siblings followed in their parents' footsteps from a young age. John took a bound collection of music with him when he went up to Cambridge; portions of the collection were passed to Thomas in 1741 (when Thomas was 16) and subsequently to Charles and James.[60] Music composition and preservation were particularly important to Granville. He spent some of his extraordinary energy on designing bookplates that emphasized music (a massive organ as backdrop to the family arms nestled among sheets of music and numerous instruments), arranging music for performance, attending madrigal society meetings, organizing the family's voluminous music catalog, and playing the six instruments he had mastered.[61] As a historian of Sharp musical activities remarked, "it is in no exaggeration to say that Granville was the brother who reveled in music," even "rediscovering" and "inventing" instruments, with one of which, the traverse harp, "he accompanied his daily singing of the psalms."[62]

Music was not just Granville's passion; the siblings shared music among them and amassed an extensive library of music (valued at over £1300) and a varied

[58] Amy Erickson, *Women and Property in Early Modern England* (London: Routledge, 1995); Amy Froide, *Never Married*.

[59] Granville Sharp, notes on Frances Sharp's estate, c.1799, D3549/23/1/33.

[60] John Frederick Lampe, "The Cuckoo Concerto," in John Sharp's music collection, Music MS 185, DCL

[61] Crosby, "Private Concerts," 65–78.

[62] Crosby, *Private Concerts on Land and Water*, 78. It is tempting to speculate that the Sharps had inherited knowledge of, if not examples of, the instruments their grandfather Wheler built during his youth. George Wheler, autobiography, 1700, MS 3286, LPA.

collection of instruments.[63] James's household alone eventually contained a spinet, two guitars, two harpsichords, a finger organ, and dozens of music volumes.[64] Preserving such a massive collection became impractical, especially after James's death in 1783 and the sale of the yachts and barges. John's and Thomas's music was combined in the Bamburgh Castle library. In 1790, William "had drawn up a witnessed agreement whereby at the death of one of them all their instruments [with some exceptions]...and music became the property of the other," and James's collection was auctioned in 1792, presumably after the family retained whatever pieces they desired.[65] The two surviving brothers equally inherited John's collection upon his death in 1792, and Granville inherited William's in 1810. However, when Granville died in 1813 and William's widow died in 1814, there were no siblings left to inherit the combined collection, and it was auctioned off. Items of personal significance went to the surviving Sharps (Jemima, niece Catherine, and James's widow Catherine), but the collection seems to have been too large to maintain within the family. Most of their library, including books and music owned by all the siblings, ultimately came to rest at the Bamburgh Castle library. Nathaniel Lord Crewe, Bishop of Durham, purchased Bamburgh Castle in 1704 and left it in a charitable trust in his 1721 will. Thomas Sharp Sr. and John Sharp were the principal trustees from then until John's death in 1792, and they managed and collected the books and music. When John willed the collection to the Crewe Trust, the musical collection alone contained nearly four hundred pieces of music.[66]

Books were important carriers of family identity, both as objects and by content. The siblings perpetuated their father and uncle John Sharp's habit of cataloging their books and music and sharing them with one another.[67] As with music, books similarly traveled between siblings' homes and were inherited from kin. A sampling of nearly two hundred books reveals 150 of them were previously owned by a member of the family. For example, Frances owned several books of sermons first owned by her grandfather and father. And that sampling included only those that had formally transferred ownership; books were loaned and traded informally as well. In the end, their collective libraries contained more than eight thousand volumes, worth at least £2000.[68]

---

[63] In one 1768 exchange, Granville explained how Catherine (William's wife) had sent him some ballads, which he added to a selection of music Judith requested and sent on to John to share with Judith. Granville Sharp to John Sharp, January 24, 1768, COLL 1891/3/19, YMA.

[64] Crosby, "Private Concerts," 70.   [65] Crosby, "Private Concerts," 64.

[66] R. Alec Harman, *A Catalogue of the Printed Music and Books on Music in Durham Cathedral Library* (London: Oxford University Press, 1968); Bamburgh Library Catalog notes by Elizabeth Sharp Prowse, *c.*1800, about the Sharp family collections, Bamburgh MS C5/1-5, PGL.

[67] John Friend, comp., "The Rev. Dr. Sharp's Durham Library," 1796, D3549/9/1/12; Crosby, *Catalogue of Durham Cathedral Music Manuscripts.*

[68] "The Bamburgh Library and the Sharp Family," finding aide, PGL, https://reed.dur.ac.uk/xtf/view?docId=ark/32150_s1w0892b02q.xml.

214   BEING SINGLE IN GEORGIAN ENGLAND

Subscription lists combined with the surviving family book catalogs and commonplace books reveal a broad taste in reading.[69] Thomas's 1748 catalog produced while at Cambridge lists titles in history, religion, classics, catechisms, his brother John's books, music, and "polite literature."[70] John's collection included musical scores and books on the English canal system, poetry, the slave trade, and sermons. Judith, Jemima, and Granville subscribed to volumes of biographical writing.[71] Elizabeth read widely on agricultural improvements, Granville read about trusts and suicide, Judith owned a book meant to "make the learning of Hebrew easy," and Frances owned memoirs of a seventeenth-century French politician.[72]

Similarly, the spiritual and intellectual inheritance contained in books was carefully cultivated and preserved. As the only surname-survivors of Archbishop Sharp, the siblings and nieces helped to preserve the legacy of their unmarried or childless paternal aunts and uncles. Their father and his brother had each inherited half of their father's library. Eventually the two halves resided in John and Thomas's hands, respectively. After Thomas died in 1772, John gave that half to the Bamburgh Castle library and then John's similarly willed half in 1792. Thus, their grandfather's books and intellectual legacy were brought back together in one location. While Jemima could have preserved the library, it was a massive collection by 1792, one that would not fit in her home in Durham. By willing the bulk of the library to the Crewe Trust, her father ensured it would be preserved beyond his lifetime, thereby allowing four Sharps spread over three generations to participate in building and leaving a legacy, even the two without descendants.[73]

Their grandfather's library was only the seed of a multigenerational effort to preserve the combined literary and musical legacy of the Sharps. Eventually the library grew to include thousands of volumes owned by the siblings and their unmarried and childless cousins. Granville, for example, had inherited the commonplace books and library of Thomas Mangey (husband of their aunt Dorothy Sharp) when their only child, John Mangey, died in 1782, unmarried and childless.[74]

---

[69] Bamburgh Castle Library catalogue, D3549/9/1/12.

[70] Thomas Sharp, book catalogue, 1748, Bamburgh Library MS A1, PGL. For a detailed discussion of the Sharps' book collection and provenance, see "Building a Library: The Sharp Family and Their Book Catalogues," April 2018 Item of the Month, Palace Green Library, https://www.dur.ac.uk/palace.green/whatshere/iotm/archive/2018/04/.

[71] John Field Stanfield, *An Essay on the Study and Composition of Biography* (Sunderland: George Garbutt, 1813), *Google Books.*

[72] McDonagh, "'All towards the improvements,'" 280, 286; Granville Sharp, commonplace books, D3549/13/4/1; Julius Bate, *A Hebrew Grammar* (London: J. Hodges, 1751), owned by Thomas Sharp Sr. and later Judith Sharp, Bamburgh F.6.22/1, PGL; *Memoirs of Maximilian de Béthune, Duke of Sully, Prime Minister to Henry the Great*, trans. Charlotte Lennox (London: A. Millar, 1763), signed by Charlotte Lennox, owned by Frances Sharp and later Catherine Sharp, SC 02749, PGL.

[73] Edward Bateson, *A History of Northumberland*, vol. 1, *The Parish of Bamburgh with the Chapelry of Belford* (Newcastle upon Tyne: Andrew Reid and London: Simpkin, Marshall, Hamilton, and Kent, 1893), 70.

[74] Reverend Thomas Mangey collection, GB 0036 ADD MS80, PGL; John Mangey, will written October 25, 1780, codicils written January 21 and August 10, 1782, proved November 29, 1782, Prerogative Court of Canterbury, PROB 11/1097, TNA, digital image at https://www.ancestry.co.uk, accessed March 18, 2016.

During their lifetimes, books and music circulated between the Sharp siblings' households, often being signed or emblazoned with a bookplate for each individual who owned the volume in sequence. As family members passed away, their libraries were combined, with Elizabeth even making a special library at Wicken to house Granville's books.[75] As with the music collection, the book collection eventually grew too large for any one household to contain it. Many of the books joined the collection housed in Bamburgh, and in the 1780s, Granville donated some of his books to their grandfather George Wheler's donated library, connecting his siblings with their maternal grandfather's ecclesiastical and literary legacy.[76]

While their proclivity for collecting and maintaining well-organized collections reflects the popular Enlightenment hobby of collecting, it was more than a hobby for the Sharps. Preserving such a massive collection meant the Sharps could perpetuate a legacy that all family members could share in, not just those with spouses and children. They became keenly aware of other ways to preserve family legacy beyond flesh and blood descendants and, in so doing, shaped the activities of their married kin. In this light, John's and William's wills, which made special mention of their never-married sister, brother, sisters-in-law, and nieces, were just the last manifestations of a lifetime spent building a legacy together with unmarried family members.[77] In addition to music and books, other objects were carefully collected, organized, and preserved. Scrapbooks, old letters, menus, and account books were willed to their nieces and preserved throughout the nineteenth century by Mary's descendants.[78]

While all Sharps, no matter their gender, wanted to preserve their intellectual and musical culture for future generations, the brothers, particularly Granville, were more invested in preserving and perpetuating that inheritance for a nonfamilial audience. Similar to Elizabeth, Granville Sharp looked to the family past to build a legacy for subsequent generations. Unlike Elizabeth, Granville thought of both familial and nonfamilial audiences for their grandfather's and father's work. In some ways the Sharps perpetuated eighteenth-century gendered attitudes about intellectual inheritance. In his will, for example, John left most of his books and music, and his father's books to Durham Cathedral, not his daughter or sisters. As discussed previously, some of this was a space constraint, but the books he did leave to his siblings tended to go to his brothers, while his sisters, and unrelated men, were given mourning rings. The brothers seemed particularly concerned with preserving their religious patrimony. Their father, Thomas Sr., had written his father's biography, and Granville and his brothers continued or began collecting

---

[75] Elizabeth Sharp Prowse, memorandum and commonplace book, October 1792–93, D3549/14/1/1.

[76] Granville Sharp, commonplace books, 1780s, D3549/13/4/1.

[77] John Sharp, will written April 17, 1792, codicil written April 21, 1792, proved May 2, 1793, Prerogative Court of Canterbury, National Archives PROB 11/1232; William Sharp, will written September 12, 1809, proved April 3, 1810, Prerogative Court of Canterbury, PROB 11/1510, TNA.

[78] Other families engaged in similar behavior. See Porter family album, bMS.2013.006, WACML.

216   BEING SINGLE IN GEORGIAN ENGLAND

their grandfather's and father's libraries and editing and preparing their papers and biographies.[79] Granville even describing his red-inked edits to his father's handwritten draft of the archbishop's life as a "farther memorial of a truly affectionate Father."[80] Additionally, John and Thomas continued the work at Bamburgh Castle that their father had begun as a trustee of Lord Crewe's in preserving the castle, managing the estate, and providing relief to the local poor.

The brothers' interest in the sermons, books, biographies, and activities of their father and grandfathers may have always been present, but it became more in evidence in the 1760s. In 1763 Granville remarked that when someone who had known Grandfather Sharp asked several questions of Granville about his grandfather, but Granville was unable to provide answers—despite being in the middle of preparing their grandfather's writings for publication.[81] His ignorance declined throughout the latter half of the eighteenth century as he and his brothers continued to work on a biography of their grandfather and publishing their father's sermons and writings—though the latter sold only "indifferently."[82] By the late 1780s whatever Granville's ignorance regarding his grandfather might have once been, it was no longer a concern. By that point Granville and John were working diligently to decipher their grandfather's shorthand in a continuing effort to publish the archbishop's writings, and were regularly exchanging information about their grandfather and father.[83] Increasingly interested in his grandfather's life, Granville also eagerly shared snippets of family stories he heard from acquaintances—stories he labeled "a Family Anecdote worthy of remembrance."[84] Additionally in the 1780s, Granville read seventeenth-century letters written by his maternal ancestor and desired to donate books to his grandfather, Sir George Wheler's library, where he was assured they would join the works of his father and paternal grandfather. By doing so he neatly connected himself to multiple generations of writers, on both sides of his family.[85]

Twilight of the Sharp Sibling Network

Sister-in-law/cousin Mary's death in 1798 and Frances's in 1799 were the last Sharp sibling deaths for a decade. In 1800, niece Mary married Thomas John Lloyd-Baker and they had six children in the first nine years of their marriage. An 1806 house party at Wicken and the short water scheme that followed were

[79] Thomas Sharp to John Sharp, December 4–5, 1761, NRO 452/C/3/2/2/6, NAW.
[80] Thomas Sharp, "Catalog of clergy of Cathedral of Durham," COLL 1891/9/1, YMA.
[81] Granville Sharp to John Sharp, April 9, 1763, COLL 1891/3/2, YMA.
[82] Granville Sharp to John Sharp, January 31, 1786 and October 31, 1790, D3549/13/1/S8.
[83] Granville Sharp, commonplace book, entries for 1789, pages 107–108, D3549/13/4/1.
[84] Granville Sharp to John Sharp, September 23, 1791, D3549/13/1/S8.
[85] Granville Sharp, commonplace book, page 36, D3549/14/1.

the last large family gatherings. Everyone was relieved at the end of 1808 when Catherine, James's widow, recovered from a severe illness, but in the coming years they were not so fortunate. In March 1809 Elizabeth and Granville, at Wicken, received word of Judith's death in Durham. Granville "set out that evening...the desire to be soon with...Dear [Jemima] as soon as possible on her great...Loss." Elizabeth departed for Durham the following morning.[86] Despite his rush, Granville arrived a day after Judith's funeral, a large procession full of ecclesiastical officers and Judith's friends and servants. She was buried in the cathedral near her parents, as well as John and Mary. Elizabeth and Granville stayed several weeks to help settle Judith's affairs. Over the summer of 1809 they were concerned for James's widow's health, but she continued to recover.

Again, they were not so fortunate in 1810. In February Elizabeth suddenly fell ill while visiting at Fulham. On the 22nd she "received the sacrament...all her own Relations & her own Servants partook" with her. The same day she dictated a letter to Jemima, Granville acting as scribe and then on the evening of the 23rd she passed away "about 20 minutes past eleven o'Clock."[87] She was 77. She was born ten months before Judith and died eleven months after Judith.

There was barely time to hold Elizabeth's funeral and have her will proved before William similarly succumbed; he died at Fulham three weeks later. It must have been sudden because Granville was not in attendance. The family circle had been reduced to one surviving Sharp sibling, the two sisters-in-law, and the three nieces. Wills perpetuated families' reputation and standing, something Elizabeth recognized.[88] Her will left the collected Sharp family archive to Granville and the nieces to preserve as they saw fit. It was not long, however, before there would be only one heir to that archive.

Unexpectedly, niece Mary died at the end of 1812 after a lingering illness, "an Event which deeply affected [Granville] & which...he never got over."[89] Catherine attributed Granville's subsequent decline to that loss. His mental and physical capacity declined in tandem; he tried to attend various committee meetings but, unable to contribute, he settled at Fulham. There, comforted by sister-in-law Catherine and niece Catherine, he spent his last days in a room decorated with family portraits, sometimes sighing, sometimes just looking at the faces of those who had predeceased him.[90] His health and mental acuity drastically declined early in 1813 and he died that July.[91] Fulham saw its last Sharp death the following

---

[86] Elizabeth Sharp Prowse, memorandum and commonplace book, March 13, 1809, D3549/14/1/1.

[87] Granville Sharp, diaries, extracted by Catherine Sharp (niece), book 4, February 1–2 and 22–23, 1809, D3549/13/4/2.

[88] Hannah Barker, *Family and Business during the Industrial Revolution* (Oxford: Oxford University Press, 2017), 49; Janet Finch and Jennifer Mason, *Passing On: Kinship and Inheritance in England* (London: Routledge, 2000).

[89] Catherine Sharp, notation in extracted diaries of Granville Sharp, book 4, page 41, D3549/13/4/2.

[90] Hoare, *Memoirs of Granville Sharp*, 465–469.

[91] Catherine Sharp, notation in extracted diaries of Granville Sharp, book 4, page 41.

218   BEING SINGLE IN GEORGIAN ENGLAND

year when Catherine, William's widow, died in February. She was buried by her husband, Elizabeth, and Granville in Fulham.

Conclusion

Legacy preoccupied both the married and unmarried Sharps. As they aged, the Sharps began to invest enormous thought and resources into their legacy. Though William, James, and John had children, they had daughters only and could not pass along their ecclesiastical heritage to a son, who could be ordained or carry on their surname. While providing a substitute posterity was especially important for the single family members, their aunts', uncles', cousins', and their own difficulty reproducing created greater impetus for additional methods of preserving their family's past and passing it on to future generations. The family portrait reflects this: single siblings were placed at the center surrounded by married and unmarried kin, and children were not grouped with their parents but jointly shared with aunts and uncles.[92]

Both Granville and Elizabeth worked to preserve a legacy, and both were kinkeepers, but in gendered ways. And their gendered pattern was replicated among their siblings. Granville concentrated on paternal lines, religious activities, and published legacy. James, John, and William helped to preserve the libraries of books and music. Elizabeth and their nieces preserved accounts of their family activities, letters, diaries, and pedigrees showing all family members, not just the fertile. While Elizabeth and Granville's behavior was not unique, it initially took a different shape from their married siblings' behavior. William, James, and John had children—physical reminders of their family's influence and values. But unmarried Granville and widowed Elizabeth looked to produce alternative physical reminders that would last into the next century. Their labor to preserve the family records and genealogy gave them a type of family power that was often reserved for spouses and children. Through their labor, Granville and Elizabeth expanded notions of inheritance and legacy to encompass other childless relatives, maternal family lines, and even fictive ties to social justice, thereby crafting a legacy meant to perpetuate their family culture and shared values in the future.[93] Eventually all the siblings, even the married brothers, took on these ways of memorializing the past for the future.

---

[92] That representation was strikingly different from more hierarchal depictions of family relationships. See Kate Retford, "Sensibility and Genealogy in the Eighteenth-Century Family Portrait: The Collection at Kedleston Hall," *Historical Journal*, 46, no. 3 (2003): 533–560.

[93] There are glimmers of similar behavior in eighteenth-century France. See Sonja Boon, "Recuperative Autobiography and the Politics of Life Writing: Lineage, Inheritance, and Legacy in the Writings of the Marquise de La Ferté-Imbualt," *Journal of Women's History*, 24, no. 3 (Fall 2012): 13–38.

In the nineteenth century the unmarried nieces, Jemima and Catherine, continued the labor of their aunts and uncles. Catherine's work with her aunt Elizabeth has already been mentioned and it appears that Granville and Jemima also engaged in efforts to preserve a family legacy, as they did in their efforts to expand and preserve the archbishop's coin collection.[94] Over time this work encompassed all of the Sharps as they engaged in a variety of activities meant to preserve a family legacy for future generations.

The Sharp siblings also enlisted their kinship network in this labor, including their sisters-in-law and Andrew Bowlt, John's long-time assistant curate. Andrew had long been a close associate of the family, living with John and Mary and traveling with the Sharps when they left Bamburgh Castle upon John's death in 1792. Andrew had also been using John's sermons as a basis for his own preaching for years. His role as a preserver of the Sharp legacy became more concrete in 1817 when he married niece Catherine and changed his surname to Sharp. As a clergyman, Andrew was more than willing to use a name that connected him to the extraordinary clerical legacy of Catherine's uncles, grandfather, and great grandfather. Assuming a wife's surname was not unprecedented, but the timing of Andrew's joining the family is illuminating. He and Catherine did not marry until they had known each other for decades, suggesting that unmarried, childless Andrew was also looking for ways to preserve a legacy. His adoption of Catherine's surname was the final action in an eighty-year effort by the Sharps—married and unmarried, with and without children—to perpetuate and preserve their family heritage. Ultimately, the Sharps passed on a legacy of shared values—of being part of a family richly endowed with talent and dedicated to sharing that abundance. All the actions, the material objects, and the preserved publications were a "mechanism for transmitting a resilient and enduring image of what [they] stood for."[95] It was a way of making sense of their own life stories and projecting that toward future generations. In the end, unmarried and married Sharps collectively created a lasting legacy.

The Sharps' management of their grandfather's coin collection illustrates how numerous family members engaged in preserving the material evidence of a family legacy, and the instrumental role single family members played in its preservation. In 1798, Granville took a visitor (a "young Mr. Sharp"), who was trying to prove his genealogy and thereby claim an estate, to visit the house where Grandfather Sharp was raised. Renovations were being carried out, and the workers gave Granville old Stuart coins they had found. He made sure to send these to Jemima, to keep with the rest of the coin collection begun by his grandfather, which was by that time a family collection stretching across four generations and

---

[94] Granville Sharp to Jemima Sharp, March 29, 1798, D3549/13/1/S6.
[95] Hunter and Rowles, "Leaving a Legacy," 328.

over 120 years.[96] Granville instructed Jemima to keep the coins in the cabinet she had inherited from her father. Her father's 1792 will had been explicit about the cabinet and the coins as representations of a family legacy. He described the mahogany cabinet filled with the coin collection and indicated it was his "Mind and Intention as the coins have been in the Family for the three Generations have passed through four several hands and have been collecting for above one hundred years...that my daughter should not part with my said cabinet out of her possession but still continue it down as far as in her lies in the Family and Name of Sharp." Then, recognizing there might be limited numbers of people who would bear the Sharp surname into the future, added "but in case she should happen to Marry a person of the Name of Sharp or one who shall change his Name to Sharp in consequence of such Marriage cabinet and what belongs to it to be retained in her Family."[97]

Jemima complied with this request in her own 1803 will; she left the coins to Granville, along with the books about coins she had inherited.[98] Jemima, however, died after her uncle Granville, meaning the coins passed to Catherine, Jemima's younger cousin. The next year, Catherine, when she married Andrew Bowlt, complied with her uncle's request and Andrew changed his surname to Sharp. However, since Catherine and Andrew died without children (not surprising, considering Catherine was 47 and Andrew 59 when they married), eventually the coins passed to Mary Lloyd-Baker's family, but the surname did not. Ultimately, though John easily maintained the coins' association with their family by passing the collection to his daughter, he recognized that unmarried and childless kin might have to go to great lengths to maintain the material familial legacy. That the single members were willing to go to such lengths, taking the time to add to the collection, storing it, collecting books about it, and providing for a potential husband to change his surname to Sharp, highlights the importance of genealogical kin-keeping to unmarried family members and underscores the importance of their efforts to do so.

---

[96] Granville Sharp to Ann Jemima Sharp, March 29, 1798, D3549/13/1/S6.

[97] John Sharp, will written April 17–May 21, 1792, proved May 2, 1793, Prerogative Court of Canterbury, PROB 11/1232, TNA.

[98] Ann Jemima Sharp, will written August 20, 1803, proved April 1, 1816, Durham Consistory Court.

Interlude 4
Epitaphs

Death was of course a constant part of life, even as mortality rates declined in the eighteenth century. The Sharps, like every family, experienced deaths in infancy, childhood, young adulthood, middle age, and old age and their burials reflected this reality. Many of the siblings who died in childhood were buried in Rothbury churchyard. Charles was buried in an unknown location either at sea or in Indonesia. Thomas was buried in Newcastle near his wife and son. Judith, John, his wife Mary, and Jemima were buried in Durham Cathedral, alongside the Sharps' parents and grandfather Wheler. James and his young son Jack were buried in the London parish where they resided when they died. Frances was buried in Berkeley, where their Prowse cousins hailed from and where she died. Niece Mary was also buried where she died, in Dawlish, Devon. Elizabeth was buried in a tomb shared by William, his wife Catherine, and Granville in Fulham. Niece Catherine, along with her mother and husband, were buried in South Mimms. No Sharp siblings were buried in Wicken, despite it being held by the Sharp female line for over a century, but the nieces commissioned a monument lionizing Elizabeth for the church wall. Similarly, no Sharps were buried in Bamburgh, but the younger Catherine erected a monument to the Sharp men who had been curates or trustees of the castle there. Much as in life, the deceased Sharps now inhabited various corners of England, forming a geography of remembrance.

The monumental inscriptions were not the only words preserved in remembrance of the Sharps. Obituaries and funeral sermons also contained epitaphs. They are not produced here because they are readily available in various online databases. Elizabeth's and William's lengthy funeral sermons and Mary's elegy to Wicken after Elizabeth's death have already been mentioned.[1] There was no funeral sermon published for Judith (who died the year before Elizabeth and William) and her death notice describes her only as the sister of Granville and John.[2]

The monuments commissioned by the nieces highlight their role in preserving Sharp family values and experiences. Catherine and her cousins' commissioning of family memorials was typical for people of their social class in the late

---

[1] John Owen, *A Discourse Occasioned by the Death of Elizabeth Prowse*; Mary Sharp Lloyd-Baker, "Wicken"; John Owen, "A Discourse Occasioned by the Death of William Sharp."
[2] "Provincial Occurrences, With all the Marriages and Deaths," *The Monthly Magazine or British Register*, 27, pt. 1 (1809), 405.

Being Single in Georgian England: Families, Households, and the Unmarried. Amy Harris, Oxford University Press.
© Amy Harris 2023. DOI: 10.1093/oso/9780192869494.003.0012

222 BEING SINGLE IN GEORGIAN ENGLAND

eighteenth and early nineteenth centuries, yet it was just one aspect of Catherine's labors. It went together with her organizing family papers and mementos, tying her desires to preserve texts associated with the deceased to the places most connected to their lives.[3] She aimed to establish, in a sense, places of pilgrimage. It did not matter that no Sharp was buried at Bamburgh or Wicken; those sites still mattered as memorials for the lives lived in those locations. By making the memorials public, she implicitly asserted that the Sharps were worthy of public veneration, part of the nation's worthy dead.[4] The African Institution of London erected a memorial to Granville to be displayed in Westminster Abbey's Poet's Corner for similar reasons: to ensure desired virtues of the past were preserved for future visitors. Catherine's memorials list the offices and public endeavors of the Sharp men, but they also emphasize familial connections to siblings and to her.[5] Strikingly, Catherine did not commission a memorial to her father, though he is mentioned on her mother's. This was likely due to Catherine's stage of life when her father died versus when she commissioned the monuments; James died when Catherine was only 13; she did not begin commissioning monuments until nearly three decades later.

The Sharp memorials were completed by some of the most renowned monument sculptors of their era. Their grandfather Sharp's memorial (1714) was done by Francis Bird, who, despite being a Catholic, created many of the figures on St. Paul's exterior. The Wicken church monument was created by John Bacon Jr. who came from a family of prominent sculptors. Granville's monument (1816), at a cost of over £60, was sculpted by Sir Francis Chantrey who also created sculptures of the king and prominent artists and politicians. Chantrey's involvement with Granville's monument might have been what made Catherine choose him for the memorials at Bamburgh and Durham. The Durham monument was completed in 1818 for £342 10s. 6d. and Bamburgh's in 1839 for £745 7s. 6d.[6] The expenditures reflected Catherine's serious commitment to perpetuating her family's legacy.

The transcriptions below include some of the notations Catherine made when she collected the inscriptions to include in her copy of Elizabeth's memorandum book. The only exception is the Bamburgh monument (upper image, Plate 8), which was commissioned two decades after her work on the memorandum book. Her additional notes about the men's professional appointments and her

---

[3] Paul Westover, *Necromanticism: Traveling to Meet the Dead, 1750–1860* (London: Palgrave, 2012).

[4] Mark Salber Phillips, *Society and Sentiment: Genres of Historical Writing in Britain, 1740–1820* (Princeton: Princeton University Press, 2000).

[5] Joanne Bailey, "The 'Afterlife' of Parenting: Memory, Parentage, and Personal Identity in Britain c.1760–1830," *Journal of Family History*, 35, no. 3 (July 2010): 249–270.

[6] Alison Yarrington, et al., "An Edition of the Ledger of Sir Francis Chantrey R.A., at the Royal Academy, 1809–1841," *The Volume of the Walpole Society*, 56 (1991/92): 2–343.

INTERLUDE 4: EPITAPHS   223

transcription of the memorials to her uncle and cousins' memorials at Wicken have not been included here.[7]

Durham Cathedral (Under the West Window)

Sacred to the Memory of Thomas Sharp D.D. son of John ArchBishop of York. He was born Dec^{er} 12th 1693, Married June 19th 1722 Judith, Daughter of the Revd Sir George Wheler, by whom he had fourteen Children. Died in 1758, and was buried at the West End of the Cathedral Church of Durham in the Chapel called the Galilee. He was Eminent not only for Piety and Prudence, but great learning and critical Judgment. He distinguished himself in the Hutchinsonian Controversy, in which his accurate knowledge of the Hebrew Tongue gave him a decided Advantage over Mr Hutchinson and his Followers. His Tract on the Rubric and Canons of the Church of England is highly Esteemed as indeed are all his Charges to the Clergy of Northumberland, over whom he presided many years as Archdeacon.

Sacred to the Memory of John Sharp D.D. the Eldest Son of Thomas and Judith Sharp. Born March 21st 1723 He Married Decr 4th 1752 Mary the Daughter of Dr Heneage Dering Dean of Ripon, by whom he had one Daughter Anne Jemima. He was a Prebendary of Durham, Archdeacon of Northumberland, Vicar of Hartburn, and Senior Trustee of the Estate of the late Nathaniel Lord Crewe Bishop of Durham, whose charities he was indefatigable in promoting. Having Repaired and Roofed the Old ruined Tower of Bamburgh Castle at the joint expense of himself and ^his^ Brother the Rev$^{d.}$ Thomas Sharp. He trod in the steps of his Excellent Father, and was Eminent for learning and Piety, and for Exemplary attention to his duties, both in his Church, and in his Archdeaconry. He died in April 1792 and was buried in the Galilee.

And in the same Place were also interred the remains of Judith, Wife of the said Dr. Thos. Sharp, and Daughter of the Rev^d. Sir George Wheler. Born 1700 died 1757; of Mary, Widow of the said D^r. John Sharp, and Daughter of D^r. Heneage Dering. Born 1720. Died 1798; of Anne Jemima, only Child of the said D^r. John Sharp & Mary his wife, born 1762. died 1816; of Judith Sharp, sister of D^r. John Sharp, born 1733 died 1809. In united Remembrance of whom this Marble is Inscribed by the only Survivor and Grand Daughter of D^r. Thomas Sharp Catherine Sharp 1816. Written by the Rev^d. Heneage Elsley.

---

[7] Catherine Sharp, monumental inscriptions of the Sharp Family, included with Elizabeth Sharp Prowse memoir, D3549/14/1/1.

Wicken Church Northhamptonshire (South Wall)

Draped urn with bas reliefs of Religion and Charity.

To the Memory of Elizabeth, Daughter of Thomas Sharp D.D. Archdeacon of Northumberland and Widow of George Prowse Esqr: late of Wicken Park who died Feb^{ry} 22nd 1810 aged 77. This Monument was erected by her three nieces Anne Jemima Sharp, Mary Baker, & Catharine Sharp as the affectionate Expression of their Veneration for her Character, and their Gratitude for her Kindness.

> Stranger whose Eyes to this Memorial turn
> Where Wicken's sorrow point to Prowse's Urn
> If grief for worth removed thy Heart reveres
> Then add they Tribute to the Village Tears
> Oh! wouldst thou Peace should cheer thy Pilgrim Way
> And Joy salute thee on thy rising Day
> Go, live like her, by God and Man carest
> Then die like her, and be forever blest.
> Written by the Rev'd John Owen

Fulham Churchyard (South Side)

Here lie the remains of Elizabeth Prowse of Wicken Parish Northamptonshire, Who died Feb^{ry} 23rd 1810 aged 77 (feb^r 22 before) and of her Brother William Sharp Esqr: of Fulham House in this Parish who died March 17th 1810 aged 81, Endeared to their Family Connexions and Society By an Amiableness of Character which has seldom been Equal^d And to Each other by a degree of mutual attachment Which has never been surpassed, "They were lovely in their Lives, And in Death they were not divided."

North side of monument

Here By the remains of the Brother and Sister whom he tenderly loved lie those of Granville Sharp Esqr At the age of 79 this venerable Philanthropist, terminated his Career of almost unparalleled activity and usefulness July 6th 1813 leaving behind him a name That will be cherished with Affection & Gratitude As long as any homage shall be paid to those principles Of Justice Humanity and Religion Which for nearly half a Century He promoted by his Exertions And adorned by his Example

West side of monument

Here also lie the Remains of Catherine, Daughter of Thomas Barwick Esq[r] and Wife of William Sharp Esq[r] who died Feb[ry] 9th 1814 aged 73. The Conduct of this Excellent Woman Under the various Relations of domestic Life Exhibited an Amiable and Edifying Example of that "Meek and quiet Spirit- "Which is, in the sight of God, of great Price"

East side of monument

The Burial Place of William Sharp Esq[re], His Wife Catharine and his Brother and Sister; Granville Sharp Esq[re] and Mrs Prowse of Whom respectively a Record will be found on the Sides and Head of This Monument.

The Inscriptions on this Tomb were all written by the

Rev[d]: John Owen-

South Mimms, Middlesex Churchyard

Beneath this Stone are deposited the mortal Remains of Catherine, Relict of the late James Sharp Esq[re] She died at Clare Hall in the Parish (where she had long resided Respected and Beloved) on the 5th day of Feb[y]: 1835 in 90th year of age Full no less of the blessed hope of Immortality than of Earthly Days "Blessed are the Dead who Die in the Lord"

Here also lie the Remains of the Rev.[d] Andrew Sharp, 43 years the respected Incumbent of Bamburgh Northumber[land] He died at Clare Hall April 30th 1835 in his 77th year, Having changed his name of Bowlt, to that of Sharp upon his Marriage in 1817 with Catherine, only Daughter of the late James Sharp Esq[re]

Bamburgh Parish Church, Northumberland (Back Wall)

Large marble sculpture against the back wall of the church. Above the memorial is a sculpture of a sitting woman, with a cross behind her and a bible under her seat. Also above is a relief sculpture of a bust of a man in profile—in clerical vestments.

This monument is erected in memory of her grandfather, her two uncles and her husband, who were successively trustees of Lord Crewes charities, or incumbents of the Parish of Bamburgh, by Catherine only child of James Sharp Esqr. of London and sole survivor of the name. A D 1839.

The venerable Thomas Sharp DD. son of John, Lord Archbishop of York, Archdeacon of Northumberland and Rector of Rothbury and prebendary of Durham, appointed trustee A.D. 1737 died A.D. 1758.

The venerable John Sharp D.D. his eldest son, Archdeacon of Northumberland, prebendary of Durahm and perpetual curate of Bamburgh: who, after rendering the ruins of Bamburgh Castle habitable, first established there a free school and dispensary and also formed a permanent arrangement for the preservation of the lives, and relief of the distresses of shipwrecked mariners. Appointed trustee A.D. 1758 died A.D. 1792.

The Reverend Thomas Sharp B.D. third son of Thomas Sharp D.D., Rector of All-Hallows in London and perpetual curate of Bamburgh. Appointed to the Curacy A.D. 1757 died A.D. 1772.

The Reverend Andrew Bowlt who took the name of Sharp on his marriage with Catherine, grand daughter of Thomas Sharp D.D. and was for 13 years the respected minister of Bamburgh.

Blessed are the dead which die in the Lord, yea saith the sprit, that they may rest from their labours and their works do follow them. Rev. cxiv. V.13.

Epilogue

An Afterlife in Documents

With the death of her aunt in February 1814, the collection of family possessions and papers that had been accumulating at Fulham since the 1780s were suddenly niece Catherine's concern. "I consider myself responsible to my family for all the papers, books, &c, which have fallen into my hands," she wrote that April. She sought the advice of Adam Clarke, a Methodist antiquarian, about organizing the voluminous pages, many dating back to the seventeenth century.[1] She may have thought she, her mother, and Jemima could work together to organize and preserve the objects and papers now stored either at Jemima's house in Durham or at Clare Hall. But that was not to be. Jemima's death in February 1816 meant only Catherine and her mother remained from their generations. Catherine continued the work she had been doing since at least the 1790s to perpetuate the family memory, and two months after Jemima's death, Catherine commissioned a monument for her and the other Sharps with ties to Durham Cathedral (see Interlude 4).

Jemima's death in 1816 might have been an additional reason for Catherine to reconsider her domestic arrangement. By marrying Andrew the following year, and convincing him to change his surname, she found a partner to perpetuate the Sharp ecclesiastical legacy as well as the surname. The connection between her marriage and perpetuation of Sharp family values was recognized by observers. In a poem written by an Alnwick watchmaker, the deceased Sharps were envisioned as witnessing the wedding:

> From their radiant spheres, lo! bending
> Sainted Sharps approve the choice
> Their gold Harps in union blending,
> And in Heavenly strains rejoice;
> Rejoice to see their only Flower
> Left to grace our wilds below,
> Transplanted to high Merit's Bower,

---

[1] Catherine Sharp, Clare Hall, to Adam Clarke, April 6, 1814, transcribed in J.B.B. Clarke, ed., *An Account of the Infancy, Religious and Literary Life, of Adam Clarke, LL.D., F.A.S., &c.* (New York: B. Waugh and T. Mason, 1833), 178.

Being Single in Georgian England: Families, Households, and the Unmarried. Amy Harris, Oxford University Press.
© Amy Harris 2023. DOI: 10.1093/oso/9780192869494.003.0013

228　BEING SINGLE IN GEORGIAN ENGLAND

The poem also admonished Catherine and Andrew to "Emulate their deeds of Glory / Who've smooth'd and pointed out the way."[2] Catherine, her mother, and Andrew lived principally at Clare Hall in South Mimms, often joined by Jane Maunsell Le Mesurier, Catherine's goddaughter/foster daughter. The group apparently enjoyed friendly and warm relationships and they spent considerable time organizing and preserving material objects and family papers, often in partnership with the Lloyd-Bakers, cousin Mary's children and grandchildren.

Families make conscious choices about which objects and records best capture the family ideology they want to preserve.[3] Collecting, preserving, and cataloging family papers and material objects had been a common practice among gentry and landed families for centuries.[4] Preserving the Sharp family papers, books, music, paintings, instruments, the coin collection, and other material objects had been a shared family concern since the at least the 1780s, if not earlier. Many letters show the recipient clearly organized and labeled correspondence at some point. A 1761 letter from Thomas to John, for example, is labeled "Bro: Tom #" in John's hand.[5] By the 1790s Catherine was heavily involved in the project. As she lost many family members in the 1810s she assumed more responsibility for preserving the families intellectual, material, musical, and religious legacy. Without heirs and without a family estate, Catherine also had to be conscientious in what she decided to keep and what she determined the Lloyd-Bakers would want to house and preserve. She then condensed and distributed family possessions previously housed in Hartburn, Durham, Fulham, and Wicken. This was a massive undertaking.

Beyond Adam Clarke, by the mid-1810s Catherine regularly corresponded with those who wanted to preserve professional papers from her male kin. Upon looking through a collection sent to her she found that the professional and family details were so intertwined in the documents that she did not "feel disposed to part with any, of which many be called the Sharp Papers, at present...wishing rather to Endeavor to get acquainted with these by degrees, in the hope of turning them to better account hereafter."[6] Her long familiarity with the family papers did not decrease the labor it took to organize all she inherited between 1814 and

---

[2] Mr. Tait, "On the Marriage of The Reverend Andrew Bowlt, of Bamburgh, with Miss Sharp," 1817, poems by various family members, D3549/24/1/3.

[3] Katherine French, *Household Goods and Good Households in Late Medieval London* (Philadelphia: University of Pennsylvania Press, 2021); Patricia Crawford, "Katherine and Philip Henry and Their Children: A Case Study in Family Ideology," *Transactions of the Historic Society of Lancashire and Cheshire*, 134 (1984): 39–73; Heather Wolfe and Peter Stallybrass, "The Material Culture of Record-Keeping in Early Modern England," in Liesbeth Corens, Kate Peters, and Alexandra Walsham, eds., *Archives and Information in the Early Modern World* (Oxford: Oxford University Press for the British Academy, 2018).

[4] Heather Wolfe and Peter Stallybrass, "The Material Culture of Record-Keeping in Early Modern England," in *Archives and Information in the Early Modern World*, 179–208.

[5] Thomas Sharp to John Sharp, February 2, 1761, D3549/9/1/4.

[6] Catherine Sharp to Adam Clarke, May 16, 1815, Add.MS 1948/5, PGL.

1816. Loose pages within Elizabeth's memoir, in Catherine's hand, show her efforts to track the location of various papers and many documents contain brief notes from her. On a sketch of an organ, for example, she noted she remembered seeing it at William's Old Jewry house (see upper image, Plate 4).

Catherine was also the recipient of numerous heirlooms and of course more books and music than she could realistically keep or expect the Lloyd-Bakers to keep. Archbishop Sharp's coin collection, for example, came to Catherine after Jemima died. Catherine attempted to find a place to donate the collection, but without luck. She had most certainly kept a miniature of Mary with her husband and children bequeathed to her by Jemima, but she sold Jemima's property in Doncaster and Durham. Catherine had no need to live in either place and given Jemima's protracted legal case over tithes from Doncaster, Catherine also had no desire to entangle herself with tenant relations hundreds of miles from Clare Hall. Instead, she concentrated on the material objects best suited to perpetuate a Sharp legacy. This included preserving Granville's anti-slavery publications, accounts about royal visits to the Sharp yacht, a journey to Scotland and to Stowe. Her work also included an effort to preserve a record of journeys and musical events as a memorial to her aunts, uncles, parents, grandparents, and cousins. John had anticipated there would not be room for his and Thomas's combined libraries—which also contained their grandfather, uncle, and father's libraries—he donated them to Crewe's charity. The entire collection was housed at Bamburgh Castle until the mid-twentieth century when they were moved to Durham University library. Elizabeth contributed to the work by compiling a catalogue of the books around 1800. This might be how some of Frances's books became included with her brothers'. Since some of Catherine's books, as well as Judith's, appear in the Bamburgh Collection, Catherine must have donated additional books in the 1810s.

On February 8, 1835, in her 91st year, Catherine's mother, Catherine Lodge Sharp, died at Clare Hall, her home for over forty years, and was buried in the local churchyard. She was followed in May by the death of 77-year-old Andrew, who was buried in the same churchyard.[7] The younger Catherine now faced a family life empty of all her Sharp relatives. There was no one left who remembered the family portrait from 1780, or the musical evenings at the house in Old Jewry. Catherine's mother was the last of her generation of Sharps and now Catherine was the last of her generation. Her cousin's children, the Lloyd-Bakers were young children when their mother, grandparents, and aunts and uncles died and had few memories of them. It is no wonder that Catherine commissioned the

---

[7] Church of England, St. Giles South Mimms, Middlesex parish registers, burial of Catherine Sharp, February 13, 1835 and Andrew Sharp, May 8, 1835, DRO/005/A/01/015, LMA, digital image at *London, England, Church of England deaths and Burials, 1813–2003*, https://www.ancestry.co.uk, accessed April 3, 2016.

230 BEING SINGLE IN GEORGIAN ENGLAND

Bamburgh monument in the wake of these losses (see Interlude 4 and upper image, Plate 8). Commissioned in 1839, it describes her male relatives who had served as curates of Bamburgh, including her recently deceased husband, but the main figure depicted on the monument is a sitting woman, perhaps praying or mourning. And its inscription describes Catherine as "the sole survivor of the name." In 1838 and 1839 she also commissioned portraits of herself, one of which passed to the Lloyd-Bakers (lower image, Plate 8).[8] These last efforts were her attempt to add a memorial of herself to all the other memorials she preserved and crafted.

The younger Catherine died in February 1843, at the age of 72. Her death notice described her as Granville's niece and the last Sharp descendant of the archbishop.[9] But there was far more to Catherine's family network and far more to the legacy she left than a surname. Her will clearly shows the financial and relational abundance she enjoyed; servants, cousins, the Lloyd-Bakers, and Jane Maunsell Le Mesurier's family were all acknowledged and generously provided for. Catherine also bequeathed all "the papers family bibles and other documents which he may wish to keep respecting my family or any of his own ancestors," to Thomas Barwick Lloyd-Baker, Mary's only surviving son.[10] Thomas Barwick kept much of what Catherine passed to him, housing it at Hardwicke Court, Gloucestershire—the home his father built in 1817–19.

The Lloyd-Bakers continued to house the Sharp items at Hardwicke Court throughout the remainder of the nineteenth and into the twentieth century, sometimes reorganizing them, sometimes making them available to biographers of Granville or Archbishop Sharp. In addition, some pieces were sold or donated during the nineteenth century.[11] Thomas Barwick's grandson, Arthur (1883–1979), was particularly instrumental in organizing the collection he inherited, not just the Sharps' archive, but also three centuries of Lloyd and Baker records. Many records contain his notations about content and provenance.[12] The Sharp legacy remained important to the Lloyd-Bakers beyond the archive stored at Hardwicke Court. They preserved Sharp names; Granville was employed as a first or middle name in each subsequent generation. And in the 1830s and 1840s, as part of a

---

[8] My thanks to Douglas Quick for details about Margaret Sarah Carpenter, who painted the portraits of Catherine and about the provenance of the portraits.

[9] "Obituary," *The Christian Reformer; or Unitarian Magazine and Review*, 1843, 10:268.

[10] Catherine Sharp, will, written July 10, 1836, codicil written January 18, 1838, proved February 27, 1843, Prerogative Court of Canterbury, PROB 11/1980, TNA. Mary had three children who survived childhood. Interestingly, though those three children married, all of them married quite late compared to their cohort; two siblings married at 33, and the third when she was 29. Additionally, typical of endogamous practice common among English landed classes, the two sisters married two brothers from the Browne family.

[11] Jeanette B. Holland and Jan LaRue, "The Sharp Manuscript, London 1759–1793: A Uniquely Annotated Music Catalogue," *Bulletin of the New York Public Library*, 73 (1969): 147–166.

[12] For example, see Mary Sharp Lloyd-Baker's 1798 diary transcripts, D3549/24/1/2.

EPILOGUE: AN AFTERLIFE IN DOCUMENTS 231

building project the family renamed places around one of their Islington properties to Lloyd Baker Street and Granville Square.

As Arthur Lloyd-Baker worked to systematize the accumulated family archive in the 1920s and 1930s, he worked side-by-side with his niece Olive Lloyd-Baker (1902–1975). Unmarried and childless, the uncle–niece duo might have been aware that they were mirroring the actions of Catherine and Granville Sharp more than a century before. They were also the last bearers of the Lloyd-Baker surname; Arthur's only uncle had died childless and his only brother (Olive's father) who died in World War I, left no sons.

It was perhaps the combination of an ever-expanding family archive becoming increasingly unwieldy to organize and a recognition that the surname line could end, that inspired Arthur to begin depositing the family papers in the Gloucestershire Record Office (now Gloucestershire Archives). Deposits were made repeatedly from the 1930s to the 1970s and the Lloyd-Bakers' executors continued to deposit family papers throughout the twentieth century. Olive also condensed family holdings by selling properties in London and Stouts Hill, a country house some ten miles from Hardwicke Court that had been in Lloyd-Baker possession since 1785. In the 1960s and 1970s she and her uncle were also able, finally, to sell the coin collection Catherine was unable to find a home for in the 1810s.[13] In the 1970s, Olive donated the Lloyd-Bakers' collection of agricultural equipment to Northleach Museum; in 1972 she attended the City of London's large commemoration of the Somerset decision; and in 1975 she permanently loaned the Zoffany painting to the National Portrait Gallery.[14]

Olive also repeated, though with a variation, something Catherine did. In 1966, Olive made her first cousin once-removed, Charles Granville Moray Murray-Browne (1945–2015), her heir. He was descended from Mary Sharp and Thomas John Lloyd-Baker through two lines—his grandparents were second cousins. When Charles Murray-Browne became Olive's heir he adopted the Lloyd-Baker surname.[15] If few families could match the Sharps' effervescence and good fortune during their lifetimes, even fewer had their memories so well preserved or for so long. That they did so, appropriately enough, is largely due to childless and unmarried Lloyd-Bakers. Whether wittingly or not, they were perpetuating patterns the eighteenth-century Sharps had refined to a perfect pitch.

---

[13] "Coins and Medals from the Collection Formed by Archbishop Sharp and His Descendants," Morton & Eden Coin and Medal Auctioneers, London, November 2017, https://www.mortonand-eden.com/wp-content/uploads/2019/02/91.pdf.

[14] Corporation of London, "Dinner to Celebrate the Bicentenary of the Prohibition of Slavery in Great Britain," July 14, 1972, D3549/13/6/10; Ann-Rachael Harwood and David Viner, "Moving to Northleach: The Lloyd-Baker Collection of Gloucestershire Agricultural History," *Folk Life*, 39, no. 1 (2000): 7–24.

[15] Nicholas Kingsley, *Landed Families of Britain and Ireland*, "(339) baker (later Lloyd-Baker) of Waresley Park, Ramsden House, Stouts hill and Hardwicke Court," August 3, 2018, https://landedfamilies.blogspot.com/.

232 BEING SINGLE IN GEORGIAN ENGLAND

The Sharps' experience might feel very distant from our twenty-first-century concerns. But their legacy is not that distant. Nicholas Kingsley, once the county archivist for Gloucestershire and historian of landed families, met Arthur Lloyd-Baker near the end of his life and met many people who knew both Arthur and Olive well. He noted that he "observed at first hand the affection and respect with which [they] were regarded."[16] I met Nick Kingsley briefly when I was conducting dissertation research at the then Gloucestershire Record Office in 2003–04. At the time I had no idea of how that encounter linked me with those who preserved the Sharps' legacy.

Much more important than that small personal interaction, has been the recent scholarly and public attention given the Sharps. The bicentenary celebrations of the end of the British slave trade (1807) and Granville's death (1813) generated a flood of books, articles, and commemorative displays telling his part in the history of abolition and celebrating his family's support. And unlike earlier eras, it has not ended with Granville's work. Zoffany's portrait of the Sharps regularly travels for exhibitions and has been central to two recent art history books about his work. In 2011, Elizabeth's stellar management of Wicken received scholarly attention and in just the last decade John and William's professional achievements have been similarly highlighted. Additionally, a popular treatment of the family's biography appeared in 2020.

*   *   *

Elizabeth's will provided for a perpetuation of the family archive, which she bequeathed to her single siblings and nieces. They, in turn, passed the items to the Lloyd-Bakers. The Sharps and their descendants preserved accounts of singular events such as family trips and the visit by the king and queen, but they also tried to preserve as much of their family culture as possible. By their middle age the Sharp siblings seemed to sense that their family mattered, that its history was worth preserving, even if it would not have a male heir to embody its perpetuation. Yes, Granville and John's work was especially important to their collection, but so was Elizabeth's kin-keeping efforts and the details of their social and emotional lives. Collectively their efforts were highly successful. Their family artifacts, musical instruments, and papers are sprinkled across the archival holdings on two continents. Mary's descendants carefully preserved the records of their social and material lives; institutions in Durham, Gloucestershire, London, Northamptonshire, Northumberland, and Yorkshire did likewise. Each year thousands of visitors view the Sharps' portrait. Commissioned by a married brother but highlighting the familial connections of the unmarried and full of all the Sharp family

---

[16] Nicholas Kingsley, "(339) baker (later Lloyd-Baker) of Waresley Park, Ramsden House, Stouts hill and Hardwicke Court."

bonhomie, the portrait remains a symbol of married and unmarried family members working together to craft an enviable family life.

In contemporary society not being in a couple is often seen as pitiable, if not pathological. The conflation of being single and being lonely has become a cliché. But no one would have ever described the unmarried Sharps as alone or lonely. Loneliness obviously existed in the eighteenth century, but it was less likely to be associated with a lack of romantic attachments. Of course, people today have many connections, perhaps even more connections than on offer in the eighteenth century, but rhetorically and culturally these are not often seen as counting as much as couplehood. This would have been an entirely foreign concept to the Sharps and most of their contemporaries. If there is anything we can learn from the exceptional Sharps, it is perhaps a fruitful way to reconsider how we define purposeful and meaningful relationships.

Select Bibliography

1. Biographies, Autobiographies, Family and Estate Records

Harman, R. Alec. *A Catalogue of the Printed Music and Books on Music in Durham Cathedral Library*. London: Oxford University Press, 1968.

Hoare, Prince. *Memoirs of Granville Sharp, Esq. Composed from his own manuscripts, and other authentic documents…With observations on Mr. Sharp's Biblical criticisms, by the…Bishop of St. Davids*. London: Henry Colburn, 1820.

Jackson, Charles, ed. "Autobiographical Memorandum of Heneage Dering, Dean of Ripon." *Yorkshire Diaries and Autobiographies of the Seventeenth and Eighteenth Centuries, The Publications of the Surtees Society*, 65 (1877): 331–350.

Lord Crewe's Charitable Trust Papers, NRO 452, Northumberland Archives.

Lloyd-Baker Family of Hardwicke Court Collection, D3549, D6919, Gloucestershire Archives.

Sharp Music Manuscripts, Durham Cathedral Library.

Sharp Papers, COLL 1891, COLL 1896, York Minster Archives.

Sharp, Thomas. *The Life of John Sharp, D.D. Lord Archbishop of York: To which are Added, Select, Original, and Copies of Original Papers*. London: C. and J. Rivington, 1825.

Thomlinson, John. "Diary of John Thomlinson." *Six North Country Diaries, The Publications of the Surtees Society*, 118 (1910).

Wicken Parish and Estate Papers, 364P, Northamptonshire Archives.

2. Secondary Sources

Abbott, Mary. *Family Ties: English Families 1540–1920*. London: Routledge, 1994.

Amussen, Susan. *An Ordered Society: Gender and Class in Early Modern England*. Oxford: Basil Blackwell, 1988.

Bailey, Joanne. *Parenting in England c.1760–1830: Emotions, Self-identities and Generations*. Oxford: Oxford University Press, 2012.

Bailey, Joanne. *Unquiet Lives: Marriage and Marriage Breakdown in England, 1660–1800*. Cambridge: Cambridge University Press, 2003.

Barclay, Katie, Jeffrey Meek, and Andrea Thomson, eds. *Courtship, Marriage and Marriage Breakdown: Approaches from the History of Emotion*. New York: Palgrave Macmillan, 2019.

Barclay, Katie and Kimberley Reynolds. *Death, Emotion and Childhood in Premodern Europe*, ed. Ciara Rawnsley. London: Palgrave Macmillan, 2016.

Barker, Hannah. *Family and Business During the Industrial Revolution*. Oxford: Oxford University Press, 2017.

Beardmore, Carole, Cara Dobbing, and Steven King. *Family Life in Britain, 1650–1910*. Basingstoke: Palgrave Macmillan, 2019.

Ben-Amos, Ilana Krausman. *Adolescence and Youth in Early Modern England*. New Haven and London: Yale University Press, 1994.

236 SELECT BIBLIOGRAPHY

Bennett, Judith and Amy Froide, eds. *Singlewomen in the European Past, 1250–1800*. Philadelphia: University of Philadelphia Press, 1999.

Benzaquén, Adriana. "Locke's Children." *Journal of the History of Childhood and Youth*, 4, no. 3 (Fall 2011): 382–402.

Berry, Helen and Elizabeth Foyster, eds. *The Family in Early Modern England*. Cambridge: Cambridge University Press, 2007.

Buxton, Antony. *Domestic Culture in Early Modern England*. London: Boydell, 2015.

Capp, Bernard. *The Ties that Bind: Siblings, Family, and Society in Early Modern England*. Oxford: Oxford University Press, 2018.

Cockayne, Emily. "Experiences of the Deaf in Early Modern England." *The Historical Journal*, 46, no. 3 (September 2003): 493–510.

Cody, Lisa Forman. *Birthing the Nation: Sex, Science, and the Conception of Eighteenth-Century Britons*. New York: Oxford University Press, 2005.

Cooper, Sheila. "Intergenerational Social Mobility in Late-Seventeenth- and Early-Eighteenth-Century England." *Continuity and Change*, 7, no. 3 (1992): 283–301.

Coster, Will. *Family and Kinship in England, 1450–1800*. London: Pearson Education, 2001.

Crawford, Patricia. *Blood, Bodies and Family in Early Modern England*. New York: Routledge, 2004.

Cressy, David. "Kinship and Kin Interaction in Early Modern England." *Past and Present*, 113, no. 1 (November 1986): 38–69.

Crosby, Brian. "Private Concerts on Land and Water: The Musical Activities of the Sharp Family, c.1750–c. 1790." *Royal Musical Association Research Chronicle*, 34 (2001): 1–118.

Davidoff, Leonore. *Thicker Than Water: Siblings and Their Relations, 1780–1920*. Oxford: Oxford University Press, 2012.

Davidoff, Leonore, Megan Doolittle, Janet Fink, and Katherine Holdon. *The Family Story: Blood, Contract and Intimacy, 1830–1960*. New York: Longman, 1999.

Day, Julie. "Household Management as a Method of Authority for Three Eighteenth-Century Elite Yorkshire Women." *Women's History Magazine*, 66 (Summer 2011): 30–37.

De Veirman, Sofie, Helena Haage, and Lotta Vikstrom. "Deaf and Unwanted? Marriage Characteristics of Deaf People in Eighteenth-Century Belgium: A Comparative and Cross-Regional Approach." *Continuity and Change*, 31, no. 2 (August 2016): 241–273.

Dickie, Simon. "Hilarity and Pitilessness in the Mid-Eighteenth Century: English Jestbook Humor." *Eighteenth-Century Studies*, 37, no. 1 (Fall 2003): 1–22.

Erickson, Amy Louise. "Mistresses and Marriage: or, a Short History of the Mrs." *History Workshop Journal*, 78 (2004): 39–57.

Erickson, Amy Louise. *Women and Property in Early Modern England*. London and New York: Routledge, 1993.

Evans, Jennifer. *Aphrodisiacs, Fertility and Medicine in Early Modern England*. Woodbridge: Boydell, 2014.

Evans, Jennifer. *Perceptions of Pregnancy from the Seventeenth to the Twentieth Century*. Basinngstoke: Palgrave Macmillan, 2017.

Ezell, Margaret J.M. "Elizabeth Isham's Books of Remembrance and Forgetting." *Modern Philology*, 109, no. 1 (August 2011): 71–84.

Finn, Margot. *The Character of Credit: Personal Debt in English Culture, 1740–1914*. Cambridge: Cambridge University Press, 2003.

Finch, Janet and Jennifer Mason. *Passing On: Kinship and Inheritance in England*. London: Routledge, 2000.

Fletcher, Anthony. *Growing Up in England: The Experience of Childhood, 1600–1914*. New Haven and London: Yale University Press, 2008.

French, Henry and Jonathan Berry, eds. *Identity and Agency in England, 1500–1800*. London: Palgrave Macmillan, 2004.

French, Henry and Mark Rothery. *Man's Estate: Landed Gentry Masculinities, 1660–1900*. Oxford: Oxford University Press, 2012.

French, Henry and Mark Rothery. "'Upon your entry into the world': Masculine Values and the Threshold of Adulthood Among Landed Elites in England 1680–1800." *Social History*, 33, no. 4 (November 2008): 402–422.

Froide, Amy. "Learning to Invest: Women's Education in Arithmetic and Accounting in Early Modern England." *Early Modern Women: An Interdisciplinary Journal*, 10, no. 1 (Fall 2015): 3–26.

Froide, Amy. *Never Married: Singlewomen in Early Modern England*. Oxford: Oxford University Press, 2005.

Gailey, Chris. "The Stillbirth Rate in Early Modern England." *Local Population Studies*, 81 (2008): 75–83.

Gillis, John. *For Better, for Worse: British Marriages, 1600 to the Present*. Oxford: Oxford University Press, 1985.

Goldie, Mark. "Voluntary Anglicans." *The Historical Journal*, 46, no.4 (2003): 977–90.

Grassby, Richard. *Kinship and Capitalism: Marriage, Family, and Business in the English-Speaking World, 1580–1740*. Cambridge: Cambridge University and Woodrow Wilson Center Press, 2001.

Griffin, Ben, Lucy Delap, and Abigail Wills, eds. *The Politics of Domestic Authority in Britain Since 1800*. London: Palgrave Macmillan, 2009.

Hardwick, Julie, Sarah Pearsall, and Karin Wulf, "Introduction: Centering Families in Atlantic Histories." *The William and Mary Quarterly*, 70, no. 2 (April 2013): 205–224.

Harris, Amy. "'She Never Inclined to It': Childhood, Family Relationships, and Marital Choice in Eighteenth-Century England." *Journal of the History of Childhood and Youth*, 12, no. 2 (Spring 2019): 179–198.

Harris, Amy. *Siblinghood and Social Relations in Georgian England: Share and Share Alike*. Manchester: Manchester University Press, 2012.

Hartman, Mary S. *The Household and the Making of History: A Subversive View of the Western Past*. Cambridge: Cambridge University Press, 2004.

Harvey, Karen. *The Little Republic: Masculinity and Domestic Authority in Eighteenth-Century Britain*. Oxford: Oxford University Press, 2012.

Harvey, Karen and Alexandra Shepard. "What Have Historians Done with Masculinity? Reflections on Five Centuries of British History, c.1500–1900." *Journal of British Studies*, 44, no. 2 (2005): 274–280.

Heal, Felicity and Clive Holmes. *The Gentry in England and Wales 1500–1700*. Stanford, Stanford University Press, 1994.

Hill, Bridget. *Women Alone: Spinsters in England 1660–1850*. London and New Haven: Yale University Press, 2001.

Hilton, Mary, Morag Styles, and Victor Watson, eds. *Opening the Nursery Door: Reading, Writing and Childhood 1600–1900*. London and New York: Routledge, 1997.

Hodgkin, Katherine. "Women, Memory and Family History in Seventeenth-Century England." In Kuijpers Erika, Pollmann Judith, Müller Johannes, and Van Der Steen Jasper, eds., *Memory before Modernity: Practices of Memory in Early Modern Europe*. Leiden: Brill, 2013.

Holloway, Sally. *The Game of Love in Georgian England: Courtship, Emotions, and Material Culture*. Oxford: Oxford University, 2019.

Houlbrooke, Ralph. *Death, Religion and Family in England, 1480–1750*. Oxford: Oxford University Press, 1998.

238 SELECT BIBLIOGRAPHY

Hunt, Margaret R. *The Middling Sort: Commerce, Gender and the Family in England, 1680–1780*. Berkeley: University of California Press, 1996.

Hunter, Elizabeth G. and Graham D. Rowles. "Leaving a Legacy: Toward a Typology." *Journal of Aging Studies*, 19, no. 3 (2005): 327–347.

Jacob, W.M. *The Clerical Profession in the Long Eighteenth Century, 1680–1840*. Oxford: Oxford University Press, 2007.

King, Steven. "Chance Encounters? Paths to Household Formation in Early Modern England." *International Review of Social History*, 44 (1999): 23–46.

Klemp, Marc, Chris Minns, Patrick Wallis, and Jacob Weisdorf. "Picking winners? The Effect of Birth Order and Migration on Parental Human Capital Investments in Pre-Modern England." *European Review of Economic History*, 17, no. 2 (2013): 210–232.

Lemire, Beverly. *The Business of Everyday Life: Gender, Practice and Social Politics in England, c.1600–1900*. Manchester: Manchester University Press, 2005.

Leonard, Amy E. and Karen L. Nelson, eds. *Masculinities, Childhood, Violence: Attending to Early Modern Women and Men*. Proceedings of the 2006 Symposium. Newark: University of Delaware Press, 2011.

Livesay, Daniel. *Children of Uncertain Fortune: Mixed-Race Jamaicans in Britain and the Atlantic, 1733–1833*. Chapel Hill: University of North Carolina Press, 2018.

McIntosh, Marjorie. "Women, Credit, and Family Relationships in England, 1300–1620." *Journal of Family History*, 30 no. 2 (April 2005): 143–163.

McKeon, Michael. *The Secret History of Domesticity: Public, Private, and the Division of Knowledge*. Baltimore: Johns Hopkins University Press, 2005.

McLaren, Angus. *Reproductive Rituals: The Perception of Fertility in England from the 16th to the 19th Century*. London: Methuen, 1984.

Morgan, Francesca. *A Nation of Descendants: Politics and the Practice of Genealogy in US History*. Chapel Hill: University of North Carolina Press, 2021.

Muldrew, Craig. *The Economy of Obligation: The Culture of Credit and Social Relations in Early Modern England*. New York: St. Martin's Press, 1998.

Newton, Hannah. *The Sick Child in Early Modern England, 1580–1720*. Oxford: Oxford University Press, 2012.

O'Day, Rosemary. *The Family and Family Relationships in England, France, and the USA*. Basingstoke: The Macmillan Press, 1994.

O'Day, Rosemary. *An Elite Family in Early Modern England*. London: Boydell, 2018.

Oldham, James. *English Common Law in the Age of Mansfield*. Chapel Hill: University of North Carolina Press, 2004.

O'Malley, Andrew. *The Making of the Modern Child: Children's Literature and Childhood in the Late Eighteenth Century*. New York: Routledge, 2003.

Ottaway, Susanna. *The Decline of Life: Old Age in Eighteenth-Century England*. Cambridge: Cambridge University Press, 2004.

Paugh, Katherine. *Politics of Reproduction: Race, Medicine, and Fertility in the Age of Abolition*. Oxford: Oxford University Press, 2017.

Pearsall, Sarah. *Atlantic Families: Lives and Letters in the Later Eighteenth Century*. New York and Oxford: Oxford University Press, 2008.

Perry, Ruth. *Novel Relations: The Transformation of Kinship in English Literature and Culture 1748–1818*. Cambridge: Cambridge University Press, 2004.

Retford, Kate. *The Art of Domestic Life: Family Portraiture in Eighteenth-Century England*. New Haven and London: Paul Mellon Centre for Studies in British Art, Yale University Press, 2006.

Retford, Kate. "Sensibility and Genealogy in the Eighteenth-Century Family Portrait: The Collection at Kedleston Hall." *Historical Journal*, 46, no. 3 (2003): 533–560.

Rosenheim, James. "The Pleasures of a Single Life: Envisioning Bachelorhood in Early Eighteenth-Century England." *Gender & History*, 27, no. 2 (August 2015): 307–28.

Scanlan, Padraic X. *Freedoms Debtors: British Antislavery in Sierra Leone in the Age of Revolution*. New Haven: Yale University Press, 2017.

Schwarz, L.D. "Social Class and Social Geography: The Middle Classes in London at the End of the Eighteenth Century." *Social History*, 7, no. 2 (May 1982): 167–185.

Seeman, Erik R. "'It is Better to Marry than to Burn': Anglo-American Attitudes towards Celibacy, 1600–1800." *Journal of Family History*, 24, no. 4 (October 1999): 397–419.

Sharpe, Michael. *Family Matters: A History of Genealogy*. Barnsley: Pen and Sword Family History, 2011.

Sharpe, Pamela. "Dealing with Love: The Ambiguous Independence of the Single Woman in Early Modern England." *Gender and History*, 11, no. 2 (1999): 209–232.

Sirota, Brent S. *The Christian Monitors: The Church of England and the Age of Benevolence, 1680–1730*. New Haven: Yale University Press, 2014.

Spicksley, Judith. "Women, 'Usury' and Credit in Early Modern England: The Case of the Maiden Investor." *Gender and History*, 27, no. 2 (July 2015): 263–292.

Stobart, Jon and Mark Rothery. *Consumption and the Country House*. Oxford: Oxford University Press, 2016.

Tadmor, Naomi. *Family and Friends in Eighteenth-Century England: Household, Kinship, and Patronage*. Cambridge: Cambridge University Press, 2001.

Thomas, Keith. *The Ends of Life: Roads to Fulfillment in Early Modern England*. Oxford: Oxford University Press, 2009.

Trumbach, Randolph. *The Rise of the Egalitarian Family: Aristocratic Kinship and Domestic Relations in Eighteenth-Century England*. New York: Academic Press, 1978.

Vickery, Amanda. *Behind Closed Doors: At Home in Georgian England*. New Haven and London: Yale University Press, 2009.

Vickery, Amanda. *The Gentleman's Daughter: Women's Lives in Georgian England*. New Haven: Yale University Press, 1998.

Wallis, Patrick and Cliff Webb. "The Education and Training of Gentry Sons in Early Modern England." *Social History*, 36, no. 1 (February 2011): 36–53.

Wallis, Patrick, Cliff Webb, and Chris Minns. "Leaving Home and Entering Service: The Age of Apprenticeship in Early Modern London." *Continuity and Change*, 25, no. 3 (December 2010): 377–404.

Webster, Mary. *Johan Zoffany*. New Haven: Yale University Press for the Paul Mellon Centre for British Art, 2011.

Weil, Rachel. *Political Passions: Gender, the Family and Political Argument in England, 1680–1714*. Manchester and New York: Manchester University Press, 1999.

Withey, Alun. "Medicine and Charity in Eighteenth-Century Northumberland: The Early Years of Bamburgh Castle Dispensary and Surgery, c.1772–1802." *Social History of Medicine*, 29, no. 3 (August 2016): 467–489.

Wright, Nancy, Margaret W. Ferguson, and A.R. Buck, eds. *Women, Property and the Letters of the Law in Early Modern England*. Toronto: University of Toronto Press, 2004.

Wulf, Karin. *Lineage: Genealogy and the Power of Connection in Early America*. Oxford: Oxford University Press, forthcoming.

Index

For the benefit of digital users, indexed terms that span two pages (e.g., 52–53) may, on occasion, appear on only one of those pages.

abolitionism 115, 121, 150–1, 182–9; anti-slavery papers 8, 92–3, 170, 183–4, 229; continuing of Granville's work into his old age 194; prison committee work and 184–5; siblings' support for Granville's work 8, 182–3, 185–6, 188, 196–7, 232; slavery in Britain 183–4. *See also* Strong, Jonathan

age. *See* birth order; childhood; marriage, age at

anti-slavery work. *See* abolitionism

apprenticeships 49, 55–8, 69–72, 112–13. *See also* education; professional careers

artwork 123–4, 135–6, 210–11. See also *Sharp Family, The* (Johan Zoffany, painted 1779–1781)

aunting and uncling 141–68; aunts and uncles of Sharp siblings 143–5; Catherine 156–8; characteristics of relationship 141–3, 161, 167–8; cousins in aunt role 48, 144–6, 161; emotional support 143, 146–7, 161, 163–4, 167–8; fertility issues and 147–51; financial support 143–5, 158; gendered expectations 142–3, 151, 158, 161, 163–5; groupings of close relationships 162–3; importance of bonds 109–10, 141–2; independence of nieces 164–5; Jack 155–6; Jemima 151–5; Mary 158–61; material benefits 141, 145–6, 153; professional support 158, 167–8; travels with nieces and nephew 151, 154–7, 159, 162–3

Bamburgh Castle, Northumberland 97–9, 108–9; charitable services at 176–9, 194–5; improvements to 173–5, 178–9; purchased by Nathaniel Lord Crewe 212–13

Bamburgh Church memorial 225–6, 229–30

Barwick, Catherine (d 1814, m William Sharp). *See* Sharp, Catherine (Barwick) (d 1814, m William Sharp)

Barwick, Elizabeth 86

Barwick, John 86

Barwick, Thomas 224

Beckford family 115

biographies of Sharp siblings 7–8

birth order 51, 58, 94–5, 123

boats: in family portrait 137; names of 164, 209–10; royal visits to family yacht 16, 208–9, 229; sale of 194. *See also* sailing trips; water schemes

books, shared collection of 124–5, 210–11; legacy, preserving 212–16, 229. *See also* published works

Booth, James 79–80

Booth, Mary (Sharp) (1715–1798, m James Booth) 48, 79–80

Booth cousins 120

Bowlt, Andrew (later Andrew Sharp) 17, 194–5, 203, 219–20, 227–30; Bamburgh Church memorial 226; South Mimms, Middlesex Churchyard memorial 225

Braidwood, Thomas 153

Cambridge, University of 4, 6–7, 22–3, 27, 46–7, 49, 72, 74–5, 90

celibacy 93–5

Cervetto, Giacobbe 138

Cervetto, James 138

charity and reform work 52–4, 169–97; at Bamburgh 176–9, 194–5; charity health services 174–9; diminution of, in 1790s 193–6; formal activities of, 1760s–1780s 174–89; foundations of siblings' efforts 171–4; gender and 189; outside formal institutions, 1760s–1780s 189–93; paternalism of 171–2, 180–1, 185–6, 188–9; political office to help push 179–82; private charity 173; reform efforts 185–7; scope of 170, 179, 190–2, 195–6; by Sharp sisters 190–3; of siblings before 1760s 172–4; siblings' intertwined 169–71, 178–9, 189–91, 196–7; transportation network improvements 180–2. *See also* abolitionism

Charlotte, Queen of England 16

childcare 41; by servants 156–7. *See also* aunting and uncling; childhood

childhood: changing attitudes about 45; formal education during Sharp siblings' 49–58; gendered expectations 51, 58; informal education during Sharp siblings' 49–58;

242 INDEX

childhood: changing attitudes about (*cont.*)
  leaving the family home 46–7, 49, 55–7,
  69–72, 105–6; modern concept of 36; Sharps'
  family culture learned in 35–7
childlessness, genealogy and 200–3. *See also*
  fertility issues; genealogical practices
coin collection 17, 210–11, 219–20, 229
communal decision-making 67. *See also*
  households, shared
conflict, in families 14, 88–90, 95, 126
correspondence xix–xx, 164–6; between
  brothers 33–4; common letters 12–13, 46–7,
  51–2, 99–100, 60–5, 205–6; to cousins 47;
  between Granville and abolitionists 184;
  in-laws join in 99–100; instruction in
  letter-writing 50–1; legacy, preserving 205–6,
  228; between nieces and nephew 155–6, 167;
  from Thomas Sharp, Sr. to his children 45–7,
  56. *See also* family papers
cousins, connections to 47–8, 120, 145; aunt role
  of elder Elizabeth Sharp Prowse 48, 144–6,
  161; emotional 146; financial 146–7. *See also
  under* Booth; Dering; Hosier; Mangey;
  Prowse; Rogers
Crewe, Nathaniel Lord 29n.60, 108, 172,
  212–13, 223. *See also* Lord Crewe's Charity

deafness, of Jemima 152–5, 164–5, 166n.108
death and loss: of Andrew Bowlt 229–30; of
  Catherine Lodge 229–30; of Catherine
  Pawson 157; epitaphs 221–6; fear of 91;
  infant and child mortality 25–6, 38–43,
  147–9; of Jack Sharp 90–1, 147, 156–7; library
  consolidation and 214–15; loss of family
  name 205; of Mary Dering 195, 216–17; of
  niece Catherine 230; obituaries and funeral
  sermons 221; of parents 73–4, 80–1, 105–6;
  of siblings 26, 42–3, 49, 91, 194–6, 198, 216–18;
  siblings' relationships following 80–1; sibling
  support during 129–31; of Thomas
  Prowse 87. *See also* miscarriages and
  stillbirths
Dering, Ann (1716–1780) 48, 146–7
Dering, Ann (d 1789) 146
Dering, Ann (Sharp) (1691–1771, m Heneage
  Dering) 22, 26–7, 75–6, 91
Dering, Elizabeth (1713–1777) 48
Dering, Heneage (1719–1802) 27, 48, 75–7,
  146–7; Durham Cathedral monument 223;
  genealogical practice of 204–8
Dering, John (1715–1774) 48
Dering, Judith (1730–1813) 48
Dering, Mary (1721–1798, m John Sharp).
  See Sharp, Mary (Dering) (1721–1798,
  m John Sharp)

Dering, Philadelphia (1723–1806) 48
Dering, Thurloe 146
Dering cousins 48, 120, 146
dining. *See* cousins, connections to; social
  gatherings
domestic masculinity. *See* gender
Durham Cathedral monument 223, 227

ecclesiastical work and influence of Sharp
  family 4, 13–14, 18–20, 23. *See also* religious
  beliefs and practice
education 4, 24–5, 49–58; apprenticeships 49,
  55–8, 69–72, 112–13; away from family
  home 47; charity school for girls founded by
  George Wheler 171–2; financial support
  for 4, 57; formal 49–58; gendered
  expectations for 39, 44, 51, 58, 171–2;
  informal 49–58; instruction in letter
  writing 50–1; in literacy 36, 51–2, 161–2; of
  nieces 159. *See also* Cambridge, University of;
  childhood
Elsley, Heneage 223
emotional support 125–7, 133–4; despite
  geographic distance 60–4; intimacy 93–4;
  through aunting and uncling 143, 146–7, 161,
  163–4, 167–8. *See also* financial support
employment. *See* professional careers
endogamy 77, 83, 148, 230n.10
epitaphs and memorials 221–6
Equiano, Olaudah 184

family culture, Sharps' 17–20, 24, 31–2, 77–8;
  family success attributed to 135; heirlooms
  (abstract meaning) 204–5; heritage, siblings'
  interest in over time 204–5 (*See also*
  genealogical practice); informal lessons in
  family identity 54; during siblings'
  childhood 35–7; Whelers' family culture 31.
  See also genealogical practices
family papers: anti-slavery focus 8; preservation
  of 166, 221–2, 227–31
family portrait (Johan Zoffany, painted
  1779–1781). See *Sharp Family, The* (Johan
  Zoffany, painted 1779–1781)
fatherhood 46, 75, 149–50, 163; surrogate 168,
  189. *See also* aunting and uncling; parenting
fertility issues 147–51; of Catherine
  Barwick 90–1, 148, 158–9, 205; infant and
  child mortality 25–6, 38–43, 147–9;
  miscarriages and stillbirths 90–1, 147–50,
  157–9, 202–5. *See also* death and loss
finances, shared 8–9, 12–13, 99, 122–4; after
  parents' deaths 74, 105–6; emotional support
  and 125–7; nieces and 174–5. *See also*
  households, shared

INDEX   243

financial stability: developing 6–7, 103, 111–13; existing, as disincentive for marriage 78–9, 87, 94–5; financial instability, conflict and 134–5; as incentive for marriage 30–1, 33, 67, 86, 91–2; of nieces 166, 230; offers comfort and entertaining opportunities 13, 98, 103–4, 106, 112–13, 210–11; of single women 6–7, 68n.8, 78–9, 87, 163, 192–3; social connections and 114–15. *See also* marriage, financial practicality of

financial support 121–2, 133–4; by aunts and uncles 143–5, 158; bookkeeping 125–6, 130; by cousins, aunts, and uncles 143–5, 158; for education 4, 57; for Granville's public service 121, 182–3; during illness and death 130; through apprenticeships 55–8; through patronage networks 4, 25, 29, 75–6, 101–2, 114. *See also* charity and reform work; emotional support; marriage, financial practicality of

Froide, Amy 10

Fulham, Middlesex Churchyard memorial 224–5

Fulham House 133

Fynney, Fielding-Best 202–3

Garrick, David 1–2, 113–15

Garrick, Eva Marie 114–15

gender 11, 14–15, 50, 133–4; in aunting and uncling duties 142–3, 151, 158, 161, 163–5; childhood 51, 58; conforming to 12, 15, 24, 53, 158, 197; domestic masculinity 14; educational opportunities 39, 44, 51, 58, 171–2; in genealogical practice and legacy preservation 199–201, 203–4, 215–16, 218; household management 11, 14, 68, 104; leisure opportunities and 101; professional prospects 145; reproduction concerns 147–51; wills and inheritances 156, 158, 205, 211–12, 215–16

genealogical practices 204, 208–9; gendered expectations in 199–201, 203–4, 215–16, 218; genealogies of Christ 202n.17; of Heneage Dering 204–8; heraldry 200, 207; names in lineage chart 39–40, 199–201, 203–4; official family pedigree 207; patrilineal 202–4; typical eighteenth-century 201–3

genealogy of Sharp family 4, 39–40; collaborative work on lineage chart 200–1, 203, 210; Elizabeth's work on 198–204, 207–9, 218; heraldry and 200. *See also* legacy, preserving

George III, King of England 16, 116

godparents 142n.4, 190

grandparents 31–2, 143–4, 164

Granville (name and surname) 20–1, 190, 200–1, 203, 230–1

Handel, George Frideric 114, 124–5

Hartburn, Northumberland 106–8

Hasleline, James 44, 143–4

health 126–7, 216–17; charity health services 174–9; deafness, of Jemima 152–5, 164–5, 166n.108; smallpox inoculation 157, 175–6, 179; of Strong 183; support during illness and death 129–33, 135–6; traveling for 82–3, 117, 129–30; traveling to visit ailing relatives 129–30, 135–6, 145

heirlooms (abstract meaning) 204–5. *See also* genealogical practices; legacy, preserving; wills and inheritances

hierarchical relationships and structures: aunting and uncling 142, 168; charity and 170; conforming to 14–15, 188–9; in genealogical practice 199; household management 134–5; lived reality as critique of 15, 67; social 14–15, 24, 55, 120, 197. *See also* gender

Higgons, Grace (1663–1703, m George Wheler) 18–22

Hoare, Prince 196–7

horizontal kinship 11, 96, 146–7; lineage chart representation of 202–3; marriage as fortification of 96. *See also* genealogical practices; sibling relations; vertical kinship

Hosier cousins 116–17, 120

household management: gendered expectations of 11, 14, 68, 104; influence on marriage decisions 11–12; informal education for 50–2; by married couples 23, 66, 104–5; by older siblings 120–1; reconfiguring, as Sharps age 193–4; servants and 98; by single men 104–5; skill of 116–17; by unmarried siblings 67–8; while single 99, 104–5; at Wicken Park 116–18

households, shared 67–8, 84, 92–3, 97–8, 100, 108; book and music collections spread throughout 214–15; co-management 122–3, 134–6; conflict over 88–9, 95; distance between sibling households 69–72; Durham home 109–10; importance of 96, 130; legacy of material objects and 210–11; travels to siblings' 111

humor 45–7; in common letters 61

infant and child mortality 25–6, 38–43, 147–9. *See also* death and loss; miscarriages and stillbirths

infertility. *See* fertility issues

inheritance. *See* family culture, Sharps'; wills and inheritances

244 INDEX

Jacobite resistance 49–50
Jacobite supporters 37

King, Steven 10

Lafayette, Marquis de 184, 188–9
Leadenhall Street home 110–12
legacy, preserving 198–220, 232–3;
  artwork 210–11; books and music 210–16,
  229; coin collection 67–8, 219–20;
  commissioned monuments and memorials
  221–2; correspondence 205–6, 228; epitaphs
  and memorials 221–6; family chronology
  compiled by Elizabeth and niece
  Catherine 207–8; family history, developing
  interest in 204–10; family papers 166, 221–2,
  227–31; family portrait 198–9, 210–11, 218,
  231–3; family stories, sharing 206; gendered
  expectations in 199–201, 203–4, 215–16, 218;
  material objects, distribution of 206–7;
  material objects, family identity and 210–16,
  218–19; material objects, passed to niece
  Catherine 227; musical instruments 212–13;
  for nonfamilial audience 215–16;
  shared households and 210–11; siblings'
  deaths 216–18. See also genealogical
  practices; names; Sharp surname; wills and
  inheritances
letters. See correspondence
lineage charts. See genealogical practices
literature and reading 36, 50–1, 53–4, 56; books,
  shared collection of 124–5, 210–16, 229;
  literacy instruction 36, 51–2, 161–2
Lloyd-Baker, Arthur 231–2
Lloyd-Baker, Olive 231
Lloyd-Baker, Thomas Barwick 230
Lloyd-Baker, Thomas John 19, 166, 216–17
Lloyd-Baker family 228; surname 202–3, 231
Lodge, Catherine (1745–1835, m James Sharp).
  See Sharp, Catherine (Lodge) (1745–1835,
  m James Sharp)
London Common Council 179–81
Lord Crewe's Charity 173–5, 178–9

Mangey, Dorothy Sharp 33, 47, 79, 145
Mangey, John (1722–1782) 47–8, 145, 214–15
Mangey, Thomas 33, 214–15
marital status, scholarship on 8–11
marriage, age at 67, 91–2; eighteenth-century
  norms 5–6, 29; of Sharps 5–6, 29, 88,
  95–6, 166
marriage, choice of 66–96; as communal
  decision 67; courtship decisions 74–95;
  endogamy 77, 83, 148, 230n.10; factors in 67,
  76–7, 95; gender and 77–9, 84, 91–2;

motivations for 72–3; nieces 166–7; social
  expectations 81. See also widowhood
marriage, financial practicality of: endogamy
  and 77; existing stability as disincentive for
  marriage 78–9, 87, 94–5; as incentive for
  marriage 30–1, 33, 67, 86, 91–2; logistics 76;
  property inheritance and 79–81. See also
  financial stability
marriages, conflict in 79–81
material benefits of siblings' mutual aid 123–5,
  133–6; through aunting and uncling 141,
  145–6, 151–3
Mincing Lane home 100–1, 105–6, 110–11, 113
miscarriages and stillbirths 90–1, 147–50,
  157–9, 205; genealogical recognition of
  stillbirths 202–4; infant and child
  mortality 25–6, 38–43, 147–9. See also death
  and loss; fertility issues; infant and child
  mortality
Mordaunt children 159–60, 163–4
music, shared collection of 124–5; legacy,
  preserving 212–13, 229
musical education 43–4, 51–2, 102; of
  nieces 158, 161–2
musical gatherings 76–7, 87, 101–3;
  chronicled for family legacy 205–6; at
  Durham 109–10; in family portrait 137–8;
  at Hartburn 106; musical guests invited
  to 114–15; nieces and nephews join in 162;
  in Old Jewry home 113–14; as siblings
  age 194; sisters-in-law and 113, 135n.166;
  water schemes 1–3, 15–16, 102–3, 106, 116,
  156–7; at Wicken Park 119–20. See also
  social gatherings

names: Andrew Bowlt becomes Andrew
  Sharp 17, 203, 219–20, 227; of boats 164,
  209–10; Granville 190, 200–1, 203, 230–1; in
  lineage chart 39–40, 199–201, 203–4;
  Lloyd-Baker surname 202–3, 231; naming
  patterns and practice 209–10;
  nicknames 45–6, 61–2, 69–72. See also
  Sharp surname
nieces and nephews: Catherine 156–8; financial
  stability of 166, 230; Jack 155–6;
  Jemima 151–5; join musical gatherings 162;
  marriage and 166–7; Mary 158–61; material
  benefits 151–2; musical education of 158,
  161–2; shared finances and 174–5; travels
  with family 151, 154–7, 159, 162–3. See also
  aunting and uncling; Sharp, Jack (1765–1771)

Oglethorpe, Elizabeth 193
Oglethorpe, James 184–6
Old Jewry home 113–14

INDEX 245

Palmer, Elizabeth (1656–1729, m John Sharp) 18–20, 22–3, 48
parenting 24–5, 142, 149; fatherhood 46, 75, 149–50, 163, 168, 189; godparents 142n.4, 190; grandparents 31–2, 143–4, 164; parental mistreatment 53; surrogate responsibilities 161, 167–8, 189–90. *See also* aunting and uncling; childhood
paternalism 171–2, 180–1, 185–6, 188–9
patronage networks 4, 25, 29, 75–6, 101–2, 114. *See also* financial support
Pawson, Catherine (1746–1771, m Thomas Sharp). *See* Sharp, Catherine (Pawson) (1746–1771, m Thomas Sharp)
philanthropy. *See* charity and reform work
portrait of Sharp family. See *Sharp Family, The* (Johan Zoffany, painted 1779–1781)
poverty, caring for people in 171–2, 174–7. *See also* charity and reform work
professional careers 57n.92, 66, 73, 84, 111–12; apprenticeships 49, 55–8, 69–72, 112–13; employment, transition to 46–7; gendered prospects 145; professional papers intertwined with family affairs 228–9; support during 169–70; support during retirement 132–3. *See also* financial stability
professional support: for Granville's anti-slavery work 8, 182–3, 185–6, 188, 196–7, 232; through aunting and uncling 158, 167–8. *See also* financial support
Prowse, Elizabeth (1735–1742) 48, 110–11, 143–5
Prowse, Elizabeth (1749–1826) 48
Prowse, Elizabeth (Sharp) (1712–1780, m Thomas Prowse) 48, 116–17, 144–6, 161
Prowse, George (1737–1767) 19, 48, 83–4, 87, 116–17, 202–3; Wicken Church memorial 224
Prowse, John "Jack" (1734–1758) 48, 73, 91–2, 116–17
Prowse, Thomas 48, 87
Prowse cousins 116–17
published works 187; genealogical, by Sharps' ancestors 204; of George Wheler 75, 204–5; Granville's, against the slave trade 92–3, 170, 183–4; preserving family legacy of 205–6; professional letters 72n.14, 111–12, 179; sermons 1–2, 25n.41, 172n.14, 176–7, 215–16

Queen Anne's Bounty (reform effort) 172

race, mixed-race unions and children 150. *See also* abolitionism
religious beliefs and practice: baptism 41; charity and 186–7; death and loss and 148–9, 157; as family value 13–14, 36–8; of household employees 119; musicianship

and 43–4; of Wheler and Sharp families 18–20, 24, 35, 37–8
reproduction. *See* fertility issues
residences, eighteenth-century homes 98–9
residences, locations of 69–72, 105–6. *See also* households, shared
retirement 132–3
Rogers children 159–60, 163–4. *See also* cousins, connections to
Rothbury 37, 44–5
Rush, Benjamin 1–2, 184

sailing trips 99–103, 116, 119–20, 136. *See also* boats; water schemes
sermons, published. *See* published works
servants 127–9, 190; childcare by 156–7
sexuality 93–4
Sharp, Andrew (né Andrew Bowlt) 17, 194–5, 203, 219–20, 227–30; Bamburgh Church memorial 226; South Mimms, Middlesex Churchyard memorial 225
Sharp, Ann (1691–1771, m Heneage Dering) 22, 26–7, 48, 75–6, 91
Sharp, Catherine (Barwick) (d 1814, m William Sharp) 19, 86–7, 111–13, 135n.166; birth of Mary 158–9; death of 217–18; in family portrait 137–8; fertility issues 90–1, 148, 158–9, 205; Fulham Churchyard memorial 224–5; as grandmother 164; Jonathan Strong and 169, 171, 183, 185, 188–9; philanthropy and 179; social gatherings and 113–14
Sharp, Catherine (Lodge) (1745–1835, m James Sharp) 19, 84–6, 112–13, 135n.166; after death of James 123, 131–3, 216–17; birth of Catherine 147, 156–7; birth of Jack 147; death of 229–30; godparenting by 190; health of 216–17; servants of 129; South Mimms, Middlesex Churchyard memorial 225
Sharp, Catherine (Pawson) (1746–1771, m Thomas Sharp) 19, 88–91, 147–8, 157
Sharp, Dorothy (1693–1755) 22, 33, 214–15
Sharp, Elizabeth (1695–1713) 22, 25–6
Sharp, Elizabeth Palmer (1656–1729) 22–3, 33, 143–4
Sharp, Elizabeth Prowse (1712–1780, m Thomas Prowse) 48, 116–17, 144–5, 161
Sharp, Grace (1726–1728) 19, 157
Sharp, Jack (1765–1771) 87–8, 150, 155–6; death of 90–1, 147, 156–7
Sharp, John (1644–1714) 18–20, 22–3, 156, 204–5, 214; autobiography by Thomas Sr. 215–16; coin collection 17, 31–2, 219–20; marriage counsel of 33–4; reform efforts 172; sermons of 216

246 INDEX

Sharp, John (1678–1726) 18–20, 22, 26–7, 33–4, 48

Sharp, Judith (Wheler) (1699–1757, m Thomas Sharp) 19, 21–2, 24–6, 48; births and deaths of her children 38–43; childhood of 50–1; death of 73–4, 80–1, 105–6; Durham Cathedral monument 223; John Thomlinson and 29–31, 77; marriage to Thomas 29–31, 33–4; musicianship of 43; parenting style 35; philanthropy of 54, 172; religious practice of 37–8

Sharp, Mary (1715–1798, m James Booth) 48, 79–80

Sharp, Mary (Dering) (1721–1798, m John Sharp) 19, 46, 48, 75–7, 84–6; after John's death 194–5; age at pregnancy 147–8; birth of daughter Jemima 151; charitable services of 174–8; conflict following Thomas's marriage 88–90; cousin connections through 120; death of 195, 216–17; death of Thomas, effect on 91; in family portrait 137–8

Sharp, Thomas (1692–1758) 4, 17, 19, 21–2, 48; births and deaths of his children 38–43; childhood of 24, 50–1; correspondence by 33–4, 45–7, 56; death of 73–4, 80–1, 105–6; death of his mother 40; death of his siblings 26; Durham Cathedral monument 223; education of 24–5; genealogical practice 204; on his parents 25; library of 53; marriage to Judith 29–31, 33–4; musicianship of 43–4; parenting style 23, 35; patronage networks 75–6; philanthropy of 52–4, 172; professional success of 38; religious practice of 37–8; sermons by 25n.41, 172n.14

Sharp Family, The (Johan Zoffany, painted 1779–1781) 137–40; description of 2–3, 137–8, 162–3, 218; legacy preservation and 198–9, 210–11, 218, 231–3; reception of 138; sociability memorialized in 135–7; Zoffany's friendship with Sharps 138–9

Sharp family crest 200, 207–8, 210. See also genealogical practices

Sharp surname 17–18, 201, 207–8; concerns about continuation of 156, 203–6, 214, 218–20, 227; musical symbol used for 12–13, 102. See also names

sibling relations 53. See also horizontal kinship; material benefits of siblings' mutual aid

Sierra Leone 187–9

single men 14, 104–5

singleness. See marital status, scholarship on

single women 10; financial stability of 6–7, 68n.8, 78–9, 87, 163, 192–3

slavery 115, 183–4, 192–3. See also abolitionism

social gatherings 23, 96; on boats and on sailing trips 99–103, 116, 119–20, 136; competition for, in London 114; dining in 100–1, 103–4, 115; in eighteenth-century homes 98–9; family portrait memorializes 135–7; financial stability and 13, 98, 103–4, 106, 112–13, 210–11; hosting 101–5; logistics 104–5, 114–15, 127; on Mincing Lane 100–1, 105–6, 113; nieces and nephews incorporation into 155–9; in Old Jewry home 113–15; servants and 127; "visiting books," 113, 138, 205–6; weddings 83; at Wicken Park 119–20. See also musical gatherings; water schemes

social hierarchy 14–15, 24, 55, 120, 197. See also gender; hierarchical relationships and structures

Somerset, James 183–4

South Mimms Churchyard memorial 225

stillbirths. See fertility issues; miscarriages and stillbirths

Strong, Jonathan 92–3, 101, 121; Catherine Barwick and 169, 171, 183, 185, 188–9; siblings' support for 171, 183, 185–6. See also abolitionism

surnames. See names; Sharp surname

Talbot, Catherine 114–15, 151–2

Thomlinson, John 29–31, 77

Thomlinson, John (uncle of John) 29–30

travels of Sharp family 73–4, 106–8, 111, 131–2; for Elizabeth's wedding 83; frequency of 106, 194; for health 82–3, 117, 129–30; independence facilitates 91–2; with nieces and nephew 151, 154–7, 159, 162–3; with parents 49, 69, 73; sailing trips 99–103, 116, 119–20, 136; sisters-in-law participate in 135–6; to sit for family portrait 210–11; the Union (yacht of William and James) 15–16; to visit ailing relatives 129–30, 135–6, 145. See also households, shared

uncles. See aunting and uncling

unmarried family members. See marriage, choice of; single men; single women

vertical kinship 11–12, 14–15, 24

voluntarism 173

Walton, Thomas 128

water schemes 1–3, 15–16, 102–3, 106, 116; nieces and nephews and 156–7. See also musical gatherings; social gatherings; travels of Sharp family

Wheatley, Phyllis 1–2, 184

INDEX   247

Wheler, George (1650–1724) 18–22, 24, 29; death of 143–4; donated library of 214–16; Durham Cathedral monument 223; on his childhood 24–5; philanthropy of 171–2; published works 75, 204–5; will of 78

Wheler, Grace (Higgons) (1663–1703, m George Wheler) 18–22

Wheler, Judith (1699–1757, m Thomas Sharp). *See* Sharp, Judith (Wheler) (1699–1757, m Thomas Sharp)

Wicken, Northamptonshire Church memorial 224

Wicken Park, Northamptonshire 116–21, 160; improvements to 190–1

widowhood 5–6, 26–7, 68n.8, 206–7; of Catherine Lodge 123, 132–3, 216–17; charity for widows 170, 172, 175, 197; of Elizabeth 6–7, 67–8, 80, 117–18, 135, 147–8, 200–1

wills and inheritances 79–81, 145–6, 206–7, 231; of Barwick, Catherine 192; coin collection 17, 210–11, 220; of Crewe, Nathaniel Lord 212–13; of Dering, Ann 146–7; of Dering, Heneage 27; of Elizabeth 217, 232–3; of Frances (no will left) 192, 211–12; gendered attitudes about 156, 158, 205, 211–12, 215–16; to godchildren 190; of James 156, 158, 205; of Lodge, Catherine 190, 192; of Mangey, John 145, 214–15; of material objects and heirlooms 210–11, 215; of Middleton, Grace 146–7; of musical instruments 212–13; of niece Catherine 230; to nieces and nephew 156, 227–30; to servants 190; of Sharp, John (1644–1714) 53; of Sharp, John (1723–1792) 17, 215–16, 219–20; to sisters 78–9; of Thomas, Sr. 51, 61–2; of Wheler, George 78

women's rights 12, 14–15, 192–3

yachts. *See* boats; sailing trips; water schemes
York, Archbishop of. *See* Sharp, John (1644–1714)

Zoffany, Johan 2–3, 137–40, 159, 231. See also *Sharp Family, The* (Johan Zoffany, painted 1779–1781)